BRITH EMETH

IN MEMORY OF

PRESENTED BY

27575 SHAKER BOULEVARD, PEPPER PIKE, OHIO 44124

MY TALKS WITH ARAB LEADERS

by

David Ben-Gurion

Translated from the Hebrew by
Aryeh Rubinstein and Misha Louvish

Edited by Misha Louvish

301.29569
B43

THE THIRD PRESS
Joseph Okpaku Publishing Company, Inc.
444 Central Park West, New York, N.Y. 10025

Published in the U.S. by The Third Press, 1973

Copyright © Hebrew edition, Am Oved Publishers, Tel Aviv, 1967
Copyright © English edition, Israel Program for Scientific Translations, Ltd., 1972

All rights reserved. Except for use in a review, the reproduction or utilization of this work or part of it in any form or by electronics, or other means, now known or hereafter invented, including xerography, photocopying, and recording, and in any information storage and retrieval system is forbidden without the written permission of the publisher.

Library of Congress Catalogue Card Number: 72-94297

SBN: 89388-076-0

First printing, March 1973

PREFACE

Leaders of the major powers have frequently declared that precipitate action in the Middle East could easily lead to a world-wide conflagration and effect the fate of humanity. But what about the leaders directly involved in the conflict?

In this book there is ample evidence that the Israel leaders, who have always been aware of the grave dangers, have constantly sought to prevent a catastrophe and to achieve peaceful co-existence with their Arab neighbors.

In spite of these efforts Israel was thrice forced to take up arms against the Arabs and notwithstanding her victories on each occasion Ben-Gurion has asserted that if a genuine peace treaty could be negotiated Israel should cede to Egypt and Jordan the larger part of the territories occupied during the Six-Day War in 1967. Genuine peace means the establishment of normal diplomatic, cultural and trade relations that exist between all friendly states including free movement in the whole area by nationals of all countries.

Though much of the material in this book is of historical interest and significance, the issues are still most topical in today's political context and the search for peaceful relations is more urgent than ever before. The major part of the book is a translation of *Pegishot im Manhigim Arviyim* published in Hebrew in 1967, but during the course of translation new material not previously released became available which shed additional light on Ben-Gurion's attempts to reach an amicable understanding with the Arab leaders. This English edition includes the account of his efforts to initiate peace negotiations with the late Egyptian President Gamal Abdel Nasser early in 1956 and again in 1962–63 just prior to his retirement as Prime Minister.

Brief biographical and other notes on persons, places, institutions, etc. mentioned in the text, are given in alphabetical order at the end of the book.

Most of the text is translated from the author's Hebrew notes. A number of passages are quoted directly from the available English documents (see Appendix).

In the transliteration of Hebrew and Arabic names, *kh* has been used for the Hebrew letter כ and Arabic خ (sounding somewhat like *ch* in Scottish *loch*), *ḥ* for Hebrew ח and Arabic ح (midway between *kh* and a strong English *h*), *ẓ* for Hebrew צ (sounding like *ts*), and *q* for Arabic ق. Generally accepted Latin-character spellings of names have been retained.

Thanks are due to the Central Zionist Archives, Jerusalem, for permission to use most of the documents listed above, and to Dr. Moshe Tavor, translator of the German edition of *Pegishot im Manhigim Arviyim*, for placing at our disposal the results of his research in checking the Hebrew text.

THE PUBLISHERS

INTRODUCTION

From the beginning of his long career David Ben-Gurion exhibited a rare combination of qualities: breadth of vision with single-mindedness of purpose. Since his early youth he worked unremittingly and uncompromisingly for the national liberation of the Jewish people in its historic homeland, but he never lost sight of universalistic humanitarian values. His undeviating dedication to the building of the Jewish National Home in the Land of Israel, open to all Jews who wished to live there out of necessity or in obedience to personal conviction, did not blind him to the needs and rights of the Arab population. He believed that the true interests of both peoples were complementary, not incompatible.

Ben-Gurion is best known to the world as a fighting statesman, a war leader who forged his country's independence in 1948 in an armed struggle with the neighboring Arab states and led it to victory in another, briefer, but even more successful campaign eight years later. And indeed, he regarded the resolute and unflinching defense, first of isolated farmsteads and urban neighborhoods, then of the achievements of the Yishuv—the Jewish community under the British Mandate—and, finally, of the State of Israel, as the first prerequisite for the building and preservation of the Jewish homeland.

Yet he made repeated and strenuous efforts to come to terms with the Arab population and the Arab world by which the Yishuv and the State of Israel were surrounded. Just over a year after the Balfour Declaration, he declared that under no circumstances must the rights of the Arabs be infringed upon; the true aim of Zionism was "not to conquer what has already been conquered, but to settle in those places where the present inhabitants have not established themselves and are unable to do so" (p. 7). He had no doubt that the national aims of both Arabs and Jews could be reconciled within the wider framework of the Middle East. Despite all setbacks and disappointments, he held fast to the faith that not only peace, but an alliance of friendship between the two peoples, would be achieved one day, because it was a necessity for both and the key to the progress and prosperity of the entire region.

This book gives Mr. Ben-Gurion's personal account of his efforts to reach an understanding with Arab leaders. It covers a period of thirty years: from 1933, when he became a member of the Jewish Agency Executive, until his retirement from the premiership of Israel in 1963.

Already in the 1930s, Ben-Gurion, together with other colleagues—notably

Moshe Sharett (Shertok), then head of the Jewish Agency's Political Department —held a series of secret talks with Palestinian, Syrian and other Arab leaders in the hope of arriving at a peaceful understanding. In return for Arab consent to Jewish immigration and settlement, he offered Jewish help in the attainment of full Arab independence and unity. He argued that a Jewish State as a member of a Middle East union could make a valuable contribution to the progress and prosperity of the region, while the rights of the Arab minority within its borders would be amply safeguarded by the Arab majority in the region as a whole. While some Arabs were prepared, in private conversation, to listen to these proposals with interest, none was willing publicly to advocate any compromise. The Arab leadership, dominated by the powerful Mufti of Jerusalem, unrelentingly demanded the stoppage of Jewish immigration (at the time when Jews were desperately trying to escape from Nazi Germany) and called for the immediate establishment of an Arab State, with a permanent Jewish minority, in the whole of Palestine.

In 1939 Ben-Gurion participated, with other Jewish leaders, in the London Conference between the British Government and delegations representing Jews and Arabs (at Arab insistence the British conferred with each separately) in another attempt to achieve a settlement. This, too, proved unsuccessful. The White Paper issued by the British at the end of the conference, imposing severe restrictions on Jewish immigration and settlement, gravely exacerbated relations between the British and the Jews and set in motion the train of events that eventually led to the end of British rule and the creation of a Jewish State.

Under Ben-Gurion's leadership, the State of Israel was established on May 14, 1948. This followed a United Nations decision of the previous November calling for the formation of a Jewish State and an Arab State within the territory of what had up to then been known as Palestine. Any hope that the Arabs would recognize the new realities and accept the United Nations decision was soon dashed. When they defied the UN and invaded the infant Jewish State, the world organization did nothing to enforce its own decision and Ben-Gurion led his people in its successful defense of its territory.

Even then he felt no bitterness or rancor, but cherished the continuing hope that now at last a *modus vivendi* would be found. In the basic principles which, as Premier, he presented to parliament after the end of the fighting, Israel's first elected Government undertook to strive for "a Jewish-Arab covenant (economic, social, cultural and political cooperation with the neighboring countries) within the framework of the United Nations Organization." Ben-Gurion repeatedly expressed, with the full endorsement of his Government, his willingness to accept the 1949 Armistice Demarcation Lines, with such minor adjustments as might be mutually agreed, as the permanent frontiers between Israel and her Arab neighbors.

But there was little response, despite the magnitude of the setback the Arabs had suffered. Every proposal for a constructive solution was rejected by their leaders, who refused to recognize Israel's right to exist.

After the Egyptian revolution of 1952, Ben-Gurion expressed initial hopes that the emergence of the new régime might provide the long-awaited opportunity for an understanding between the two peoples. But he was destined to be disappointed. Egypt took the lead in hostility to Israel and the danger to her very existence increased. This book describes how President Eisenhower sent a special emissary early in 1956 to try to arrange a meeting between Nasser and Ben-Gurion or some other Israel representative, in order to discuss the possibility of a settlement, or, at least, to find ways of relaxing the tension that had grown as a result of the flow of Soviet arms to Egypt. The failure of these negotiations was followed by the Sinai Campaign, which gave Israel a modicum of quiet on her border with Egypt for a period of ten years.

In 1962 Ben-Gurion made another attempt to arrange a meeting with Nasser —this time through the mediation of President Tito of Yugoslavia. Despite his friendship with Nasser, however, Tito felt unable to undertake the task and the situation in the Middle East continued to deteriorate. On April 17, 1963, Egypt, Syria and Iraq signed a treaty of alliance in Cairo unifying the armies of the three countries and proclaiming their major aim to be the "liberation of Palestine"— the usual Arab euphemism for the destruction of Israel. Two months later, Ben-Gurion resigned from the premiership and became a private citizen.

David Ben-Gurion has often been hailed as a modern prophet and his words often have the ring of biblical prophecy, both in their moral imperatives and their political sagacity. His vision of peace in the Middle East, which he strove for but was unable to implement when in office, will continue to guide the people of Israel until it becomes a reality.

MISHA LOUVISH

CONTENTS

PREFACE		iii
INTRODUCTION		v
1	Before World War I	1
2	The Weizmann-Faisal Agreement—1919	4
3	Early Statements on Arab-Jewish Relations	6
4	Labor Becomes Largest Zionist Party—1931–33	11
5	Talks with Musa Alami and Others—1933–34	14
6	Brit Shalom and Its Policies	21
7	Another Talk with Alami—August, 1934	24
8	More Talks with Alami—August, 1934	29
9	Talks with Syrians—September, 1934	35
10	Arab Demands—1935–36	40
11	Talks with Antonius—April, 1936	42
12	Third Talk with Antonius—April, 1936	55
13	Arab Unrest; Proposals of "the Five"—1936	63
14	Smilansky's Version—June, 1936	73
15	Sharett Talks to Alami—June, 1936	84
16	Sharett and Joseph Talk to Alami—June, 1936	93
17	The Memorandum of "the Five"—June, 1936	97
18	Attempts to End the Arab Strike—1936	104
19	The Arab Strike Ends—October, 1936	113
20	Talks with Fuad Bey Ḥamzah—April, 1937	121
21	Talks with Philby and Armstrong—May, 1937	127
22	The Hyamson-Newcombe Proposals—1937–1938	141
23	Sharett Corresponds with Magnes—1937–1938	152
24	Magnes Answers Criticisms—February, 1938	162
25	Meeting with Musa Ḥusseini—February, 1938	182
26	Ben-Gurion Replies to Magnes—March, 1938	186
27	Talk with Saudi Ambassador—August, 1938	195
28	London Conference Opens—Feb. 2, 1939	199

29	Weizmann's Address—Feb. 8, 1939	202
30	British Meet Arab Delegations—Feb. 9, 1939	214
31	Malcolm MacDonald's Proposals—Feb. 10, 1939	217
32	MacDonald Answers the Arabs—Feb. 11, 1939	223
33	Nuri Sa'id's Speech—Feb. 13, 1939	226
34	The McMahon Letters—Feb. 14, 1939	228
35	Discussion on Strategy—Feb. 14, 1939	230
36	Jordanian and Yemenite Speeches—Feb. 15, 1939	238
37	Discussion on Immigration—Feb. 15, 1939	240
38	Meeting with Chamberlain—Feb. 16, 1939	247
39	Proposals to the Arabs—Feb. 16, 1939	250
40	British Proposals Rejected—Feb. 17, 1939	255
41	Executive Discusses Policy—Mar. 7, 1939	256
42	British, Jews and Arabs Meet—Mar. 7, 1939	258
43	Britain's Final Proposals—Mar. 15, 1939	263
44	Jewish Agency Says "No"—Mar. 17, 1939	265
45	The Arab War Against Israel—1947–53	266
46	The Growing Threat from Egypt—1954–55	270
47	The President's Emissary Arrives—January, 1956	274
48	The Arab Refugees	283
49	Cease-fire and Direct Talks—Jan. 24, 1956	287
50	Clarifying the Positions—Jan. 24, 1956	290
51	The Emissary Returns from Cairo—Jan. 31, 1956	296
52	Letter to Eisenhower—Feb. 14, 1956	309
53	The Emissary's Last Visit—Mar. 9, 1956	312
54	The Sinai Campaign and After—1956–1962	325
55	Approach to President Tito	327

BIOGRAPHICAL AND OTHER NOTES   331
APPENDIX   342

1 BEFORE WORLD WAR I

Not one of the great thinkers who dreamt and wrote about the national rebirth of our people in its ancient homeland Ereẓ Israel, the Land of Israel, had the least apprehension that from its very first day this renascence would be accompanied by a military attack by the Arab nations, and that the sovereignty of Israel would be established through the victory of Jewish arms.

Of the three great visionaries of the Jewish State in the nineteenth century only one, Moses Hess, in his book *Rome and Jerusalem*, from the very start linked the revival of Jewish independence to Ereẓ Israel. Leon Pinsker, in his *Auto-Emancipation*, and Theodor Herzl, in *The Jewish State*, initially did not consider that Palestine was necessarily the country in which the redemption of the Jewish people would take place, and it was only their contact with the Ḥibbat Zion movement that drew them to the Promised Land. Pinsker contented himself with small things, with extending assistance to the handful of settlements that had been established in the country. Herzl's was a grander vision. He advocated a Jewish State, founded the World Zionist Organization and transformed the Jewish people into an international political factor. However, after the establishment of the Zionist Organization, he no longer spoke of a Jewish State but of "a publicly and legally assured home in Palestine," as it was worded in the Basle Program, and of a Charter. The "practical" Zionists, who would not wait for a Charter but demanded settlement activity in Palestine under any conditions, ignored almost completely the problem of how Jewish immigration and settlement would be possible in a country not under Jewish control. Their historical instinct convinced them that a Jewish population must be established in Palestine, irrespective of the circumstances, and to the maximum possible extent. However, even the "political" Zionists like Herzl and his disciples considered only the problem of the *ruler* of the land, and not that of the *inhabitants*. Their political efforts, like Herzl's first steps, were aimed at gaining the goodwill of the ruler—the Ottoman sultan. Before World War I the Arab countries were an integral part of the Ottoman Empire, and Palestine, like all of its neighbors, belonged to that empire. When Herzl despaired of winning the sympathy of the sultan, he turned to England, and in 1902 he conducted negotiations with the British Government over Jewish settlement in el-'Arish. Lack of water and the opposition of Lord Cromer, the British High Commissioner in Egypt, put an end to this plan. Joseph Chamberlain, the British Colonial Secretary, then offered Herzl Uganda, but the Russian Zionists and others objected to this, and the proposal caused a rift in the Zionist Organization. In 1904 the seer of the Jewish State died—of a broken heart.

One of the first Bilu pioneers, Ze'ev (Vladimir) Dubnow, brother of the Jewish historian Simon Dubnow, who reached Jaffa with the second Bilu group on September 21, 1882, took a practical view of the vision of rebirth—and we may assume that his comrades did likewise. In a letter to his brother, who was not happy about his having left the university and immigrated to Palestine, Ze'ev Dubnow wrote:

"Do you really think that my sole motivation in coming here is to better myself, with the implication that if all goes well I will have achieved this aim and that if it does not then I ought to be pitied? No. My ultimate aim, like that of many others, is greater, broader, incomprehensible but not unattainable. The final goal is eventually to gain control of Palestine and to restore to the Jewish people the political independence of which it has been deprived for two thousand years.

"Don't laugh; this is no illusion. The means for realizing this goal are at hand: the founding of settlements in the country based on agriculture and crafts, the establishment and gradual expansion of all sorts of factories, in brief—to make an effort so that all the land, all the industry, will be in Jewish hands. In addition, it is necessary to instruct young people and the future generation in the use of firearms (in free, wild Turkey anything can be done), and then... here I too am plunging into conjecture—then the glorious day will dawn of which Isaiah prophesied in his burning and poetic utterances. The Jews will proclaim in a loud voice and (if necessary) with arms in their hands that they are the masters of their ancient homeland. It doesn't matter whether that glorious day comes in another fifty years or more. Fifty years are but a moment for such an enterprise. Agree, my friends, that this is a sublime and magnificent idea..."[1]

Ze'ev Dubnow was then working as a hired laborer at Mikve Israel, together with his Bilu comrades. They earned one franc a day.

In all the writings of the leaders of the movement, both of Hovevei Zion and of the Zionists, it is hard to find a definition of the vision of the rebirth as pointed, brief and comprehensive as that given by this young *halutz* in a private letter to his brother and friends more than eighty years ago, $65\frac{1}{2}$ years before the establishment of the State of Israel and the War of Liberation. This was at a time when Palestine contained only one-quarter of one percent of world Jewry, approximately 20,000 souls, and the only Jewish village, which had

---

[1] The letter appears in A. Druyanov, ed., *Writings on the History of Hibbat Zion and the Settlement of Erez Israel*, [Hebrew], III, 495.

been founded four years earlier with the significant name of Petaḥ Tikva (Gate of Hope), had been abandoned by its inhabitants owing to malaria and the stench of the swamps. In that letter Ze'ev Dubnow no doubt expressed the views that were current among his Bilu comrades. But these words did not reach the general public.

I first came into contact with Arabs when I was working as a hired laborer in Sejera in 1907–09. Actually, I had come across Arabs earlier, in the year of my arrival in the country, 1906, when I was working in the Judean village settlements of Petaḥ Tikva and Rishon le-Zion, where most of the laborers were Arabs. There we waged a struggle for Jewish labor. We regarded Arab labor in the Jewish villages as a grave danger, for we knew that the land would not be ours if we did not work it and develop it with our own hands. But there we never clashed with the Arabs or experienced Arab hatred. In Sejera all the work was done by Jews—and it was this fact that drew me to the place. But it was there that I first became aware of the seriousness of the Arab problem. In those days there were only four Jewish settlements in all of Lower Galilee, but in three of them most of the work was done by Arabs, though this was less true of Yavne'el than of Menaḥemiya and Kefar Tavor. Sejera, which consisted of an ICA (Jewish Colonization Association) farm on the hilltop and of the houses of young farmers on the slopes, was then the only settlement in the country in which Jewish labor prevailed. The farm director, Eliahu Krause, understood the importance of Jewish labor and was helped in this matter by his brother-in-law, Yehoshua Hankin, "the redeemer of the soil." It was here that the first "collective" (as it was then called) was organized, i.e., a group of workers who assumed responsibility for doing all the work on the farm and who shared in the profits. This "collective" was the nucleus of the kibbutz movement which developed after the founding of Degania in 1911. Guard duty, too, which in Sejera had at first been performed by Circassians, was turned over to Jewish hands as a result of pressure by the workers, and there was no need here to fight for the principle of Jewish labor. But it was here that I saw for the first time the acuteness and dangers of "the Arab problem."

Under Ottoman rule there was a good deal of anarchy in the country, and Beduin attacks on peasants were a frequent occurrence, as were wars between one tribe and another. But Sejera had its full share of Arab enmity. It was surrounded by aggressive armed Arab villages, like Lubiya and Kafr Kana, and by the Ẓabuaḥ tribes, and here, for the first time, we all saw Jews being murdered—it was on the last day of Passover 1909—simply because they were Jews.

I first encountered Arab political opposition to Jewish settlement in spring 1915, after Turkey had entered the war on the side of Germany. At that time, Izhak Ben-Zvi and I were law students at the Turkish University in Constantinople. I had friends and acquaintances among the Turkish and Arab students, but we never discussed Jewish affairs. As we were on our way back to Palestine at the beginning of August 1914, during the university recess, the war broke out, and Jamal Pasha, who headed the Southern Command of the Ottoman Empire, arrived in Syria and Palestine. He began to suppress the Arab nationalist movement, and in Beirut he had a number of Arab leaders hanged. In Palestine he struck at the Zionist movement, and when our names—Izhak Ben-Zvi's and mine—were discovered in a list of delegates to the Zionist Congress we were interrogated by a Turkish officer, following which Jamal Pasha ordered us banished from the Ottoman Empire, "never to return." We were imprisoned until we could be deported, but since we were students at a Turkish university, we were treated with civility and during the day were permitted to stroll about in the compound of the administrative complex in which the jail was located. There I met an Arab student, Yiḥya Effendi, with whom I had been friendly back in Constantinople. When he asked me what I was doing there, I told him that I was imprisoned and that there was an order banishing me from the country. My friend Yiḥya Effendi responded with these words: "As your friend, I am sorry to hear it; as an Arab, I am glad." This was the first occasion on which I encountered an expression of political hostility on the part of an Arab.

2   THE WEIZMANN-FAISAL AGREEMENT—1919

After the defeat of the Central Powers in World War I, Turkey lost all of its Arab territories, including Palestine. The British army, under the command of General Allenby, which included four Jewish regiments composed of Jews from England, the United States, Canada and Palestine—the first Jewish regiments in our times—had conquered the country. In November 1917 the Balfour Declaration was issued; though addressed to Lord Rothschild, it had been achieved mainly through the efforts of Dr. Chaim Weizmann. Even before the Jews obtained the Balfour Declaration, Sir Henry McMahon, the British High Commissioner in Egypt, had promised Sherif Hussein of Mecca, on Britain's behalf, to liberate the Arab countries from Turkish rule and to recognize the Sherif as their ruler. It was true that the area of Palestine had been excluded from the terms of the

McMahon correspondence, but a statesman like Weizmann could not ignore the significance of the declaration or the growing self-assertion of the Arab peoples. He tried to reach an agreement with Faisal, son of Sherif Hussein. On January 3, 1919, the two signed an agreement pledging friendship between a Jewish Palestine and its neighbor, the promised Arab State. The agreement stated:

"Article II
"Immediately following the completion of the deliberations of the Peace Conference, the definite boundaries between the Arab State and Palestine shall be determined by a Commission to be agreed upon by the parties hereto.

"Article III
"In the establishment of the Constitution and Administration of Palestine all such measures shall be adopted as will afford the fullest guarantees for carrying into effect the British Government's Declaration of the 2nd of November, 1917.

"Article IV
"All necessary measures shall be taken to encourage and stimulate immigration of Jews into Palestine on a large scale, and as quickly as possible to settle Jewish immigrants upon the land through closer settlement and intensive cultivation of the soil. In taking such measures the Arab peasant and tenant farmers shall be protected in their rights, and shall be assisted in forwarding their economic development."

Even before that, on December 12, 1918, the London *Times* had published the following statement by the Emir Faisal to a Reuter correspondent:

"The two main branches of the Semitic family, Arabs and Jews, understand one another, and I hope that as a result of interchange of ideas at the Peace Conference, which will be guided by ideals of self-determination and nationality, each nation will make definite progress towards the realization of its aspirations. Arabs are not jealous of Zionist Jews, and intend to give them fair play, and the Zionist Jews have assured the Nationalist Arabs of their intention to see that they too have fair play in their respective areas."

However, this agreement had no practical value. Not only the Arabs of Palestine, but also those of the neighboring countries, and even of Iraq itself, where Faisal had been enthroned, regarded it as a worthless piece of paper. Faisal's agreement did not bind a single Arab. Weizmann was compelled to rely exclusively on the Balfour Declaration and the British Mandate, and he thus concentrated his political activity in England, but he never ignored the Arab problem and never failed to emphasize the blessing that Jewish settlement in the country would bring to the Arab nation.

The demand for a Jewish State was first expressed after the Balfour Declaration at the founding convention of the Zionist Socialist Association of the Workers of Ereẓ Israel—Ahdut Ha'avodah, which met in Petaḥ Tikva in March 1919. The convention resolved to demand "an international guarantee of the establishment of a free Hebrew State in Ereẓ Israel which, until the creation of a Jewish majority in the country, would be under the aegis of a representative of the League of Nations." But the convention did not consider the possibility that the establishment of a Jewish State might meet with opposition on the part of the Arabs in Palestine. The general assumption then prevailing in the Zionist movement was that our settlement enterprise would prove a benefit to the Arab community, and the same view was current among the Jewish labor movement in Palestine. It was therefore believed that the Arabs would welcome us with open arms or, at all events, would acquiesce *post factum* in our growth and independence, since there was sufficient room in the country both for the existing Arab community and for the immigration and settlement of millions of Jews.

3 EARLY STATEMENTS ON ISRAEL-ARAB RELATIONS

At the time of the Balfour Declaration, Izhak Ben-Zvi and I were still living in exile in the United States. Shortly after the publication of the Declaration, I wrote in the Po'alei Zion organ in America (on November 14, 1917):

"The great miracle has come to pass. The greatest of the Powers, whose army is approaching the gates of Jerusalem, has officially proclaimed 'the establishment in Palestine of a national home for the Jewish people.' After 35 years of pioneering enterprise in the country, which has clearly proved the ability of the Jewish people to reconstruct the ruins of its land, after 20 years of political propaganda, which revealed to the world the aspirations of the Jewish people for its homeland, the most powerful nation in the world has proclaimed that it officially recognizes the existence of the Jewish people and undertakes to aid in the establishment of its national home in Palestine.

"England has not returned the land to us. Precisely now, at the moment of our great triumphant joy, this must be given particular stress: *England is not capable of returning the land to us.* Not because she is not, or not yet, in control of the country. Even after the whole country, from Dan to Beersheba, is conquered by England, it will not become ours again simply because England has agreed to it, even with the approval of all the other nations. A people acquires a land only by the pains of labor and creation, by the efforts of building and settlement. England has done much: she has recognized our existence as a political entity and has endorsed our right to the country. The Jewish people itself must convert this right into an established fact; it is obliged to devote its strength and its wealth to establish its national home and to implement its national redemption to the end."

About a year after the Balfour Declaration and a year before the founding of Aḥdut Ha'avodah in Petaḥ Tikva, while I was still living in American exile, I wrote:

"The Jewish State will not arise overnight, even if it is proclaimed and recognized by a council of nations. But until its full realization it does not remain a fiction, a mere international legal statement that exists only on paper. The sovereign rights of the Jewish people are based on a vital, united force. All Jews who express in an organized manner their desire for a Jewish homeland in Ereẓ Israel are the real founders and makers of the future State."

But I added:

"With the international endorsement of the right of the Jewish people to its land, and with the recognition of the political authority of the Zionist Organization to realize that right, the Zionist Organization does not become the ruler of the country. Palestine is not an unpopulated country. Within the territory that may be regarded—historically, politically, ethnographically and economically—as Ereẓ Israel, and which covers an area of 55,000–60,000 square kilometers on both sides of the River Jordan, there is a population of slightly over one million. In Cisjordan alone there are about three-quarters of a million. *By no means and under no circumstances are the rights of these inhabitants to be infringed upon*—it is neither desirable nor conceivable that the present inhabitants be ousted from the land. That is not the mission of Zionism. The true aim and real capacity of Zionism are not to conquer what has already been conquered, but to settle in those places where the present inhabitants of the land have not established themselves and are unable to do so. The preponderant part of the country's land is unoccupied and uncultivated. According to the figures of the Turkish Ministry of Agriculture, only 5.28 percent of the land in the Jerusalem district is under cultivation. In the vilayet of Beirut, only 9.76 percent of the land is under cultivation, while in the vilayet of Damascus not more than 3.47 percent. According to an estimate of Prof. Karl Ballod, the country's irrigable plains are capable of supporting a population of six million, to be sure under conditions of intensive cultivation and using proper, modern irrigation methods. It is on these vacant lands that the Jewish people demands the right to establish its homeland. The demand of the Jewish people is based on the reality of unexploited economic potentials, and of unbuilt-up stretches of land that require the productive force of a progressive, cultured people. The demand of the Jewish people is really nothing more than the demand of an entire nation for the right to work.

"However, we must remember that such rights are also possessed by the inhabitants already living in the country — and these rights must not be infringed upon. Both the vision of social justice and the equality of all peoples that the Jewish people has cherished for three thousand years, and the vital interests of the Jewish people in the Diaspora and even more so in Palestine, require absolutely and unconditionally that the rights and interests of the non-Jewish inhabitants of the country be guarded and honored punctiliously.

"In analyzing the rights and interests of the Jews and non-Jews in Palestine, we note a characteristic difference between the two. The non-Jewish rights consist of *existing* assets, material or spiritual, which require legal guarantees for their preservation and integrity. The Jewish interests, which also include some existing assets, consist mainly of the *age-old* opportunities offered by the country, the economic and cultural potential of this semi-desolate land, the hidden wealth of natural resources and the soil which the Jewish people is destined to uncover and exploit through a creative effort and the investment of wealth and toil.

"The non-Jewish interests are conservative; the Jewish interests are revolutionary. The former are designed to preserve that which exists, the latter — to create something new, to change values, to reform and to build." [2]

In those days there was considerable confusion with regard to the boundaries of Palestine. Even Zionists expressed the opinion that Transjordan was not part of Palestine, a view that stemmed from their complete ignorance of the history and nature of the country. The Hebrews, as we know, settled the territory east of the Jordan before they conquered the land to the west. When the Israelites crossed the Jordan for the first time under the leadership of Joshua, the eastern part was already in their hands. The first Hebrew conquest that we know of from the Bible narrative was the conquest of "the land that was on this side of the Jordan, from the river of Arnon unto mount Hermon . . . All the cities of the plain, and all Gilead, and all Bashan, unto Salchah and Edrei, cities of the kingdom of Og in Bashan" (Deut. 3:8–10).

Contemporary scholars are divided over the veracity of the accounts given in the Bible of the wars of Sihon, king of the Amorites, and Og, king of Bashan. But they all agree with the Biblical tradition that the Jews first settled on the east side of the Jordan. Nor was the settlement of the Hebrews

---

[2] These observations were written on January 29, 1918, and were first published in *Der Yiddisher Kempfer*. They were reprinted in D. Ben-Gurion, *We and Our Neighbors* [Hebrew], Tel Aviv, pp. 31–33.

in Transjordan a temporary affair, until such times as they conquered the western part. It is true that the centers of the nation were all located in the western part of the country, that most of the historical events recorded in our ancient literature took place in those parts of the country that lie between the Jordan River and the Mediterranean Sea, and that the mark made by Transjordan on our history has not been as prominent as that of the western part. But from the aspect of Hebrew settlement there was no difference between the two parts of the country. During the period of the Judges, two judges of Israel were from Transjordan—Jair the Gileadite and Jepthah the Gileadite, and one of our greatest prophets also came from these parts—Elijah the Tishbite, who was an inhabitant of Gilead. Of the six cities of refuge that the Israelites set apart for those who committed murder unintentionally, half were in Transjordan and half in Cisjordan (Joshua 2:7–9).

Even when, in the days of Pekah ben Remaliah, king of Israel, the Jews of Transjordan were banished by Tiglath-Pileser to Assyria, the remnant of Israel was not exiled, and after the return of the exiles from Babylonia the Jews again settled in Transjordan. Judah the Maccabee fought his wars against the Greek rulers of Syria not only in the western part of the country but also in the east (Maccabees 1:5). Alexander Yannai subdued all parts of Transjordan, and during his reign both sides of the Jordan were united into a single kingdom. When the Mishna divides Erez Israel into three lands, it always lists Judea, Transjordan and Galilee.

After the San Remo conference in April 1920 had conferred the Mandate over Palestine on Britain in order to establish the Jewish National Home in that country, we submitted in November 1920, on behalf of the World Union of Po'alei Zion, a memorandum to the British Labour Party (it was written by me and was signed by S. Kaplansky and myself, who were then the representatives of the Union of Po'alei Zion in London).

We wrote that we were aware of the support the Labour Party had given to the establishment of Palestine as the National Home of the Jewish people and that we therefore wished to clarify the vital question of the boundaries of the country, which would shortly be determined by Great Britain and France. The Balfour Declaration, which had been endorsed by the French Government, had automatically nullified the Sykes-Picot Agreement of 1916 and changed the entire situation.

In accordance with the Balfour Declaration, we said, the question of the boundaries of Palestine could be solved in only one way: to turn it into an economic-political unit in order to establish the Jewish Commonwealth. The implementation of this goal—which in view of the present misfortune of East European Jewry had become a matter of life and death for the Jewish masses who were seeking work—was possible only by the vigorous and complete development of all the agricultural and industrial resources of Palestine. An impetus was needed for the activity of the Yishuv, which would pave the way for large-scale immigration and for mass settlement of the Jewish working class. The first and most basic condition for this mass settlement was a just solution to the question of the boundaries in the north and east.

Palestine was not a large country, the letter continued. Its area was approximately 33,000 square miles (55,000–60,000 square kilometers), in which we wished to settle hundreds of thousands of status-less Jews who were seeking work. If we wished to prepare the country in a brief time to absorb the majority of these masses, its area should not on any account be artificially reduced. It was also essential that the water resources, on which the entire future of the country depended, should not be cut off from the Jewish Homeland to be established. Nor should the fields of the Hauran, on which the country depended for its daily bread, be detached from it. For that reason, we had always insisted on the obvious demand that Palestine must include the southern bank of the Litani, the sources of the Jordan as far as the Hermon, and the Hauran District up to the al-Uja River, south of Damascus.

The northern district of Transjordan, which the Sykes-Picot Agreement had allotted to France, had always been an integral part of Palestine, and it was this district that provided grain for the whole country. Whereas the western districts of Transjordan had a population density of approximately 26 persons per square kilometer, in the Hauran District the density was not more than 12–15, yet it had always been Palestine's granary. The growth of the Jewish community in Palestine would increase the demand of its inhabitants for grain from Transjordan, and without the intensive cultivation of the Hauran and large-scale settlement of workers there, Palestine would never be able to feed its inhabitants. Despite the great importance of the northern and eastern parts of Palestine for the growing of cereals, they were even more important as a reservoir for the country's water resources.

Palestine was an arid country, we pointed out, and without artificial irrigation a large increase in the Jewish population was out of the question. The country had no coal, and industry would depend mainly on water power. All the country's rivers flowed from east to west, or from north to south, and this explained the importance of Upper Galilee and the Hauran for the entire country. The main rivers of the country were the Jordan, the Litani, and the

Yarmuk. Not only did the country need them to supply its water, but all its industrial possibilities depended on the hydroelectric power that could be harnessed from these three rivers. These rivers were not important to the northern districts of Syria, since they flowed from north to south. Only Palestine could exploit them for large-scale immigration. The possibility of using these rivers freely was a basic condition for mass settlement in Palestine and for the country's economic independence.

Great Britain had not been given the Mandate over Palestine in order that it should become a British colony. The Jewish workers would oppose with all their might any attempt to convert the Mandate into an instrument for imperialist ends. We were sure that the Socialist International, which had recognized our nationalist demand for Palestine, would extend us practical help in this matter. We concluded the letter by expressing the hope that the British and French workers, who had never failed to take the side of justice, would exert all their influence with their Governments in order to ensure the establishment of the Jewish National Home in an undivided Palestine, capable of economic development and self-sufficiency.

4 LABOR BECOMES LARGEST ZIONIST PARTY—1931-33

From the beginnings of the renewed Jewish settlement in Palestine there was always the assumption in Zionist ideology that the return of the Jewish people to its land was bound up with a great mission of making the East blossom and of engendering friendly cooperation between the Semitic peoples, who in the Middle Ages were the torch-bearers of progress and science. The great Jewish thinkers of the Middle Ages wrote their philosophic works in Arabic. The poet Judah Halevy wrote *The Kuzari* in Arabic, and Maimonides wrote his *Guide for the Perplexed* in that language. In fact, however, the Arabs in Palestine in recent times did not respond to this ideology. There were, it is true, individual Arabs who admitted that Jewish settlement has proved of benefit to their people, but the Arab nationalist movement, which came into being almost at the same time as political Zionism, adopted a hostile attitude to Jewish immigration. As Jewish settlement in Palestine increased so did Arab opposition to it. To a considerable degree, the Zionist enterprise became an auxiliary factor, if not a decisive one, in the strengthening of Arab nationalism, which regarded the war against Zionism almost as its main task.

After the Balfour Declaration, efforts were made on the part of the Executive of the Zionist Organization to explain to the Arabs the benefits and the blessings of cooperation between Jews and Arabs, and an attentive audience was found on occasion. In general, however, the Arabs showed hostility to Jewish settlement and from time to time even attempted to combat it with force.

I am one of those who believed, and who still believes, in the great blessing that cooperation will bring to both peoples. But from the time I started to work in the country as an agricultural laborer almost sixty years ago, I had to carry a rifle on my shoulder when I set out with my comrades to plough the fields of Galilee, and I also stood guard at night in an isolated Hebrew village (Sejera) that had previously been attacked. That was in the period of Ottoman rule. The attacks grew in number and intensity during the British Mandate. At one of the Zionist Congresses in the 'twenties, I was asked by one of the Polish Zionist leaders (he came from my birthplace, Plonsk), who was friendly to the Palestine labor movement and was opposed to Dr. Weizmann, even though he was a General Zionist, why we, the representatives of the workers, supported Weizmann and were so insistent on cooperation with the Mandate Government. This was after the slaughter of the *halutzim* in Jaffa in 1921. I told him that what we had suffered at Arab hands up to then was child's play compared with what we might expect in the future. My descriptions were not very far from what actually came to pass in the years 1936–39 and in the months following the adoption of the Partition resolution by the United Nations General Assembly in November 1947. Therefore, I said, we needed British help. My interlocutor answered that if he were to go about plagued by such thoughts he would go out of his mind. I said that if we did not prepare for these catastrophes we would forfeit our lives, that so long as we were few and weak (there were then less than 100,000 Jews in the country) we must try to maintain the Mandate regime, and that cooperation with the Mandatory Government was thus of vital importance for increasing our numbers and our strength in the country. At the same time, I told him, we must make every effort to find a common language with the Arabs of Palestine.

The late Chaim Arlosoroff, who was elected to the Zionist Executive as director of the Political Department in Jerusalem in 1931, as a result of his political activity arrived at pessimistic conclusions both with regard to the international situation and to the value of the Mandate. In a private letter to Dr. Weizmann on June 30, 1932, discussing the unsatisfactory alternatives that confronted the Zionist movement, he wrote:

"The fourth possible conclusion would be that Zionism cannot, in the given circumstances, be turned into a reality without a transition period of the organised revolutionary rule of the Jewish minority; that there is no way to a Jewish majority, or even to an equilibrium between the two races (or else a settlement sufficient to provide a basis for a cultural centre) to be established by systematic immigration and colonisation, *without a period of a nationalist minority government* [my italics—B. G.] which would usurp the state machinery, the administration and the military power in order to forestall the danger of our being swamped by numbers and endangered by a rising (which we could not face without having the state machinery and military power at our disposal). During this period of transition a systematic policy of development, immigration and settlement would be carried out."[3]

Arlosoroff did not explain in that letter how we would come to power (there were then less than 200,000 Jews in the country). Would we forcibly evict the English and seize the government? Or would the English voluntarily cede us dictatorial rights over the country? Nor did Arlosoroff take into account that there existed neighboring Arab states who might go to war against a Jewish dictatorship that rested on a handful of Jews in the country, particularly if it had been established in opposition to England; the opposition of the League of Nations also should have been taken into account.

This proposal of Arlosoroff's was never submitted for discussion to the Zionist Executive or to a meeting of party members, and even his closest friends had no knowledge of the letter, which was written at a time when Weizmann was not serving as president of the Zionist Organization.

About a year later Arlosoroff was murdered, and in the elections to the 18th Congress, in 1933, a radical change took place in the relative strength of the parties in the Zionist movement. For the first time, the Labor Palestine faction was the largest. Whereas at the 17th Congress, in 1931, Labor had 69 delegates out of 240, it now had 132 delegates out of 306. The General Zionists declined from 80 delegates to 70, and the Revisionists from 47 to 40. An Executive was formed of Labor and Radical Zionists, with Labor in the majority. I was elected to the Executive. That was the year Hitler came to power in Germany and I regarded the stepping up of immigration as the main task of the Zionist movement. At the first meeting of the Histadrut Council after the Congress, I said:

"At a difficult and dangerous hour, a heavy responsibility for the fate of Zionism has been placed on our movement, such as it has never borne previously. The catastrophe that has befallen German Jewry is not confined to the boundaries of

---

[3] Chaim Arlosoroff, *Jerusalem Diary* [Hebrew], p. 341

Germany. Hitler's rule places the entire Jewish people in jeopardy. Hitlerism is fighting not only the Jews of Germany but the Jews of the whole world. Hitler's regime cannot long continue without war, a war of vengeance against France, Poland, Czechoslovakia and the other countries where a German population is to be found, or against Soviet Russia with its vast expanses. The Jewish people is not a world factor capable of preventing or averting this danger. However, there is but a single place in the world where we constitute a major factor, if not yet the decisive one, and that place prescribes our entire future as a nation. What will be our strength and weight in that place on the awful judgment day, when the great catastrophe bursts upon the world? Who knows—perhaps only four or five years (and possibly even less) stand between us and that terrible day. During this period we must double our numbers, for the size of the Jewish community then may determine our fate in that decisive hour. That is why we must regard the question of immigration as central to all other questions." [4]

We did, in fact, succeed in increasing immigration in those years, which attained a peak of 61,000 in 1935; mention should be made here of the High Commissioner, General Wauchope, who was a great help in those days.

However, as the person responsible for Zionist policy, I could not ignore the Arab problem, and after I was elected to the Executive I initiated talks with the Arab leaders in Palestine and with representatives of Syria, Lebanon, Egypt and Saudi Arabia. My object was to find a common platform for the aspirations of the Zionist movement and those of the Arab nationalist movement.

5 TALKS WITH MUSA ALAMI AND OTHERS—1933-34

My first contact with the British Prime Minister, Ramsay MacDonald, was at Chequers, his official summer residence, on July 12, 1931. During the 17th Zionist Congress held shortly before, the stormiest of them all, Dr. Weizmann had asked Lewis Namier and me to meet with the Prime Minister in order to discuss the main points of his Palestine policy. The meeting was arranged, and the Prime Minister's son, Malcolm MacDonald, was also present. Among other things, I suggested that the Prime Minister arrange a round table at which Jewish and Arab representatives could try to arrive at mutual understanding and cooperation. Meanwhile, the Cabinet committee that had drafted the famous "MacDonald Letter" should continue to meet with us and discuss the

---

[4] D. Ben-Gurion, *From Class to Nation* [Hebrew], 1955 ed., pp. 474f. •

questions of Transjordan, land policy, immigration, and the role of the Jews in the development plan. MacDonald evinced sympathy for our proposals and noted that the Balfour Declaration and the Mandate had not implied that the Jews were to obtain only half of the country, since after the war the Arabs had already received a number of countries (Hejaz, Iraq, Syria), while the Jews had only Palestine. He promised to appoint a new High Commissioner satisfactory to us (and he was true to his word). As for a round table with the Arabs, he thought it desirable but he could not commit himself at the moment.

It should be recalled that it was at the 17th Congress that non-confidence was expressed in Dr. Weizmann, and Nahum Sokolow was elected president of the Zionist Organization.

Two years later, at the 18th Congress (1933), I was elected to the Zionist Executive, together with Moshe Sharett (then Shertok) and Eliezer Kaplan, and I decided to do what I could to reach an agreement with the Arabs.

I knew that the Arabs in Palestine had no authorized spokesmen and that the leaders were divided in their views and attitudes. After consulting with Moshe Sharett, with whom I shared responsibility for the political affairs of the Zionist movement, I decided to meet a certain Arab, who had a reputation as a nationalist and a man not to be bought by money or by office, but who was not a Jew-hater either. The man was Musa Alami, who was serving at the time as Attorney General in the British administration.

The prevailing assumption in the Zionist movement then was that we were bringing a blessing to the Arabs of the country and that they therefore had no reason to oppose us. In the first talk I had with Musa Alami, together with Moshe Sharett (the conversation took place in Sharett's home, because I then did not have an apartment in Jerusalem), that assumption was shattered. Musa Alami told me that he would prefer the land to remain poor and desolate even for another hundred years, until the Arabs themselves were capable of developing it and making it flower, and I felt that as a patriotic Arab he had every right to this view. Our conversation was frank, and Musa Alami gave me the impression of a sincere, straightforward and sensible man. He complained that the Jews showed contempt for the opinion of the Arabs, and that the previous members of the Executive had acted unfairly, before the disturbances of 1929. He particularly emphasized the pessimistic feeling that prevailed among the Arabs: they were gradually being ousted from all the important positions, the best parts of the country were passing into Jewish hands (while Arabs were also benefiting from this, the situation of the masses was desperate), the Jews had acquired the large concessions, the national budget was expended on defense, for which the Arabs had no need, there was an abundance of high-salaried British officials—and all for the sake of a Jewish national home; an Arab Palestine had no need for this officialdom. This was the reason the tax burden was steadily increasing. Perhaps the Jews were compelled to come here, but for the Arabs all was bleak and bitter. They were also apprehensive about their political future, but Musa Alami was concerned above all about the economic positions, and these were collapsing one by one.

I asked whether there was no possibility of agreement and mutual help instead of hatred and sterile opposition. The fact was that the Arab fellah and the Arab laborer were better off here than in Transjordan, where there wasn't a single Jew, or in the neighboring Arab countries. Musa Alami conceded that this was so, but said that the Arabs did not want outside help and in the meanwhile to lose important positions. I said that we would seek a common political platform, and then I put to him the crucial question: "Is there any possibility at all of reaching an understanding with regard to the establishment of a Jewish State in Palestine, including Transjordan?" He replied with a question. Why should the Arabs agree? he asked. Perhaps the Jews would manage to achieve this even without Arab consent, but why should they give their consent to this? I answered that in return we would agree to support the establishment of an Arab Federation in the neighboring countries and an alliance of the Jewish State with that federation, so that the Arabs in Palestine, even if they constituted a minority in that country, would not hold a minority position, since they would be linked with millions of Arabs in the neighboring countries.

After brief reflection, Musa Alami said that the proposal could be discussed, but what would happen in the meantime? The English were proposing the establishment of a Legislative Council, but it was a mere deception. All the power would remain in the hands of the English, while the elected representatives—Arabs and Jews alike—would be able to do nothing but talk; the Government would do as it pleased. Nevertheless, the Arabs would apparently participate in the Legislative Council, because they had gained nothing from their refusal to join the council established twelve years before.

I asked him whether the Arabs would agree to parity. His answer, as I had anticipated, was absolutely negative. Why should they? he asked. Did the Arabs not constitute four-fifths of the country's population? Were they not the indigenous population? Why should they make such a concession?

I said that I could well understand that stand, but possibly another proposal was feasible. Instead of a council without any real power, perhaps we should together demand a share in executive authority. The English were surely not keen on having us participate in the government, but if the Jews and Arabs agreed among themselves and presented a joint demand, the English might be forced to consider it—and the Jews would agree to such a demand if they were assured of parity in the government. Would the Arabs agree?

Such a plan might serve as a basis for discussion between the Jews and the Arabs, Musa Alami replied.

The hour was already late, and we parted.

The Arlosoroff murder trial began around that time, Musa Alami served as assistant to the chief prosecutor, and we were unable to meet. After the trial was over, he took sick, and again a meeting was ruled out.

Knowing of the eagerness of Dr. Judah L. Magnes for negotiations with the Arabs in order to seek an agreement, I met him and asked whether he had spoken with any Arabs on the subject and whether he thought there was hope of reaching any agreement. He replied in the negative. He had lost heart. It did not seem to him that the Jews were interested in an understanding with the Arabs. He had no authority to interfere in political affairs (he was president of the Hebrew University), and he had therefore stopped meeting with Arabs some time before. I told him of the conversation with Musa Alami and of my wish to continue the discussion with him, and said that I thought that this period of increased immigration was a good time for negotiations. I expressed the hope—based on my acquaintance with the man—that the High Commissioner, General Wauchope, would help us in the negotiations.

Meanwhile, Moshe Sharett went to Lebanon and met with Riad al-Sulh, a Lebanese leader who later became Prime Minister. The latter promised to visit Palestine for another talk, and he did come to Jerusalem at the end of May or the beginning of June 1934. I met him together with an official of the Political Department, Aharon Haim Cohen, who was of Persian origin. Riad al-Sulh declared that he was willing to work for Jewish-Arab understanding, to begin with among small groups of his friends. He asked what kind of an agreement we had in mind.

I proposed five points:

1) Freedom of Jewish immigration with no political limitation, including Transjordan.
2) All the Palestinian Arabs to remain in the country, and systematic aid to be extended in order to improve their economic and cultural position.
3) Participation of Jews and Arabs in the government, so long as the Mandate existed, on a parity basis.

4) Jewish independence in Palestine.
5) A link between the Jewish State in Palestine and the independent Arab Union in the neighboring countries.

Riad al-Sulḥ said that he considered my proposal to be a basis for negotiation. The leaders of Istiqlal were mainly interested in the last point, even though they saw no possibility of Syria's uniting with the other Arab countries without a new world war. He would meet with the other leaders and talk to them. Meanwhile, our talk must remain secret. He asked me to let him have my proposal in writing, and Aharon Ḥaim Cohen prepared an Arabic version.

A few days later I met Dr. Magnes and told him of my talk with Riad al-Sulḥ. I asked him whether it would be possible to meet one of the Palestinian leaders, and added that I had in mind people who were Arab patriots and honest men who could not be bought. Not long thereafter he invited me to his home to meet Auni Abdul Hadi, the Istiqlal leader in Palestine. The meeting took place on July 18, 1934, at nine in the evening. That was my first meeting with Auni. My initial impression was not encouraging. His face was not very pleasant. After Magnes introduced us, he started the conversation. Speaking broken English, he opened with the land question. The Jews were buying up the best lands and dispossessing the Arabs. All the valleys were in their hands: the coastal valley, the Jezreel valley, the Ḥule. Weizmann and others were always proclaiming goodwill toward the Arabs—where was this goodwill? In what form had it actually been manifested? Do you think you can fool us with sweet-sounding proclamations? What have you done to prove your goodwill? The settlement of the Jews undermines the existence of the Arabs. It is of no benefit to us. Individuals among us have become rich, but the people are losing their positions. The Jews have introduced speculation into the country. They pay exaggerated prices for land, and even if a few Arabs do plant orange groves with the Jewish money they have obtained, who can guarantee that in the end those groves will not be sold too? Who can resist the insane prices paid by the Jews? The English are helping to dispossess the Arabs from the land, contrary to the Mandate. He was planning to go to court to protest the illegality of the Jewish purchases. He knew that he would lose, for there was no justice in the land, but he wished to try. The terms of the Mandate provided that the Jews be helped without causing any harm to the Arabs. But the sale of land did cause harm, and it was thus a violation of the Mandate. The behavior of the Jewish National Fund was particularly reprehensible. It did not leave the Arabs any trace of land, he said, citing as an example the land purchase at Um-Ḥalad, an Arab village north of Netanya.

Both Dr. Magnes and I tried to prove to him that the settlement of the Jews was a blessing to the Arab fellahin in the coastal valley and in other areas: their farms had developed, yields had increased, working methods had been improved, and their income was much larger than it had been previously. Auni disputed this. He maintained that in any case the land was being transferred to the Jews, and even though the Arabs might not need it at the moment they would require it in a generation or two, when their numbers would be greater.

I said that if he was opposed to all land purchases under any conditions there was of course no possibility of a mutual understanding. We had been compelled to come and settle without the consent of the Arabs, and we would continue to do so in the future if necessary, but we would prefer to act on the basis of an understanding and mutual agreement. This was conceivable if the Arabs recognized our right to return to our land, while we would recognize the right of the Arabs to remain on their land. By developing the country we would make possible a larger and more firmly established population. Thirty years back, a farmer, Jewish or Arab, required a minimum of 250 dunams for subsistence; now, as a result of improved farming methods, 50 dunams were sufficient, and yielded an even greater income than before. With irrigation, even 25 dunams or less would be enough, and the income greater still. On the basis of our settlement experience and of detailed scientific research, we were convinced that there was room in the country both for Arabs who would gain their livelihood from their land and for large-scale Jewish settlement. We wanted all the Arabs that were working the land to remain where they were.

But under Jewish ownership? Auni asked.

No, I replied, we wanted to acquire the surplus. There was plenty of land in the country that was entirely uncultivated and unpopulated, and it should be put under intensive cultivation to permit a greater population density.

Auni had his doubts, and he returned to the arguments the Arabs had put forward before the Shaw Commission, which had been sent to Palestine after the disturbances of 1929.

I told him that, while the land question was of great importance, to us as well as to the Arabs, it would be impossible to arrive at an understanding on that matter unless there were grounds for agreement between us on the central issue. And the central issue was: Is it possible to reconcile the ultimate goals of the Jewish people and the Arab people? Our ultimate goal was the independence of the Jewish people in Palestine, on both sides of the Jordan, not as a minority but as a community of several millions. In my opinion, it was possible to create over a period of forty years, if Transjordan was included, a community of four million Jews in addition to an Arab community of two million. The goal of the Arab people was independence, and the unity of all Arab countries. If the Arabs agreed to our return to our land, we would help them with our political, financial and moral support to bring about the rebirth and unity of the Arab people.

Auni became enthusiastic when he heard this and said that if with our help the Arabs would achieve unity he would agree not to four million, but to five or six million, Jews in Palestine. He would go and shout in the streets, he would tell everyone he knew, in Palestine, in Syria, in Iraq, in Damascus and Bagdhad: Let's give the Jews as many as they want, as long as we achieve our unity.

When his enthusiasm abated he reverted to his mocking and sceptical tone and asked what guarantees the Arabs would obtain. The Jews in Palestine would increase in number to four million, while the Arabs in the other countries would be left with the English, the French, and the promise given by the Jews. Did we think the Arabs could rely on our promises and declarations?

I told him that if we should reach agreement on the main point we would seek together practical means whereby each side could insure the interests of the other. Even we had not yet attained four million in the country, the realization of Zionism was a long process, and the rebirth of the Arab people would also not come about overnight.

Auni asked whether we would help the Arabs get rid of France and England.

I answered that I had to speak frankly on this matter too. We would not fight against the English. We, too, had grievances against the Mandatory Government, perhaps no less than those held by the Arabs. But the English had helped us, and we wanted them to continue to do so. And we were faithful to our friends. The building up of the Arab economy, the raising of the level of culture, public education, the development of the various Arab countries—all these preceded and conditioned political liberation. In that positive task we were prepared to render all possible assistance to the Arab people. The only question was whether the Arabs were prepared to let us to work peacefully and undisturbed in Palestine.

Dr. Magnes framed the question as follows: Were the Arabs willing to sacrifice Palestine in order to attain the broader goal in the other Arab countries?

I commented that we did not wish the Arabs to "sacrifice" Palestine. The Palestinian Arabs would not be sacrificed so that Zionism might be realized. According to our conception of Zionism, we were neither desirous nor capable of building our future in Palestine at the expense of the Arabs. The Arabs of

Palestine would remain where they were, their lot would improve, and even politically they would not be dependent on us, even after we came to constitute the vast majority of the population, for there was a basic difference between our relation to Palestine and that of the Arabs. For us, this Land was everything, *and there was nothing else.* For the Arabs, Palestine was only a small portion of the large and numerous Arab countries. Even when the Arabs became a minority in Palestine they would not be a minority in their territory, which extended from the Mediterranean coast to the Persian Gulf, and from the Taurus Mountains to the Atlantic Ocean. The situation was similar to that of the English minority in Scotland. They were not a minority, because they were part of the United Kingdom, where they constituted a majority. For the Jewish people, it was essential that they be the majority here, as otherwise they would not be independent. But the Arabs could not turn into a minority.

Dr. Magnes asked whether the Arabs in the various countries really felt their unity.

Auni answered that, while this might not yet be true of the masses, the Arab intelligentsia in all countries—Syria, Iraq, Saudi Arabia, Tunis, Morocco—did feel that they belonged to one culture, one past, one nation.

The talk lasted three hours, and we parted on very friendly terms.

At a meeting with the High Commissioner, General Wauchope, on July 30, 1934, I related to him the gist of my conversation with Auni, and to my great surprise he asked me to proceed with these talks.

The next day I saw Dr. Magnes, who was about to leave on a trip abroad. I mentioned to him about my meeting with the High Commissioner, and the latter's comment. Magnes informed me that after our conversation, Auni had met Musa Alami, who told him of his meeting with me and Moshe Sharett. Musa Alami had been impressed by my frankness. One of the difficulties in a rapprochement with the Arabs had been the absence of personal confidence. I had won Musa Alami's confidence, and he—Magnes—set great store by that fact.

6 BRIT SHALOM AND ITS POLICIES

The two proposals that I made to Musa Alami in the early part of April 1934 —parity in the government under the Mandate, and afterwards a Jewish State —were no improvisation offered on the spur of the moment. I had expressed the same ideas orally and in writing previously in the debate with the Brit

Shalom organization and in discussions in the 'twenties with Aḥdut Ha'avodah, which, to the best of my knowledge, was the first Zionist party to call for the establishment of a Jewish State.

In the fall of 1924, at a meeting called by Brit Shalom, which advocated a bi-national state, I argued:

> "What is meant by the formula, a bi-national state? Sprinzak says we don't want to become a majority, but only to become many. How much is many? A hundred thousand? A hundred and fifty thousand? Many in relation to whom—to the Arab community in Palestine, or to the Jewish communities in the Diaspora? Does it imply a restriction on our increase to become a majority in the country? Yes or no? Will we agree to such a restriction? For me, an Arab question exists only when I adopt a Zionist stance, when I want to solve in Erez Israel the question of the Jewish people, that is, to concentrate it in Erez Israel and make it a free people in its land. Without this Zionist basis there is no Arab question in Erez Israel but a Jewish question, just as there is a Jewish question in all countries of the Diaspora, even where we are many. We are many in Russia, in Poland, in America. There are millions of us there—and yet the Jewish question exists. There are vital historic needs of the masses of the Jewish people that are the foundations of Zionism, and the Jewish people will not hear of this. The Jewish people wants to be a free people in its land, to be its own master, and that means—a Jewish State." [5]

At a second meeting with members of Brit Shalom, in December 1929, I said:

> "The formula of a bi-national state, which the Brit Shalom members have been advocating, has no meaning and lacks any political content. If the intention is merely to signify the fact that in Palestine there are Jews and Arabs, I have nothing against such a signification. But even in regard to this fact, I am afraid that there is a difference of opinion between us and Brit Shalom. What is the nature of this fact? Is it static or dynamic? However, if by your formula you wish to affirm that the country has equal value for the Jews and the Arabs, again you are missing the point and distorting the truth. Erez Israel for the Jewish people and Palestine for the Arab people are not one and the same thing.
>
> "Our land is only a small district in the tremendous territory populated by Arabs —most sparsely populated, I might add. Only one fragment of the Arab people —perhaps 7 or 8 percent, if we take into account only the Arabs of the Asian countries—lives in Palestine. However, this is not the case with respect to the Jewish people. For the entire Jewish nation this is the one and only country with which

---

[5] D. Ben-Gurion, *op. cit.*, pp. 76f.

are connected its fate and future as a nation. Only in this land can it renew and maintain its independent life, its national economy and its special culture, only here can it establish its national sovereignty and freedom. And anyone who blurs this truth endangers the survival of the nation." [6]

At the merger convention of Aḥdut Ha'avodah and Hapo'el Haẓa'ir in January 1930, which resulted in the formation of Mapai, the Palestine Labor Party, I spoke on Zionist policy and said:

"The rights *of the Hebrew people and of the non-Jewish inhabitants of the country* present a unique constitutional problem, which cannot be solved by analogy with, or precedents from, other countries, not even mandated ones. In order for the government in Palestine to be just, in conformity with the Mandate, the recognized aspirations of *the Jewish people* and the legitimate interests of the Arabs, it must fulfill the following conditions:
1) Enable the performance of the obligations of the Mandate by the incumbent, without any interference.
2) Prevent the domination of the Arabs by the Jews, or of the Jews by the Arabs.
3) Let the inhabitants participate in government.
4) Aid in rapprochement and cooperation between Jews and Arabs." [7]

Afterwards I drafted what I called "Postulates for Establishing the Governmental Regime in Palestine." [8] There I proposed three stages in attaining independence which, on the one hand, would insure the rights of the Jewish people in its entirety, the right of the Jewish people to national independence on a par with all other nations, and, on the other hand, would guarantee equality of rights to all citizens as individuals and as groups. In the first stage the foundation would be laid for self-government in local (urban and rural), communal (religious and national), and countrywide affairs, with the power of decision vested in the Mandatory Government. In the second stage there would be district autonomy with broad authority. In the third stage, when the Jews would have attained a majority, the Mandate would be abolished and a federal state established, with independent cantonal units, as in Switzerland: independent Jewish cantons and independent Arab cantons. There would be a bicameral federal parliament, consisting of a House of the Nations, where Jews and Arabs would be represented on an equal basis, and a House of the Inhabitants, in which the

---

[6] *Ibid.*, p. 99
[7] *Hapo'el Haẓa'ir*, Nos. 7–8. Nov. 28 and Dec. 5, 1930.
[8] *Ibid.*, No. 22, March 20, 1931.

cantons would be represented in proportion to their population (as in the United States of America).

I prepared this plan as early as November 23, 1929, shortly before the merger of Aḥdut Ha'avodah and Hapo'el Haẓa'ir. However, after further consideration, I came to the conclusion that it would not be feasible, and that after a Jewish majority was attained in the country a Jewish State should be established. While the Mandate continued, the participation of Jews and Arabs in the government on a parity basis should be insured, and when the Jewish State came into being it would be a member of a Semitic Federation, together with all the neighboring Arab countries.

When I spoke at the merger convention, in January 1930, I said:

> "Our opposition to Brit Shalom does not stem from any negative attitude on our part to the idea of peace and understanding with the Arabs. Even before Brit Shalom was founded, the Jewish labor movement in the country insisted on the need for joint action with the Arab worker. Neither has the Arab question ever disappeared from the political horizon of the labor movement, though the solution is not yet clear to this day. We are wrestling with the Arab question only from a conception of greater Zionism, and only from a recognition of the historic necessity that the masses of Israel settle in this land and here become a nation that is its own master. That nation will encounter hundreds of thousands of Arabs dwelling in this land, and Arab nations and kingdoms that surround us in the neighboring countries. And we must approach the Arab people, not with words of falsehood and deceit, not with any concealment of our Zionist aspirations, but with words of truth and peace. We will put it clearly: Come what may, we will not budge from here. No attack or obstruction will weaken the efforts of the Jewish people to settle once again in its land. But we recognize your needs, and we know of your nationalist aspirations. Peace, mutual understanding and joint undertakings with the Arabs of Palestine and the surrounding area—these are part of the very essence of Zionism." [9]

7 ANOTHER TALK WITH ALAMI—AUGUST, 1934

After the conclusion of the Arlosoroff murder trial and Musa Alami's recovery from his illness, I sent him a letter (on August 13, 1934), in which I said that I was about to go abroad and would like to meet him before my departure. He replied that the state of his health did not permit him to leave his village,

---

[9] *Ibid.*, No. 8, October 2, 1930.

but that he would be happy to meet me the next day at any hour if I could come there.

At 3 o'clock the next afternoon (August 14, 1934), I left for the village. Musa Alami was waiting for me in the courtyard, and we sat down to talk under an ancient oak tree, which my host described as being the oldest and biggest oak in the country. For three hours we spoke and thrashed out all the basic questions relating to a Jewish-Arab agreement. Both of us spoke with complete frankness, and I think with sincerity as well. Musa Alami concentrated mainly on the economic questions, and I on the political ones.

He began with the land question. More than anything else the Arabs feared that they would be dispossessed if the land passed to Jewish ownership. The great majority of the Arab people earned their living from agriculture, and without their own land the Arabs would have no livelihood.

I proposed a comprehensive, general development plan that would increase yields, bring much fallow and empty land under cultivation, and improve the position of the farmers. There would be enough land for the Arabs, while land would be gained for large-scale Jewish settlement. I related what we had accomplished in Degania, for example. There we had begun in 1911 with the establishment of a small *kvutza*, of less than twenty people, and we now had on the same area three *kvutzot*, each consisting of about one hundred people, and we had still not reached the ultimate point of improvement and population density. True, such a great increase was not possible everywhere in the country, but by our joint efforts we would be capable of turning the entire land into a flourishing economy and bringing under cultivation tremendous areas that were now completely desolate. We would teach the Arabs and the new settlers modern work methods, we would introduce new strains of dairy animals, we would improve the sanitary conditions, we would open schools in every village (here Musa Alami commented that there were no Arab teachers), we would open teachers' colleges for promising Arab youngsters. The basis of the agreement would be that if we purchased land we would insure that an adequate area remained for the tenant farmers and would help improve the Arab economy. We would make an effort to establish Jewish model villages near Arab villages, to serve as an example.

We would also establish factories by our joint efforts. The Arabs would participate with their capital and labor.

Musa Alami asked why we were fighting for Jewish labor.

I told him of the talk I had toward the end of the 'twenties with Sir John Chancellor, the High Commissioner who came to Palestine from Rhodesia.

As secretary general of the Histadrut labor federation, I requested him to allocate part of the Government's construction jobs to the Jewish worker. Chancellor remarked that it was inconceivable that Jewish workers would engage in unskilled physical labor: they should concentrate on light, skilled work. I told him that we did not want to create a situation such as existed in southern Africa, where the Whites were the lords and masters while the Blacks were the workers. If we remained merely the owners of the land, without doing all the necessary work with our own hands, easy and hard, skilled and unskilled, this would not be our homeland. I told Musa Alami about the builders of the first villages—Petaḥ Tikva, Rishon le-Zion, Zichron Ya'akov and Rosh Pina—and about the Bilu settlers. They had come here driven by the impulse to revive our homeland and our independence, but in the course of time many of them had forsaken these ideals and employed only Arab laborers, who were cheaper (because they had fewer needs) and more subservient, whereas the Jewish workers, most of whom had come with a vision of redemption, regarded themselves as no less important than the farmers. I explained that in the Diaspora we were cut off from the land and were accused of living on the toil of others. Even the Arab Executive had sent a memorandum to the League of Nations, in which it asserted that we were not at all suited to agriculture, since the Arabs were doing all our work. And when in 1923 I was sent by the Histadrut to visit the agricultural exhibition in Moscow, a letter was published in *Emes*, the newspaper of the Jewish section of the Communist Party, signed by a Jewish (non-Zionist, of course) Communist, claiming that all the samples of agricultural produce I had brought to display were the fruit of Arab labor. I explained why we regarded work as the basis of life and the foundation of national renascence.

All this was like the revelation of a new world to Musa Alami. I asked him whether the plan for improving the conditions of the Arab peasants and workers would not come up against the opposition of the Arab landowners and moneylenders. He assured me that there were no such groups in the country. The large landowners were mainly Syrians, while the moneylenders had virtually disappeared. It was true that the peasants were deep in debt, but they were no longer receiving loans—there was no one to loan them money.

I expressed my surprise that the Arab nationalist movement was not trying to do something to raise the level of the Arab masses, not in the economic sense but in the cultural one.

Musa Alami sadly admitted that their movement possessed no positive content.

The political questions I divided into two: 1) the constitutional arrangement during the transition period; and 2) the eventual arrangement.

For the transition period I proposed the participation of Jews and Arabs in the executive branch of the government, on a parity basis, together with the British, and the extension of local autonomy (in the towns and villages).

Musa Alami saw no difficulty in such an arrangement.

As the final arrangement I proposed that Palestine would be an independent Jewish State connected with an Arab Federation.

Who would guarantee this connection? Musa Alami asked. The Arabs would not rely either on the British or on the League of Nations, who had deceived them more than once. And without an adequate guarantee it would be impossible to agree to Jewish immigration. He therefore suggested that the order be reversed: first establish the federation, with free immigration throughout it, and not limited to Palestine alone.

I explained to him that for us as a people only Palestine could be considered our homeland. Individual Jews would be free to settle in Iraq or Syria if they so wished. But we regarded as our land only Palestine, including Transjordan. I told him that at the beginning of the century Joseph Chamberlain had offered us Uganda in Africa for Jewish settlement, but that the Zionist Congress had rejected this proposal, although Dr. Herzl supported it.

As for guarantees, I asked him to state what guarantees were wanted and would be acceptable. We could not postpone our immigration until the federation was functioning.

Musa Alami said that without a firm guarantee regarding the federation, it was unlikely that the whole idea would meet with acceptance.

The Arabs, he said, were actually not thinking of a single state. As they saw it, there were three blocs: 1) Syria and western Palestine; 2) Iraq and Transjordan; 3) Arabia:—Hejaz, the Negev and Yemen. Both dynastic considerations and cultural differences would interfere with the creation of a single Arab state (even if imperialistic factors were not involved). Since the death of Faisal, there was no one personality that could be regarded as the representative of all the Arabs. The Hashemite dynasty was not respected. Ibn Saud was a rising star, but there was no inclination on the part of Syria to join his kingdom. The great obstacle to the unification of the Arab countries was the French occupation, and for that reason it was unrealistic for the time being to speak of an overall federation. What was feasible at the moment was the union of Iraq, Transjordan and Palestine, i.e., all the countries under British rule. Musa Alami also added the Kingdom of Saudi Arabia to the "English" countries.

In answer to my question as to the Arab elements that should be taken into account in negotiations, he replied that there were three groups:

1) The Istiqlal. In Palestine, this group was small and without influence, except among the youth, because the leaders were not trusted.

2) The main power in Palestine was the Mufti. Although the Jews regarded him as their principal enemy, he was really not so terrible. His influence was decisive, and he was held in high esteem in the Moslem world as well as by Arabs outside of Palestine. The Istiqlal outside of Palestine would do nothing without the Mufti's knowledge. For his part, the Mufti took into account the views of the Istiqlal outside of Palestine, particularly the opinions of the Syrians, Iḥsan Bey el-Jabri (Musa Alami's father-in-law) and Shekib Arslan (who was a Druze, but an Arab "assimilationist").

3) The opposition. Its leaders were corrupt and uninfluential, and only a few of them were worth anything at all. They took no interest in the general problems but were concerned only with local matters. One of the grievances of the Arabs was the intervention of the Jews in the Jerusalem municipal elections in support of Nashashibi and against the Husseinis (the Mufti's men).

I commented that there was opposition among the Jews to this intervention.

Musa Alami suggested that I meet the Mufti. Of course, the meeting would have to be secret, and if nothing came of it and no agreement was signed by the two parties, whatever passed between the two of us would be null and void. The Arabs still remembered the unfair conduct of Colonel Kisch and his associates who, before the Seventh Arab Congress, urged the Arabs not to adopt an anti-Zionist resolution, promising that in return the Jews would show goodwill toward the Arabs. The Seventh Congress met and, through the influence of Iḥsan Bey el-Jabri, did not adopt any resolution against Zionism. Meanwhile, the disturbances of 1929 took place, and when the Shaw Commission came to Palestine the Jews exploited the fact that no anti-Zionist resolution had been adopted to prove that the Arabs were not opposed to Zionism.

The testimony of Sacher[10] before the Shaw Commission concerning Auni Abdul Hadi had likewise aroused anger and suspicion.

I promised Musa Alami that my conversations with him and with any other Arab leader would remain strictly confidential. For the time being I too was

---

[10] Sacher asserted before the Commission that the Arabs were not hostile to Zionism, citing the resolutions of the Arab Congress which said nothing against Zionism. As this subject had been omitted at the request of the Jews, the appearance of Sacher before the Commission aroused the ire and distrust even of those Arabs who had shown an inclination to reach an agreement with the Jews.

speaking in a private capacity and had not yet discussed all these matters with my colleagues.

I suggested that the meeting with the Mufti be postponed until I conferred with my colleagues abroad, and that I first meet the Istiqlal leaders (Jabri and Arslan) in Switzerland. I would meet the Mufti when I returned.

While we were talking, Musa Alami's father-in-law (Jabri) and Ta'alabi of Tunis arrived. The latter had the look of a Jewish scholar. They did not speak English, but French; between themselves, of course, they spoke Arabic. Musa Alami introduced me to them. Later, the Turkish consul arrived, and at six in the evening I left for Jerusalem.

The next morning I met Edwin Samuel (the son of Herbert Samuel and then a senior official in the Mandate Government) and, without mentioning names, I gave him the gist of the conversations and the elements of the agreement discussed. In his opinion all these talks were worthless. The Arabs had no representative who could speak with authority. These individuals were dabbling in politics simply to gain public stature for themselves. The British Government, in his view, would pay no attention to such an agreement, but would maintain that, even if an agreement were signed, a new party might arise the next day which would fight Zionism and proclaim as traitors those who had signed on behalf of the Arabs, and we would be back where we started.

I asked Samuel whether he didn't think a Jewish-Arab agreement would be of some value. No, he answered. The only thing for us to do was to work among the fellahin and laborers: health services, loan funds, joint organization. That was what the Government was doing too. The High Commissioner visited the villages and won the peasants over. We must do the same. But there was no hope to be expected from the Arab leaders.

That same evening I met the High Commissioner, and I decided to put the matter before him, again without mentioning names, and to sound out his opinion. I was happy to hear that the views of the High Commissioner were quite different from those of Edwin Samuel.

8 MORE TALKS WITH ALAMI—AUGUST, 1934

On August 27, 1934, I had another meeting with Musa Alami at his home. He had come to Jerusalem to be examined by a doctor I had recommended, and afterwards he drove me in his car from my hotel to his home. This time he put a number of questions to me, and not very easy ones either.

The first related to the Mosque of Omar. If the Jews became the majority in Palestine and it was declared a Jewish State, who would guarantee the Mosque of Omar, the holiest Moslem shrine outside of Hejaz?

I asked whether there were truly intelligent Arabs who feared that we wanted to take the Mosque of Omar.

Indeed there were, Musa Alami replied, adding that there was foundation for this apprehension. Among those who held this fear was the Mufti. There were a number of facts and documents that testified to the intention of the Jews to rebuild their Temple on the site of the Mosque. Had Sir Alfred Mond (later Lord Melchett) not made a speech about the building of the Temple? True, Herbert Samuel—who had been High Commissioner at the time—had written to Mond asking him why he had mentioned such a thing, and Mond had replied that what he meant was a spiritual temple, but that answer did not satisfy the Arabs. In 1920 an Englishman by the name of Shelley approached the Arabs with the proposal that they sell the Mosque to the Jews for a million pounds and use the money to build schools. Shelley was head of the Jerusalem chamber of commerce, a Christian missionary, and a man who hated Islam and the Arabs. The Arabs were convinced that he spoke on behalf of the Jews.

I answered that the Orthodox Jews did believe—and this was no secret—that the Temple would be rebuilt, but that would be only after the coming of the Messiah. This was a religious belief, and the faithful were certain that it would take place by way of a miracle, and not in a natural manner. But it did not occur to any Jew to touch the holy places of other peoples, and if any guarantees were necessary that no such intentions existed with regard to the Mosque of Omar, they would certainly be given.

Musa Alami then asked whether I would agree that Iraq, Transjordan and Palestine should constitute a single state. I replied in the negative. The independence of the Jewish people was inconceivable without Palestine as an independent political unit, that is, a Jewish State.

He then asked whether I would agree that the three states be linked to one another.

I replied that we wanted to see only two states: Palestine, including Transjordan; and Iraq.

He commented that even under the Mandate Transjordan was not included in the Jewish national home.

I answered that our Zionism did not spring from the Mandate or the Balfour Declaration. In any case, the Jews and the Arabs were not in any way bound by the Mandate. The Mandate was binding on Britain, not on us or the Arabs.

However, if we were assured of unlimited immigration and settlement in Transjordan we would be prepared to discuss a special arrangement, temporary or permanent, regarding Transjordan.

(It is worth noting that when I spoke to the High Commissioner on August 14, 1934, after my previous talk with Musa Alami about Transjordan as part of a Jewish State, the High Commissioner noted that the status of Transjordan could not be like that of Cisjordan, since the terms of the Mandate concerning a national home did not apply to the former territory. I replied that our settlement in Transjordan was a condition to the agreement, and the nonapplication to Transjordan of the paragraphs dealing with the national home was not absolute or permanent, but temporary, as stated specifically in Paragraph 25 of the Mandate.)

Musa Alami then asked a third question: Would I agree to the restriction of Jewish immigration during the next ten years so as to insure that the Jewish population at the end of that period would not exceed one million.

I replied in the negative, and I asked what was the point of such a restriction.

He answered that the Arabs would be unable to progress sufficiently in the next ten years, and if the Jews were to increase without any limitation the country would become completely Jewish, without the Arabs being able to safeguard their future in it.

I said that instead of impeding our growth, it would be preferable for us to work out a plan together in order to accelerate Arab development. We would open schools in every village, we would teach the Arabs new working methods, we would improve their farms, we would establish model Arab villages, and so forth.

Musa Alami doubted whether the Arabs would be capable of progressing so rapidly. There were no teachers, and they would thus be unable to rise to the level of the Jews.

I commented that without Jewish help he might well be right, but if we formed an alliance and invested manpower, organization, technology and money in the development of the Arab economy, as we had done for the development of the Jewish economy, the entire economic and cultural condition of the Arabs might change. The alliance between us had to be built on mutual aid and not on mutual hindrance. We would assist not only in the development of Palestine and Transjordan, but also in that of Iraq. That country offered tremendous possibilities, it had an abundance of fertile land and of water. We were interested in its maximum development, both politically and economically.

I asked Musa Alami how the agreement would come about; who would sign for the Arabs?

He replied that the question was not merely a Palestinian one. There could be no solution to the Jewish-Arab dispute within the borders of Palestine alone; only within a general Arab framework would a final answer be possible. In Palestine it would be necessary, first of all, to negotiate with the Mufti, and outside of Palestine, with the Istiqlal. If agreements were reached, a general Arab Congress would be convened, with delegates coming from Syria, Palestine, Iraq, Saudi Arabia and Yemen. The delegates would elect an executive committee, and its members would sign the agreement.

I told Musa Alami that I would be leaving for London shortly and would submit the entire matter to my colleagues. From London I would travel to Geneva, where I would meet the Syrian committee: Shekib Arslan and Ihsan Bey el-Jabri.

He commented that they would first confer with the Mufti and would do nothing contrary to his wishes. He asked whether I would like him to speak to the Mufti about the matter, and I said it would be most desirable, even before I left.

Musa promised to meet the Mufti and to visit me in Jaffa before I sailed. As to Arslan and Jabri, he was prepared to give me a letter to them. I said it would be preferable if he wrote to them about the content of our talk.

On August 29, Musa Alami telephoned me in Jerusalem to say that he would meet me in Jaffa the next day. He had already spoken to the Mufti. The next day, however, I was informed that he would not be able to come, and the meeting was fixed for August 31 in Jerusalem.

At 10 a.m. on August 31, 1934, I met Musa Alami in his home in Jerusalem. He had seen the Mufti in his village and reported to him on the content of our talks. This came as a bombshell to the Mufti. He had not imagined that there were Jews who sincerely wished an understanding and an agreement with the Arabs. Up to then no such approach had ever been evident. He, Musa Alami, had assured the Mufti that I was speaking honestly and sincerely and that he could rely on me. The Mufti heard the plan with great interest, and replied as follows:

Up to now he had not believed that the Jews felt any need for an understanding with the Arabs. For his part he had no objection, so long as it would be possible to safeguard the religious, economic and political interests of the Arabs of Palestine. Naturally, he would have to give the plan further consideration. It was all so surprising and so sudden. For the moment he could not take a single step. Arab public opinion was far removed from such a proposal, and no leader could do anything behind the Arabs' backs. Public opinion had to be changed, a different atmosphere created. Some public declaration was needed that would influence Arab public opinion.

It was Musa Alami's opinion that I should first of all meet Jabri and Arslan. He would write to them about his talk with the Mufti. The Mufti attached much weight to their opinion, and they to his. Afterwards a public declaration should be made, without going into details and without yet hinting at any negotiations. The talks for the time being must remain absolutely secret.

I agreed. We clarified the general lines of the declaration: the Palestine question was a matter of concern not only to the Arabs and Jews living in the country but, on the one hand, it was the affair of the entire Jewish people and, on the other hand, it was a general Arab question; the complete realization of the aspirations of the Jewish people in Palestine did not conflict with those of the Arab people: on the contrary, the two complemented one another; cooperation between the two peoples would be of benefit both to Palestine and to the other Arab states; measures would be taken to insure that Jewish and Arab press reactions to the declaration would be friendly, and we would go on from there. I invited Musa Alami to visit our collective farms, and he gladly accepted.

On September 2, I sailed for London. From the boat (the *Sphinx*) I sent a letter to Dr. Magnes on September 7, 1934, in which I wrote:

"I am en route to London. I left the country on the 2nd, and in four days time I shall be in London (I shall stop over in Paris for a day or two). After your trip, I met several times with Musa Alami, and we clarified the fundamental lines of an Arab-Jewish pact. The two peoples would recognize each other's national aspirations, and would help bring about their *full* realization to the maximum degree possible. Without dispossessing the Arabs living in the country, the Jewish people's right to return to Ereẓ Israel *and to settle there without any numerical restriction* would be recognized. The Jews would also be given the right to immigrate to Transjordan, and to settle there. Together we would draft a comprehensive development plan with the aim of clearing and preparing land for intensive Jewish settlement and of raising the standard of the Arab agricultural workers to a modern European level. Land purchases by the Jews would be with the assurance that the Arab peasants would be allotted sufficient land to gain a livelihood. In the development of industry, Jews and Arabs would participate jointly, both with capital and labor. The right of Jewish labor in the Jewish economy would be recognized. The Arab peasants would be offered assistance in the spheres of science, organization, health and finance. As to the political aspect: during the transition period, Jews and Arabs would participate in the executive branch on a parity basis. The ultimate arrangement would be an independent state linked to the Arab Federation, and with British interests protected. The Jews would help—politically, morally and financially—in the development of the Arab countries (Iraq and Transjordan above all) and in the attainment of Arab unity. The status of Transjordan still required clarification—whether it would constitute an integral part of the State of Erez Israel or would have some special, intermediate status between Erez Israel and Iraq—but Jewish settlement without any political restriction would be assured there too. Adequate guarantees would be given for the protection of the Moslem holy places in Palestine (particularly the Mosque of Omar).

"This, of course, is only a general sketch that still requires clarification on a number of important points. When the two sides reach agreement a general Arab Congress will be convened, with representatives from all the countries: Palestine, Syria, Iraq, Saudi Arabia, Yemen. An executive will be elected which will sign the agreement.

"Musa Alami has submitted the plan to the Mufti. He told me the Mufti was amazed to hear of this. He had not believed that there was a sincere desire on the Jewish side to reach an understanding and agreement with the Arabs. His answer was: if it would be possible to safeguard the religious, economic and political interests of the Arabs then he was for an agreement. However, this matter was so remote from Arab public opinion that no leader would now dare to do a thing. A change in atmosphere was necessary. For that reason a declaration on the part of the Jews was needed.

"I discussed the outlines of such a declaration with Musa Alami. He has written about the entire plan to his father-in-law [Jabri] and to the Emir [Arslan], who are now in Geneva, informing them that I will be going there to meet them. He also conveyed to them the Mufti's views on the matter.

"Meanwhile I have spoken to the High Commissioner [General Wauchope] about a plan for a Jewish-Arab agreement along the above-mentioned lines, without mentioning the names of the men with whom I have been in contact. He was pleased to learn of this and requested me to continue. He informed me that if we would arrive at an economic agreement, the Government would adopt it as a Government plan. As to the political agreement, he said that while he could not commit the Cabinet he was sure that it would view with favor any Jewish-Arab agreement.

"I shall have to stay in London for about two weeks. On the 20th or the 25th of the month, I shall travel to Geneva to meet the two gentlemen [Jabri and Arslan]. In my opinion it is very important that you should take part in these talks, and I request of you to let me know in London whether this is possible and where you will be at this time.

"Please write to me care of the Zionist Executive in London."

I received a reply from him saying that he had to be in the United States at this time and would be unable to come to Geneva to participate in the talks.

9 TALKS WITH SYRIANS—SEPTEMBER, 1934

I stayed in London for about two weeks, and on September 22, 1934, I left for Paris in order to meet up with Marc Jarblum who was to act as my interpreter in Geneva. I knew that the two Arab leaders did not know English, and I was not accustomed to conversing in French. (I studied French when I was a student in Constantinople before World War I and I read French literature, but I had never had the opportunity to speak the language.) In Paris I tried to contact Nahum Goldmann, who was in Geneva, but there was no answer. I looked for Jabri's telephone number, but it transpired that he had no telephone. I traced Arslan's telephone number, and a girl answered that he was not at home. My schedule called for my departure for Geneva that evening. Before leaving I phoned Arslan once again, and this time he was in. He said they could meet me the following evening, and I therefore decided to postpone our departure until the next morning. At noon on September 23 we set out for Geneva; and I had sent a telegram to Jabri informing him that we would meet at Arslan's home at 9.30 p.m.

When we arrived at Arslan's, Jabri was already there. Arslan lived in a spacious and lavishly decorated apartment. I was acquainted with Jabri from Palestine, and he greeted me warmly. "The Lion" (*Arslan* in Turkish means lion) gave the impression of a slow-moving old man, but when he spoke his vigor and fervor came to the fore. After a brief conversation about common acquaintances —in the French Socialist Party—we came to the point. Jabri said that he had received a letter from Palestine about the talks held with me, but he wanted to hear details. There was a language difficulty. We started in Turkish, but since Jarblum did not know the language we switched to French. That was the first time in my life that I took part in a lengthy, serious conversation in that language. Jarblum, of course, helped me. So did the two hosts, who knew a little German. Every once in a while they would provide the word I was groping for.

The talk in Arslan's home lasted until one in the morning. I went over the main points I had discussed with Musa Alami. Arslan immediately adopted an extreme position. Without a promise from us that the Arabs in Palestine would remain a majority he was not prepared for any negotiations. As to our assistance in achieving the unity of the Arab countries outside of Palestine—unity of that kind was nothing but a dream. Before that came about, a hundred or who knew how many years would pass. Meanwhile, the Jews would be the majority in Palestine while the Arabs would become an insignificant factor. I said that I was not so pessimistic about the unity of the Arab countries. As for the Palestinian Arabs, they were after all only a small percentage of the total Arab population, and even if we became the overwhelming majority in Palestine, more than two-thirds, the Arabs of Palestine would not feel themselves a minority, because they would be surrounded by Arab states that were linked with the Jewish State. Arslan changed his line of reasoning and said that the unity of the Arab peoples was assured in any case. He himself had helped bring about a rapprochement between Ibn Saud and the Imam Yiḥya in Yemen. Iraq and Saudi Arabia were also about to draw closer. If a world war should break out, Tunisia, Algeria, Morocco and the other countries would gain their independence, so why did the Arabs need Jewish help, and what would it actually give them? If the Jews needed a Jewish State, why did they not go to one of the larger, unpopulated countries? I told him that similar advice had been offered us at the beginning of the century, not by a private individual, but by the representative of a world empire, by Joseph Chamberlain, who was then Colonial Secretary and had offered us Uganda—and we had rejected it. I explained what Ereẓ Israel had meant to the Jewish people for some four thousand years. Arslan insisted emphatically that he could not approach the Arabs of Palestine with a proposal that they should eventually become a minority. He did not see any value whatsoever in Jewish assistance, and he was also certain that the English would never permit us to become a majority or a great force in Palestine. England wanted a Jewish community in Palestine in order to make it easier for her to dominate the Arabs, but she had no interest in creating a Jewish Palestine. Even if such a Palestine should be created, the Arabs would never acquiesce. After all, surrounding Palestine there were tens of millions of Arabs. He was prepared to enter an agreement only if we would undertake to remain a minority. He also denied our right to settle in Transjordan. That area had not been promised to us in the Mandate, and we had no claim on Transjordan even from the English standpoint. He asked me, by the way, whether the English agreed to our settling in Transjordan. I said that the exclusion of Transjordan from the Jewish national home was temporary and had been introduced a few years after the Balfour Declaration, which applied to all of Ereẓ Israel, eastern as well as western.

When Jabri spoke, he made no attempt to contradict Arslan, but it was obvious from his questions that he was more willing to compromise: he valued the Jewish factor more and understood the historic tie of the Jewish people to Palestine. He asked me whether we were empowered by the Jewish people or the Zionist Organization to make an agreement. I said that for the time being the conversation was private and, as he already knew from the letter he had received, also confidential.

After our talk was over, Jabri escorted me to the railway station. On the way he said that the last word had not been spoken and that the discussion would continue.

I spent a few more weeks in Europe (I also visited Warsaw) and returned to Palestine in December 1934. When I arrived I was amazed to learn that the November issue of *La Nation Arabe*, published by the Syrian-Palestinian delegation in Geneva, carried a report of my talk with Arslan and Jabri, even though it had been stipulated that it would remain confidential. And it was not without distortions either. The headline read: "MR. BEN-GURION'S VISIT TO THE SYRIAN-PALESTINIAN DELEGATION IN GENEVA." And this was the story that followed:

> "Following the pressing appeals of a number of friends, we agreed to receive Ben-Gurion in Geneva. He wished to talk to us about the Jewish problem in Palestine and to propose a number of practical solutions which had been put before his committee.
>
> "To tell the truth, we hesitated a long time before agreeing to the visit, because we suspected that it might have been planned as propaganda for the Zionist movement. But after receiving information as to Ben-Gurion's serious nature, we decided that it would be worthwhile to hear his proposals while at the same time learning of the real aim of Zionism from an authorized source.
>
> "Naturally, the talks had no official character. This was an informal exchange of views without any commitments on either side. The meeting took place on September 23 in Geneva, the time being fixed in a telegram that Ben-Gurion sent to us from Paris. He was accompanied by a Jew of that city.
>
> "We told Ben-Gurion that we would listen to his proposals with the greatest attention. He opened with an introduction which included the causes of immigration to Palestine, the aims of the Zionist movement, and the urgent motives for Jewish settlement in that country. He detailed the various stages the Jews have gone through in different countries, and he concluded with the absolute necessity of making Palestine a Jewish homeland and a Jewish State. That could not be prevented, he declared, but he believed that it was necessary to reach an agreement with the Arabs.
>
> "We asked him how many immigrants the Zionist agency intended to bring into the country and what he thought was the maximum absorptive capacity of the

country. He stated frankly that their claim applied not only to Palestine but to Transjordan as well. According to their experts, the two countries can absorb between six to eight million Jews. He explained in greater detail the material and spiritual factors that draw the Jews to Palestine. He had come to ask quite simply what compensation the Arabs might demand for an agreement on the establishment of a Jewish State in both of these countries, immediately adding the promise that the Arabs who did not wish to emigrate from their country would be free to remain and that their land would not be stolen from them.

"We felt it our duty to ask him whether he was talking seriously, for we could not keep from smiling when we heard such nonsense. Nevertheless, we wanted to get to the bottom of the matter and we asked Mr. Ben-Gurion what compensation the Jews would make to the Arabs in return for their sacrifices. He answered: 'We will extend political and economic aid to the Arabs. The political aid will come from the mobilization of the Jewish forces on behalf of the Arabs in Syria. The economic aid will be in the form of capital investment in Iraq, Saudi Arabia, and Yemen, looking to their economic development.' We replied: 'In short, you are proposing to us the evacuation of seven or eight million inhabitants [*sic!*] from the country in return for some vague political assistance and economic aid of which these Arab countries have no urgent need.' More precisely, we explained to him frankly that France, in view of her international obligations, would not be long in reaching an understanding with the Syrian nation.

"Furthermore, we told him, you are well aware that France has officially declared to the League of Nations that she recognizes the ability of Syria to govern itself. And as you see, events in Syria are developing normally, without the need of any Jewish help. Iraq, for its part, has already achieved independence and, thanks to its oil and other natural resources, is in the full swing of economic development. There is no capital shortage; the Government only has to ask, and money is forthcoming. As for Hejaz and Yemen—at this time, at any rate, they have no intention of seeking foreign capital, and Jewish capital least of all.

"You can well see that Arab dependence on the political and economic aid of the Jews is not a necessity. Indeed, an absolute zero is offered in return for driving a million and a half Arabs to abandon their birthplace, the holy land of their fathers, in despair and wander into the desert; in return for the Arab nation of twenty million souls accepting this humiliation of evacuating the land, every grain of which is saturated with the blood of their fathers, and which is so holy from the religious aspect. Such a proposal should not be presented before it is weighed and examined with great care.

"If anyone has such arrogant and impudent ideas, he should not assume that he will obtain the consent of his adversary. It would be better for him to continue, with reliance on British bayonets, and create the Jewish State, but at least he should not contemplate an agreement with the Arabs, an agreement that the English and the Jews do not cease talking about in order to deceive world public opinion. "We therefore informed Mr. Ben-Gurion that there was no point in continuing this fantastic conversation. These are the facts.

"Mr. Ben-Gurion has good reason for his boldness in making such childish and illogical proposals, for the tremendous backing of the British Government and the inaction of the Arab forces in the face of the growing dangers and the assaults of the Jewish enterprise have made it possible for the Zionist representatives to amuse themselves with the most daring notions.

"Mr. Ben-Gurion's step is really a most important act, revealing the true aim of the Zionists, which can be explained by their faith that their dream will soon be realized. It is a warning not only to the Arabs but also to the British, who ought to ponder the results of Jewish expansion of this type."[11]

When I read the periodical on my return to Palestine, I immediately recorded the following:

1) The talk was private and confidential. It was stipulated that the content of the talk would not be made public. Iḥsan Bey el-Jabri was the first to emphasize this condition.

2) Since the talk was reported in brief, statements were not rendered accurately. However, in certain parts there were deliberate distortions:

a. I did not say that "all the Arabs who did not wish to emigrate or leave the country would be free to remain." I had said exactly the opposite. Before the start of Jewish settlement many Arabs, particularly Christians, left the country and emigrated to America, Argentina, etc. That emigration ceased with the settlement of the Jews. And not only was it not our intention or in our power to push the Arabs out, but intentionally and unintentionally we are improving their condition. And the proof is the large increase of the Arabs after the war.

b. I did not say that "we will mobilize the Jewish forces to help the Arabs in Syria." On the contrary, I criticized the Arab nationalist movement, which was based on negation alone, for it was concerned solely with the fight against foreign domination. And I said that we would have no part in that. Our movement was based on positive goals—on economic and cultural activity. And we would be prepared to help the Arab people in such activity, since only the raising of the economic and spiritual level of the Arab people would lead it to true national freedom.

---

[11] *La Nation Arabe*, Organ of the Syrian-Palestinian Delegation to the League of Nations, edited by the Emir Shekib Arslan and Iḥsan Bey el-Jabri, No. 2, December 1934.

When I showed the pamphlet to Musa Alami he was filled with shame and humiliation. He said that henceforth it would be difficult for him to show his face in public. I knew that he said this with sincerity and was truly sorry.

10 ARAB DEMANDS—1935-36

Meanwhile our political situation changed. On November 25, 1935, a united Arab delegation presented the High Commissioner with a memorandum which he forwarded to the Colonial Office. In it the Arabs put forward three main demands: 1) the establishment of a national Government elected by the inhabitants of the country; 2) the complete stoppage of Jewish immigration; 3) the prohibition of land sales to the Jews.

On January 9, 1936, the High Commissioner informed the members of the delegation in writing that the Secretary of State for Colonial Affairs had received the memorandum and was studying it carefully and that the two of them would discuss it as soon as possible.

On January 29, the High Commissioner summoned the members of the delegation and informed them that he had received a cable from the Secretary authorizing him to give them answers to their three demands, as worded in the following official communique:

> "a) The demand for the establishment of a democratic Government has been answered by the communication on the part of the High Commissioner to the Arab leaders of proposals for the establishment of a Legislative Council with a large unofficial majority, in the composition of which the elective principle is recognised.
>
> "b) There can be no question of the total stoppage of Jewish immigration into Palestine. The guiding principle as regards the admission of immigrants is a policy of economic absorptive capacity and His Majesty's Government contemplates no departure from that principle.
>
> "In order to ensure that the closest possible relation is maintained between the number of new immigrants to be admitted and the absorptive capacity of the country, both now and in the future, a statistical bureau has been set up under the charge of a highly trained and experienced statistician from Canada. It is intended that this bureau should carry out periodical surveys of trade, industry and agriculture and should keep the High Commissioner in close touch with the changing economic situation in the country.
>
> "c) The Secretary of State approves in principle of the enactment of legislation whereby, except in the sub-district of Beersheba and in urban areas, and also except

as regards land planted with citrus, no land owner shall be permitted to sell any of his land unless he retains a minimum area which is sufficient to afford a means of subsistence to himself and his family; as a safeguard against collusive sales this minimum area shall revert to Government if it ceases to be cultivated by the owner occupier. The legislation próposed will be of general application so that outside the excluded areas the sale of land to any person would be subject to the restrictions indicated.

"The High Commissioner shall retain the power to approve the sale of a subsistence area if he is satisfied that to do so will be in the interests of the public good, for example, where a subsistence area is needed for sub-urban development or is blocking development of rural land or an important irrigation or drainage scheme."

The High Commissioner said that in connection with the Legislative Council he was considering the observations and criticisms of all the parties represented at the meeting of November 25; he would reply in writing, after which, if necessary, a further discussion might take place.

In commenting upon the land sales problem, he reminded those present of his long-standing interest in the happiness and prosperity of the rural population of Palestine and of his desire to ensure, without arresting development or disturbing the credit system of the country, that the cultivator should not suffer by transfers of ownership. This was why he had enacted in 1933 the Protection of Cultivators Ordinance, which gave a measure of security to rural tenants. He went on to say:

"That Ordinance did not, however, affect the position of the small owner, whose position at that time was in no way critical. The situation is, however, changing and in view of increasing land sales some protection is now needed for smallholders as well as for tenants. At present, little difficulty is experienced in obtaining alternative employment. But that state of affairs may not continue indefinitely, and the natural increase of the population is another factor which will add to the difficulties of the situation if no measure is taken at a fairly early date. In the circumstances I am satisfied that the process of sale of lands by smallholders can no longer safely be allowed to go unchecked."

The High Commissioner did not state what would be the minimum sub-area the sale of which would be forbidden. For the time being he announced only two assumptions pertaining to this question:
1) The minimum would not be the same throughout the country. In places where cultivation was extensive the minimum would be greater, and where cultivation was intensive it would be smaller.

2) If land should be improved or irrigation possibilities develop, the minimum would be reduced.

Before the High Commissioner met the Arab delegation on January 29, he sent the Jewish Agency the text of the statement he had prepared, and in another letter he recalled the talk he had had a year before, on February 12, 1935, with Dr. Arthur Ruppin, Moshe Sharett and the present writer. We had then discussed the necessity of protecting the Arab peasant as well as the tenant farmer, and the High Commissioner noted that in the past five years Jewish land purchases had increased. (According to the Government's figures, the Jews bought 19,365 dunams in 1930, 18,585 dunams in 1931, 18,893 dunams in 1932, 36,991 dunams in 1933, 62,114 dunams in 1934, and 73,000 dunams in 1935.)

The Arabs were not satisfied with the Government's reply, and the Jews were certainly not. Both groups objected—though for the opposite reasons —to the proposed Legislative Council. This "joint" opposition did not bring the Jews and Arabs any closer.

After the failure of the talk with Arslan and Jabri in Geneva (and I must say that Musa Alami regretted the publication of the story no less than I did), I did not meet with Arab leaders for more than a year and a half, since the proposal of the Legislative Council was pending all the time.

In April 1936, Dr. Magnes suggested that I meet George Antonius, a Christian Arab who in a sense was the theoretician of the Arab nationalist movement. The meeting took place in Antonius' home, which was on the road to Mount Scopus. Dr. Magnes was present, and occasionally took part in the conversation.

11 TALKS WITH ANTONIUS—APRIL, 1936

Our first talk was held on April 17, 1936, at 10.30 a.m., and lasted an hour and a half. Dr. Magnes said that in his opinion we should start from the assumption that Jews and Arabs were in Palestine by right and not on sufferance, and that there was need for contact and cooperation. A legislative council would be of value, for there Jews and Arabs would meet, and he regretted that the Jews were opposed to such a council.

Antonius complained that the Jews had mobilized "the whole world" against the council. The first step toward mutual understanding had to be taken by the Jews, since they were the aggressors. In the entire eighteen years of British rule not a single step had been taken by the Jews that gave the Arabs the impression that the Jews were interested in their goodwill. He understood all the arguments of the Jews, but the Arabs had no other course but to fight against the "flooding" of the country by the Jews, which would undermine the very existence of the Arab people. He himself thought that the Arabs must accept the fact of the existence of the Jews in the country, and that they must therefore limit their aims. On the basis of the full aspirations of the Arabs and the Jews mutual understanding was out of the question, since these aspirations conflicted and there was no way of reconciling them. If understanding was sought it would be necessary to curtail these aspirations. Each side would have to yield something, and only then was understanding conceivable. But there was no indication that the Jews were willing to forego any part of their objectives, and he therefore did not believe that mutual understanding was possible.

I said that I rejected the assumption that the aspirations of the Jews and Arabs were incompatible. There was no essential and inevitable contradiction. The point of departure should be that the question was not one that involved only the Jews of Palestine and the Arabs of Palestine—in this limited area there really was a conflict that was difficult to reconcile—but that the Jews constituted one world bloc and the Arabs another. I believed that there was no essential contradiction between the national aspirations of the Jewish people and those of the Arab people, which might not be clear or definite but would undoubtedly crystallize in the course of time. My reason for thinking so was that we were interested only in this country, but this was not true of the Arabs; and no matter what happened in Palestine the world status of the Arab people would not be changed. I understood the national aspirations of the Arab people—aspirations for a cultural and economic renascence and political independence. And I believed that the full realization of the aims of both peoples was conceivable without any inner conflict between them. For even if Palestine, as a result of immigration, became a predominantly Jewish country, there was no danger to Arab culture or freedom. Even when the Arabs became a minority in the limited area of Palestine they would not be a minority as members of the greater Arab nation, for that nation would have dominion over its broad territory; and the aspirations of the Jews, even when they would be realized to the full, did not in the least endanger or undermine the future of the Arab nation. I understood that the Arabs wanted Palestine, too, to be completely Arab. For us, on the other hand, it might be more convenient if there were no Arabs there at all. But there were facts that had to be faced. It was not out of mere emotion or caprice that we were returning to this country. For us it was a question of survival, a matter of life and death. We had come here and would continue to come—with or without Jewish-Arab understanding. Pogroms would not stop us. If we had to choose between pogroms in Germany, Poland or some other Diaspora country and pogroms in Ereẓ Israel, we would choose pogroms in this country. But I posed a question: what was better for both sides—to fight one another or to help one another? It was my conviction that we had a common interest in mutual aid. War would bring no benefit to either side.

Antonius asked whether we were prepared for some restrictions, for unless we were, and the Arabs too, no mutual understanding would be possible. He had said to his friends on a number of occasions that the Arabs must consider the Jews, that their presence in Palestine was a fact, and that their existence in the country necessarily restricted the aspirations of the Arabs. But the Jews must also announce that they were prepared for such restriction.

I replied that I disagreed with that premise, and that I saw no need for any restriction.

Antonius asked how many Jews we wished to bring to the country.

I said that I could not give a round number as an answer and that I could not agree to any numerical limitation. I wanted to settle in Palestine that number of Jews for whom it would be possible to create new possibilities of existence without ousting the Arabs or reducing their ability to support themselves. That was the only restriction we accepted, and we accepted it willingly and from conviction, for both moral and political reasons.

Again Antonius asked: if it should become evident—as it was already obvious to him—that the aspirations of the two sides were irreconcilable, would we be prepared to modify our goal?

I said I did not wish to answer that hypothetical question, especially as I was convinced that there was no contradiction, unless one saw a contradiction in our very return to Palestine.

Antonius said that he did see a contradiction, in that a Jewish State stood in opposition to the aspirations of the Arabs.

I asked: "What is a Jewish State?"

He replied that a Jewish State meant that all of this country would be handed over to Jewish rule, with the Arabs merely tolerated; the state would be sovereign and separate, and none of the Arabs would have any share in it.

I commented that if in his opinion that was the only definition of the Jewish aspirations, and if these were blocking the possibility of an understanding, I was willing to consider a change in the definition.

Antonius replied that that was an important statement, and one which opened a way to a clarification.

I said that the time had not come to give legal definitions to the ultimate aspirations of the two peoples. We should try to see to what extent cooperation was feasible without either side demanding that the other give up anything, until it became obvious that without such a demand cooperation was impossible.

Dr. Magnes again raised the question of the Legislative Council.

I said I was prepared to consider the question only on a parity basis, but I did not believe that without a basic understanding on the important issues it would be possible to reach agreement on current policy.

After a further exchange of views it was agreed that we would meet again on the following Wednesday (April 22, 1936), in order to examine thoroughly whether there was a possibility of reconciling the national aspirations of the two peoples. It was arranged that the meeting would take place at Dr. Magnes' home.

Two days later, on Sunday, April 19, 1936, Arab riots broke out in Jaffa, and 16 Jews were murdered. Under the circumstances, I doubted whether our talks would continue, but I made up my mind that I would not be the one to call them off. On Wednesday morning I telephoned Dr. Magnes, who said he had not heard from Antonius. He therefore suggested that I come as scheduled. The meeting had been set for 5 p.m., and I arrived five minutes early in order to discuss the situation with Magnes. He told me that Antonius had telephoned in the afternoon to enquire whether the meeting was still on, and Magnes told him that it was. At five o'clock sharp Antonius arrived.

At first the atmosphere was tense. Dr. Magnes asked Antonius whether the Arab delegation which the High Commissioner had suggested should go to London would indeed leave, and what was the mood of the Arab leaders. Antonius replied that it was about a week since he had seen the Mufti or anyone else other than Musa Alami, who had told him that most of the members of the delegation were opposed to the trip. He thought that the delegation would not leave for the time being, even though the High Commissioner was exerting pressure on them.

Dr. Magnes expressed his regret at this news. I said I had been told that the delegation had decided unanimously to postpone the trip. Antonius showed surprise and commented that the majority had apparently won over the minority.

Nearly two months earlier, on February 26, 1936, there had been a debate in the House of Commons on the proposed Legislative Council in Palestine, and a similar debate was held in the House of Commons on March 24. The Government was criticized concerning the Legislative Council in both debates, not only by the Opposition but also by a number of its loyal supporters. Two proposals were put forward in the debate: 1) the appointment of a Royal Commission to examine the question of the council; 2) inviting the Jews and Arabs to a round table in London. Both were aimed at rejecting the Legislative Council, if not absolutely then at least temporarily. The Government did not accept either of them, for obvious reasons. The Government's proposal to establish a Legislative Council had been made in order to appease the Arabs, and it had no desire to adopt a resolution that was designed to nullify or postpone the council idea. As to the round table suggestion, the Government knew that the Arabs would not agree to it, for under the conditions prevailing in Palestine, Syria and Egypt, the Arabs were in no mood to compromise with the Jews or to meet them at a round table. Thus was born the idea of inviting an Arab delegation to London. The Arab leaders were summoned to the High Commissioner on April 2, and he proposed that they send a delegation to London. They accepted the invitation unanimously. However, when the Arab public learned of this, the idea of a delegation met with opposition. The Arab functionaries who had no chance of being included in the delegation did not like the idea that the five or six leaders chosen by the High Commissioner should be the representatives of the Arab people. But the objection was based on more than personal grounds. The extremists, who had opposed the Legislative Council all along, did not agree to a delegation, whose main task would be to persuade the British Government to establish the council.

Until the outbreak of the disturbances on April 19, those who favored sending a delegation held the upper hand. But the riots in Jaffa immediately changed the situation. After the murder of 16 Jews in Jaffa for no reason at all, the Arab leaders well understood that this was not the most opportune moment to visit London. If, when things were quiet in Palestine, the British Parliament had opposed the proposal of a Legislative Council on the grounds that it could only interfere with the establishment of the Jewish national home, after the wanton murder public opinion in England would certainly not agree to the handing over of legislative power to this Arab majority. On April 22, the Arab leaders unanimously rejected the idea of a delegation and proclaimed a general strike.

The Arab general strike was proclaimed under three slogans, which had already been formulated in the memorandum submitted to the High Commissioner in November 1935: cessation of immigration; prohibition of land sales; establishment of a national government responsible to a parliament elected by the country's inhabitants. According to the formal proclamation, the strike was to last until the three demands were met.

After a brief exchange about the events in Jaffa and about the Government, I asked Antonius whether there were any Arab leaders who sought a mutual understanding.

Antonius replied in the negative. The Arab representatives—the dignitaries and the men of influence—believed that the Jews were totally indifferent to the views and needs of the Arabs and that there was no course open but to fight against Jewish immigration. True, there were some Arabs—not leaders or functionaries, but thinkers and intellectuals—who held that the Jewish question could not be ignored, but even they doubted whether there was any possibility of an understanding. He himself had read the writings of the recognized Zionist leaders, he had spoken to a number of them, and he followed the trends of events—and he thought that the Zionists could be divided into three classes:
1) Those who wanted a spiritual center. With them it would certainly be possible to reach an agreement, since the Arabs had no objection to them.
2) Those who wanted the Jews and Arabs to live in the country as two separate peoples, with Palestine a bi-national state.
3) Those—they constituted the vast majority of the Zionists and their number had recently been growing—who wanted to bring as many Jews as possible to Palestine without any consideration whatsoever for the Arabs. This group was composed not only of the majority of Zionists but also of a number of non-Zionists, including some who had previously opposed Zionism and were very anxious to take the Arabs into account but who, after the developments in Germany, felt that there was no choice, that there was no other refuge for the German Jews but Palestine, and that as many Jews as possible should immigrate to that country. With this third group it was impossible to reach an understanding. They wanted a one hundred percent Jewish State, while the Arabs would remain in the shadows.

I asked Antonius whether he, as a student of the nationalist movement and of the life of the Arab people in Palestine and the neighboring countries, believed that a Jewish spiritual center would be possible in this country.

Antonius answered that there was no point now in speaking of a spiritual center, since the Jews already had achieved more than that. Four hundred thousand Jews were hardly a spiritual center. Eighteen years before one could talk about a spiritual center, and he was certain that there was not an Arab who would not have accepted the idea willingly.

I told him that I had never believed in a spiritual center, and still did not. If I was convinced that that was all that could be achieved in Palestine I would not advise a single Jew to come here. Not only because a spiritual center not based on the reality of masses of Jews would be valueless, but because I was certain that, given the political, social and cultural conditions of this country and its surrounding area, no Jewish spiritual center could survive. I expressed surprise that an expert like him thought that it would be possible to establish a spiritual center of any value here.

Why? Antonius asked.

I explained that if a spiritual center meant not simply a school or a university, but a Jewish community that served as a model and an example to the Jewish people in the Diaspora, this implied that the Jews, who would constitute the spiritual center, would here create important social and cultural values. Would such values arise—and if they did, would they be able to last—in the present Arab environment? I did not think that the Arabs would remain in their present condition forever, but the situation would not change so quickly either. And was it conceivable, for instance, that two of our basic values—the equality of women and the value of work—could survive in this environment?

Antonius replied that he was sure that a Jewish spiritual center with modern values could exist here, and the Arabs would do nothing to its detriment. There was development among the Arabs too. In Egypt there was a high level of culture. There were intellectual forces. Naturally, the Arabs could not agree to the principle of pure Jewish labor, and they did not yet have any labor movement of their own.

I said that I had been referring not only to the value of hired labor but to the value of labor in general, including that of the farmer. We were creating communal farms, new forms of living. And it was strange that he thought that even a small spiritual center did not have the right to sustain itself by Jewish labor.

Antonius commented that in Egypt the fellah had developed.

I asked whether the fellah no longer subsisted on two piasters a day. In any event, I added, the argument was academic, since a spiritual center was not the point at issue. I agreed with him—though not for his reasons—that there was no sense in talking about a spiritual center, and that there must be some other basis to our discussion. I could not subscribe to any of the three types he had listed. Not to the first type, because I denied the possibility and value of a spiritual center; not to the second, because it offered no solution to our problem; and not to the third type either, because in my Zionism there was no element of domination.

Antonius remarked that that was a very interesting point.

Dr. Magnes made the personal comment that I belonged to the class of young

Zionists of the previous generation who had come to Palestine from schools and universities in order to work the land.

Antonius asked me a number of questions about my birthplace and background. For a while the conversation centered on my work and activities before the war, my studies in Constantinople, Islamic law, relations with the Arabs before the war, Turkey, and so forth. Then we returned to our subject: What was the basis for a mutual understanding?

When the question was put in these terms, Antonius said that as matters stood the Arabs had no option but to fight against the flooding of the country with Jews (in 1935 over 65,000 immigrants had arrived), whether they would succeed or not. Within Palestine proper he saw no possibility of a solution. It seemed to him that it was also not convenient for us to have the problem limited to Palestine. It was a small country without elbow room, with no space to move about in, either for the Jews or the Arabs. Greater expanses were necessary. We should discuss Syria, Greater Syria, which stretched from the Taurus Mountains to the Sinai Desert. That was a single unit, and it incorporated much vaster expanses.

Dr. Magnes expressed his agreement and said it would be a good thing for the Jews to go to Syria too. I answered in jest that although I belonged to the Zionist extremists I was not an imperialist like Magnes. I was aware of the fact that the Arabs regarded Palestine as part of Syria, as southern Syria. Palestine for us lay at the southern border of Syria, and Syria for us was foreign territory, theoretically no different from America or any other foreign country. We were by no means interested in scattering the Jews in countries outside of Palestine but wished to concentrate them in this country, and we were concerned only with the area known as Erez Israel. If there would be a mutual understanding we would certainly extend assistance, whatever help we could offer, also to the Arab countries outside of Palestine, but our settlement would be concentrated in this country.

Antonius said that the Syrians would gladly accept Jewish capital and Jewish industrialists to develop all of Syria.

I asked him why he limited the discussion to Syria, and excluded Iraq. That he excluded Saudi Arabia was understandable, but Iraq was a nearby country, with great possibilities. If we were thinking in terms of a broad settlement—and I accepted the view that the more we broadened the sphere of discussion the easier the solution would be—then we ought to consider three countries: Palestine, Syria and Iraq.

Antonius answered emphatically—and his reply was rather surprising—

that there was no connection between Iraq and Syria. In Iraq a feeling of Iraqi nationalism prevailed. "I am an Iraqi!"—one heard this from every Arab in Iraq.

I asked whether there was an Iraqi self-awareness as there was an Egyptian self-awareness.

Even more so, was his answer. The Iraqis had always been a people unto themselves. They had never had ties with Syria. Between the two countries there lay a great desert, and it had been a great mistake on the part of Faisal to try to unite them. Iraq was very much under Persian influence. It was in another bloc entirely, and there was no point in talking of the unification of Iraq and Syria. For both the Syrian Arabs and the Palestinian Arabs the big question was the unification of Syria as far as the Sinai Desert. This was one land. There was no natural barrier between Palestine and Syria, and there was no difference between their inhabitants.

I asked him how he envisaged the unification of Syria and Palestine without a world war and the defeat of England or France, or both. We Jews had ties with England, and we would not do anything against England, or without her consent. There were two reasons for this, I explained. The first was political, and there was surely no need to elaborate. But the second reason was just as important. Although we were an Oriental people, we had been Europeanized, and we wanted to return to Palestine in the geographical sense only. We intended to establish a European culture here, and we were linked to the greatest cultural force in the world, at any rate so long as the cultural foundations of this part of the world did not change and so long as the political organization of the world did not change.

Antonius said he understood my question and saw the difficulty, but he believed that if the Jews and Arabs would become united with the consent of England, England could force France to leave Syria altogether. The unity of the Jews and Arabs would constitute a tremendous moral force that would conquer world public opinion. All America would back the common demand of the Jews and Arabs, and the two could obtain whatever they wanted.

That was the first time during the conversation that I sensed feeling and sincerity in his words.

I asked him what part the Jews would have in this united Syria.

He replied that two restrictions were involved, one applying to numbers and the other to area. If the Jews would agree to these limitations, the Arabs would consent to a Jewish "establishment" in that part of Syria then known as Palestine.

I replied that only a restriction of area could be discussed. We would not agree to any prior limitation on numbers. We accepted the necessity of an objective limitation: more Jews should not be brought to Palestine than the country could absorb, taking for granted that the Arabs would not be dispossessed.

Dr. Magnes supported me vigorously on this point. He said that the Jews might discover natural resources or might by other means create new possibilities for absorbing large numbers of people, so why should the number of Jews be restricted?

Antonius remarked that there was no reason why new opportunities revealed in the country should be for the Jews alone. Arabs should benefit from them, too, otherwise the country would be filled with Jews. The Jews would also appear beyond Palestine. The Jews had money, energy, education; they would conquer everything, and the country would become Jewish.

I said that if he thought that we would agree in advance, as a political principle, to remain a minority even in a limited territory, he was mistaken and there was no point to our discussions. I was not presenting any prior demand as to numbers. I was not saying one million, if there was no room for a million, and I was not saying not more than four million if there was room for more. We had taken it upon ourselves, and would continue to do so—agreement or not—that our immigration and settlement in the country would not be at the expense of the Arab community and would not encroach upon it. I told Antonius that if, thirty years before, we had discussed how many Jews could come to Jaffa, which then had a population of 20,000 or 30,000, he would undoubtedly have said: only 15,000. We had already brought 130,000, but this had not been at the expense of the Arabs in Jaffa, but thanks to our new creative enterprise in Tel Aviv. And there were now more people in Tel Aviv than in Jaffa.

That was what the Arabs wanted to prevent, he remarked, that the Jews should not gain control of Jaffa.

I said we had no wish to control Jaffa, and that we had not followed that course. We had established a new Jewish city in a desolate place, and we had brought there as many as we could, and we would bring as many more as we could. For example, I saw no reason why we should not build a Jewish city of half a million people in the Haifa Bay area.

Antonius said it would not be good for the Jews if they became a purely urban community.

Of course not, I said, I agreed wholeheartedly. Without land there could be no independence or national future. By means of agricultural development we wanted to create opportunities for a large Jewish settlement, without ousting the Arab farmers from their land.

But these opportunities, Antonius repeated, must be available to the Arabs too.

Here Dr. Magnes intervened again and disagreed with Antonius. The Jews would discover new opportunities and would settle in the areas which they ameliorated for that purpose.

The only limitation that I agreed to, I said, was one of area.

"What is the area?" Antonius asked.

"The area is Ereẓ Israel," I replied.

He asked what the boundaries of Ereẓ Israel were, and I answered that they were known from history.

Antonius said that a border was an artificial thing, today it was here, tomorrow it was there.

Those who regarded Palestine and Syria as a single country considered the border as something artificial, I said, but we regarded Palestine as a historical and geographical unit and, while there might be many possibilities as to the exact boundary lines, the area itself was fixed and permanent.

"What is the area?" he asked again.

"It is the land between the Mediterranean to the West and the desert to the East, and between Sinai to the South and the source of the Jordan to the North."

"Do you also include Transjordan?" Antonius asked in surprise.

"Of course," I answered. "Is the Jordan the boundary of Ereẓ Israel? It is a river of Ereẓ Israel."

"In other words, you want more than the Mandate territory that was given to you by England," he retorted.

I asked what the boundaries under the Mandate had to do with determining the territory of Ereẓ Israel. That had been an artificial partition and it did not constitute the basis of our discussion.

"Then you also include the Hauran," he said with even greater astonishment.

I said that I did not mean to include the part that had been outside of Ereẓ Israel, but that both Gilead and Bashan belonged to it.

"You are in fact proposing that what England didn't give you, you should obtain from us," Antonius said.

I replied by asking whether he imagined that Transjordan would be out of bounds to us, and that in the united Syria that was to arise there would be a

Pale of Settlement for the Jews, as there had been in Czarist Russia. Could he really suggest to us that we be citizens of the country without even having full civic rights throughout the state, there being places where we might not go.

Antonius became a bit confused. He did not mean to say that a Jew might not go to Transjordan. What he meant was to rule out permanent settlement.

I repeated my question: Was it conceivable that Jews would not be permitted to settle in certain parts of a country of which they were citizens?

Individuals yes, but not masses, Antonius replied with some embarrassment.

I asked what difference there was between individuals and masses. If many individual Jews went to Transjordan and settled there, they would become masses.

Dr. Magnes added that Jews would also go to Syria and settle there.

I commented that I did not equate the other parts of Syria with Erez Israel. Of course, any Jew who wanted to go to Syria might do so, but we had no interest in their going there.

Antonius said he was not talking about what individual Jews would do. He was referring to a Jewish establishment. That establishment would be only in Palestine.

I observed that "Palestine" had nothing to do with it. For us Jews there was no such thing as Palestine, there was Erez Israel. And even for the Arabs, he himself had said, there was no such thing as Palestine.

He said he agreed that the Jewish establishment be called Erez Israel, the Arabs would also call it Erez Israel and not Palestine, but this would include what was then known as Palestine, and not Hauran and not Transjordan.

I said that if it were clear that we would have an absolute right to settle in Transjordan, not only in the part under the British Mandate but also the part under the French Mandate, I would be willing to defer for the time being the clarification of our status as a people in that part, if we could reach agreement as to the nature of the Jewish establishment, to use his expression.

Antonius said that if the Jews agreed that they would not be the ones to determine how many Jews might enter Erez Israel, it would not be difficult to reach agreement on this matter.

I could understand his objection to letting the Jews alone decide that question, I said, but we could not let that decision rest solely in Arab hands.

Antonius said that Syria must become a sovereign state, and its government, which would also contain Jews, would decide this question.

I said that it was not as simple as that. We did not agree to a Legislative

Council, because we were not willing to hand our fate over to the Arab majority in the country, and he could not suggest that we entrust our future to the Arab majority in Syria.

Dr. Magnes again supported me. He said there must necessarily be some limitation on Syrian sovereignty, and that the decision must be in the hands of a neutral body.

Antonius declared emphatically that a limitation of sovereignty was out of the question. Nothing would offend the Arabs more than talk of that kind.

I said I understood, but that he too must comprehend that there could be no talk about restricting the Jews. That not only offended our feelings, it threatened our very existence and our future.

He said that it was an Arab country and the Arabs had a right to complete sovereignty. I agreed that this was true of Syria, but stressed that we had been in Erez Israel before the Arabs. We were returning to our own land.

This touched off an historical argument.

I observed that in the discussion of the political points at issue I attached value to the scientific foundation. There could be only one basis for an agreement: recognition of the needs of the two peoples. The size of our population in Erez Israel would determine our fate, but the size of the Arab population in Erez Israel would not determine the fate of the Arab people. Nor was the question only one of the number of Jews, but also of their autonomous political status. And if one spoke of Syria, then it was not only our problem that was involved but also that of other groups, who would not accept the absolute rule of the majority.

Antonius commented that sovereignty did not negate autonomy; there would be provinces with special rights, and one of them would be "Erez Israel."

I said that that might serve as a basis for discussion. Before that, however, we would have to solve the problem of international guarantees and an external force to protect our rights so long as "Erez Israel" did not exist.

Antonius said he recognized the need for guarantees, and that we would have to decide this issue without using the term limitation of sovereignty.

I summed up the discussion: A single Syria, which would include "Erez Israel," that name to be used in Arabic too. Jewish immigration without numerical restriction. The claims on Erez Israel are restricted to its territory. The question of Transjordan requires further discussion. Freedom to the Jews to settle in all parts of Syria. International guarantees. Assistance by the Jews in the liberation and development of Syria. Arab assistance to Zionism.

Dr. Magnes offered to prepare an outline of these points, which he would submit to us for checking.

We both objected to this, on the grounds that the points had not yet been sufficiently clarified and that they should not be formulated in writing, even tentatively. Only in the course of further discussions would we attempt to put something on paper.

At the end I asked: "Are there Arab leaders who will accept this scheme as a basis for negotiation?"

Antonius replied that although he was speaking in a private capacity he was familiar with the views of the leaders both in Syria and in Palestine, and he thought that something like this might be acceptable to them.

We agreed that our next meeting would take place on Wednesday, April 29, at 5 p.m., in Antonius' house.

12 THIRD TALK WITH ANTONIUS—APRIL, 1936

A quarter of an hour before the appointed time I called for Magnes, and we went together to Antonius' house. The date was April 29, 1936. Magnes told me that he had seen Musa Alami after our first meeting with Antonius. Musa Alami was most depressed by the state of affairs. With all his heart he wanted to see the two peoples come to an understanding, and he saw no prospect of an agreement except on a broad scale: a federation of Palestine, Syria and Iraq. His attitude toward me was one of confidence and esteem, and he regretted that his father-in-law (Jabri), owing to attacks in Arab newspapers, had been forced to publish a report of our talk in Geneva. He would be leaving shortly for a two-month vacation abroad.

When we arrived at Antonius' home we found several Arab visitors there. He ushered us into a different room. Magnes asked him what the strike situation was, (after the riots in Jaffa began the Arab Higher Committee proclaimed an Arab general strike, which included a stoppage of work, the closing of stores and the closing down of Jaffa port). Antonius said that the strike had not yet reached its peak and that it was hard to say how long it would last.

I asked him whether we should start off by discussing the paragraphs of the agreement, in continuation of the deliberations at our second meeting, or whether we should first take up the question of the procedure for maintaining the agreement. Antonius suggested that for the time being we continue to discuss the paragraphs of the agreement.

Magnes took a piece of paper from his pocket on which he had outlined the main points agreed on at our second meeting, with some additions of his own. The following points were listed:

1) A Greater Syria will be established, as the beginning of an Arab Federation.

2) Greater Syria will be composed of Syria, Lebanon, Palestine and Transjordan.

3) Throughout all of Syria as defined above there will be provincial autonomy, with a central parliament of Greater Syria.

4) In Palestine the Jewish people will have a special national status, and the country will be called Ereẓ Israel.

5) The boundaries of Ereẓ Israel would be fixed in the course of the negotiations.

6) Jewish immigration to Ereẓ Israel would not be restricted on any political grounds but would be fixed in accordance with the country's absorptive capacity.

7) England, France and the International Labor Office would from time to time determine the absorptive capacity of Ereẓ Israel.

I commented that the first point was not accurate, since at our previous meeting we had not agreed on a federation outside of Syria. Antonius also objected to this paragraph.

I also pointed out that at our previous meeting I had not consented to the removal of Transjordan from Ereẓ Israel. Magnes answered that he had neither excluded nor included Transjordan, since the borders of Ereẓ Israel were yet to be fixed, and that part of Transjordan could be included within the borders.

Antonius raised no objection to this answer.

I next pointed out that there was no clause dealing with the equality of the citizens of Syria and Ereẓ Israel in all parts of Syria. Magnes replied that that was self-evident. I said it should be explicitly guaranteed, and Antonius agreed with my proposal.

My fourth comment was that I did not think it was a good idea that the three parties mentioned should determine the country's absorptive capacity.

Magnes explained that nothing had actually been said on this subject at the previous meeting and that it was his own suggestion. He considered it sound to place the question of absorptive capacity on a scientific basis and to turn the question over to some non-political body like the International Labor Office. England would participate as the mandatory in Palestine, and France as the mandatory in Syria.

Antonius said that he too objected to this proposal. Syria must be independent, and France and England should not interfere.

Magnes asked: In that case, who will determine the size of Jewish immigration?

Antonius said he had given thought to the matter. He had no answer, and a way must be found to do this without infringing on Syria's sovereignty or on the interests of the Jews. Syria must be like Iraq: its own master. In Iraq the mandate had been abolished and an agreement signed with England guaranteed British interests in that country. The same thing had to be done here. There would be an agreement with France, which would ensure French interests and a French sphere of influence in Syria, and a French envoy would remain in Syria. Similarly, an agreement would be signed with England, ensuring England's interests in Palestine, and there would be a British envoy in the country. He would decide.

I pointed out that this was a political solution to the question of France and England, but not to that of immigration. Immigration should be discussed separately.

It was agreed that meanwhile we would discuss the other issues.

Dr. Magnes asked about the authority of the autonomous entities and what powers would be vested in the central parliament.

Antonius replied that in his opinion the autonomous provinces would enjoy the maximum authority; only the bare minimum, national in its very nature, would be turned over to the central parliament. For example, roads were a local matter, with the exception of one or two that extended over the whole country. Military and foreign affairs would be the domain of the state. All other matters would be in the hands of the provinces, as in North America and Switzerland.

I said that I was inclined to accept that principle. However, America and Switzerland were not the same in this respect, since the Swiss canton was more independent than the American State; I preferred the system that was in force in Switzerland.

The question arose as to how many autonomous entities there would be in Syria.

Dr. Magnes expressed the opinion that the Alawites, the Lebanese and the Druze should have separate provinces, in addition to Transjordan and Erez Israel.

Antonius said he did not think it was necessary for the Alawites to have an autonomous government, and perhaps not the Druze either.

I asked what Lebanon's role would be in the negotiations then taking place in Paris.

He replied that the Syrian leaders, without exception, were not then demanding the inclusion of Lebanon, so long as Lebanon itself did not wish to be joined to Syria. All the Syrians insisted on was that the artificial enlargement of Lebanon by the French after the war, be annulled. Tripoli must be returned to Syria, while Lebanon could retain Rashaya, Hasbaya, Tyre, Saida (Sidon) and Beirut. He thought the Syrian leaders were acting wisely; Lebanon should not be coerced into joining Syria, and the hour was not really ripe for the unification of the two countries. In the course of time the desire to join Syria might develop spontaneously in Lebanon.

I said that the autonomy of Erez Israel, as I saw it, would differ from that of the other autonomous provinces in three respects: 1) immigration; 2) development; 3) language and culture.

Antonius replied that he did not see three points of difference. The matter of language and culture was obvious. Erez Israel would be Hebrew. Development would be the concern of each individual province, with no distinction between Erez Israel and the others. The aspect in which Erez Israel would differ from the other Syrian provinces was that of immigration.

Magnes asked what form of government there would be in Erez Israel.

Antonius replied that it would be the same as that in the other provinces.

Magnes: "There's a difference. Here there are two peoples."

Antonius: "Representation will be in accordance with population."

Dr. Magnes said that first of all there was the question of whether the elections would be by communities, or by districts as in the United States. Communal elections meant a split along national and communal lines.

Antonius said that while there was indeed a disadvantage to communal elections the time was not far when communal elections would have to be instituted throughout Syria.

Magnes asked what would be the basis for representation. If it were the size of population, the Arabs would hold a majority.

Antonius: "Could there possibly be any other basis?"

Dr. Magnes said there was a proposal of parity without regard to the size of population. Whether the Arabs in Erez Israel were more numerous than the Jews, or the Jews more numerous than the Arabs, the parliament of Erez Israel should consist of an equal number of Jews and Arabs.

Antonius asked who, then, would decide.

"The English," Magnes replied. The British envoy would decide. But he thought it would preferable to have three Englishmen rather than one, for if there were only one the decision would be a personal one.

Antonius commented that neither the Jews nor the Arabs would accept this proposal. For the Jews it was imperative that they be the majority. It was essential that in one place they could do as they pleased, and not be dependent on others. Therefore, the boundaries of Ereẓ Israel should be so arranged as to give the Jews a majority.

Magnes asked how that would be possible.

Antonius answered that there would be an Ereẓ Israel with a Jewish majority, and another part, to be called Palestine, with an Arab majority. Ereẓ Israel would extend from Haifa to Gaza and the Jezreel valley, while Palestine would stretch from Hebron to Nablus.

Dr. Magnes: "That means cantons?"

Antonius replied that he was opposed to cantons; these would be two countries. Otherwise it was difficult to conceive that the Arabs and Palestinians would agree.

I said that such a proposal could not be considered. If we were considering a Greater Syria that would include Ereẓ Israel, we could not talk about a part of Ereẓ Israel. His proposal was one for the cantonization of Ereẓ Israel, and to that we would not agree. From the Zionist viewpoint, the focal question concerning Ereẓ Israel was not the constitution of the country as it now was. Jewish immigration was a dynamic factor, and the main question for us was how to ensure this dynamism. In the other parts of Syria the political issue was that of the political form and constitutional relations between static elements. But for Ereẓ Israel the cardinal question was the *function* of autonomy: the development of the country in order to make possible greater absorption of immigration. Ereẓ Israel in a static state could not be a land of immigration. To absorb immigration, it would be necessary to develop the country. That is why I had said at the beginning that the question of development distinguished Ereẓ Israel just as much as did the question of immigration, for the latter depended on the former. If there was to be a Jewish-Arab accord there would have to be an agreement on the development of the country which, on the one hand, would raise the standard of living of its inhabitants and, on the other hand, would make possible large-scale Jewish immigration and settlement. Raising the level of the Arabs in Ereẓ Israel was also a matter of importance to us—and not necessarily from altruistic motives. We were coming to the country with a European culture and standard of living, and it would not be to our benefit if the Arab population remained at its primitive level. There was a basic difference between the Jewish nationalist movement and the Arab nationalist movement. The Arab movement was political only and almost entirely negative in nature. It had done nothing for the development of the country, and the Arab leaders were not even contemplating any such activity. The essence of Zionism was that it was a creative movement. We were creating national-cultural values in agriculture and industry. We were developing the country and only thus could we make immigration possible. In order that immigration might continue and that its dimensions would provide an answer to the Jewish Question, it was necessary for us to develop all of the country's potentialities. I could therefore not conceive of a Jewish-Arab accord without a comprehensive agreement on the development of the country. We had to work out a plan for developing the coastal area, the hill regions, the Jordan Valley, the Negev, and Transjordan.

Antonius commented that he saw the point. He agreed with my criticism of the Arab nationalist movement and he saw the connection between the country's development and immigration, but how would the size of the immigration be set?

I answered that if we accepted the development plan, it could constitute the basis for fixing the size of the immigration. Naturally, the size of the immigration must not be stipulated precisely. A minimum and a maximum could be prescribed for a given period of years, and a neutral and objective body would be agreed on to determine from time to time, in accordance with the pace of development, the range between the minimum and maximum. At the end of the period a new minimum and a maximum would be laid down for the next period.

Antonius asked what would happen if something occurred to lower the minimum.

I replied that it was also conceivable that something would happen to raise the maximum, and that we should make provision for an instrument to which either side could turn if it wished to introduce a change in the size of the immigration. In that case, however, the burden of proof would be on the side appealing.

Antonius asked whether it would not be better to stipulate a specific number in advance. How many Jews did we wish to bring into Ereẓ Israel?

I said it was impossible to answer that question. We would like to bring in all the Jews, but this was not something solely reliant on our wishes. It depended on the economic possibilities, and the economic possibilities were not predetermined but were dependent on various factors. The possibilities could be expanded or curtailed. When I spoke of a Jewish-Arab agreement I did not have in mind merely that we should put an end to overt war and tolerate one another, but that there should be an active agreement, an accord of mutual aid. We would help the Arab people to attain its maximum productivity, we would aid it morally, politically, financially and organizationally. And the Arabs would help us achieve the maximum of our national aspirations, that is, they would aid us in developing Erez Israel to the utmost, so that they would have a good life in this country and so that we might bring in the maximum number of Jews. What the size of that maximum would be could not be fixed in advance.

Dr. Magnes suggested that in order to avoid arguments we should set an arbitrary figure and agree that eventually a million Jews would immigrate.

Antonius supported that proposal.

I said that in my opinion this was no proposal, and it seemed to me that neither the Jews nor the Arabs would accept it. Were I an Arab I would not accept the proposal. If it was important for the Arab people that not more than one million come, there was no guarantee that after a million Jews had arrived and constituted a powerful force in the country—while, on the one hand, Jewish influence in the world remained as it was and, on the other hand, Jewish misfortune likewise remained unchanged—the pressure of the desire for Jewish immigration would not be intensified, and it would then be impossible to prevent such immigration, just as it was impossible to prevent it now. And even if the Jews were now to sign an agreement that they would not demand more than a million, I, as an Arab, would not rely on that signature. How many agreements in our times had been torn up before the eyes of the whole world? But of course the Jews would not agree. One million would not solve the Jewish Question in the Diaspora, nor would it satisfy national aspirations within the country. And why one million? Why not half a million, or two million? There were historical reasons for Zionism, and there were vital factors that induced and impelled Jewish immigration. Neither I nor any other Jewish representative could set artificial limits to it. On such a shaky foundation no viable agreement was conceivable. Only if the agreement met the historical needs of the two peoples could it come about and last. My own faith in a Jewish-Arab accord was based on the conviction that cooperation between the two peoples could be an historic blessing for both of them. We were capable of building up this country, and we could do great things here, if only the political obstacles were removed. The Arab people had great potentialities: Syria and Iraq were countries with tremendous possibilities, and the help of the Jewish people could be of great benefit in advancing the Arab people in those countries. There were historical grounds for an alliance of the two peoples in order to achieve these two national goals. Perhaps it was still too early, since we were yet few in number. However, only if far-sighted Arab leaders recognized this mutual interest could a true and viable understanding be reached. Therefore, there was need not only for a political accord on Syria, but also for an economic agreement on a comprehensive development plan for Ereẓ Israel, which would raise the level of the Arab community in the country and would offer the Jews the maximum possibilities for immigration. The size of this immigration would be determined solely by the economic potentialities that we would create in the country with the support and the help of the Arabs.

Dr. Magnes said that there was no need for a perpetual agreement. We could draw up an agreement for twenty or twenty-five years and stipulate that in that period a million Jews would enter.

I replied that we could not make a temporary agreement if we were prepared to become part of Greater Syria and that we would not agree to an *a priori* determination of the size of the immigration. If in the course of twenty years only 500,000 Jews could immigrate then only 500,000 would immigrate and no agreement could increase that number. But if during those twenty years two million or four million could immigrate, without encroaching upon the Arabs, there was no basis for or possibility of renouncing this.

It was almost seven o'clock, and Mrs. Antonius entered the room. Antonius expressed his regret that he had to leave, and asked that we fix a time to continue our talk. We agreed that two questions were still pending—the form of government in Ereẓ Israel and the determination of the size of the immigration—and I asked what would be the next step after we found an answer to these two questions.

Antonius said that there were two alternatives. We could either first approach the Government and find out whether it was prepared to endorse our plan, or each of us could confer with his associates and learn whether the plan was acceptable to them.

I expressed the view that we should first clarify with the leaders of the two sides whether they were inclined to enter an agreement on the basis of such a plan, and only then turn to the Government. On that note we parted.

The time of the next meeting was to be fixed through Dr. Magnes. Meanwhile, each of us would discuss the plan with his associates.

A few days later Magnes informed me that Antonius had left for Turkey.

I never saw him again.

13 ARAB UNREST; PROPOSALS OF "THE FIVE"—1936

The year 1936 was a turning point in a number of respects, both with regard to the Arabs and to the Mandatory Government. On November 25, 1935, an Arab delegation called on the High Commissioner and presented, as described above, three main demands: 1) the establishment of a national government elected by the inhabitants; 2) the complete cessation of Jewish immigration; 3) the prohibition of land sales to the Jews. The High Commissioner promised the delegation an answer after the Government in London took a decision on these questions.

As the High Commissioner informed the Arab delegation, the land issue had engaged the attention of the administration over the past twelve months, i.e., even in 1935. In a talk with Moshe Sharett on February 1, 1935, the High Commissioner raised the question for the first time and expressed the opinion that the protection given to tenant farmers must be extended to petty independent farmers. He was therefore about to promulgate a law to the effect *that every land transfer would require the consent of the High Commissioner*, and that such consent would not be given unless the owner of the land retained for himself that portion of the land required for his subsistence. Sharett stated immediately that we would oppose the idea, and on January 12, 1936, a meeting took place between the High Commissioner and three representatives of the Jewish Agency Executive: Dr. Arthur Ruppin, Moshe Sharett, and the present writer. We explained to the High Commissioner that only through active and systematic assistance in raising land productivity, improving work methods, and installing irrigation facilities wherever feasible would the Government fulfill its obligation to both the Jews and the Arabs. We stressed that the problem of land and settlement on the soil was for us a question of life and death, that our return to Ereẓ Israel was above all a return to working the land, and that under the terms of the Mandate it was the Government's obligation to aid actively in our dense settlement on the land; negative measures, such as restricting the freedom of sale, would be of no benefit to the peasants but would add to their plight. If the peasant were not free to do as he liked with his land, he would fall prey to the usurers who sucked his blood, and his farm would remain as primitive as ever. Even Sir John Hope Simpson, the Government's emissary in the country at the beginning of the 'thirties, had reached the conclusion that the Government would fulfill its obligations toward the Arabs and the Jews only through "an active policy of agricultural development, designed for dense settlement on the land and for intensive cultivation by both Arabs and Jews." The Jewish Agency was therefore opposed to any negative measure of the Government, but offered its aid in drafting a *positive* plan to advance Jewish settlement and improve the position of the Arab fellah.

The High Commissioner then declared that it was by no means his intention to interfere with the continuation of Jewish settlement; on the contrary, he wished to advance it. Even if the principle of a "subsistence unit" were adopted, this unit would not be something fixed and immutable, but would be changed from time to time in keeping with the pace of development in the country, and the proposed law would not interfere with the expansion of Jewish agricultural settlement.

Earlier, on October 15, 1935, there had been a meeting in London between representatives of the Government and the Jewish Agency. The Government was represented by the Colonial Secretary, Malcolm MacDonald; his Deputy, Lord Plymouth; and the High Commissioner. Dr. Chaim Weizmann and I represented the Jewish Agency. The discussion centered on the problem of land and immigration, but the Government's representatives did not give the slightest hint that they were planning in any way to restrict the freedom of land purchase. Even after the High Commissioner returned from his vacation in London at the end of 1935, this matter was not brought up in any of his meetings with the Jewish Agency Executive. Meanwhile, however, a new Colonial Secretary, J. H. Thomas, had been appointed, and the memorandum presented by the Arabs on November 25, 1935, aroused our apprehensions. On January 26, 1936, the High Commissioner met with us—Dr. Weizmann, Dr. Ruppin, Sharett and myself; Weizmann was the chief spokesman. He pointed out that the land question cut to the core of our existence. The issue was not a new one. It had been raised in Passfield's White Paper of 1930, and it had caused a storm. The Government (this was the Labour Government with Ramsay MacDonald as Prime Minister and Arthur Henderson as Foreign Secretary; Ernest Bevin was instrumental in getting the Government to act and he, in turn, was influenced by Dov Hoz) then appointed a Cabinet committee headed by Henderson, a faithful friend of the Zionist movement. The committee's discussions resulted in the White Paper being interpreted in such a way that its content was actually changed. That interpretation was known as the MacDonald Letter, which was sent to Dr. Weizmann. The President of the Zionist Organization quoted the obligations set forth in the letter and which were in clear contradiction to the new intentions of the High Commissioner concerning land restrictions. Dr. Weizmann emphasized the fact, well known to the High Commissioner, that as a result of Jewish settlement, the condition of the Arab peasants in the neighborhood of the Jewish settlements had been bettered.

Weizmann announced that the Jewish Agency was prepared to cooperate, as it had in the past, in any constructive activity for the good of the Jews and the Arabs, but that we would fight to the end against any restrictions.

While the Arab delegation derived no satisfaction from the statement of the High Commissioner, they were greatly encouraged by the concessions on the land question and by the proposed establishment of a Legislative Council. After the murder of 16 Jews in the Jaffa riots of April 19, 1936, the Arab Higher Committee decided (on April 22, 1936) on a general strike that would apply to all employment, commerce and transport. The Arab community was called upon to close stores, to stop all work, and to halt all transport until the three demands were met: the complete cessation of Jewish immigration; a prohibition of sale of land to Jews; and a government elected by the inhabitants of Palestine.

The strike itself did not affect the Jewish economy. The closing of Arab stores, the strike of Arab taxis and buses, and the withholding of Arab agricultural produce from the Jews did not harm the Jewish economy but actually strengthened it. However, it was clear that the murders in Jaffa were not the last word in the Arab assault against the Jewish community. There were a number of factors that had intensified Arab opposition and strengthened the hand of the extremist leaders. The year 1935 had been a record year for Jewish immigration. Including tourists who decided to settle in the country, Jewish immigration that year amounted to over 65,000, the highest figure attained throughout the Mandate period. In 1936 the French Government opened negotiations with the Arab leaders in Syria looking to the abolition of the Mandate and to an agreement between an independent Syria and France, along the lines of the arrangement worked out between Iraq and Britain. The Italian-Ethiopian dispute, which had worsened, also exerted an influence, as did the growing feeling that a new world war might soon break out.

At the beginning of 1936, Sir Arthur Wauchope was appointed to a second five-year term as High Commissioner. When Dr. Weizmann arrived in the country in January 1936, I met with him, together with Moshe Sharett, and informed him that ever since the High Commissioner returned from London I had had the feeling, which was gradually turning into a certainty, that there had been a change in policy. I sensed that we would soon be faced with a new version of the Passfield White Paper of 1930. Besides the formation of the Legislative Council, substantial reductions in immigration and serious restrictions on land purchases were being planned. Sharett informed Weizmann of the immigration restrictions the Government was devising. "Capitalists" would now require twice as much as before in order to obtain an immigration visa: LP 2,000 instead of LP 1,000. Tourists would have to deposit a larger sum with the authorities for an entry permit. Apparently, the Government feared a repetition of the large-scale immigration of 1935.

I said I did not think it was the 60,000 immigrants that the Government feared but the complex world situation. The British were apprehensive about a European war and wanted to appease and win over the Arabs. Sharett agreed.

Meanwhile the disturbances in the country increased. The Arab terror spread to all parts of the land. At a meeting of the Jewish Agency Executive on May 19, 1936, I tried to analyze the political situation and the conclusions we should draw from it:

> "We cannot content ourselves with a day-to-day reaction to events. Nor can we be satisfied with a negative policy. We must show political initiative, primarily vis-à-vis England, but also vis-à-vis the Arabs. The disturbances are not yet behind us; there is still the threat of more riots. There is still the danger of a revision to our disadvantage. True, in the last two or three days the situation has cleared up to some extent. The unloading at Tel Aviv port, the immigration quota, yesterday's statement[12] by Thomas [the Colonial Secretary] go some way toward meeting our demands and averting the pressing dangers that threatened us. Nevertheless, we have not rid ourselves of two dangers: of terrorism—serious terrorism—or a revision policy by the Government. Obviously, the initiative for the inclination toward a revision comes from Palestine and not from London. And it preceded the disturbances. There are those who conclude from this that we should fight for the dismissal of the High Commissioner. It is not so simple. We don't know who will be appointed in his place. I do not regard the present Commissioner as one of the worst that England has sent us up to now. He is not an enemy. True, he has reached the point of revision. But he has been here five years. He has allowed us to do great things. And he has come to revision. What accounts for this inclination? To my mind, there is fear here. There is fear of the Jews, and there is fear of the Arabs. The fear of the Jews—if their growth continues at the present tempo they will constitute an anti-English force. If I were an Englishman—and I am trying to put myself in the place of an Englishman at this moment—and I saw how the Jews failed to appreciate the positive aspects of our administration, and how they exaggerate the negative aspect, with their interminable suspicions, I too would fear

---

[12] On the appointment of a Royal Commission of Inquiry into the causes of the disturbances in the country, which would hear the grievances of the Jews and the Arabs.

that they would not go along with us. If we wish to lay down a political line it is not enough for us to see the facts as they appear to us, but we must also see them as they appear to others. The English have grounds for believing that the Jews are an anti-British element. The second fear—and it is the greater one—is of the Arabs. There are many reasons for this fear. There is apprehension about riots, which will be a blot on England's reputation. This applies not only to the Arabs of Palestine, but also to those in other countries. There is another threat—the situation in the Middle East. That is why there is a desire to restrict immigration and the expansion of our settlement enterprise. The riots were an additional factor. The way I see it, the source of the riots is the Italian-Ethiopian war. The disturbances in Syria and Egypt were a consequence of that war. There is one basic factor: the Arab fear of our growing strength. Again, I want the members of the Executive to see the situation through Arab eyes, and it is immaterial whether the Arab view is a correct one or not. The fact is that is how they see things. If Samuel declares that eventually there will be three million Jews in Ereẓ Israel, in the eyes of the Arabs they are already here. They see the Jewish economy gaining strength. They see the electric company and the Dead Sea Works in Jewish hands—the largest enterprises in the country. They see that England identifies itself with Zionism. The debate in Parliament went against the establishment of a Legislative Council. The Government proclaimed and undertook the establishment of this council—and along comes Parliament and opposes it. Isn't this conclusive proof that England is in the hands of the Jews? They see that British commissions were here: the Shaw, Simpson, and French commissions. All of them were against us, and although there was no foundation for what they said, in the eyes of the Arabs they expressed truth and justice. Then Passfield's White Paper appears. And all these findings are nullified: no White Paper, no French conclusions, no Simpson report, no Shaw report. Doesn't this prove that England is in the hands of the Jews?

"Now they are fighting for the cessation of immigration. A Jewish High Commissioner halted immigration when there were riots. At that time there was quiet all about us. Now Syria is in turmoil, and so is Egypt. France is giving in to the Syrians, and England—to the Egyptians. Here they are not demanding the ending of the Mandate but only the stoppage of immigration—and even that is not granted. That is the way things look to the Arabs, and that is the fear. Nevertheless, I think that the present situation could have been averted if the Government had stepped in and taken the necessary steps. I am not saying that the Government aided the riots, but since it is evident to me that the High Commissioner had notions about revision before the riots—and London did not immediately agree with him—there was no great desire to use force in preventing them. Fear of the Arabs is an important factor. Will it be possible to overcome this fear by negotiating with them? Here, too, one must envisage the difficulties. Economic conflict, although it exists only in their imagination, is a factor to be reckoned with. They fear for their economic future, because they see the tremendous ability of the Jews in this area. We see our poverty, they see our affluence. But in this sphere the conflict is imaginary, and the fear can be removed. The serious conflict, however, is the political one. They regard this land as theirs, and we regard it as ours. We do not come here the way we came to Poland or Spain. However, even this conflict is not absolute or eternal. Our wishes are opposed to those of the Arabs of Erez Israel, but they are only a small part of the Arab people as a whole. Today, the Arab people is weak, suppressed, and disunited. The same was true in the past of a number of European nations, such as Italy and Germany, which succeeded in uniting and in freeing themselves of a foreign yoke. A Jewish Erez Israel will not interfere with the liberation and unification of the Arab peoples. On the contrary, if there is an alliance between us and the Arabs we can help liberate and develop the Arab peoples. But it is doubtful whether such an accord, a political agreement, is possible at this time. Only if a Jewish Erez Israel becomes a fact will an understanding be conceivable. Even then, they won't want to enter an agreement unless we can prove to them that they will benefit from it. But we won't be able to prove this so long as they believe they can prevent our growth.

"At this moment there is a quarrel between us and the Arabs. For the Arabs it has possibly come too late. For us it has come a little too early. They are a bit late, because we already constitute a force in the country which it will not be easy to liquidate. For us it is too soon, because we are not yet strong enough to face this struggle alone. To a large extent the continuation of our efforts depends on England. England is now the decisive force—I refer to external forces. I should add that I believe—and this has always been my deep conviction—that the decisive factor in all situations and under all conditions is the Jewish people. But the external factor today is England. Not Geneva [the League of Nations], not Poland, not Germany —but England. Poland and Germany will not fight against England on our behalf.

"We are staking everything on the Balfour Declaration. That declaration is a broken reed. I value the Mandate and the Balfour Declaration, but in themselves they are a broken reed. Since the issuance of the Balfour Declaration, the Versailles Treaty has been torn into bits, the Covenant of the League of Nations, signed by 34 states, has been rendered valueless, the Assyrians and the Armenians have been deceived, and the Locarno Pact has been nullified—a pact guaranteed by England, Italy and France, three powerful states. Italy [in Ethiopia] has violated the law in the face of the entire world. This piece of paper in itself is not enough. England has violated an agreement signed by Baldwin and the President of the United States. It may be a paradox, but it is a fact that it is not so easy to violate an agreement with the Jews. The Armenians were promised a national home—and this promise was reneged. The Armenians are a Christian people, and a million of them were slaughtered during the war. We now face a great political decision—I won't say it is the last. I don't know whether this is the last battle. But the decision this time will be very difficult. Two factors have now come to the fore: the Arab opposition; and the need of masses of Jews for Ereẓ Israel. Yesterday J. H. Thomas [the Colonial Secretary] announced that the Mandate is still in force. In reply to a question by Lord Winterton it was stated that the Royal Commission would discuss the interpretations to be given to the Mandate. We know what the meaning of interpretation is. In our times the document itself is nothing. What counts is the interpretation.

"From the outset, we adopted a negative attitude to the Royal Commission, because we had bitter experience with the Shaw Commission, even though the Arabs claim the same. But now a change has taken place. The Commission is obliged to hear the complaints of Jews and Arabs. We have now been given the legal opportunity of presenting our complaints and demands, and we will strive for a Jewish-English agreement. In order to increase the possibility of a such an agreement we must be prepared for a Jewish-Arab agreement. We must consider an urgent political question, that of the government of the country now. The Government has proposed a Legislative Council, which we opposed. But we cannot deny completely the right of the Arabs to participate in the government of the country. I have no doubts about our full right to a Jewish State in Ereẓ Israel. I have perfect faith in its possibility, but I do not believe that it is possible to deny all rights to the Arabs. We have no moral right to do that. We opposed a Legislative Council, and we succeeded in demonstrating the justice of our stand in England too. But it is not enough simply to say No. I am for parity, but parity that gives something real both to the Arabs and to us. With a Legislative Council the whole government is actually in the hands of the High Commissioner. A Legislative Council on a parity basis gives nothing to the Arabs. But a parity partnership in the Government, so long as the Mandate is in force, would give something to the Arabs and to us. I spoke about this with a wise, honest, intelligent Arab, who is close to the Mufti and other Arab circles. I told him that our aim was a Jewish State but that, so long as there was the Mandate, one Jew and one Arab, or two Jews and two Arabs, should be co-opted to the Government. He said that that was something to talk about. I don't know whether the Arabs will accept this, whether the English will agree to it. But this may well serve as the basis for a Jewish-English agreement and a Jewish-Arab agreement. I have also discussed with other Arabs the possibility of parity participation in the Government during a transition period to be followed by a Jewish State allied with an Arab Federation. The High Commissioner told me to proceed with these talks, although he mentioned explicitly that he was not speaking on behalf of the Government."

After the debate in the Executive that lasted two sessions it was decided that I should go to London. Dr. Weizmann had returned to London even before that. I arrived in London on May 29. In Paris I had met with Jarblum. He, together with Nahum Goldmann and Longuet (of the French Socialist Party), had seen Riad al-Sulh, a member of the Syrian delegation that was negotiating with the French Government over the termination of the Mandate. Riad complained that the Jews remembered the Arabs only when there were riots. According to him, the Jews were opposed to the liberation of the Arabs from a foreign yoke. Someone told him that Weizmann had been in Paris and had spoken with the French Government, urging them not to grant independence to Syria. If the Jews wanted understanding with the Arabs they must first of all publicly declare their support for the Arab liberation movement. Only then would it be possible to discuss an agreement. Riad had apparently forgotten our talk of two years before, which took place when things were quiet in the country, and that he had considered the proposals I then made as the basis for a Jewish-Arab agreement.

In small print in *Le Matin*, I saw a cabled item reporting that Ormsby-Gore had been appointed Colonial Secretary in place of Thomas.

In London I found Dov Hoz and Lewis Namier, a Polish Jew who had become the greatest English historian of his time. He was Weizmann's faithful assistant, but more extreme than he, and in practically all the differences between Dr. Weizmann and me he took my side. Namier was not pleased with the appointment of Ormsby-Gore, even though he had been known as a devout Zionist ever since he was sent as the British liaison officer to the Zionist Commission headed by Dr. Weizmann. In Namier's opinion, Ormsby-Gore was weak. Namier was displeased with the entire Government (then headed by Baldwin). England's international situation was difficult. She was not armed and Baldwin, he thought, was not the leader needed at that hour.

A few days after my arrival in London, I received the stenographic transcript of the meeting of the Jewish Agency Executive held in Jerusalem on June 2, 1936, at which Moshe Sharett had said the following:

"As the members of the Executive well know, even before the disturbances we made various attempts to meet with Arab circles and discuss with them the possibility of a Jewish-Arab agreement. We renewed these efforts at the time of the riots. In recent weeks such attempts have also been made by private individuals. About a week ago, Judge Gad Frumkin told me about a talk he had had with two important Arabs, one of them being a leader with whom Ben-Gurion and I had already met several times. Frumkin said that the Arabs had begun the conversation, not necessarily with the intention of finding a way out of the strike and the present imbroglio in the country, but with the aim of later reaching an agreement between Jews and Arabs for a given period. He explained, however, that if the schedule [the immigrant quota that had been approved] had not yet been adopted, the Arabs would undoubtedly have proposed that we forgo it in order to bring the strike to an end and to facilitate the negotiations. Since the deed was already done they did not speak of a way out of the strike, but on the bases of an agreement for the future, of which there were three: the question of immigration; land; and the form of government in the country.

"Meanwhile, the question of the agreement has begun to interest other Jewish personalities. Pinhas Rutenberg proposed to the High Commissioner that the Jews themselves should attempt to reach an agreement with the Arabs, and then perhaps there would be no need whatsoever for a Royal Commission. Shertok [Sharett] had warned him, indeed, against presenting such proposals, since they might weaken the will of the High Commissioner, who in any case was given to fluctuations, to suppress the riots with force, and even dispose him to put the blame on us in the event that the effort failed. Nevertheless, Rutenberg had had his say, and this had a follow-up in a talk between the High Commissioner and Shertok in the orange grove of Kfar Hanoar.

"In the course of these talks and efforts, a meeting of five people (Magnes, Novomeysky, Rutenberg, Moshe Smilansky, and Frumkin) was held in order to consult on the question. Already at their first session they had agreed, as Rutenberg informed Shertok, that when they reached accord among themselves they would inform the Jewish Agency Executive of their stand and would take no action without our approval. At their second meeting they decided to confer with Shertok and delegated Rutenberg and Frumkin for that purpose. Rutenberg also invited Berl Katznelson. The meeting took place in Tel Aviv and four persons thus participated: Rutenberg, Frumkin, Katznelson and Shertok. Information was given there on the formation of this group and on its meetings. It transpired that between their first and second meetings Dr. Magnes had met with the same Arab with whom members of the Executive as well as Frumkin had spoken, and who served as the link with those Arab circles that might decide on the question of an agreement. This time they had discussed matters more specifically. They not only deliberated, but Dr. Magnes formulated their ideas in writing as the outlines of a proposal and both of them, Dr. Magnes and the Arab, had agreed to the formulation.

"The document agreed on between Dr. Magnes and his interlocutor consists of a preamble and the clauses of the agreement. As Shertok recalled, the preamble read as follows: 1) Negotiations between the two sides are desirable. 2) The negotiations should begin immediately; it is preferable that they be conducted without the intervention of the English Government. Approval should be sought only after agreement is reached between the Jews and Arabs. 3) In order that the negotiations may be conducted in a quiet atmosphere, it is necessary that the strike be ended. However, since it would make the position of the Arab leadership difficult if the Government were to end the strike by suppressive measures, and perhaps rule out the possibility of negotiations, it was therefore desirable for the Jews to make a symbolic gesture for the sake of peace *and agree to forgo the use of the immigration certificates they had already received* during the period of the above negotiations [italics mine].

"Three clauses follow: 1) immigration; 2) land; 3) government.

1) With regard to immigration. Jewish immigration of 30,000 a year for the next ten years is being spoken of. The assumption is that natural increase in that period will amount to 100,000 Jews, so that at the end of ten years the Hebrew community will number 800,000, or twice the present size. The Arabs will then number 1,200,000 (their present 900,000 plus 300,000 natural increase), and the Jews will thus number 40 percent of the country's population, or about 70 percent of the Arab community. Another paragraph in this clause says that the Jews undertake to employ an agreed percentage of Arab workers in their enterprises.

2) With regard to land. The Jews undertake not to purchase from a fellah all the land he owns. An example is given: if an Arab has 100 dunams, 75 may be bought from him, while at the same time the Jews undertake to aid with money and technical assistance in the development of the land that remains in his hands.

3) Government. The Jews and the Arabs jointly enter the Palestine administration, in such a way that if one department is headed by a Jew his deputy will be an Arab, and vice versa. Secondly, a Legislative Council on a parity basis.

"Shertok reported that B. Katznelson had analyzed the draft agreement in a conversation they had in Tel Aviv. He agreed to the third clause (government), but rejected the proposal on immigration, as well as the promise of Arab employment, firstly because there was no way of ensuring that Arab labor would not exceed the agreed percentage, and, secondly, because no political body was in a position to coerce private individuals. On the land question we were prepared to ensure that a portion of the land remain in Arab hands, but it was out of the question to burden our limited financial resources with additional expenses for the development of the Arab farms. With regard to Arab labor he was willing to agree to the principle that the Arab worker would not be boycotted, on condition that the Arabs would not boycott Jewish labor or products and also that there be no Arab immigration from other countries.

"On the Sabbath, Rutenberg and Novomeysky visited Ussishkin and reported the matter to him. Ussishkin was shaken by the proposal on immigration. The five gentlemen mentioned requested a meeting with the members of the Jewish Agency Executive, and yesterday a meeting was held at Shertok's house. All five were present, as were also Ussishkin, B. Katznelson, E. Kaplan, and Dr. Dov Joseph. Shertok read the 'revised version' and emphasized that the proposal for 'the cessation of immigration' was to be found here, albeit in a different form. It transpired that there had been a difference of opinion among the group ('the five') on this point. Smilansky announced that at first he had been strongly opposed to the cessation of immigration, but the grave security developments in the past few days and the impossibility of relying on the English called for a concession on this point."

Before I received the transcript of the meeting of the Executive, from which only three of the 16 pages are quoted here, the director of the London office of the Palestine Electric Corporation, Mr. Bradley, forwarded to me a cable from Pinhas Rutenberg. It stated that the situation in Palestine was serious. There was a real danger that the entire Near East would rise up against the Europeans, and we would appear as the cause in the eyes of the world. It was essential to negotiate immediately with the Arabs along the lines he had outlined to Sharett. The High Commissioner was aware of this. The negotiations would not affect the taking of firm action against the disturbances. He demanded telegraphic authorization to continue negotiating contrary to the prevailing view in the Executive. He also thought that my immediate return was vital.

I asked Bradley to reply as follows: The decisive factor was not the Arabs, but England. There were no grounds for panic, although the situation might deteriorate. We must not leave our fate in the hands of the Arabs and be dependent on their agreement. Negotiations with them were desirable, but no proposal for the discontinuation of immigration, even temporarily, could be discussed and that also applied to the fixing of immigration below the level of 1935. As to my return, I would only be able to decide the following week.

14 SMILANSKY'S VERSION—JUNE, 1936

One of "the five," Moshe Smilansky, has given many details about the activity of the group in his book *Tekumah ve-Shoah* (Revival and Holocaust), 1953.

According to Smilansky, Pinhas Rutenberg submitted a memorandum to the Jewish Agency solely in his own name, and in it he stated the following:
1) The aim of any serious attempt to find a way out of the Arab-Jewish imbroglio should not be a temporary agreement with Arab leaders in Erez Israel but a permanent settlement with the Arab world.
2) In order to achieve that goal, the Jews must put forward definite, comprehensive, and frank proposals.
3) Economic concessions alone will not now suffice to appease the Arab nationalist movement. The concessions must be in the area of politics as well as in the area of economics.

4) No practical settlement of value will be achieved unless the area to the east of the Jordan is included in the sphere of Jewish interests; Erez Israel and Transjordan must be regarded as a single unit.

5) The British Government, Erez Israel and Transjordan must be the parties to any agreement between the two communities.

To these postulates Rutenberg appended, as Smilansky tells it, a number of economic and political proposals.

Economic proposals:

Immigration: The immigration question must be discussed by a tripartite committee consisting of representatives of the Jews, the Arabs and the English. The country's absorptive capacity must be the basic principle, in accordance with which the annual quota of Jewish immigrants will be determined. The number of unemployed in the country, to be calculated every six months, will serve as a criterion of the country's absorptive capacity. In computing the number of unemployed only those persons who actually depended on wages for their livelihood should be taken into account. Farmers and nomads will not be reckoned. If the number of unemployed equals 10 percent of all wage earners, the situation is to be regarded as normal and will not affect the immigration quota. The entry of immigrants of the capitalist type and relatives of agricultural settlers will not be affected by unemployment.

Land: A joint committee of Jewish and Arab experts must survey the land now owned by the Jews and the Arabs and reach agreement on the purchase of land, as follows: Districts in Erez Israel and Transjordan must be delimited in which the Jews will have the right to acquire land, and the scope of the purchase must likewise be determined. It must be decided what minimum area of land may not be sold, in order to prevent cases in which fellahin remain landless when they sell their land to Jews or Arabs. The committee may stipulate circmstances under which the sale of land will be forbidden altogether, and also permit land exchange.

Labor: In all Jewish villages and in the Jewish industrial enterprises, with the exception of those financed and operated by the Jewish national institutions (the Jewish National Fund, Keren Hayesod, the Jewish Agency) Arabs are to be hired as well as Jews. The ratio of Arab labor must be 25 percent in Erez Israel and 50 percent in Transjordan. All Government departments, public works, posts and telegraph, the railroad, the port, the customs house, etc. must undertake to employ Jews in numbers not less than the proportion of their population in the country (at present 30 percent of the total population).

Joint activity in commerce and industry: Whenever a new enterprise is started—commercial, industrial or transport, over a certain limit, say an enterprise with capital exceeding LP75,000—Arabs should be given the opportunity to participate, in the management as well, in proportion to the money they invest. In an enterprise with capital of LP25,000, one place on the board of directors should be offered to an Arab representative, even if Arabs have no part in the enterprise. When existing enterprises decide to increase their capital they must allow Arabs to participate and must ensure them representation in the management of the company in accordance with the capital they invest, and one place on the board of directors even if they do not participate in the financial investment. Every commercial, industrial or transport enterprise whose capital exceeds LP25,000, with the exception of those financed by the Jewish public institutions or under their patronage, must employ up to 25 percent Arabs on their clerical staffs. Arab enterprises are obliged to employ the same proportion of Jews on their clerical staffs. The Government is under obligation to employ Arab and Jewish officials in accordance with their numbers in the country. Ways and means must be found for joint activity by Arab and Jewish cooperative enterprises—both in those already in existence and in those to be established in the future. The Government must find a way of including Erez Israel among the dominions and colonies that enjoy preference in all the markets of the British Empire.

Political Proposals:

A Legislative Council should be established in Erez Israel on the basis of Arab-Jewish equality, including the power to enact laws. This equality will not be affected in the future by changes in the size of the population of the two peoples. The chairman of the council will be appointed by the High Commissioner from a list of candidates approved by both groups, Arab and Jewish. Problems relating to immigration, land and labor will come before the council only after agreement on them between the Jews and Arabs has been reached in committees, in accordance with the above rules. The High Commissioner for Erez Israel and Transjordan will be appointed only after consultation between the two groups, Jewish and Arab, and the candidate will be appointed only with their approval. Erez Israel and Transjordan will have dominion status as laid down at the last Imperial Council; in other words, they will have the right to withdraw from the British Empire if both groups of peoples so decide. The entry of Erez Israel and Transjordan as an independent member into an Arab union, should it be established, may be considered, but such a decision will be based on the following conditions:

1) The British Government, alone or together with the French Government, must guarantee the security of the country, the observance of the Constitution and the rights of the Jews:

2) No discrimination will be permitted in the countries of the union against the Jewish population in Ereẓ Israel and Transjordan, and the Jews living in all those countries must be treated like the rest of the population in matters of their employment in agriculture, commerce and industry; or at least their rights will not be inferior to those of nationals of other countries, in accordance with the law.

Smilansky does not say what happened to these proposals. It is not clear whether anyone on the Jewish or Arab side agreed to this plan.

On the other hand, he tells of a version agreed on between Dr. Magnes and Musa Alami, which differs slightly from that described by Moshe Sharett at the Jewish Agency Executive meeting on June 2, 1936. According to Smilansky's story, Magnes and Musa Alami drafted the following aide-mémoire:

"An agreement will be made between the Jews and Arabs, to be valid for from five to ten years. It will be concluded immediately and without the intervention of the Government, but with its consent afterwards. The agreement is on questions of economics and politics, and these are its details:

1) *Immigration:* Arab laborers will not be permitted to enter the country from the neighboring countries. Certificates for bringing in Jewish workers will be issued in accordance with the country's absorptive capacity and on condition that a certain number of Arabs will be employed. Capitalists and relatives will be permitted free entry. Jews will be employed in public works in proportion to their numbers in the country. In determining absorptive capacity the number of unemployed will be taken into account but only those who subsist on their wages, and not agricultural workers or nomads. It should be understood that Jewish immigration to the country during the period of the agreement will not raise the number of Jews in the country to more than 40 percent of the total population.

2) *Land:* A fellah may sell only three-quarters of his land; he is prohibited from selling the last quarter. And he must be aided in the rational cultivation of the remainder of his land. If land held by tenant farmers is sold, there is an obligation to leave a parcel in their possession from which they can subsist, or to give them a parcel of land somewhere else in the country, and the purchasers of the land are obliged to help them cultivate their land rationally.

3) *The political aspect:* The establishment of a Legislative Council on the basis of equality between the two peoples, and in such a way that neither side can dominate the other. It is essential that Jewish and Arab participation in the central government

in the country steadily increase. As a start, one Jew and one Arab should be placed at the head of two important Government departments, and one Arab and one Jew should participate in the supreme executive of the country's government."

When the five negotiators approached the Jewish Agency about arranging the agreement, they were informed, on June 16, 1936, that the Jewish Agency would agree to fixing an immigration quota for a given period, but only one equal to that of the previous year (1935), i.e., not less that 62,000 a year, and that the negotiations must be conducted by the Political Department of the Jewish Agency. Furthermore, the cessation of immigration for a certain period could not even be considered.

What is interesting about Smilansky's story is the way in which he expected to reach an agreement with the Arab leaders.

"He [Smilansky] did not take part in the negotiations with the Arab leaders in the city, but he knew in his heart that nothing could be accomplished in an open and straightforward way. True, Musa Alami was a man of integrity, and perhaps there were one or two others who had no ulterior motives, but neither the members of the Arab Committee nor of the Mufti's party would do a thing unless it would be to their personal benefit—and if the Arab Higher Committee refused, no agreements would improve the situation. While his [Smilansky's] friends were striving to find a way to an agreement with the best of the leaders, Yehuda [the name by which Smilansky refers to himself in the book] knew that although such an agreement might serve as a 'paper bridge' to bring the official Arab functionaries closer to the desired goal, there was also need for a 'silver bridge' to influence people in the way it is customary in the East, and not only in the East, even if they are in a position to impose their authority by force. He [Smilansky] consulted with his friend, Abdul Raḥman Tagi, about how to go about building this second 'bridge.' His friend referred him to his neighbor in Nes Ziona, Tufiq Bey Ghussein, whose son was one of the ten members of the Arab Higher Committee, and although the latter represented the nationalist youth, among whom there were those with clean hands, he himself had neither clean hands nor a pure heart. His friend's advice appeared sound to Yehuda and he thought to himself that if he succeeded in buying off the members of the Arab Executive Committee through one of them it would no doubt help Magnes and his friends to reach an agreement with Musa Alami and his colleagues. Yehuda wasted no time. He met with Tufiq Bey a few times and spoke frankly to him, and the two were not long in coming to an understanding. The Bey understood matters thus: 'You have an innocent soul who acts from idealism—Magnes; and we have one too—Musa Alami. The two of them have worked out a nice draft that will win people's hearts, and we practical men will help them by reaching a "formulation" of our own that will have appeal.' And the 'formulation' proposed by the Bey, after several trips to Jerusalem and after his son brought a few members of the Arab Higher Committee to his father's house, was as follows: The Jews would pay LP 50,000, to be divided among eight of the members of the Arab Committee—LP 5,000 each—while he, the Bey, would receive LP 5,000 for his trouble and his son an additional LP 5,000 for 'expenses.' In return, the members of the Arab Higher Committee would agree to the High Commissioner's proposal—to end the strike and go to London with the Jewish representatives for negotiations based on the agreement that Magnes and Musa Alami would draft. The money would be deposited in trustworthy hands, or in some bank under an assumed name, until the Arab Higher Committee fulfilled its obligation.

"'Why only eight members of the Arab Higher Committee, when they are ten?' Yehuda asked. The Bey laughed and said: 'The other two are Haj Amin and his cousin, Jamal. The first obtains sums from the Italians and the Germans that the Zionists cannot match. And the second is a fool; he doesn't take money.'

"The entire negotiations, and the man with whom he had to bargain, disgusted Yehuda, but he knew that it was only through such underhand dealings that they would be able to break out of the present impasse, and he promised the Bey an answer as soon as possible. Yehuda knew that he must not tell his friends in Jerusalem anything: they had no way of raising the money, and Magnes would reject all such negotiations with revulsion. He made up his mind to consult Rutenberg. He went to Haifa to see him, and Rutenberg listened attentively. Without hesitation, he agreed to the idea as such. Without such measures, accepted in the East, things would not budge. He also agreed to give LP 25,000 for this purpose from the funds of the Electric Corporation; the Jewish Agency would have to supply the rest. Weizmann, who again headed the Zionist movement [this was a year after he had been re-elected President of the Zionist Organization after a period out of office], was then living permanently in Rehovot, and Yehuda asked Rutenberg if he was willing to go with him to see Weizmann. Rutenberg agreed on condition that Weizmann invited him. Weizmann's attitude to the entire matter was favorable, and he said that even great and powerful countries resorted to such measures when necessary. He contacted Rutenberg immediately and asked him to come. Rutenberg again expressed his willingness to provide half of the required sum, if the Jewish Agency would put up the other half. Weizmann undertook to persuade the Agency people, but he was unsuccessful."

This story of Smilansky's came to my knowledge thirty years after the events dealt with in his book. At the time I had no idea that anyone was planning to build a "bridge of silver" between us and the Arabs. In all my contacts with Arab leaders I avoided meeting and conducting negotiations with people who could be reached by such a "bridge"—and not for moral reasons alone. I knew that the Arab people as a whole could not be bought for money, and I was convinced that notables such as the Bey, with whom Smilansky negotiated, did not represent this people and that any agreement with them would be worthless since the Arab people would not follow them. Other details that Smilansky relates—the failure of the attempt to end the strike at Jaffa port by means of a "silver bridge"—only prove his misjudgement in this matter, even though in his book he does not go into the significance of this failure.

I learned about the activities of "the five" only when I received the transcript of the meeting of the Jewish Agency Executive held on June 2, 1936, at which Sharett reported on the initiative taken by Magnes, Rutenberg, Smilansky, Novomeysky and Gad Frumkin. In a letter to the Executive in Jerusalem dated June 9, commenting on the subject discussed by the Executive after hearing Sharett's report, I wrote as follows:

"First of all, I must correct two statements made by Shertok. He says [in a later part of the transcript than the passage quoted above]: 'Mr. Ben-Gurion continued the activity and included Dr. Magnes in the talks.' Magnes was never present at the talks I was then holding with the Arab in question [the reference is to Musa Alami]. No one else participated in these talks. The subject of the discussion was a Jewish-Arab agreement on the establishment of a Jewish State in Erez Israel, west and east of the Jordan, and the ties between that state and an Arab Federation. The Mufti knew about these negotiations, which ended in Geneva with my meeting with the Emir Shekib Arslan and Iḥsan Bey al-Jabri. The negotiations came to a halt after those two gentlemen published our conversation—with distortions—in their French organ, *La Nation Arabe*.

"Magnes knew about these talks. Sometimes he heard about them from me, sometimes from my Arab interlocutor, but never did he take part in them.

"The one talk I did have in Magnes' presence was not with the Arab in question but with Auni Abdul Hadi. That was on July 18, 1934. I reported the details of that conversation to the High Commissioner, who requested me to continue with the talks, but to this day I have not managed to meet Auni again.

"Shertok likewise erred in his conjecture that Magnes had told me he intended to continue the talks with Antonius. My talks with Antonius were discontinued because he left for Turkey, and neither explicitly nor implicitly was it ever hinted that the talks would be continued without me. Only after Antonius' departure did I meet the same Arab [Musa Alami] in Magnes' home, and he [Alami] asked whether it was possible that immigration be halted. I gave him a clear and resolute answer that the proposal was not even being considered. He then asked me whether it was possible that we would halt land purchase for a certain period of time, and to this proposal, too, he received from me a clear and emphatic reply in the negative.

"As to the issue itself: perhaps the whole idea of an agreement is not in the realm of practical reality. Not only because of the bitterness and enmity that were intensified in the course of the disturbances, but because of the fundamental political conflict between us and the Arabs, above all on the question of immigration. For the Arab leaders there is no value to the economic aspect of the development of the country, even if they admit—and not all of them do—that our immigration brings a *material* blessing to the land. They say—and from an Arab viewpoint I think rightly so—'None of your honey, none of your sting.' Of course, there are Jews who do not believe in Zionism, and they live in fear and are willing to compromise at the expense of the future of the Jewish people. Such Jews are only likely to spoil the chances of an agreement, because they will mislead the Arabs into thinking that the Jewish people will relinquish Erez Israel and thereby intensify Arab intransigence. It is not in order to establish peace in the country that we need an agreement. Peace is indeed a vital matter for us. It is impossible to build a country in a state of permanent war, but peace for us is a means. The end is the complete and full realization of Zionism. Only for that do we need an agreement. The Jewish people will never agree to, and dare not agree to, any agreement not designed for that purpose. And the question is: Is *such* an agreement with the Arabs at all conceivable, and is it possible at this time?

"To the first question I answer in the affirmative; to the second question a negative answer is possible, but it is not definite or absolute. For two types of agreement must be considered: a comprehensive agreement regarding the final objective, and a temporary one. A comprehensive agreement is undoubtedly out of the question now. For only after total despair on the part of the Arabs, despair that will come not only from the failure of the disturbances and the attempt at rebellion, but also as a consequence of our growth in the country, may the Arabs possibly acquiesce in a Jewish Erez Israel. Individual Arabs have already almost reached the point of despair, but their opinion will not be accepted, nor will they dare to voice it publicly.

"However, I think that it is not entirely impossible for us to reach a temporary agreement. The chances are not great. I doubt whether the odds are one to ten. Nevertheless, I think that there is a small possibility.

"We are full of complaints—most of them just and some of them unfounded—against the British Government. At times we think that the Government is entirely on the side of the Arabs, and we take no account of the fact that in the eyes of the Arabs the picture is quite the opposite. The Arabs are certain that England is definitely on our side. They are sure that the English press is captive to our cause, that the Cabinet invariably does our bidding, and that Parliament is always influenced by us. The legend of the domination of the world by the Jews is for them a fact, and they see the rise of Leon Blum to power as a further and conclusive proof. They are certain that our financial ability is unlimited, and who appreciates power and the value of money as they do? It doesn't matter in the least that these suppositions are ridiculous and both factually and politically baseless. This is the source of the great fear that grips all the Arab leaders. And although this fear causes us a lot of trouble, it may also serve as a stimulus and an incentive to an agreement. For if we can mitigate their fear somewhat by means of certain arrangements, it is not out of the question that they will accept a temporary agreement which contains a blessing for us and at the same time reduces the danger to them, *as they picture it in their minds*, even though this danger does not really exist or is much smaller than they envisage it.

"The question is: Are we interested in such a temporary agreement? In my opinion there are two weighty arguments in its favor:

1) Political grounds. From the aspect of *external* politics the decisive party for us is England. There is no need to ignore the importance of other political factors (Poland, Czechoslovakia, America, the League of Nations, and the like) in order to comprehend this elementary truth. And we have to deal with England as she is, not with an imaginary England as we might like her to be. And this England has certain qualities that we must take into account, and she has certain interests that we dare not overlook. Balfour was not England, but one Englishman. And even if he were in the Colonial Office, I don't know whether he would not be different in practice than he was in theory. And England is not wholly in accord with our enterprise, as we would like. She is full of hesitation, apprehension and self-conflict. She wants the friendship not only of the Jewish people but also of the Moslem and Arab world. She wants both of them to be dependent on her, and not the other way round. The difficulties that are incapable of frightening us are very likely to deter her. If we succeeded in removing the growing obstacle of Arab opposition, we would immeasurably strengthen our political position vis-à-vis England. This is of particular importance now, when England is involved in fateful questions on the international scene and is not headed by a strong Government, and perhaps not even a stable one. I consider it an act of extraordinary heroism on the part of the British Government that it has not—at least until now—temporarily suspended immigration. Getting the schedule this time was for us a political victory of the first order, one which perhaps we have not adequately appreciated. However, by their very nature our interests cannot be achieved by a one-time act, and the great danger—the like of which never before existed—to the fate of immigration has not completely passed; perhaps we have not yet reached it. We are living in the year 1936, and the scale of immigration in the fifteen years preceding 1934 is now devoid of any real value for the Jewish people. The great, decisive struggle over the scope of immigration is still before us. And it will not be an easy contest. An agreement with the Arabs will give us a tremendous advantage.

2) Economic grounds. Our situation is totally different from that of the Arabs. They wish to maintain the status quo; we want to change it. Our fate depends on

the possibilities of building, and building on a large scale. The Arab economy is primitive, and it will not be destroyed even under conditions of disturbances, riots and disorder. The Arabs can exist without the Jewish market. The Jews need the markets of Syria, Egypt, etc.

"Normal relations with our neighbors are not only a moral and political necessity, but also an economic one. And if there is any chance at all, even a shadow of a possibility, we must not overlook it and let it slip by. We must constantly strive to reach some sort of agreement, particularly now.

"I am opposed to an agreement for a period of ten years. If a comprehensive agreement based on our ultimate goal is possible—fine; but if we are talking about a temporary agreement then five years should be the maximum. We do not have the right to bind ourselves now to constitute only 40 percent in ten years' time. Actually we may not even reach this figure. No one can determine this in advance. But at no price am I prepared to undertake that ten years fron now we will not exceed 40 percent. Our immediate task is to double our numbers, and all our efforts in the future should be aimed at achieving this within the next five years. Of course, I don't mean that we must take a watch in hand and insist on this to the last digit. But this should be the framework of our aspirations. It is approximately on these terms that we should be prepared to come to an agreement. In any agreement, I think that the immigration figures for 1935 should be taken as the basis.

"I reject absolutely the condition of the employment of Arab labor. I do not object to joint enterprises—joint both in capital and in labor. But we cannot and must not forgo 100 percent Jewish enterprises and settlements.

"We can and must, I think, agree to the condition of the retention of an adequate portion of land by each fellah who is prepared to sell us his excess land, if in return for this agreement we will get rid of the Government law.

"We can propose parity in government. I see no harm in the participation of Jews and Arabs in the actual government, on condition that this will be parity participation, and provided that every Jew has an Arab deputy and every Arab a Jewish deputy. The English will probably not be pleased by such a proposal. But if the two sides are united, they will be able to impose their will on England in this matter.

"If we ever get down to a serious discussion on an agreement, the question of Transjordan must not be ignored. I would suggest that Abdullah be given supreme religious authority over all the Moslems in Erez Israel, in return for opening Transjordan to us, even if the formal status quo of Transjordan is not changed for the time being. On this point we will come up against the opposition of the Mufti, and I doubt whether any agreement is possible without him.

"Another important question is who will conduct the negotiations. This difficulty is particularly great for the Arabs, but even on our side it is not easy. It is impossible at this stage to conduct official negotiations, that is, in the name of the Jewish Agency. For the time being they must be informal, but even informal negotiations cannot be entrusted to anyone. Only someone who has the following two qualities should be considered:

1) Someone who has a deep faith in Zionism; someone for whom adherence to the fundamentals of Zionism (such as: Jewish labor, national immigration, land) is an indispensable condition; someone who regards maximalist Zionism as the essential minimum for the Jewish people; someone who sees the realization of Zionism as the life and death question of the Jewish people.

2) Someone who understands the soul of the Arab; someone who respects his national aspirations; someone who is capable of seeing events through Arab eyes.

"And another point: Anyone who enters negotiations out of panic is bound to err and mislead. For this reason it appears to me that not one of 'the five' is suited for these negotiations.

"We are facing a political battle such as we have never known before, and that is why we must take care of all the fronts and every sector on each front.

"For that reason, let us not desist from any effort, and let us not belittle the slightest chance."

I must add to the above letter that my faith in the possibility of reaching an agreement with the representatives of the Arabs on the *fundamental* issue was badly shaken. While my first talks with Musa Alami, and also with Riad al-Sulḥ and Auni Abdul Hadi, had strengthened my belief in the possibility of a mutual understanding, the meeting with Shekib Arslan had dashed my hopes. True, the talks with Antonius had in a way restored my faith, but I knew that while Antonius was a theoretician of the Arab nationalist movement he did not represent this movement. His true interest, as I sensed it in our talks, was the fate of Syria, but not that of Ereẓ Israel. A few weeks before the meeting with Antonius, I had visited Magnes (it was on March 11, 1936), who told me that two weeks before he had approached an Arab notable "of considerable influence" to arrange a meeting between me and Jamal, and that Jamal had said he saw no *practical* value in such a meeting (Jamal had no doubt heard from his brother-in-law, Musa Alami, about my Zionist outlook). This was the same Jamal who, according to Smilansky's story, was "naive" like Magnes, and the only member of the Arab Higher Committee who could not be made to cross the "bridge of silver." However, despite the disappointments, I regarded it as our moral obligation, which was also our political duty, to meet as many Arab leaders as possible who could not be bought, even if they were incapable of rising to the moral height of Musa Alami. Even though it would not be easy to reach a temporary or permanent agreement there were benefits to be gained from the meetings as such. There was value to every frank clarification, for in that way we could see the Arabs as they were and learn to understand them, and the same held true for the other side. Such an acquaintanceship, sincere and true, held promise even if it did not immediately lead to mutual understanding and an agreement. For that reason I cabled Sharett, two days before sending the above letter: "REGARD CONSTANT CONTACT WITH ARAB LEADERS OF UTMOST IMPORTANCE AND IF OFFICIAL NEGOTIATIONS IMPOSSIBLE CONTINUE PRIVATE TALKS."

15 SHARETT TALKS TO ALAMI—JUNE, 1936

The activity of "the five" during the Arab strike at the end of April 1936 and thereafter created difficulties for the members of the Jewish Agency Executive in contacting Arab leaders. At a meeting of the Executive, while I was in London, there were differences of opinion as to whether we should negotiate with the Arabs on the volume of immigration, At a meeting between Dov Joseph and Musa Alami at that time the latter declared that without a discussion of the volume of immigration there was no possibility of negotiations between the Arabs and the Jews. At the same time a certain Englishman approached a Jewish functionary (not one of "the five") and suggested that he meet one of the Arab leaders to discuss the possibility of peace arrangements. At Sharett's suggestion, the Jewish functionary met with this Arab leader. The Arab advised the Jew to arrange a preliminary meeting with Musa Alami. Moshe Sharett thereupon decided to get in touch with the other himself, and on the morning of May 21, 1936, he telephoned Alami and asked whether he was willing to meet him. Musa Alami agreed at once and invited Sharett to his home. Sharett hurried over (he recorded the talk in English).

Sharett was given a friendly reception, and he reminded Musa Alami of the previous meeting together with me two years earlier. He noted that since that time a number of attempts had been made to arrange meetings between Jews and Arabs, mostly unofficial meetings. Sharett asked him if he was willing to have a discussion with him without intermediaries. Musa Alami replied that he saw no reason why the two of them should not maintain direct contact with one another. Sharett commented that in that case he preferred to renew the talks himself, adding that Bernard [Dr. Dov] Joseph was his associate in the Political Department of the Jewish Agency and that the talk that Joseph had had with him had been with Sharett's knowledge.

Musa Alami replied that he had been aware of this, but since it had not been stated explicitly until now he had not felt he had the right to tell Joseph that he had previously met with members of the Jewish Agency Executive.

Sharett then asked him directly whether in his opinion there was a chance that his friends would sit down with the members of the Executive to discuss the future.

Musa Alami replied that, if the truth be told, he had almost despaired of that lately. The suspicions that his friends had always harbored had lately begun to weigh upon him too. It seemed to him that the Jews were not in fact interested in reaching an agreement with the Arabs, since they depended on the English, and as soon as their situation improved somewhat they completely forgot about the existence of the Arabs. He felt obliged to mention that a few weeks before he had spoken with several of his Jewish friends and had hoped that the talks would continue. But suddenly it appeared to him that all those friends were steering clear of him.

Sharett expressed his amazement at this impression. He said that Musa Alami surely could not accuse him or me of forgetting the Arabs when things were going well. He well knew that the two of us were the first to meet with him, and that we had done so when the Jewish community was flourishing and everything was quiet. Immigration had then reached a record figure. Even on that very day, Sharett said, he had got in touch with him after receiving a report of the debate in Parliament, which could be regarded as a Jewish victory, and something that ought not to prompt an overture to the Arabs. But such thinking was far from our minds. No success in England could bring us to ignore the Arabs, with whom we would have to live together down the years; that was why we had to reach an understanding with them, regardless of the state of our relations with the British.

Musa conceded at once that he had never doubted the sincerity of Sharett's intentions or of mine. In fact, he had been happy to hear Sharett's voice on the telephone that morning. But he must be frank and say that, despite all his respect and esteem for me, it could not be denied that I was intransigent. He always had the impression that while I was genuinely anxious to reach an agreement with the Arabs I insisted that they accept my Zionist program one hundred percent. An agreement must necessarily involve give and take; it could not possibly be based on the consent of one side to accept all the demands and aspirations of the other.

Sharett reminded Musa that when the three of us had met at Sharett's house it had been agreed that Musa would find out from his friends whether it would be possible to broaden the circle of individuals participating in the discussion on the Arab side—and that we had not yet received an answer.

Sharett returned to Musa's allegation that a number of his Jewish friends had been avoiding him, and that contact had been severed. Sharett explained that the matter had really become involved and that some time would be needed to straighten things out. Two or three different persons had spoken to him, and it was not clear whom they represented. For that reason he felt it necessary to find out from him whether he preferred direct contact or not.

Musa agreed that this was something that should be clarified immediately. He told Sharett about his talks with Judge Frumkin, who had been the first to make contact with him. He confessed that he had been taken aback somewhat to see Judge Frumkin involved in politics. He had not expected a judge to play such a role. He was even more surprised to hear Frumkin say he was sure he could obtain authorization from the Jewish Agency to negotiate on its behalf, should that prove necessary. He had then turned to Dr. Magnes with whom he had talked on a number of previous occasions. He not only respected Magnes but also regarded him as a good friend. Even among his closest Arab friends he doubted whether there was anyone he liked as much as Magnes. But he knew very well that Magnes did not represent the Jews, and on several occasions he had told Magnes that an agreement with him had no real value, for he would not succeed in persuading the Jews to accept it.

Sharett said that all these separate preliminary efforts at negotiation caused him much anxiety. He recalled that Musa Alami had told Bernard Joseph that he had heard from someone that there was no point in discussing a Jewish-Arab agreement with the members of the Jewish Agency Executive, since they were all under the influence of Dr. Weizmann, who in recent years had become an extremist.

Musa Alami admitted that he had heard that from a friend—on this occasion he said it was a British friend, although Joseph definitely remembered his mentioning a Jewish friend on one occasion.

He pressed his thumb on the table to demonstrate the position of the Agency Executive under Dr. Weizmann, as it had been described to him.

Sharett said that without going into a discussion of the relations between the Executive and Dr. Weizmann, the fact was that we had all been elected by the Zionist Congress. And although Dr. Weizmann as President had the supreme authority, never had he tried to impose his will on the Executive. All questions were decided on jointly, and it was nothing but a distortion of the truth to describe Dr. Weizmann as someone who was trying to prevent us from reaching an agreement with the Arabs. Dr. Weizmann was constantly pressing us to persist in these efforts of ours, and more than once he had expressed concern that we were not sufficiently active in seeking contacts with the other side.

Sharett explained to Musa Alami how much damage could be caused by such distortions. Whether the members of the Executive were intransigent or not was a matter of opinion. In any event, they and only they were in a position "to deliver the goods." To say that there was no point to discussions with them about an agreement was tantamount to saying that there was no point in discussing an agreement, because any deliberation other than with the Agency Executive was valueless. In talks with members of the Executive there was no possibility, at any rate, of being misled or deceived. If they agreed to an arrangement they were in a position to have it approved and implemented. If they considered certain conditions unacceptable they would say so straight out, and the two sides could part without any impairment of their mutual respect. But if unauthorized persons conduct negotiations there is always the danger of false hopes that will cause disappointment and bitterness. If participation of a particular Jew in the negotiations was desirable that could be arranged, but only with the knowledge and consent of the Jewish Agency.

Musa Alami agreed.

That same day Moshe Sharett reported to his colleagues on the negotiations with the Arabs. He said the following:

"In the matter of negotiations with the Arabs there are continuous new developments. I shall here deal with four points:

"1) Ragheb Nashashibi. There has been intermittent contact with Ragheb through a reliable person, and it is not clear exactly what Ragheb wants. There is no doubt that he is in great distress and is embittered; he has got himself into a mess. He sees the Mufti deceiving him and settling all sorts of matters with the authorities behind his back. He has a strong desire to extricate himself somehow from the morass. There was a time when Ragheb expected the Government to banish him. Now he sees a way out for himself by going to London, but such a trip would not be of his own accord. He would like to go to London to serve his people, as he understands it, in opposition to the Mufti. Ragheb's mood can be described roughly as follows: he wants to help the general cause of the Arab people—and instead the strike has turned into a tool serving the clique of the Mufti. He is in despair over this, and will go to London to seek an honorable way of serving his people. Obviously, his first need is for money to cover the travel expenses. Ragheb owns an orange grove. Now, if he could immediately sell the coming year's crop for ready cash, the way would be clear for the trip to London. It is not clear how much of this comes from his own initiative and how much has been put into his head by the Jews who meet him, including the Jew he considers most trustworthy. In any case, the fact is that over a period of time attempts were made (under Rutenberg's guidance, and which I opposed) to offer this man money—and he turned down the offers. He did not reject them with disgust, but said that for the time being he had no need of them. In other words, if he should need funds he would say so. When the proposal of selling the fruit of the orange grove was put to him, and he was told that the matter could be arranged and a price was quoted, this made an impression on him.

"Meanwhile, in the course of the talks between the two (Ragheb and the Jew whom he trusts), a second Jew, a confidant of Ragheb's obviously closer to Ragheb than to us, made the following proposal to him: Since the entire issue is the suspension of immigration, and the present schedule has already been approved, action can be taken with regard to the next schedule. It can be announced that the next schedule will be deferred until the arrival of the Royal Commission. This in effect is a variant of a proposal that is being bandied about among the officials on which I have already reported, the idea being that perhaps in this manner a way out of the impasse may be found. To this proposal Ragheb answered that he must confer with another party, the mayor of Jaffa. In order to do so he must travel to Jaffa, and to get to Jaffa now is very difficult, because the road is dangerous, people are fired on without distinction. But the upshot was that he may go to Jaffa after all. Tomorrow he will give an answer. The Jew said to Ragheb, 'If you agree to this proposal, I will speak to the Jews about it.' However, it should be clear that if there was any chance of deferring the next schedule as a way out of the impasse, after Ormsby-Gore's speech in Parliament it no longer has any basis. The High Commissioner is no longer able to do this, and the Central Government has announced that it does not undertake to act in accordance with the recommendations of the Royal Commission. I do not now ascribe any value to this proposal. But if Ragheb agrees to it, we shall see what must be done.

"2) The anonymous Jew who proposed an Arab national government to Dr. Khalidi today came up with a new suggestion, which he has already put to Khalidi. He proposed a sort of 'round table' with an odd composition and authority. Instead of the Royal Commission he suggests a Jewish-Arab committee, to consist of three Arabs, three Jews, and an Englishman. And the Arabs will not be the Mufti or Alami, but three names, such as Ibn Saud, the Prime Minister of Iraq, and the like. (Interjection: 'Ataturk!') By the way, there is also some connection with Ataturk. An Englishman who is an expert on questions of the East came to Weizmann and said that he has ties with Ataturk, and that he is prepared to influence him to advise the Arabs to make peace with the Jews. Weizmann asked Ben-Gurion, and Ben-Gurion writes in this connection that it is worth trying anything in order to break the strike. I wrote to Ben-Gurion that I was opposed to this scheme, which was not a serious one but had a dangerous aspect, and I referred to what I had written previously about the fear of Turkish imperialism that prevailed in Syria. The Arabs already believed that we were interfering with their interests in France and England, and if they started thinking that the Zionists were hatching some plot against them involving Turkish imperialist ambitions, that would be the last straw. All this is by the way. Going back to the plan that was suggested to Dr. Khalidi, our side was to be represented by personalities such as Leon Blum, Brandeis, and the like. Both sides would undertake in advance to abide by the decisions of this body. According to the Jew who initiated the proposal, it made a powerful impression on Dr. Khalidi, who immediately got in touch with four people by telephone and told them about it. Who they were we don't know, but Khalidi repeated that the matter must be given thought. According to the Jew, Khalidi was enthusiastic about the proposal. When I was told about it, I said that it merited consideration, but my first reaction was negative. For if people who are familiar with the issue convene, then each one knows what he can offer and what he cannot. But if the meeting is between uninformed parties, there is no hope that anything substantial will emerge.

"3) Three days ago an Englishman, not from Government circles, approached Dr. Thon. He apparently spoke about the suspension of immigration, and proposed that Dr. Thon meet with Dr. Kan'an. Thon asked me whether I thought this was advisable. I answered affirmatively, but said that if the question of the suspension of immigration came up he should say no, absolutely, while if other questions were raised he should listen without going into the terms of the agreement; he should only talk about the procedure of the negotiations: how to meet and with whom. Thon went, and their talk ended with Dr. Kan'an suggesting that a meeting be held with Musa Alami. B. Joseph visited Musa Alami twice, but he did not succeed in finding him in. Thon suggested that it would be better if somebody else were to meet with Musa Alami, rather than us. However, since we (Ben-Gurion and I) had already met Musa Alami and spoken to him we saw no point in now introducing a new intermediary in our contacts with him.

"4) This morning I saw Musa Alami at his office and we had a talk.

[Sharett's report of this meeting started with the points already mentioned on pp.84–87.]

"M.S.: '. . . It is not easy for me to telephone you. I don't know how you would take it—perhaps I might be causing you difficulties. But Joseph tried to get in touch with you and did not succeed.'

"M.A.: 'I didn't know that Joseph was trying to see me about these matters. I thought he needed me in connection with legal affairs.'

"M.S.: 'In brief, do we have something to talk about or not?'

"M.A.: 'Your side does things that obstruct the possibility of an agreement, and I don't understand why you have to act in this way. I don't know what point there is in your constantly emphasizing that the Arab movement is supported by Italian money. First of all, let me inform you that this is a lie. Perhaps I am not aware of everything that is being done within the movement, but nevertheless I am in the know. I'll put it this way: if it turns out that there is Italian money here this would come as a great surprise to me. You stress this point all the time, and it is also voiced in Parliament. It is obvious that this is at your prompting; you teach the members of Parliament how to speak.'

"M.S.: 'It isn't true that only we talk about this. The Government talks also. This matter has also filtered through from the Foreign Ministry in England. Even before the disturbances, during the Abyssinian war, the Government issued clear statements that Italy was spending a lot of money here in the country.'

"M.A.: 'The only case was nine months ago. Two young fellows went to Egypt and obtained one or two hundred pounds under false pretences; they embezzled the money, and never carried out what they promised. As far as I'm concerned, it's permissible to accept money from abroad too, but I deny that this is actually happening. There was only this one case of two young fellows misappropriating funds. In fact, you saw that during the Abyssinian war our entire orientation was pro-British.'

"M.S.: 'That doesn't alter the fact that Italy has expended considerable money for propoganda, because it pays for Italy to irritate England.'

"M.A.: 'There was another case in which a newspaper obtained money, and as a result stopped attacking Italy. You have to understand the feeling of the Arabs. The people live with the feeling that they are sacrificing their blood, and if it is said that they do this only for the sake of Italian money—there is no greater insult. I request you in all sincerity to stop this talk about Italian money.'

"M.S.: 'I wholly agree with you that the movement that has now arisen cannot be explained *only* by Italian money. But at the same time we are certain that there *is* foreign money.'

"M.A.: 'If it emerges that this is the case it will be a great surprise to me. The second thing I cannot understand is this: Why do you attack the Mufti personally? This is done in Parliament too, and it is obvious that you feed these words into the mouths of Members of Parliament. Don't you realize that in this whole affair the Mufti is not the worst person with whom you will have to deal? In such a situation is it possible to speak about an agreement? Don't you understand that there is no hope for an agreement to which the Mufti does not consent? And you make his position difficult by your personal attacks.'

"M.S.: 'On the contrary, we strengthen his position, we make a patriot out of him.'

"M.A.: 'No, the attacks on the Mufti oblige the Government to act and come to his defense, and nothing can harm him as much as his defense by the Government. That is more damaging than your attack. Don't you know what a crooked policy the High Commissioner is following with regard to the Mufti? You don't have to believe me, but what I am about to tell you is as true as the fact that I see you before me: *the Mufti is opposed to violence.* He has undergone a tremendous change in the last few years. He now understands many things he failed to comprehend before. Perhaps it is a result of aging, but he is much more tolerant now. I am telling you what he told me. Perhaps the Mufti is the incarnation of the Devil. Maybe he is only acting, but he told me that he is opposed to violence, because violence will not lead to any positive results, because when it comes to violence the Government is in a stronger position, and it will suppress us by force, and it has the ability to do this. The Mufti's idea was: a peaceful strike. But a protracted strike. He believes that this is the sharpest weapon against you, for the strike is bound to destroy your position in the country, and it will harm you more than the Arabs. Perhaps he is wrong, maybe be doesn't understand economics, but that is his credo. He holds that the strike is bound to force you to leave here, and will at any rate keep others from coming here. He believes that the second stage after the strike must be an economic boycott against you. By such measures he plans to fight you.'

"M.S.: 'In that case the Mufti is making the same mistake as the High Commissioner, who also thinks that a strike is possible without acts of violence. Now he sees that this is impossible.'

"M.A.: 'Perhaps the Mufti has erred. The High Commissioner ruined the whole business with his vacillating policy. He has caused the present catastrophe in the country and there is no way out. Either, or. When the High Commissioner summoned the Arab Higher Committee and threatened to take strong measures he should have carried out his threats, or not have threatened at all. But by the very threats that he uttered he already forced the Higher Committee to disobey him. [This came into the conversation as follows: When I said that the strike had led to acts of violence, Musa Alami said that this was not so; the police by using force against Arab crowds had introduced the element of violence. The police had lost all sense of proportion and had provoked the crowd, thus leading to bloodshed.] The High Commissioner all along has been trying to compromise the Mufti's position. I know that it is Andrews who is advising him to follow this course. Let me give you an example. Some time ago there was the business with Sheikh Ḥasan Abu Saud [one of the preachers in the Mosque of Omar]. Last week the police wanted to arrest him, and all the sheikhs gathered together and said that without the Mufti they would not permit him to be taken. One of the sheikhs read a call for a Jihad [Holy War] but the matter was hushed up. The High Commissioner summoned the Mufti and spoke to him about some trifling matters, but he let the impression be created that the Mufti had come to him to appeal for the cancellation of the warrant against that sheikh. When it was learned that the Mufti had been to the High Commissioner, people said: "Aha! he was at the High Commissioner's, which means that he is ceding something to the Commissioner"—and there is no confidence in him. In the recent debate in Parliament it was said that the Moslem Council is not striking—and that, too, in order to cast aspersion on the Mufti. His position is becoming untenable. Now he is opposed to carrying on with this matter but he doesn't know how to extricate himself. He is against its continuation because: a) it has led to violence, and violence in his opinion harms the national interest; b) acts of violence are bound to lead to suppression by force, and if the movement that has now arisen is forcibly suppressed it will not be easy to raise it up again; c) his personal standing is being adversely affected. That is why he is interested in bringing the matter to an end.'

"M.S.: 'And so, in short: is there anything for us to talk about or not?'

"M.A.: 'But what will happen? Is there any way out of the situation? Perhaps you have some ideas.'

"M.S.: 'When you say "way out" you mean the suspension of immigration. On this issue there is nothing to discuss. I will tell you why. Now you have the Mosque of Omar, and let us assume that you don't want violence and come to the conclusion that the Friday prayers at the Mosque are the source of all the disturbances in the country, and that as long as services continue there will be unrest. And assume that we would approach the Moslems and suggest that in order to end the disturbances the Mosque should be closed for a month. There is nothing to be afraid of, the keys remain in their hands, but close it temporarily. Would they agree?'

"M.A.: 'No!'

"M.S.: 'Why would they not agree? Would this be only on religious grounds? It would not be just for religious reasons but because they would see this as a symbolic renunciation of their rights. The same holds true for the suspension of immigration. You say: "Immigration causes disturbances; stop the immigration. What does it matter to you? After all, the keys to the immigration remain in your hands, the schedule remains in your hands even for the future, but for the sake of peace halt the immigration temporarily." To that we say: "Immigration is our fundamental right; you are attacking that right. The suspension of immigration is an act that symbolizes our capitulation, and no Jew can agree to that." [He was impressed by the analogy. When I told Ussishkin about this conversation half a year ago he said: "What! You said, 'Your Mosque'? You should never say to them, 'Your Mosque.'"] We cannot now discuss an agreement in general, it is not the proper time for that. We can discuss a way out of the situation—do we have anything to talk about or not? If it is impossible here let's go to Egypt, we will meet there, but we must know if there is something to talk about or not.'

"M.A.: 'We must discuss some general principles before I make an attempt to influence people.'

"We fixed a meeting on general principles for Wednesday of this week at a neutral place. I informed him that Joseph would also participate.

"You have read Ben-Gurion's letter to the Agency Executive concerning the negotiations with the Arabs. There was a further discussion in the Executive on this question, mainly on the issue of setting norms for immigration, and we reached some agreement. Only Fishman maintains his opposition, but Greenbaum agreed that for the purpose of sounding we may also talk about immigration figures. Ussishkin formulated his position thus: We say, 'Immigration in accordance with absorptive capacity,' and if they ask what that means we should answer, 'Immigration at the level of 1935, for five years.' Thus, he has changed his position.

"In the same letter of Ben-Gurion's to the Executive, he writes that we can agree to the fixing of the immigration figure at 60,000 to 80,000 a year, which is a concession on our part, and in return for that concession the Arabs must agree to our settlement in Transjordan. That is a certain conception, but it has no connection with the real background against which one can sit down with Musa Alami to discuss agreement. Obviously our agreement to fixing the number of immigrants is a concession. But for Musa Alami to agree to this would be a far greater concession and entirely unrealistic. I believe that we can and should speak about immigration at the level of 1935 for the next five years. I think that we should talk to Musa Alami about that at Wednesday's meeting and see what his reaction is. If the whole thing bursts—it bursts. But if it doesn't, and even after that it is possible to go on to other issues and talk about matters of government and land—then we must do that.

"To complete the information on this matter I must add that in Egypt there is one man who took an active part in the affairs of Palestine. He is completely identified with the Mufti, traveled with him to the Arab countries, and was Minister of Education in one of the Governments in Egypt. This man [Muḥamad Ali Aluba Pasha] met Vilensky in Cairo and asked him whether it was possible to talk about negotiations between Arabs and Jews; he was prepared to bring Jews and Arabs together in Egypt. Vilensky told him that the Jews would agree to negotiations on condition that the Arabs recognized the Mandate and the Balfour Declaration. I asked Vilensky to tell the Egyptian that the Jews agreed to negotiations *without* prior conditions. The Egyptian reported this to the Mufti too, and the latter replied that he was prepared for negotiations *after* the suspension of immigration. Then the Egyptian said that he saw that the Jews were willing to reach an agreement while the Arabs were not."

16 SHARETT AND JOSEPH TALK TO ALAMI—JUNE, 1936

Three days later, on Monday, June 24, 1936, Moshe Sharett and Dov Joseph met with Musa Alami at the King David Hotel, and this time it was Dov Joseph who took notes:

> "M.S. and I met M.A. at the King David Hotel by appointment. Prior to the meeting M.S. and I discussed the line we should pursue. He said that in view of the strong opinion against negotiating on the basis of fixed dimensions of immigration he thought we should explain how difficult it is to fix any total figure as there were categories of immigrants not subject to our control, and that we should, instead, explore other guarantees required to allay Arab fears. We might then discuss

first the questions of land and constitution leaving out immigration for the time being.

"I proposed that instead of discussing any principles we might first tackle the question of procedure. We should take the line that it was not fair of him to expect us to put forward concrete proposals until we know that Arab leaders agreed to meet to negotiate with us, and that we should limit the discussion to a clarification of his status and the likelihood of his being able to get support among Arab leaders for his views and efforts. We might talk about governmental institutions and land in a general way but should decline to discuss immigration or to make concrete proposals for the reason stated. We agreed on this course.

"M.S. opened the conversation by enquiring whether M.A. was satisfied that he would be able to obtain the support of recognised Arab leaders for any proposal that he might consider reasonable as a basis of settlement. It was well known that there were differences between different Arab parties and it was important to know whether M.A. could hope to arrange at least for those leaders whose agreement was essential to cooperate in negotiation with the Jews. The question was whether they were prepared to do so or whether they would refuse to entertain any such proposal, either because they themselves thought an agreement out of the question or because they were afraid of being denounced by their rivals. Our people would, before negotiating on the merits of the differences between Jews and Arabs, like to know whether M.A. could 'deliver the goods.' Otherwise we would be wasting our time in discussion. The Jews had a definite organisation whose decision could be regarded as one which would bind the Jews. The Arabs had no such organisation. He was not suggesting that they must or should have. But we had to be assured that he would have the backing of the recognised permanent leaders of Arab affairs for any understanding reached.

"He replied that it was remarkable how the Jews and the Arabs agreed in mistrusting each other. He on his part knew that the same doubt existed in Arab minds as to the usefulness of conducting discussions with the Jews. Before the disturbances he had often heard the opinion expressed among Arabs that an effort should be made to come to an understanding with the Jews. Even certain Istiklalists considered that it was better to come to terms with the Jews than to rely on the British. But now no such suggestions were any longer made. The Jews were regarded as being intransigeant. We need have no concern about the Arab leaders being disunited. If a programme of cooperation were put forward which was acceptable to the Arabs it could be arranged that despite their differences the responsible leaders should accept it. He had not been in touch with Arab leaders and had not disclosed to them that he was having discussions. He had thought it was wiser to wait until he had a definite proposal which he considered acceptable. He was much more moderate than the others and could understand much of the Zionist point of view. He thought that could be a fair test; if he could not be satisfied the others would surely not be.

"He wished however to draw attention to something which was making discussion difficult. It seemed a number of Jews were conducting negotiations with Arabs at the same time and that reduced the value of his attempts to assist in finding a solution of our differences. A certain Jew, he did not know his name, had approached Tewfiq Bey Ghussein, again about going to see the High Commissioner jointly. This morning his son, Jacob Ghussein, had returned from Cairo where proposals had been made to him by Jews there. Dr. Khaldi [Khalidi] told him he had been approached by a Jew who claimed to speak with the authority of the Jewish official bodies.

"I pointed out that we could not stop Jews from talking to Arabs but it was clear that with regard to the Jews no one could speak for them except the Agency. Nor could Government recognise anyone but the Agency as representative of the Jews. The Arabs could, therefore, disregard any interference by Jews other than the Agency. But with regard to the Arabs the position was different. I wished to put the matter bluntly. He should be fair to M.S. As he knew, not all Jews were agreed as to the usefulness of such negotiations. Many thought it was a mistake to enter upon them as the Arabs would never agree to our minimum and we would not agree to their demand, and, therefore, it was better not to begin. They thought Arab leaders would never agree to meet Jewish leaders to discuss matters. If we were to come to terms with him and then the Arab leaders would be unwilling to take up the agreement, these Jews would say 'We told you so!' and this would expose M.S. to serious criticism. We knew that any agreement would entail a certain amount of give and take. Otherwise no agreement would be reached. We believed that there was a chance of our being able to convince him to agree upon certain proposals, otherwise we would not be wasting our time talking to him. But much as we might like to talk to him in a friendly spirit we could not now afford the time to hold conversations with someone who might turn out to be the equivalent among the Arabs of Dr. Magnes among the Jews—a very charming person eager to see Jewish-Arab differences settled but representing no one and having no right to speak for the Jews. We knew or believed that he had the confidence of the Mufti and Jamal, but would that be enough for the purpose? For that reason it was necessary that he should arm himself with authority from the Arab leaders. They might not wish at this stage to meet Jewish leaders. They might prefer that the discussions should be between representatives of themselves and of Jewish leaders until the negotiations had reached a point where agreement was in sight. I did not think we would object to this. But we must know that he and other representatives were authorised to speak for certain Arab leaders.

"M.S. pointed out that we did not say he had to be armed with the authority of all the ten members of the High Committee. We did not regard that committee as a permanent organ. But he should speak for the recognised leaders of permanent standing and authority in Arab affairs; we would leave it to his judgment as one interested in the cause as to whom to approach and how. I observed that clearly the Mufti and Jamal would have to be among the leaders represented.

"M.A. said that he saw our point of view. Perhaps we were right and if we wished he would speak to certain Arab leaders and ascertain whether they would agree to discussions being carried on either by him or other representatives on the understanding that if a settlement of a reasonable nature were proposed by us they would agree to consider it and to meet to discuss it. He was also friendly even with Ragheb Nashashibi. But as for the others like Abdul Latif Salah and Jacob Ghussein they didn't count. If the Mufti and Jamal and the Istiklalists agreed on a policy a way could be found to make the others accept it. There would also be no difficulty, he was sure, of getting the Mufti himself to meet with us if an agreement were in sight, nor would it be necessary to have the meeting outside of Palestine as had been suggested. The important thing was to get them to believe that the Jews were willing to make some sacrifice for the sake of peace. They all felt the Jews were intransigeant like Mr. Ben-Gurion had proved himself in the conversations in Geneva some two years ago with Sheikh Arslan. He admired very much the candour and straightforwardness of Mr. Ben-Gurion. It was perhaps right that he should state clearly what he intended. But it had frightened the Arabs. What in effect he had said was 'You give us all we ask for now and in return we shall at some future date, which might never arrive, help you in the matter of an Arab Confederation.'

"M.S. said that it was a mistake to regard the Jews as intransigeant. He agreed, however, that any discussion should be about Palestine as presently constituted. It would be well for Jews and Arabs to make clear to one another what their views were about the eventuality of an Arab Confederation but that should not be a major matter of discussion. M.S. also made it clear that we did not consider the discussions should be about the present situation. The Arabs had got themselves into an impasse from which the Jews could not extract them. The discussions should be about the relations between Jews and Arabs after things settled down.

"I added that the Jews had more than proved their readiness to negotiate by the very fact that M.S. had agreed to take the first step and came to meet him. But we could do no more than that. We also had to have regard to matters of prestige. Moreover Jewish leaders were ready at any time openly to meet Arab leaders around a table to discuss matters and had said so. This was not the case with regard to Arab leaders.

"M.A. admitted that was so. He had been very much impressed by the fact that M.S. had again taken the first step in ringing him up. He asked whether we wanted him to go to the Arab leaders expressly to put the matter before them or whether he should find a convenient casual opportunity of doing so. We replied that we left that to him to decide, but, although we could not press him to act with haste, he would appreciate that time was an important factor in the present situation and there should be no undue delay.

"The conversation then turned to the subject of the High Commissioner. M.S. asked whether the Arabs did not regard the High Commissioner as a friend of their cause.

"M.A. said that on the contrary H.E. had told him that in forming his policy he had had to take account of the fact that it was considered to be in the interests of the British Empire to foster the Jewish National Home. He would not be surprised to learn that H.E. had told us he was compelled to have regard to Arab considerations elsewhere than in Palestine.

"M.S. replied that the Jews believed the same thing as to factors influencing H.E.'s policy in the opposite sense, and no doubt H.E. must have mentioned that he had to have regard to the Arab factor in the light of neighbouring Arab countries.

"I said that I never held two views on the matter. H.E. was essentially and entirely pro-British and neither pro-Jewish nor pro-Arab. He clearly should have regard to both Jewish and Arab influences and public opinion if he were to fulfil his task wisely.

"M.S. asked whether the Arabs did not realise how eager H.E. was to assist in Arab development.

"M.A. replied that on the contrary they thought his prime concern was to help develop the Jewish National Home. In fact he was to the Arabs the most hated man in Palestine. They would be happy if he were removed from office tomorrow. They regarded him as their greatest enemy.

"There was further conversation of a general nature and inter alia it was made clear to M.A. that Jonathan Blumenfeld who had spoken to Dr. Khaldi [Khalidi] had no right whatever to speak for anyone and when he reported to us what he had suggested he was told that his suggestion was too preposterous to be entertained.

"During the conversation M.A. mentioned that he had met Dr. Magnes to discuss an Arab-Jewish rapprochement several weeks before the disturbances had broken out. No one dreamt any such thing was going to happen or develop in that way. In fact he had arranged to go on leave just before the troubles began.

"It was agreed that in a few days' time M.A. would let me know what success he had met with at the hands of the Arab leaders and whether they agreed to the discussion of the merits of an Arab-Jewish understanding being entered into."

17 THE MEMORANDUM OF "THE FIVE"—JUNE, 1936

Meanwhile "the five" met—Judge Gad Frumkin, Dr. Judah L. Magnes, Moshe Novomeysky, Pinhas Rutenberg and Moshe Smilansky—and prepared the following memorandum which they duly submitted, in June 1936, to the Zionist Executive:

"Soon after the beginning of the Arab Strike of this year, it became evident that the disturbances would be prolonged and might result in Governmental measures detrimental to Zionist aims and interests. The undersigned met in order to exchange views on the situation and to see if a reasonable program of negotiations with influential members of the Arab Community could be worked out, with a view to ending the present Strike through a truce and perhaps subsequently, to a lasting peace arrangement between the two races.

"The undersigned have been living in the country for a number of years. All of them have in different ways had close contact with leading members of the Arab communities of Palestine, Transjordan, Egypt, Syria and Iraq. They have had many opportunities of hearing Arab views on the burning question of Jewish-Arab relationships. All of them have been in touch with Government officials whose views and feelings on the subject of Jewish-Arab relations they regard themselves as competent to interpret.

"The exchange of views between the undersigned through verbal discussions and written memoranda, brought to light, that, although differing in details, they were united on fundamental points of approach as follows:

"1) The successful upbuilding of the Jewish National Home cannot be accomplished without coming to an agreement with the Arab Community of Palestine.

"2) Even if this upbuilding, notwithstanding Arab opposition, were possible, with inevitable disturbances and riots entailing loss of life, enormous loss of material values, frustration of many endeavours and the great loss of time necessary for recovery, Jewish colonisation with Arab consent offers incomparably more advantages than this work in opposition to the Arab Community.

"3) Although there is more difficulty now than 10–15 years ago, during which time a new generation of nationally minded Arabs has grown up, in reaching an agreement with the Arabs, the undersigned from their experiences with responsible Arab leaders before and during the present disturbances were convinced that even now it was possible to come to an understanding with influential leaders of the Arab Movement, and these leaders in their turn would be prepared to use their endeavours to make this understanding acceptable to the majority of their Community.

"4) All classes of the Arab Community without exception believe that, with the present rate of Jewish immigration, there will soon be a Jewish majority in Palestine with the Arabs a subject race. The undersigned were convinced that a basis for discussion with the Arabs could be found only if the question of the fixation of Jewish immigration over a limited period formed the central point of the discussion.

"5) From recent private conversations of some of the undersigned with prominent Arabs, they became convinced, that the fixation of immigration at an average maximum of 30,000 Jewish immigrants per annum over a period of 10 years, resulting in a Jewish population of 800,000 at the end of the period or 40% of the total population of 2,000,000, could have formed the basis of discussion with Arab leaders with considerable hope of success. Although these figures had already had considerable Arab assent, the undersigned felt that once the two sides met, having agreed in advance on the principle of the fixation of Jewish immigration over a limited period, the number of Jewish immigrants and the period of the truce might well be the subject of further discussions.

"6) The undersigned further believed, that an agreement on the main question—immigration—might have led to a peace settlement between the two communities on such other outstanding questions as the regulation of land purchases, employment of labour and staff, and arrangements in the political field on the basis of the equality of both Nations.

"From the outset the undersigned agreed that no steps be taken in furtherance of their views without the knowledge and consent of the Jewish Agency—the body authorised to deal with political affairs. Therefore, having coordinated their views on fundamental points of a possible agreement with the Arab Community, the undersigned communicated the result of their information and deliberations to the members of the Jewish Agency responsible for conducting its political affairs and offered them their assistance, if desired.

"A Memorandum embodying the agreed views of the undersigned was drawn up, consisting of two parts: 1) the substance of the proposals which might form the basis of discussion with Arabs; and 2) the procedure to be followed.

"Following conversations which Mr. Frumkin and Mr. P. Rutenberg each had privately with Mr. Shertok on the subject, both of them together, on behalf of the undersigned, had on 29th May in Tel Aviv a joint conference with Mr. Shertok and one of the leaders of the Histadruth, who were informed of the undersigned's proposals and their desire to have a formal meeting with members of the Jewish Agency in order to place these proposals before them.

"On Monday, the 1st of June, this meeting took place. There were present on behalf of the Jewish Agency: Messrs. Kaplan (in the chair), Shertok, Ussischkin, B. Joseph and Berl Katznelson; on behalf of the group—Messrs. Frumkin, Magnes, Novomeysky, T. Rutenberg and M. Smilansky.

"A memorandum was submitted and discussed. Copies of this memorandum are attached hereto. In regard to its second part—procedure for arranging a conference with Arab leaders—the undersigned explained why they thought it preferable that preliminary stages should be conducted through unofficial channels. It was, however, emphasized that the procedure to be followed was a matter to be decided by the Jewish Agency, the chief interest of the undersigned being in the substance of the proposals.

"The representatives of the Jewish Agency decided to call a meeting of its Executive and undertook to inform the undersigned through one of its members of the decision taken.

"A few days later Mr. Shertok informed one of the undersigned, that the Executive had decided unanimously in favour of negotiation with the Arabs, that the question of the possibility of waiving under certain carefully thought-out circumstances the right to utilise the immigration certificates already issued could not be discussed, being entirely inacceptable, and that on the question of the fixation of immigration, the views of the members of the Executive were equally divided and the opinions of the members at present in London—Dr. Weizmann and Mr. Ben-Gurion— were to be sought by cable and telephone and that the undersigned would be informed of the results in a few days. Mr. Shertok was urged to give a speedy reply, as the disturbances were developing and deepening and the opportunities which seemed to be favourable at the moment might not be available as time passed.

"On the 8th of June another meeting took place between Mr. Shertok and Messrs. Rutenberg and Novomeysky at the Hotel Gat-Rimon in Tel Aviv. Mr. Shertok was again urged to act in the matter of negotiations with all possible speed, to start negotiations themselves on their own, if they did not want to agree to the proposals of the undersigned.

"On the 16th June a meeting took place between representatives of the Jewish Agency, Messrs. Shertok and Kaplan, and Mr. Novomeysky, representing the undersigned. Mr. Novomeysky was informed that a majority of the Executive of the Jewish Agency was now in favour of fixation of immigration over a limited period, but that the annual figure which they would be willing to consider was that of 1935, namely, 62,000. As to the procedure, the Executive was against the proposal to empower the undersigned to start unofficial negotiations with Arab leaders. The Political Department of the Agency was the only body to conduct negotiations, and this Department would be glad to receive any useful information from private persons.

"On the 20th June Messrs. Rutenberg and Novomeysky had a meeting with Mr. Ussischkin to clarify the situation. Mr. Ussischkin undertook to arrange for another meeting of the Agency's Executive.

"On the 24th June at the invitation of Mr. Ussischkin a meeting took place at his home, at which Mr. Kaplan and Mr. Shertok of the Jewish Agency and Mr. Novomeysky representing the undersigned were present. Mr. Ussischkin summarised the decision of the Executive in regard to the proposals of the undersigned, as follows:

"1) The Executive welcomes these proposals of assistance in negotiations with Arab leaders.

"2) The proposal in regard to the fixation of immigration is accepted, but it should be formulated so that the absorptive capacity of the country remains the main basis for the calculation of immigration figures. On this basis the figure of 1935, namely, 62,000 should be accepted for a limited period of 10 years.

"3) The possibility of a waiver of the right to utilise certificates already granted should not be raised.

"4) The undersigned may meet those Arab leaders with whom they have been in contact, but they should remain in close touch with the Executive, mutually exchanging information and discussing steps to be taken.

"Mr. Novomeysky, although expressing doubts, in view of the great change the Arab Strike Movement had undergone since the undersigned had first discussed the question with the Executive and in view of the fact that certain Arab leaders were absent either from Jerusalem or the country, nevertheless expressed his satisfaction with Mr. Ussischkin's proposals and asked to be informed of the actual procedure to be followed and the next step to be taken.

"Mr. Shertok stated, that he was unable to give a definite reply immediately or even the following day, but he expected to be able to do so in two or three days, after he had consulted some of his friends.

"Four weeks have now passed since that meeting. The Chairman of the Agency Executive, Mr. Ben-Gurion, has in the meantime returned to the country and left again for England and the undersigned have received no communication from members of the Agency.

"The undersigned wish to put on record their deep regret and concern over the attitude of the Executive. Another eleventh hour opportunity has thus been lost for initiating a course for the undisturbed building up of the Jewish National Home."

Signed: G. Frumkin
J. L. Magnes
M. Novomeysky
P. Rutenberg
M. Smilansky

"I. THE AGREEMENT

1) A period of from 5 to 10 years.

2) The Agreement is to be made at once and without the intervention of Government, but with its ultimate approval.

3) The Agreement to cover both the economic and the political aspects of the question at issue.

"II. IMMIGRATION

4) No free entrance into the country of Arab workmen from other countries.

5) Jewish Labour Immigration in accordance with the absorptive capacity of the country, but on condition that in new openings for labour by Jews a proportion to be allotted to Arabs.

6) No change in reference to Capitalist immigration or relatives.

7) Jews to be employed on Government undertakings in a proportion not less than their numerical strength.

8) Among other factors in determining capacity, the number of unemployed taken half-yearly should be an index, only wage-earners to be counted and not agricultural labourers or Bedoui.

9) In case the above is insufficient to secure agreement, a temporary fixation of immigration over 5 to 10 years to be conceded, provided that at the end of the period the Jewish population may reach approximately 40% of the total population.

"III. LAND

10) No acquisition, except on the principle that an Arab cultivating the land as owner or tenant should not be displaced without his consent, or that land of equivalent value in the same neighbourhood or any other place with his consent be placed at his disposal for development.

11) Only a given proportion (75%) of land, owned and cultivated by a fellah is to be sold by him and a lot viable is to remain to him in inalienable possession and the necessary financial and scientific aid is to be given him for the development of his land by Government, with possible Jewish participation.

12) If land cultivated by tenants is sold, a portion of it or some other land to be allotted to them, and they to be helped to acquire and develop this land by Government, with possible Jewish participation.

"IV. POLITICAL

13) A Legislative Council upon the basis of parity, thus showing that neither people is to dominate the other.

14) The principle is adopted of increased Jewish and Arab participation in Government administration as Heads of Departments and as members of the Government Executive. As a beginning, a Jew and an Arab as heads respectively of two Government Departments and a Jew and an Arab as members of the Executive Council.

"V. STAGES OF THE NEGOTIATIONS

1) The Executive of the Jewish Agency is to authorise the unofficial Committee consisting of five persons which may coopt any other persons by mutual agreement with the Executive of the Jewish Agency to canvass with unofficial Arabs the possibility of coming to an understanding on the main points of Immigration, Land and Legislative Council.

2) Should those private talks indicate that there is the possibility of agreement on the main points, the above mentioned unofficial Committee shall with the consent of the Executive of the Jewish Agency come together with a similar unofficial Committee of Arabs for the purpose of preparing a text for submission to both Jewish and Arab official bodies respectively.

3) The Executive of the Jewish Agency and the Arab Supreme Committee are to consider this text and to inform the unofficial Committee of their attitude.

4) Should an agreement be reached on the main points—Immigration, Land,

Legislative Council—the Executive of the Jewish Agency and the Arab Supreme Committee are then to meet and to issue an announcement something like the following:

" 'The Executive of the Jewish Agency and the Arab Supreme Committee have decided to enter into formal negotiations and during the progress of these negotiations the strike is to be called off by the Arab Supreme Committee as from June . . . . . and the Jewish Agency is to postpone the carrying out of the new labour schedule.

" 'The formal and official negotiations between these two bodies will begin on . . . . .'

"APPENDIX.

"Although the following figures were examined in 1938 they will help make clear what was intended by the ten-year agreement mentioned, so that the number of Jews at the end of the stipulated time would be 40 percent of the population of the country.

"The Arab population in 1948 will be approximately 1,240,000. If the Jewish population constitutes 40 percent of the total population, it will be two-thirds (40/60) of the Arab community, or about 825,000. This necessitates an average annual immigration of 29,000 beginning with 1938. With that quota of immigration and the natural increase of Jews and Arabs, the country's population after 1940 would be roughly as follows:

Year	Total Arabs	Total Jews	Total Population
1940	1,040,000	480,000	1,520,000
1941	1,065,000	520,000	1,585,000
1942	1,090,000	560,000	1,650,000
1943	1,115,000	600,000	1,715,000
1944	1,140,000	650,000	1,790,000
1945	1,165,000	690,000	1,855,000
1946	1,190,000	735,000	1,925,000
1947	1,215,000	780,000	1,995,000
1948	1,240,000	825,000	2,065,000"

The memorandum of "the five" ended with this table.

It may be of interest to recall the results of the first population census taken in the State of Israel, on November 8, 1948, in the limited area of the state, covering only three-fourths of Western Erez Israel alone. In that area there were then found to be 782,000 persons, of whom 713,000 were Jews and 69,000 non-Jews. Arab inhabitants of Galilee and the Negev, who numbered between 30,000 and 50,000, were not counted.

18 ATTEMPTS TO END THE ARAB STRIKE—1936

The talks of "the five" yielded no results. The Arab strike proclaimed on April 22 with the aim of halting Jewish immigration, banning the sale of land and establishing an elected government, did not achieve its object and led to open opposition between the bulk of the Arab population and the official leadership. The paralyzation of Arab trade, labor and transport was to the serious detriment of the Arab masses, while it had only a minor effect on the economy of the Jewish community. The shutting down of Jaffa port, where not a single Jew worked, did cause some damage, because it handled mainly Jewish imports and exports. However, as the High Commissioner did not agree to opening the port by force, he gave permission, on May 15, 1936, to load and unload goods on the Tel Aviv shore, and a pier was built which served as a port of sorts. Its great importance lay in the fact that Jewish workers began to engage in the loading and unloading of ships and all other port jobs. The opposition of the Arab masses to the continuation of the strike increased, but the leaders did not dare to end it until they had at least achieved temporary suspension of immigration. However, they failed to attain this goal, since the Government in London, under the pressure of British public opinion, as expressed in the debates in Parliament, refused to halt immigration, either during J. H. Thomas' term as Colonial Secretary or during that of his successor, Ormsby-Gore. The Arab leaders then appealed to the Arab kings and emirs to help them out of the impasse.

As early as April 29, 1936, shortly after the strike was proclaimed, Yusuf Yassin, the representative of King Ibn Saud, expressed to the British representative at Jedda the wish that the Government would to some extent meet the demands of the Arab leaders in Palestine, so that they could end the strike. Ibn Saud's representative said that while the king did not wish to do anything that would clash with British policy, a "general Arab feeling" impelled him to draw near to Egypt, Yemen and Iraq, and this should also be taken into account with regard to Palestine. The British representative firmly advised him not to interfere in Palestinian affairs, since there was a difference between a Mandated territory and the countries he had mentioned.

The Arab leaders turned to the Emir Abdullah of Transjordan and requested his mediation. The Emir asked what their minimum demand was. They replied that they had called for the suspension of immigration, a ban on land sales, and a national government. The Emir again asked what was their *minimum* demand. They answered: a temporary halt of immigration. The Emir advised them to send to London the delegation suggested by the High Commissioner.

On May 16 the Emir requested Colonel Kirkbride to tell the High Commissioner and His Majesty's Government that the Arabs' demand ought to be met so that the delegation could go to London.

On June 6 the Arab leaders again approached the Emir, and he insisted that they stop all acts of terror so that the Royal Commission that had been decided on in London might come to the country.

On June 13 High Commissioner Wauchope was asked by London whether he was in favor of the British High Commissioner in Egypt receiving an Arab delegation from Palestine. Wauchope objected to this on the grounds that it would create the impression that the Government was irresolute, and the disturbances would increase in intensity.

On the same day, June 13, the British representative in Transjordan recommended to the High Commissioner in Jerusalem that Abdullah should not be prevented from telling the Arab leaders that the Jews would never attain such numbers through immigration that they would become a majority over the Arabs.

The High Commissioner in Jerusalem noted on July 7 (apparently after consulting London) that he must ask the Chief Secretary to make it clear to the British representative in Transjordan what the British position would be if that suggestion were carried out. It would constitute a plain obligation vis-à-vis the Emir, which meant an obligation to all the Arabs, and one for which there was no justification.

In the middle of June the British Acting High Commissioner in Egypt spoke with the Prime Minister, Naḥas Pasha, about Palestinian affairs.

On June 16 Nuri Sa'id reported in Baghdad on a long talk with Dr. Weizmann, in which the latter had agreed to request His Majesty's Government to suspend immigration for a year. High Commissioner Wauchope on June 20 asked Colonial Secretary Ormsby-Gore if that was so.

On June 22 Naḥas Pasha addressed a public meeting on the question of Palestine, and expressed regret that the British High Commissioner had not been instructed to receive a Palestinian delegation. He was confident that immigration would be temporarily stopped. In the opinion of the British representative in Egypt there was no feeling of true solidarity between Egypt and the Palestinian Arabs and the propaganda was artificial. Neither was there any anti-Jewish feeling in Egypt.

On June 29, Naḥas Pasha again asked the British representative if he had any information on the suspension of immigration. He received a negative reply.

In early July the British informed Ibn Saud that if he could succeed in influencing the Arabs of Palestine to end the disturbances he would be doing a service not only to His Majesty's Government but also to the Palestinian Arabs themselves. Ibn Saud replied that it would be best if he worked together with King Ghazi of Iraq and the Imam of Yemen, and he offered to approach both of them, but only with the knowledge of His Majesty's Government. On July 3 he was informed that His Majesty's Government gladly consented. Meanwhile Ibn Saud received reports that Saudi and Transjordanian Beduin were about to demonstrate on behalf of the Palestinian Arabs, and he ordered his governors to prevent that. In reply to the petition of the Palestinian Arabs that he intervene, he stated that he appreciated their position but that so long as the disturbances continued His Majesty's Government could not yield, and that they must therefore first of all stop violating the law. A Palestinian Arab replied that at first they had had no quarrel with His Majesty's Government, only with the Jews. Ibn Saud asked what their grievances were, and they answered: the freeing of the prisoners, the abrogation of collective punishment, and the suspension of immigration.

Ibn Saud replied that in his opinion they must give in first, since His Majesty's Government could not consider their grievances otherwise. The Arabs answered that if they obtained assurances on those three points they would end the disturbances.

Ibn Saud was prepared to give instructions to Fuad Bey Ḥamzah, who was then in Syria, to go to Palestine in order to persuade the Arabs there, and the British representative in Jedda requested the Palestinian Government to grant Fuad permission to enter the country. High Commissioner Wauchope welcomed the suggestion but expressed his opinion that before Ḥamzah began negotiations with the Palestinian Arabs there was need for an accord between Ibn Saud and the other Arab kings publicly demanding that the Palestinian Arabs end the disturbances without any prior political concessions. Before Ḥamzah entered the country it was necessary that Ibn Saud undertake to issue a demand for unconditional surrender, otherwise the Palestinian leaders would influence Ḥamzah, and not he them.

Ibn Saud wished to have the Emir of Transjordan and Prince Mohamad Ali of Egypt participate in this step, but there was opposition in London to the latter's participation. The British representative in Egypt was also against the idea, since he feared that the outcome might be that the Arab rulers would come to be regarded as responsible for implementing the conditions for ending the disturbances in Palestine, which in turn might strengthen the coordination of the Arab position vis-à-vis Britain.

On July 5 the Egyptian prince asked the British representative in Egypt whether the situation in Palestine ought not be rectified. The representative answered in his private capacity that perhaps a general truce should be arranged, i.e., the disturbances would end and the English would proclaim a temporary stoppage of all Jewish and Arab immigration to Palestine until the arrival of the Royal Commission which had been decided on in May.

Meanwhile Fuad Bey Ḥamzah took sick and was unable to travel to Palestine. Two candidates were proposed in his stead: Kamil al-Khasab, who was living in Palestine, and Shukri Bey al-Kuwatli of Syria.

On July 15 the High Commissioner replied that he preferred Fuad Bey Ḥamzah, since in his opinion the two persons proposed in his place were not suited for such a delicate mission. He also feared that the French would be annoyed, for Sheikh Kamil al-Khasab had been president of the committee of national defense under King Faisal which had once organized an uprising against the French, and Kuwatli was now president of the Syrian bloc and supported the revolt of the Druzes.

Meanwhile Ibn Saud contacted the Imam of Yemen and the King of Iraq. The Imam advised Ibn Saud that if His Majesty's Government would promise the suspension of immigration he was willing to go along with the step proposed by Ibn Saud. Ghazi answered that he would participate if: 1) His Majesty's Government would halt immigration until after the report of the Royal Commission; 2) it would restrict immigration and land sales, and would discuss with the Arabs the establishment of a national government.

Ibn Saud thought that Ghazi's second condition was out of place. But he hoped for the suspension of immigration.

Three Egyptian newspapers—*Balag*, *Siasa*, and *Mokatem*—published articles at the end of July praising the decision of Parliament in favor of the Palestinian Arabs. Naḥas Pasha tried to moderate the stand of the newspapers, but they continued publishing extreme articles against the policy pursued by Britain in Palestine.

On July 20 the Saudi Ambassador in London was informed that until the disturbances were brought to an end the Government was not prepared to make any announcement concerning Jewish immigration. The Ambassador asked whether they would discuss the freeing of prisoners and the abrogation of collective punishment. He was told that those two demands were apparently linked with the suspension of immigration, and that it was therefore doubtful whether, without the suspension of immigration, the Arab leaders in Palestine would be contented. The Saudi Ambassador agreed.

Ibn Saud transmitted this answer to the Imam of Yemen and to Ghazi of Iraq, and he notified London that he would try to use his influence over the Palestinian Arabs.

On August 11 the Saudi Ambassador informed the Foreign Office in London that since Ibn Saud had no direct contact with the Palestinian Arabs he had spoken with their representatives in Egypt, Syria and Iraq and had called upon them to end the disturbances. Their answer was that they would like to follow his advice but that there was panic in Palestine owing to the widespread belief among the Arabs that the Zionists sought a monopoly over Palestine, to the exclusion of all Arabs. The leaders had lost control over the public, and without the suspension of immigration and the release of the prisoners they were powerless. In Ibn Saud's opinion these two demands should be met. The reply given to the Saudi Ambassador was that it was to be doubted whether His Majesty's Government could agree to concessions at that time.

Nuri Pasha informed the British Ambassador in Baghdad on August 17 that in two or three days he would be leaving for Jerusalem en route to Ankara, where he hoped to obtain the help of the Turkish Government in the resettlement of the 8,500 remaining Assyrians who were prepared to leave Iraq. He would be staying in Jerusalem two days and was prepared to make every effort in order to bring about the restoration of normality. He would speak to the Palestinian Arabs as an Arab and not as a member of the Iraqi Government.

On August 21 Wauchope informed the Colonial Secretary (Ormsby-Gore) that on August 5 he had received from Emir Abdullah a letter about the visit of the Arab Committee in Amman. The Emir had succeeded in organizing a "nucleus" of moderation and had been assured of the help of the newspapers *Falastin, a-Diffa* and *al-Gami'ah al-Islamiah*. But the moderates would take no action unless there were concessions to the Arabs. The main concessions demanded were:
1) The gradual release of the prisoners held at Sarafand;
2) The abrogation of the punishments imposed on villages;
3) A general amnesty to all persons now bearing arms, the quashing of the charges against all persons caught with weapons on their person during the disturbances, or accused of similar offenses, and some hope of clemency for those already sentenced, although no official announcement was expected on the last points;

4) The extension of the amnesty, insofar as possible, to persons charged with or tried for murder;

5) The publication of an announcement that immigration would be suspended during the visit of the Royal Commission in Palestine.

As a result of the steps taken by the Emir, Wauchope continued in his report to the Colonial Secretary, the terror had intensified. On August 14 the Mayor of Hebron had been murdered, perhaps because he belonged to the moderates, and it was clear that no general amnesty could be proclaimed. However, if the disturbances subsided, the following steps could be taken:

1) The release of selected individuals from Sarafand;

2) Announcement that fines would be remitted after order was restored, except those imposed upon persons who were involved in serious crimes;

3) Amnesty for persons who were caught bearing arms, if they were not charged with a criminal act, and the stoppage of police searches for suspects, except in murder cases. After order was restored he would consider the question of an amnesty for such persons also.

4) As for the halting of immigration, he had made no promise but he had pointed out to the Colonial Secretary that the latter's statement of July 29 could be interpreted as hinting at a temporary stoppage of immigration, which might be decided on when the time came. In a letter to the Emir on August 5, Wauchope had noted that the stoppage would cover all immigrants and not the workers' quota alone. (In a letter to the High Commissioner on August 12, the Emir had said that he did not believe that the suspension of immigration was an essential condition for the cessation of the disturbances.)

Nuri Pasha was invited to Government House and he told the High Commissioner that the leaders did not dare to end the strike without obtaining some assurances in advance. Both the Mufti and Ragheb Nashashibi feared for their lives. Nuri Pasha told the High Commissioner that he had advised the leaders that they must take the first step, since no government could negotiate with rebels. He hoped (on August 22, after his talks with the Arab Higher Committee—"the Ten") to persuade them to end the strike and the disturbances on the basis of the memorandum he would send to the Higher Committee. He would assume no obligation and would not send the memorandum until the Committee explicitly undertook to end the strike and the disturbances. Nor was he proposing that his Government approach His Majesty's Government until the action of the Higher Committee was manifestly effective.

The High Commissioner on August 22 requested authorization from

Ormsby-Gore to inform Nuri that His Majesty's Government welcomed this mediation. Since Nuri would be staying in the country only a short time and the situation was deteriorating, he requested an immediate reply by telegram. Any delay was liable to strengthen the extremists. Nuri Pasha also intended at a later stage to have Ibn Saud and the Emir take part in his mediation efforts "in a less formal manner."

Nuri's memorandum stated that the Government of Iraq, motivated on the one hand by racial ties with the Palestinian Arabs, and on the other hand by bonds of friendship and a treaty with the British Government, felt obligated to mediate with the aim of ending the disturbances in Palestine. His Government believed that it was incumbent upon it; 1) to bring the Arab Higher Committee to adopt a decision about the termination of the strike and the disturbances; 2) to use its good offices to persuade the British Government to grant all the just demands of the Palestinian Arabs, whether these stemmed from the current disturbances or were fundamentally connected with the general policy in Palestine.

On the evening of August 23 the Chief Secretary summoned Nuri. Nuri said that Auni and Izzat Darwazah had agreed to his plan for ending the disturbances. A fully attended meeting of the Arab Higher Committee had been held and Nuri had explained his proposals. After considerable debate the Committee—according to Nuri—had agreed unanimously to accept his proposals and asked for two days' time in which to "prepare the ground." After that the Committee would issue a proclamation ending the strike and the disturbances.

The next day (August 24) Nuri intended to visit the Emir in Amman and then fly to Alexandria. His plan was to return to Palestine on Thursday (August 27), to find out from the Higher Committee whether the ground had been "prepared," and the proclamation ending the disturbances was to appear on Friday (August 28).

Nuri asked Hall (the Chief Secretary) to permit Auni and Izzat Darwazah to come to Jerusalem to seek medical advice, and while in Jerusalem to receive two or three leaders. Nuri also requested permission for Ḥilmi Pasha and Amin Bey Tamimi to visit Sarafand and speak freely with a number of the prisoners. He further appealed that during the next two or three days, while the Committee of Ten was "preparing the country," the Government refrain from punitive action, such as the demolition of houses and collective punishment. He did not propose that the Government refrain from attacking armed bands or from punishing persons shooting at soldiers, policemen or civilians. Before taking leave from Hall he said he had read in the papers that the Royal Commission would arrive in October and he, Nuri, would have to come to Jerusalem to testify before it. He added laughingly that as a mediator it was important that he appear before the Commission. Hall made no comment.

On the morning of August 24 Nuri informed the High Commissioner that at a full meeting of the Arab Higher Committee the previous afternoon they had all agreed to accept his mediation to end the disturbances "unconditionally," and that in the next two or three days they would do everything to persuade the local committees to accept this. The High Commissioner passed this on to Ormsby-Gore, adding that he was not responsible for the truth of Nuri's report. But he requested authorization to inform Nuri that His Majesty's Government accepted his mediation on the basis of his memorandum.

The next day, August 25, Ormsby-Gore replied by cable that Nuri's proposal differed materially from what His Majesty's Government had agreed to in connection with the intervention of Ibn Saud. It had agreed that Ibn Saud, together with other kings, would use their influence over the Arabs to end the disturbances, without His Majesty's Government being obliged to announce anything about the Arab demands before the cessation of the disturbances. Para. 2 of Nuri's memorandum alluded to the intercession of the Iraqi Government with His Majesty's Government to grant the demands of the Arabs, and the consent of His Majesty's Government to this memorandum, which was to be sent to the Higher Committee, would become public knowledge and would be interpreted to mean that His Majesty's Government agreed: 1) that the Iraqi Government was authorized to intervene in Palestinian affairs; 2) to undertake in advance to accept the Arab demands.

His Majesty's Government could not agree to the official mediation of the Iraqi Government, and Nuri's memorandum was therefore inappropriate. Nuri in Baghdad had promised that he would speak to the Palestinian Arabs as an Arab and not as a minister. In the view of His Majesty's Government, it was essential that he continue in his role as a prominent Arab but not as the representative of a foreign Government. Apart from this the memorandum did not take account of the Royal Commission. It was only in accord with the conclusions of that commission that any change could be made, and Ormsby-Gore proposed that the memorandum should be worded as follows: 1) Nuri was certain that His Majesty's Government desired a fair and honest solution to the Palestine problem; 2) a precondition to that was an impartial investigation by the Royal Commission; 3) he would appeal to the Arabs to end the disturbances, so that the Commission could begin its work.

On August 27, apparently after Wauchope pointed out that Nuri's services as a private individual would be valueless—and that his mediation was desirable for the restoration of peace—Ormsby-Gore changed his mind and proposed that Nuri's memorandum make it clear that the mediation of the Iraqi Government would be "informal." The two objects of that mediation, he thought, should be stated as being: 1) to influence the Arab Higher Committee to adopt a decision to end the strike and all the present disturbances; 2) to use its good offices with respect to the means that the Royal Commission was likely to recommend in order to meet the just demands of the Palestinian Arabs which stemmed from the internal factors that had led to the recent disturbances.

Nuri returned to Jerusalem the same day (August 27), at the request of the Higher Committee, which had accepted his proposals. That day the High Commissioner sent a telegram to Ormsby-Gore (before receiving the latter's telegram). Nuri confirmed the High Commissioner's view that as an individual his mediation would have no value. He told the High Commissioner—who reported it to Ormsby-Gore by telegraph—that the Arabs had lost confidence in the good intentions of His Majesty's Government, and that they were convinced that all the proposals of the Commission in favor of the Arabs would be rejected under the pressure of the Jews. The only way to end the situation was to promise that the Iraqi Government would look after the interests of the Palestinian Arabs in the coming months and would use its influence with His Majesty's Government as a counterweight to the influence of the Jewish Diaspora.

He was convinced that nothing less than the formula in his memorandum would suffice to persuade the leaders to end the disturbances, and that the restriction of the phrase "its good offices" by the word "informal" would preclude Arab acceptance of the memorandum. He had no intention of arrogating to the Iraqi Government any general or permanent right to mediate on behalf of the Palestinian Arabs, or of doing more than giving his general support to their demands before the Royal Commission and also in London and Geneva after the Commission submitted its report. He agreed that a letter be sent to him which he, as Foreign Minister, would endorse, if his Government approved, in which the limits of the Iraqi mediation would be set forth. It was desirable that this letter should later be made public. He said that it was not his aim to intervene but to help. In his opinion nothing short of his proposal would bring about the end of the disturbances, unless His Majesty's Government was prepared to suspend immigration before order was restored. If His Majesty's Government did not accept his proposal he would leave. He had to travel to

Ankara on August 30. Like all the Palestinian Arabs, he understood Ormsby-Gore's reply in Parliament on July 22 to mean that immigration would be suspended after order was restored, and it was solely out of faith that he had offered to mediate, since he believed that only the suspension of immigration would restore the confidence of the Arabs in His Majesty's Government.

If Nuri's efforts failed because His Majesty's Government could not accept the representations of the Iraqi Government, the chances of a rapid termination of the disturbances would be very remote. The High Commissioner was certain that the Arabs wanted peace, but because they believed that their distress was great they were prepared to continue the struggle until they saw a real indication of the goodwill of His Majesty's Government. The letter to be sent by His Majesty's Government should make the following points:

1) The proposed mediation by the Government of Iraq would be carried out on the basis of its strong ties of friendship with Great Britain, and was not to be interpreted by the Government of Iraq as a claim to intervene in the affairs of Palestine;

2) The mediation proposed by the Government of Iraq would consist of:

a. The presentation of certain friendly proposals to His Majesty's Government designed to increase goodwill in Palestine, if the Arab Higher Committee succeeded in terminating the strike and all the disturbances;

b. The presentation, through Nuri Pasha to the Royal Commission, of evidence pertaining to the grievances of the Arabs;

c. The presentation, after publication of the Report of the Royal Commission, of its views to His Majesty's Government with regard to those recommendations of the Commission pertaining to the future status of the Palestinian Arabs;

d. The exercise of its rights as a member of the League of Nations to support the recommendations of the Royal Commission after these were presented to the League of Nations.

19 THE ARAB STRIKE ENDS—OCTOBER, 1936

The Government and the Prime Minister of Iraq backed Nuri Pasha, although the Prime Minister in Baghdad did not identify himself completely with the demands put forward by his Foreign Minister in Jerusalem.

On the day Nuri returned to Jerusalem (August 27, 1936), the Iraqi Prime Minister contacted the British Ambassador in Baghdad, after receiving a telegram from Nuri requesting authorization to continue his efforts in the name of King Ghazi and the entire Iraqi Government. The Prime Minister was willing to give Nuri all necessary support, but the Council of Ministers wanted to know the stand of the British Government before committing itself and King Ghazi. The Prime Minister told the British Ambassador that Nuri had proposed the establishment of an Iraqi office in Jerusalem, composed of Nuri, Maj'afar, and Rustum Heidar, to represent the Arab demands and to operate as a mediating agency during the period that the Royal Commission would be in the country. The Prime Minister was of the opinion that Nuri had gone too far; the Iraqi Government did not wish to become too deeply involved.

We saw in the last chapter that Ormsby-Gore suggested to Wauchope that the wording of Nuri's memorandum be altered. On August 28, the High Commissioner in Jerusalem replied to the Colonial Secretary saying that he had consulted with Nuri, who feared that any change in the formulation of the memorandum would arouse the suspicion of the Arab leaders and would create new difficulties at a moment when success was assured, to his way of thinking. Wauchope accepted Nuri's opinion and cabled London emphatically urging that the original text be left as it was; if that was impossible then he and Nuri agreed to make a slight amendment to Para. 2 of Ormsby-Gore's letter, so that it would say that after the Arab Higher Committee had been persuaded to end the strike and the disturbances, the British Government would make use of their help, first of all with regard to the *urgent steps* required to increase good feeling in Palestine, and afterwards with regard to the measures to be proposed by the Royal Commission in order to meet the just demands of the Palestinian Arabs.

And the "urgent steps" were: 1) an amnesty to the rebel bands returning to their villages and to minor criminals; 2) the cessation of immigration. The High Commissioner requested immediate telegraphic approval, for time was pressing.

The High Commissioner did not agree to Baghdad's proposal of a three-man Iraqi office for the duration of the stay of the Royal Commission, but only to Nuri's appearance before the Commission.

Ormsby-Gore cabled Jerusalem and Baghdad on August 29 to the effect that the entire matter would be brought before the Cabinet on September 2, and that no statement should be issued in the interim period that would in any way commit His Majesty's Government to the suspension of Jewish immigration.

Before leaving for Istanbul on August 29, Nuri told the High Commissioner that the lives of the Arab leaders in Palestine would be endangered if the strike were ended without immigration being suspended. Only by introducing Iraqi mediation would it be possible to extricate the leaders from the difficult position, and Nuri called on Ormsby-Gore, "who understands the Arab mentality," to weigh whether it was worth sacrificing the life of a single British soldier for what in his opinion was simply a formal objection. The High Commissioner added that he subscribed to Nuri's appeal for Iraqi mediation.

On August 31 the Foreign Office cabled Jerusalem and Baghdad that Nuri had overstepped the mark. At first he said that he had come to Jerusalem as an individual—and now he was appearing as the representative of Iraq. There was a difference between private mediation and the recognition of an official status in Palestine.

It was obvious that Nuri was taking advantage of the present situation in order to create a maximum scope for future Iraqi intervention in Palestinian affairs and to advance his pan-Arab ideas.

The entire matter would be brought before the Cabinet on September 2, and meanwhile no formula should be accepted that would bind His Majesty's Government. Ormsby-Gore sent a telegram the same day concerning his talk with Chaim Weizmann and myself.

On September 2, Ormsby-Gore cabled that the Cabinet was of the opinion that any decision on the suspension of immigration would be interpreted, after the manifesto of the Arab Committee, as submission to violence. The War Secretary, Duff-Cooper, was about to send another division to Palestine. The next day the Colonial Secretary cabled to inform Nuri Pasha that negotiations would not be resumed until the disturbances ended. The Cabinet had studied the High Commissioner's letter of August 22 and all the telegrams pertaining to the Iraqi mediation. The Government had come to the conclusion that British prestige in the world had been damaged in the Ethiopian affair,[13] and that an agreement with the Arab Higher Committee would be interpreted as British weakness. Therefore, drastic measures should be taken to apprehend the armed bands, to punish criminals, and to show the Arab leaders that the British would not be intimidated. This meant a state of war, if not

---

[13] In connection with the imposition of sanctions on Italy after its attack on Ethiopia.

throughout the country then at least in certain areas. General Dill had left for Palestine. A reasoned statement was being prepared on the new course to be adopted.

A third cable notified two decisions of the Government: 1) To emphasize its previous decision that order must be established in the country, and that British authority in the country must be quickly restored; 2) No decision would be taken at this time on the temporary cessation of immigration.

The British Ambassador in Baghdad cabled London on September 8 that the Iraqi Prime Minister believed that the course resolved upon by His Majesty's Government was apparently the only possible one and that Nuri's mediation had ended. However, Nuri was prepared to return to Jerusalem or to London in order to prevent a blood bath, although he (the Prime Minister) believed that Nuri's intervention would create difficulties for His Majesty's Government, and he had instructed Nuri to go to Geneva and to maintain contact there with the British delegation.

On September 10 Wauchope cabled London to say that he had met separately with the Mufti, Ragheb Nashashibi, and Auni Abdul Hadi. He had warned them of the gravity of the situation and demanded that they call a stop to the strike and the disturbances. They replied that they would so do without any prior conditions if the request came from the kings, i.e., Ibn Saud, Ghazi and the Imam of Yemen. Otherwise, they would not comply. The Mufti suggested that His Majesty's Government invite the kings to appeal to the Palestinian Arabs through the Arab Higher Committee. Since he (the High Commissioner) planned to meet with the Arab Higher Committee on September 12, he was asking Ormsby-Gore how he should act on the suggestion that His Majesty's Government invite the kings. If the Colonial Secretary thought it best not to involve the kings, he was prepared to try to persuade the Arab Higher Committee that they themselves should demand the ending of the disturbances, although he did not hold great hopes that the Committee would do so, or that, even if it did, the people would obey.

Ormsby-Gore replied to the High Commissioner on September 11 that His Majesty's Government did not approve of his proposal because such a step might be misinterpreted. The Arab Higher Committee had the right to consult with others of its race as it saw fit, but for His Majesty's Government to undertake such action or to assume responsibility for an appeal to a foreign power was out of the question. His Majesty's Government had announced its policy and would adhere to it.

This had been the unanimous decision of the six Ministers whom it had been possible to convene on that day. Eden, who was absent from the meeting, agreed to the decision by telephone.

On September 12, the High Commissioner met with the Arab Higher Committee and informed them of the decision of His Majesty's Government and of the expected arrival of General Dill the following day. Ragheb Nashashibi asked whether Emir Abdullah was included among the kings. The Mufti asked whether the Government would object if the Arab Committee were to invite the Arab kings to come out with a demand that the strike be ended. The High Commissioner replied that they themselves could appeal to the kings, but without the encouragement of His Majesty's Government.

The same day the High Commissioner cabled the Colonial Secretary that, as a result of a meeting that morning with the Arab Higher Committee, he was very hopeful that if the Arab rulers were requested by the Arab Committee and felt free to advise the Palestinian Arabs to end the disturbances, the Arab Higher Committee would issue a satisfactory proclamation within the next few days. The strike would end, and acts of violence would greatly diminish. Without the help of the Arab kings it was feared that the Arab Higher Committee would be unsuccessful.

Ormsby-Gore replied on September 15 that he had no objection to the Emir's joining in the proclamation of the Arab Higher Committee, on the explicit condition that he did not identify himself with any proclamation hinting at the possibility of concessions or promises made by His Majesty's Government.

Meanwhile, Nuri arrived in Egypt and wished to continue with his intercession. The Mufti had cabled Ibn Saud that the Arab Higher Committee would welcome his mediation.

The British Ambassador in Baghdad cabled his Government in London on September 21 that the Iraqi Minister of Interior had told him that the Arab Higher Committee four days before had notified King Ghazi directly and through the Iraqi Embassy in Egypt that, after consulting with the High Commissioner in Jerusalem, they had arrived at the conclusion that the only way to overcome the present obstacle was the issuance of a declaration by the Arab rulers. The Ambassador had received a telegram from Ibn Saud on September 17 saying he was willing to join in the proclamation with King Ghazi and the Imam of Yemen.

The Ambassador reported that the Council of Ministers in Baghdad was concerned about the increasing enmity toward the Jews, and that one prominent Jew, a friend of the Prime Minister's, had been murdered four days before.

Meanwhile, Ibn Saud inquired of London whether His Majesty's Government would object to his intervention, and whether an amnesty would be granted after the disturbances ended. He was told that nothing could be promised before the end of the disturbances.

Nuri Pasha meanwhile met with Lord Cranborne in Geneva and discussed the question of Iraqi intercession with him. Vansittart, the Permanent Undersecretary of State for Foreign Affairs, informed Eden that a Cabinet meeting had been held that morning at which the situation in Palestine had been discussed. The Ministers were of the opinion that Nuri's proposal should not be accepted, but that there was no objection to a proclamation by the kings. The British Ambassador in Baghdad also reported that the acting Prime Minister had told him that Nuri's proposals had not obtained the approval of the Iraqi Government.

On September 25 the British Foreign Office cabled Jedda, Baghdad, Cairo and Jerusalem to the effect that His Majesty's Government could not give any undertaking or promise, and that the disturbances must end unconditionally. It added, however, that if the kings issued a proclamation and the strike and the disorders ended, the Royal Commission would leave for Palestine, and that the Arab rulers would of course have the right to present to His Majesty's Government any claim they felt necessary for the good of the Palestinian Arabs, provided they were submitted through diplomatic channels. It was further emphasized, however, that His Majesty's Government could not state what its stand would be with respect to such proposals, and King Ibn Saud should not assume that if he succeeded in ending the strike he would have a right to expect the implementation of every recommendation he made.

In reply to his question, Ibn Saud's representative was told that his king would have to submit to His Majesty's Government his proposals on behalf of the Palestinian Arabs after the cessation of the disturbances and before the publication of the conclusions of the Royal Commission. To the question whether, after the disturbances had ended, Ibn Saud might request an amnesty and the suspension of immigration, the king's minister was told that the difficulties in the way of an amnesty or the temporary halting of immigration seemed to be tremendous.

The same cable was also sent to the Egyptian Prime Minister, Nahas Pasha, who was in Berlin at the time.

On September 27 the Iraqi Prime Minister received a cable from the Arab Higher Committee saying that they would be grateful if the King of Iraq would issue a proclamation calling for an end to the disturbances, if he were certain

that after the disturbances ended:
1) a general amnesty would be proclaimed;
2) Jewish immigration would be suspended;
3) mediation would be agreed to on the basis of Nuri Pasha's proposals.

Meanwhile, Nuri Pasha met with the British Foreign Secretary, Anthony Eden, in Geneva on September 24, and proposed that the question of Jewish immigration be settled in such a way that the number of Jews in Palestine would never exceed one-third of the Arab populace; he also demanded the suspension of immigration. Eden replied that before the disturbances were stopped there could be no talk of any promise. Nuri said that he understood this, but he explained that the Arab Committee could not end the strike without showing the Arab public that it had achieved something. Eden replied in the negative. Nuri then asked Eden for an assurance that he would appear before the Royal Commission. Eden explained that this was a difficult matter.

On October 3 the Iraqi Prime Minister gave the British Ambassador in Baghdad details of the proposed proclamation. The Iraqi consul cabled from Haifa that Husseini had hinted that if the proclamation would appear the strike would be ended. The Iraqi Government had contacted Ibn Saud and the Egyptian Government, but they would not wait for the latter's consent. The Prime Minister wished to obtain an undertaking from the Mufti that when the appeal of the Arab Higher Committee was published no announcement would be made by the Committee hinting at promises relating to future activities of His Majesty's Government allegedly obtained by the Arab rulers.

The Iraqi Prime Minister spoke by telephone with Auni Abdul Hadi in Amman and explained to him that there was no point in trying to wrest any commitment whatsoever from His Majesty's Government as a condition for ending the strike and the disturbances.

The Prime Minister prepared a proclamation worded as follows: "In the name of the King of Iraq, we are gravely distressed by the present situation in Palestine, and, in consultation with our brother Kings and Emirs, we call upon you to restore peace and order so as to put an end to further shedding of blood, and to rely on the sense of fair play of His Majesty's Government and on its declared intention of fulfilling its undertakings. Be assured that we will continue in our efforts to help you."

Meanwhile General Dill arrived in Palestine, and on October 6 he sent a cable to the War Office in London. Both he and the High Commissioner were anxious for a quick end to the talks with the Arab kings. While he appreciated the political considerations involved, from a military viewpoint it was highly desirable that, after the arrival of the first division with much fanfare, some firm action should follow immediately. The role of paper tiger for the army would not evoke respect for Britain, nor would it be effective. He urged that the next step be speeded up, for unless he was entirely mistaken a state of war would be needed to restore order.

The next day Wauchope cabled Ormsby-Gore to urge that the proclamation of the kings be speeded up, as any further delay would be detrimental. On October 11 authority would be divided between him and General Dill. He added that it was essential to disarm a few thousand Arabs who were serving in the British Army and were threatening Jewish colonies. They must learn a lesson, and this measure of disarmament was necessary for the future security of the country. Another argument in favor of strong action was that this was likely to prevent even worse riots in the future, should the work of the Royal Commission prove disappointing.

On October 8 the British Ambassador in Baghdad reported that Ibn Saud had agreed to the wording of the proclamation. The text was already in the Mufti's hands. Through a telephone call to Cairo it was learned that the Egyptian Government would not be a partner to signing the proclamation.

On October 9 Auni informed the High Commissioner in writing that he believed the situation existing in Palestine would come to an end in the next two days. On the same day the High Commissioner wrote to the British representative in Transjordan requesting him to inform the Emir Abdullah, inter alia, that unless the strike and violence ended before October 14 it would be necessary to announce that as from that date special powers would be granted to the commanding general.

On October 10 the High Commissioner cabled Ormsby-Gore that the proclamation of the kings had been accepted and that on the following day the Arab Committee would call for the ending of the strike and the disturbances on October 12. And, indeed, on October 11, 1936, about six months after the strike began, the Arab Higher Committee proclaimed that, in accordance with the demand of the Arab kings and emirs, it must be ended. To most Arabs in Palestine the strike had long since become unpopular, for it had caused considerable damage to the Arab economy, and many of them were not observing the strike. But the entire Arab community breathed a sigh of relief that the strike could now be ended with the consent of their leaders and that of the Arab kings in the neighboring countries.

Meanwhile something had occurred to exacerbate the political situation. The Governor of Galilee, L. Andrews, was murdered in Nazareth by Arabs, and the Government made mass arrests among the Arabs. Even two members of the Arab Higher Committee were placed under detention: Dr. Khalidi, the mayor of Jerusalem, and Fuad Saba. When Dr. Dov Joseph met with the Acting High Commissioner (Wauchope was out of the country at the time), the latter told him that the Government had decided to dismiss the Mufti from his position as president of the Supreme Moslem Council (to which, it will be recalled, he was appointed by the Jewish High Commissioner, Sir Herbert Samuel, against the wish of a majority of the Council). Most of the members of the Arab Higher Committee had fled the country.

The Royal Commission arrived in Palestine a month after the strike ended, on November 11, 1936.

Even before the arrival of the Commission, the Colonial Secretary announced in Parliament that immigration would not be suspended during the Commission's hearings, as the Arab Higher Committee had hoped and Nuri Pasha had demanded. The Arab Committee therefore decided to boycott the Commission and refused to appear before it. However, in the first week of January 1937 the Arab Committee lifted the boycott, and in the middle of that month a representative of the Committee testified before the Commission.

The Royal Commission, as we know, recommended the partition of the country into a Jewish State and an Arab State, and the Government, headed by Neville Chamberlain, accepted and approved these recommendations. Meanwhile, however, the danger of a world war increased and in 1938 the Government, in effect, revoked its decision to establish a Jewish State. At that time renewed attempts were made to arrive at an agreement between the Jews and Arabs.

20 TALKS WITH FUAD BEY ḤAMZAH—APRIL, 1937

The following two conversations with Fuad Bey Ḥamzah, Director of Foreign Affairs in Ibn Saud's Government, were recorded by Eliahu Epstein (Elath). The first talk was conducted by Epstein and the second by the present writer.

"The meeting between the undersigned [Eliahu Epstein wrote] and Fuad Bey Ḥamzah took place at the latter's home in Beirut on April 8, 1937. I have known Fuad Bey since 1933, and we have corresponded from time to time on scientific subjects. It was thus not difficult for me to meet with him this time as an emissary of the Political Department of the Jewish Agency.

"Fuad Bey Ḥamzah is a Druze of Lebanese birth, 38 years old. He is a graduate of the American College at Beirut and of the Jerusalem Law School. In 1925 he was invited by King Ibn Saud to be his children's tutor. His knowledge of European languages stook him in good stead, and he was appointed, at first Secretary, and later Director, of Foreign Affairs in the Saudi Arabian Government. He has carried out various diplomatic missions on behalf of Ibn Saud, and in the latter's name has signed political and commercial agreements with the Governments of England, France, Italy, etc. The British Government has knighted him.

"He is a pleasant and intelligent conversationalist. Speaks fluent English. Wears Beduin garb. Has published two books on Arabia, of limited scientific value. He was once suspected of having excessive sympathy for the Italian side, but he later supposedly changed his stand, and he now supports Saudi friendship with England. In the competition between the brothers Saud and Faisal, Ibn Saud's sons, for decisive influence in their father's court, Fuad backs young Faisal, in contradistinction to Sheikh Yusuf Yassin, King Ibn Saud's private secretary, who supports Crown Prince Saud. The relations between Fuad and Philby are not good, and I have heard Fuad express sharp criticism of Philby's scientific research in Arabia. Fuad has built a beautiful house in Beirut, and here he spends his vacations with his family.

"When I arrived at Fuad's home I explained the purpose of my visit on behalf of the Jewish Agency. I said that we appreciated Ibn Saud's interest in Palestinian affairs, but that the King's information and conclusions on this subject were up to now based on a one-sided approach. The Palestinian question, I said, was weighty and complex, and a person who wished to be an honest critic should know it from all aspects. We respected the political talents of King Ibn Saud, but how could he discuss Palestinian matters without having first heard at first hand about the Zionist aims and our enterprise in the country, and he had no way of learning of those aspects which the Arab leaders in Palestine had not called to his attention or had deliberately obfuscated. The Jewish Agency, I told Fuad, would be glad to take advantage of his stay in Beirut in order to transmit to King Ibn Saud, through his person, our position concerning our relations with the Palestinian Arabs in particular and the Arab people in general, and we would be grateful if he would assume this task.

"Fuad replied that his King, Ibn Saud, took a great interest in the Palestinian question for the following reasons: 1) Most of the inhabitants of Palestine were Moslems; 2) From the desire to help England, a state with which Ibn Saud had friendly relations, solve the problem of its relations with the Palestinian Arabs; 3) Owing to the fact that Palestine was a neighboring country of Saudi Arabia.

"Ibn Saud, said Fuad, is a King who observes the Arab tradition that one must hear all the sides involved in a matter in order to be sure of one's conclusions. He would therefore be happy to obtain information from us. He, Fuad, could not meet with us officially before getting permission from his King and also informing the French representation about an official meeting taking place in their protectorate.

It would also be necessary to notify the local British authorities about the official meeting between us. On the other hand, he was willing to meet privately with a representative of the Jewish Agency, and he would later report the content of the conversation to Ibn Saud.

"I replied that at the moment all I had in mind was a private meeting with him, for we knew that his visit to Beirut was strictly private, and that in any case we regretted disturbing him during his vacation.

"He interrupted me to say that it would not inconvenience him if a private meeting were held, for he himself was very interested in the Palestinian question, and his King would also be happy to obtain information from him.

"I turned to fixing a time and place for the meeting. He asked that the meeting take place within the next few days since he would shortly be returning to Saudi Arabia. He suggested that the meeting be held in Beirut, as this was a more convenient venue than Palestine. He then asked me who would take part in the talk—Mr. Shertok? I told him of Mr. Shertok's absence from Jerusalem and said that Mr. Ben-Gurion would come. He asked me for a few details about Ben-Gurion's personality and his position in the Jewish Agency, and he expressed his satisfaction that he would be able to transmit to his King the views of the head of the Jewish Agency Executive. He regretted that Shertok would not be able to be there; he had met him in Jerusalem and esteemed his knowledge of Arabic.

"In reply to his question I gave him various details about the Zionist movement, the Jewish Agency and the organization of the Jewish community in Ereẓ Israel.

"The meeting was most friendly, and lasted about an hour."

"The meeting between D. Ben-Gurion and Fuad Bey Ḥamzah, with the participation of the undersigned [Eliahu Epstein], took place on April 13 at Fuad's home.

"Fuad wore European dress this time, and he received us not only with the traditional coffee but also with tea, which was served English style.

"The beginning of the conversation was devoted to personal exchanges. Fuad spoke of the four years he had lived in Palestine, before being invited to Saudi Arabia by King Ibn Saud, and about his visits to the country on various occasions. He later recalled a chance meeting with Ben-Gurion in a Jerusalem book shop fifteen years back.

"After a few questions by Fuad regarding the present situation in the country, and about the Royal Commission and the rumors surrounding it, the conversation turned to Zionism and the problems of our relations with the Arabs of Palestine and outside of the country. When Ben-Gurion asked him what they thought in Saudi Arabia about the Palestine problem, Fuad presented himself as a private individual, unauthorized to speak in the name of anyone else, and said he personally would like to clarify matters in the light of the claims of the Palestinian Arabs in order to learn our answers to each one of them separately. The Palestinian Arabs, Fuad said, put forward three main arguments, pertaining to immigration, land and political rule in the country. Immigration was the most important, and to a large extent the answers to the other questions troubling the Palestinian Arabs also depended on it. The question of immigration was for the Palestinian Arabs a political problem and not merely an economic one. The Jews aimed to become the majority in Palestine, and what good to the Arabs was the economic prosperity that came in the wake of Jewish immigration if they should be turned into the minority and lose their control over the country. Who had ever heard of a people voluntarily renouncing their political rule as a majority in any country for the sake of another people? The assertion of the Jews, as worded by Ben-Gurion, that it was possible to establish in Palestine a political system based on the non-domination of one people over the other without taking account of the numerical ratio between them was not a practical argument. Today, when the Jews were a minority in Palestine, they put forward this proposal. But when they became the majority, and new leaders had replaced the present ones, it would be natural for them to wish to draw conclusions from the new situation and not to honor promises given earlier, when the Jewish community was a minority in the country.

"Ben-Gurion commented that it was an error to analyze the question in that light. The guarantee of the non-domination of one people by the other in Erez Israel depended not only on a formal agreement between the two peoples, but on the existence of Arab states east, north and south of Erez Israel, which constituted the periphery within which there was no danger to the Palestinian Arabs, and they had no reason to fear the fate of a national minority. Jewish immigration, which would continue in accordance with the possibilities of economic absorption, and without dispossessing the non-Jewish inhabitants of their present habitations, could not endanger the social, national or political status of the Arabs, who in Erez Israel constituted only a small part of a large and decisive Arab community in this part of the world. Looking at the issue of the Palestinian Arabs from an overall Arab viewpoint, this was merely a question of a land less than 2 percent of the total area occupied by the Arabs in the East, and containing 3 percent of the total number of Arabs in the world, whereas for the Jews it was a question of their national past and future. Obviously, even the tiniest part of its territory was dear to any people, and the storm that was aroused in the Arab world over the Alexandria affair was understandable; but there was no comparing the value of Erez Israel for the Arabs with the importance it held for the Jewish people.

"Here Fuad commented that for the time being the Arab world was divided into any number of separate states, and there was no knowing when that Arab Confederation would come about that would break down the barriers separating the Arabs of Syria and the Arabs of Iraq, Saudi Arabia and Palestine. At the moment every Arab state had its own government; only the Arabs of Palestine did not enjoy independent rule because of Zionism. It could not be said that Palestine was inferior to Transjordan, or even to Iraq, with respect to its preparedness for self-government. It was thus no wonder that the Palestinian Arabs were dissatisfied with their present situation in this area.

"With regard to the rights of the Jews to Palestine, Fuad observed that from an historical viewpoint one could also justify the right of the Arabs to Spain, and so forth.

"Ben-Gurion explained the difference: Spain was a country that had been conquered by the Arabs, but it had never been the birthplace of Arab culture and nationalism, whereas in Erez Israel the Israelite nation had been born, there its culture created, and with it the Jewish people had been linked by thousands of spiritual and material ties throughout the thousands of years of its exile.

"Fuad tried to interpret Ben-Gurion's remarks as a proposal to solve the problem of the emigration of seventeen million Jews in the world, and he said that Palestine could not absorb that tremendous number, so that Zionism would obviously develop into a movement of territorial expansionism at the expense of the neighboring Arab countries.

"Ben-Gurion in his reply discussed the history of the Zionist movement from the aspect of its historic ties with Erez Israel and with no other country, and he cited as an example the Uganda offer, which had been rejected by the Zionists of Russia, a country where the Jews were suffering perhaps more than anywhere else. Not all the Jews would want to leave their present homes, and we had agreed to immigration in accordance with economic absorptive capacity. It was true, however, that we were increasing and expanding the country's absorptive capacity and were obliged to do so, for we did not wish to dispossess even a single Arab. We were increasing the absorptive capacity by improved technical measures, by raising agricultural productivity, by the creation of industry, by engaging in shipping and fishing and by introducing capital and suitable organization.

"Fuad then asked how many Jews could still be brought into Palestine on the basis of these plans.

"Ben-Gurion replied that it was impossible to state numbers in advance. For everything depended on the conditions under which the immigration and absorption occurred; however, on the basis of the intensive method of settlement in agriculture alone, it would be possible to settle 100,000 families in the coastal region.

"Fuad commented that the Royal Commission would probably provide answers to all the questions in dispute.

"To that Ben-Gurion replied that with all his great respect for the Commission and its members he was not sure that it would be possible for them to solve the problem of Erez Israel, and he feared that it would remain without a decisive or final solution so long as the Jews and Arabs failed to reach a mutual agreement. To the regret of the Jews, no statesman had yet been found among the Arabs in Erez Israel itself, or outside of it, who could comprehend the problem and see its solution in the light of the benefit it would bring to the country and to the entire Arab people. The late King Faisal had understood this, and at Versailles the Jews and Arabs had appeared as friends and partners, and not as enemies or opponents. The Jews constituted an important force in the world and they could be of great help to the Arab people in various spheres: economic, cultural and political. The situation in the world and in the East was tense, and the Arabs ought not to belittle the Jewish factor and the aid they were likely to bring to the entire Middle East if an agreement were effected between the Jews and Arabs for cooperation in all areas of life, so that there would be no interference with the absorption of Jews in Erez Israel and that not a single Arab would be dispossessed, but on the contrary the economic and cultural position of the Palestinian Arabs would be improved.

"Fuad paid close attention to Ben-Gurion's words and he observed that the interested party in the whole affair was first of all the Palestinian Arabs themselves, and they would never agree to conduct negotiations with world Jewry on the determination of the fate of Palestine. They recognized the rights of the Jews already living in Palestine, they would not question the right of other Jews from abroad to come and visit their national home temporarily, but they would object strenuously to converting Palestine into a national home that would lead to the creation of a Jewish majority in the country.

"Ben-Gurion commented that he saw no way out of the situation so long as the discussion of the relations of Jews and Arabs in Erez Israel did not break out of the narrow framework in which it was now confined and if a broader view were not taken of the interests of the two peoples in their full scope.

"Fuad for his part tried to limit the issue and to establish it as one involving the Palestinian Arabs alone, on the grounds that the Arab world was divided into several states, and that the question should therefore be discussed realistically in the light of the present situation.

"After a lengthy debate Ben-Gurion posed the question whether Ibn Saud, who was a great statesman in his country, was also capable of penetrating to the heart of issues remote from his land and of expressing an opinion about how to solve the Jewish-Arab question in Erez Israel. This was not an appeal to Ibn Saud to be a judge in this matter, since as a Moslem and an Arab he was not an objective party. But there was a desire to hear what a great personality like Ibn Saud could propose after he fully understood the problem, having become acquainted with it also from a Jewish source.

"Fuad answered that he could not say with certainty before asking the King whether he agreed to this undertaking, but as far as his personal qualities were concerned, Ibn Saud was capable of penetrating to the heart of the problem and of giving it serious consideration.

"He, Fuad, would be returning to Saudi Arabia in a week's time. On his arrival he would discuss the matter with the King at once, and he would transmit his reply to Ben-Gurion. Meanwhile he thought it would be worthwhile for representatives of the Jewish Agency to meet the Saudi Crown Prince, Saud, who was traveling to London for the coronation.

"In reply to my question, Fuad said that he was prepared to recommend to Saud and Yusuf Yassin, who would be accompanying the Prince to London, that they meet with representatives of the Jewish Agency. Fuad would meet them at Port Said and would pass this on to them.

"At the close of the conversation Fuad thanked Ben-Gurion for his remarks, and said he would report them to the King. The talk lasted three hours."

A few days later I went to London, and there I got in touch with two Englishmen close to Ibn Saud: St. John Philby, the well-known writer, who had been converted to Islam, and Captain Armstrong. Both spoke Arabic and were friends of Ibn Saud, but it would be difficult to imagine two such opposites as belonging to the same people.

Philby had embraced Islam and settled in Saudi Arabi. He spoke as though he were an Arab himself. As he saw it, a Moslem was an Arab. He hated England—to judge from his talk, at any rate. He denounced and abused the British Government, and identified himself completely with the interests of the Arabs. Armstrong, on the other hand, spoke like a British imperialist: he was not concerned either about the Arabs or the Jews, and he said so frankly.

When I arrived in London I contacted both of them and arranged to meet them on the same day, first Philby and then Armstrong, each in his own club.

21 TALKS WITH PHILBY AND ARMSTRONG—MAY, 1937

I met Philby for lunch at the Athenaeum Club on May 18, 1937. Our conversation lasted about two hours. Immediately afterwards I met Captain Armstrong at the Automobile Club. There was no conflict in what the two had to say about facts and people, but each of them complemented the remarks of the other.

The talk with Philby began with the recollection of common acquaintances in Palestine and with mention of archeological discoveries. He told of his travels in Yemen and the discovery of Amharic and Hebrew inscriptions. He did not know what they contained, since he could not read those languages, but he had copies of all of them and was about to publish them. We then passed on to the subject of Palestine. In Philby's opinion, the present calm, after the termination of the strike, was only temporary. When the Mufti was in Mecca, Ibn Saud had asked him to influence the Arabs to refrain from all acts of violence until the publication of the findings of the Royal Commission. And he knew that as soon as the Mufti returned he would immediately issue a proclamation calling for the maintenance of order. However, it was obvious to him that as soon as the Commission's report was published—regardless of what it contained—"the rebellion" would break out again. In the terms of reference of the Royal Commission it was explicitly stated that the Mandate must not be impinged upon, and it was clear that British rule would continue and that the Balfour Declaration would remain in force. And that meant war: war between the Jews and the English on one side and the Arabs on the other. Palestine was part of Arabia. The Jews wanted to establish a Jewish State there. If the present situation continued, in another ten years the Jews would constitute a majority, and that meant a Jewish State. When he had come to Palestine in 1919 there were only 60,000 Jews in the country. Today they numbered 400,000. In the last six years their numbers had doubled. In another five years their numbers would double again, and the Arabs would become hewers of wood and drawers of water, for they could not compete with the diligence, the education and the financial power of the Jews. The fault lay not with the Jews but with England. England wished to turn Palestine into a crown colony. In effect, it had already done so. Ormsby-Gore had said a few days before that England had no intention of leaving that country. There was nothing left for the Arabs to do but fight. It was not only the battle of the Palestinian Arabs: the entire Arab and Moslem world would rise in arms. Randall of the Foreign Office had been in Jedda recently to learn about Ibn Saud's stand on the Palestine question. Ibn Saud informed him of his total opposition to Zionist policy. He, Philby, had asked Ibn Saud whether the Jews had no rights in the country, whether their coming to Palestine had the force of "law" or was *talm* (an injustice). Without hesitating, Ibn Saud answered: *talm*. Ibn Saud had influenced the Palestinian Arabs to end the disturbances. The intercession of the other kings had been valueless. Ghazi was only a pawn in England's hands. Emir Abdullah was a nonentity, and lived by the grace of England. Ibn Saud was the only independent Arab ruler. Arabism and Islam were identical in Philby's eyes. He wished to give the Royal Commission a chance. He wanted quiet so that the Commission could come. But the Commission was not competent to abrogate the Balfour Declaration or the Mandate, and as soon as its report was published the "war" would be renewed. Even in June 1935, when the country was supposedly quiet, he had told acquaintances in England that if matters continued as they had there would be bloodshed—and what had occurred was no mere chance.

He did not come out with all this at one time, in the form of a lecture, but in reply to my answers and objections. When I commented that it was not the appeal of the kings that had ended the disturbances, but other causes—the suffering of the Arab masses, the undermining of their economic position—and that the appeal had aimed only at saving the face of the Arab rulers, Philby stubbornly stuck to his opinion that it was Ibn Saud's intervention that had brought the disturbances to an end. One could never know what would have happened had that intercession not been forthcoming. I should not be so sure that the disturbances would have ended for the reasons I had mentioned. There might also have been some other development.

I said that the Jews of Palestine could withstand the country's Arabs, if only the Government did not help the Arabs.

Philby replied that it was not the Palestinian Arabs with whom the Jews had to contend but the entire Arab world. True, the Government sided with the Jews, but no one could tell what would yet happen in the world. The hatred of the Jews among all the Arab peoples was tremendous, and one could not rule out a slaughter in which all the Jews of Palestine would be annihilated. The Jews were the victims of the English. England should get out of these countries; this was an Arab country.

I said to him: "This is our land, this was our land, and this will be our land." We did not wish to evict the Arabs, nor were we in a position to do so, but we were returning to the country as a matter of right, and if a war should break out we would fight, although our aim was peace and we wished to sign a treaty of agreement with the Arabs.

"On what basis?" he asked.

I said I saw three elements in the agreement: 1) Jewish immigration unrestricted in numbers or for political reasons, with the exception of the non-eviction of the Arabs; 2) the country's independence in internal affairs; 3) ties with an Arab federation or confederation.

He asked animatedly whether I really believed in this. And when I replied in the affirmative, he asked: "And what do the Jews think? Will they agree to it?"

I said that this was a private conversation. I was only expressing my opinion as an individual. From my knowledge of our movement, I was aware that many would agree to the third point if the first two points were assured.

Philby said that a Jewish-Arab agreement was conceivable only if England were completely removed. The Jews and Arabs could work things out according to my proposal, but England would not allow it. She wanted the country for herself. She had turned Iraq into an English country and she would not leave Palestine.

I said that we would make a treaty with England. After all, England had left Egypt and contented herself with a treaty.

Philby laughed bitterly. England had left Egypt? She was fortifying herself in Egypt and would not agree to leave the country.

I told him about my talk with Auni Abdul Hadi and with the High Commissioner, and that the latter had informed me that although he was not authorized to speak on behalf of the Cabinet he believed that if we and the Arabs got together on an agreed proposal the Cabinet would also consent.

Philby said he did not believe the English. They had made promises to the Jews, they had made promises to the Arabs, and they would not keep either.

I said that without the consent of the British a Jewish-Arab agreement was inconceivable. I did not accept his view that the English and the Jews were on the same side—we perhaps had more grievances against the English than the Arabs had—but I did not think that British consent was out of the question if Jews and Arabs really arrived at a common understanding.

Philby commented that if the agreement were based on complete realism, without any English intervention later on, then it was possible. As far as he knew Ibn Saud—he was not speaking on his behalf at the moment but he knew his way of thinking—he would give his consent to such an agreement. Ibn Saud was a great man. He was not only brave but he loved people. Yemen had been at his mercy, but he did not wish to exploit his victory, for he knew that a large part of the population would hate him as a foreign tyrant.

But what was this Arab federation? Who would head it? He could conceive of only one man: Ibn Saud. First of all, Palestine and Transjordan should be united. This division was artificial. It was a single unit. Palestine without Transjordan was a misfortune; Transjordan without the West was not viable. He had always been opposed to the separation of Transjordan. This unification was necessary both for the Jews and the Arabs. Abdullah was a cipher. He had no strength, no will, no ability. When he, Philby, had been British Commissioner in Transjordan he wanted Abdullah to be the real ruler. Even then Philby had been in favor of complete Arab independence. He had told Abdullah: "I won't interfere—you be the ruler." But Abdullah was lazy and frivolous; he was fond of splendor and self-adornment, he loved money and enjoyed squandering it, he liked to show others his wealth and munificence, but he did not wish to bear the burden of governing. And when Philby's replacement arrived in Transjordan he received instructions from London to retain all the reins of power in his own hands and to allow Abdullah to be Emir in name only. The only man who could head such a confederation was Ibn Saud.

I asked whether he had in mind that Ibn Saud's rule would also extend to Palestine. Of course, he replied, otherwise Ibn Saud would be unable to assure the Jews what they wanted.

That was something we had never considered, I said, adding that I doubted whether there was anyone, not only among the Jews but even among the Arabs, who would agree to Ibn Saud's rule.

"Leave the Arabs to me," Philby said, "we'll manage with them." The Jews were demanding internal independence for Palestine. But it was necessary that Ibn Saud be in such a position that he would be able to uphold the agreement. He was the only man. What alternative was there? Abdullah? He was not a bad man, but he had no power, and could not be relied on. If Ibn Saud gave an undertaking, one could be sure that he would stick to it. He did not make decisions quickly, he weighed everything from all sides, but once he decided he did not waver.

"Is it possible to stake so much on one man," I asked. "And what if something should happen to Ibn Saud?"

Philby said he had been asked that question twenty years before. At that time Ibn Saud was not yet the great king, but Philby was sure then that he was the only man in the Arab world who could unite the Arabs, and not the Sherif of Mecca. Then, too, Philby had been asked, "And what if Ibn Saud should die?" His answer had been that Ibn Saud was forty years old, healthy, was living a normal life, that there was no reason why he should not live for many more years, and that what happened in his lifetime would be important. The King was now 57, an age at which many Arabs became senile, but he was in perfect physical and mental condition, and there was no reason to think that he would not live another fifteen or twenty years. (Philby proved to be right in this prediction: Ibn Saud lived until 1953.)

"Why should Ibn Saud agree to immigration?" I asked.

The Jews could be an asset to the Arab world, Philby said, and there was no doubt that Ibn Saud would see that too. The Jews were now hated and feared. Whenever a foreign company proposed some enterprise the first question asked was: "Are there Jews behind it?" But if there were an agreement and a federation, the Jews would prove of benefit to every Arab. The country had to be developed; roads, highways and railways were needed; Arabia made a living from pilgrims. The railway had been destroyed by England. Money was needed, and the Jews could supply all that. They would also settle in Khaibar.

I interrupted him to say that I recalled having heard rumors about incitement by the Mufti to the effect that the Jews also planned to conquer Medina and Khaibar, where Jews had lived in former times. I said that we wanted to be concentrated in Erez Israel. It was enough that we had a community in Yemen. Uganda had been offered to us, and we had rejected it. We would not go to Arabia.

He agreed that there were Jewish settlements in Baghdad, Yemen and Damascus.

I said that it was not such settlements that we had in mind. In Erez Israel we wanted an entirely different community. Philby said he knew and understood. But the help of the Jews to all the Arab countries could be important. Take Medina. This had been a city of 75,000 inhabitants, but now there were only 1,500. It had been destroyed by the lack of roads. Ibn Saud knew the need for development, but Arabia was poor. Help from England or France meant subservience. The Jews could play a great role, and Ibn Saud would appreciate that.

Did he really think, I asked, that the Christian world would acquiesce in placing Palestine under the rule of Ibn Saud?

He asked why I spoke about the Christian world. It was England's affair. This was an English colony. Ibn Saud would agree to nothing if a trace of British rule remained. He was not like Fuad or Faisal or Abdullah. He did not want make-believe rule. He had been offered the position of caliph, but he had asked whether the Egyptians or the Indians would obey him. What was the caliphate without real power?

Would England really abandon its imperialist interests in Palestine? I asked.

He asked what I was referring to, and I said I meant the oil pipelines, air transport, the port.

Ibn Saud would certainly not agree to any special privileges for England, he replied. Anyone could fly, anyone could buy oil, but special privileges—no! That would be English rule.

I asked about Saud, the crown prince.

He was respected by the tribes, but he was not Ibn Saud, Philby said. Ibn Saud had come to power after a war and a difficult struggle; Saud had been born to royalty. Nothing was done in Arabia without Ibn Saud's knowledge. He decided everything. Not his son, not a minister. He himself made the decisions. And everyone waited to hear what he had to say.

I said that when we Jews had thought about an Arab Federation, and even when we discussed it with our Arab friends, we had never meant Ibn Saud. We had thought first of all of Erez Israel, Transjordan and Iraq.

Philby did not want to hear of Iraq, and I asked him why he excluded that country. Syria, I could understand, since it was tied to France. But Iraq? Did it not rank among the first countries to be considered?

Philby refrained from speaking about Iraq, even though I returned to the subject a number of times during the conversation.

Finally I told him about my talk with Fuad Ḥamzah.

He asked whether Crown Prince Saud and Yussuf Yassin, Ibn Saud's representative, who were in London, knew about this.

I said that as far as I knew Fuad had not met with them, but that he had promised me that he would speak to Ibn Saud himself.

He insisted that Ibn Saud was living in great fear that England would turn his country into a British colony. When I showed surprise at this, he said that there was basis for this apprehension. After Burma was separated from India, Aden had been proclaimed a British colony and placed under the Colonial Office. England was now trying to extend the boundaries of that colony at the expense of Ibn Saud, and there was a serious dispute. Of course, Ibn Saud would not yield, but he knew that England would not be content with Aden alone.

I tried to raise the question of Italy and the danger it presented. He belittled this. The real danger was England.

Philby said it might be a good idea for us to meet with some of Ibn Saud's people here. He would think it over and let me know. He paid for the meal despite my protestations, for it had been I that had invited him to have a talk.

Our conversation ended at 3:40, and from the Athenaeum I went straight to the nearby Royal Automobile Club to meet Captain Armstrong, as we had arranged.

In appearance, too, the two men were quite different. Armstrong did not smoke at all, although his countenance was that of a heavy drinker. In my presence he drank only tea, though he offered me whisky; I told him I had never imbibed whisky. I don't know whether it was on my account that he took nothing else or whether, despite his appearance, he really was not a drinker. He had already met Weizmann twice.

He asked me about the situation and about the chances of the Report of the Royal Commission. I said I didn't know but that I was afraid it would satisfy neither the Jews nor the Arabs.

"We are in a mess," he said.

That was why I had come to him, I said. The situation would be eased for the British if we succeeded in reaching an agreement with the Arabs.

He stated at once that neither side was important in his eyes; what mattered was the British interest, and it would no doubt be to Britain's advantage if the two sides were to reach an agreement. He wanted to know how he could help.

I said that one of the difficulties in the negotiations with the Arabs was the quarreling and competition between their leaders. Each was afraid of the others, and even if one thought it worthwhile to sign a treaty with the Jews he was afraid his opponents would denounce him as a traitor. What was needed was a man of influence who would delve deeply into the matter, and I thought that Ibn Saud might be such a man.

Ibn Saud, he answered, was a wise, cautious and honest man. He adopted a realistic approach to things, took the facts into account. Though he was a devout Moslem, he was not a fanatic. He smoked in private. He was a truly frank person. He never deceived anyone. If he was asked something he might refuse to answer, but if he said yes or no, his yes was a yes and his no was a no. He was able to control his passions; he loved women, but he stayed within Moslem law and never had more than four wives, even though he changed them frequently by divorce.

In reply to a question of mine, Armstrong said that Ibn Saud would not do anything against England. There was no danger that he would send an army to Palestine if disturbances broke out. Ibn Saud would not provoke England. When he appealed to the Palestinian Arabs to end the strike this had been done with the consent of the British Government. His people here had no influence with the exception of one man, the Ambassador, Ḥafiz Wahbah. Ibn Saud decided everything on his own. He would let no one act in his name.

Philby was not Ibn Saud's political adviser, though he was his friend. Philby had supported Ibn Saud before he came to power, and Ibn Saud was faithful to his friends. But he considered every issue by himself and weighed everything in his mind. Philby was hated by Ibn Saud's entourage because he was rude to them. He was given to cursing and abusing people. The Wahhabis were careful not to use profanity, and Ibn Saud himself would never curse anyone. He might slap a man in the face, or cut off his hands, but he would not curse him, and that is why Philby was disliked, since he was a Wahhabi Moslem.

I asked how sincere he was in his Islamic beliefs.

Armstrong answered that Philby had previously been an atheist. If he had been a Christian or a Jew he could not have become a true Moslem. But because of the very fact that he was never a Christian it was possible that he was faithful to Islam, but his mediation might be harmful.

Fuad Ḥamzah was an intelligent man, and there was sense in his argument that only after the publication of the Report of the Royal Commission could a meeting take place with Ibn Saud on seeking a way to an agreement. He, Armstrong, was prepared to sound out Ibn Saud's emissaries in London as to whether a meeting would be worthwhile.

Ibn Saud's government and power were strictly personal. After his death the whole structure might disintegrate. There was no peace between his sons, and not one of them was capable of continuing his work. However, it was worth meeting with Ibn Saud, for despite his success he kept a level head. In this respect he resembled Mustafa Kemal Ataturk, who was also a cautious man.

Armstrong knew about the Mufti's visit to Mecca but, in his opinion, he would not succeed in inciting Ibn Saud against England.

I had a second luncheon meeting with Philby at the Athenaeum. He had spoken at length with Yusuf Yassin and proposed that the three of us meet. Yassin had replied that in accordance with Ibn Saud's personal instructions he was not permitted to speak to anyone in London on political matters, even if it was to the benefit of the Arabs. For that reason he would be unable to meet me. But we should continue our discussions, and if we arrived at some conclusion we should write direct to Ibn Saud. Philby suggested that we try to present our ideas in writing. We agreed to do so that very afternoon.

Philby proposed that we send a joint letter to the newspapers on the main points of the agreement.

I said that was out of the question, since, although I was speaking to him in a private capacity, I was also chairman of the Jewish Agency Executive, and if I published a letter, even if signed by me as an individual, it would to some extent bind the Executive, whereas his signature would be binding on no one.

He argued that he was known as an ally of the Arabs and that it would make a great impression if he came out in public in favor of the enterprise of the Jews in Palestine. I said that everything depended on the wording of the letter. For the time being there were still deep-seated differences between us, though we were in agreement on a number of points, and we must see if it would be possible to propose a joint formulation. He asked me to submit my comments on his draft of an agreement.

Philby said he would be leaving London on Saturday. He was going to Wales to write a new book. He would return in July and travel to Geneva for the meeting of the Mandates Commission. He would return to Saudi Arabia in November.

I asked Philby if he was serious in his intentions to abolish the British Empire.

A hundred and fifty years ago, he replied, the Americans fought against us and broke away. Have you ever met a single American who regretted that America was outside the Empire?

They broke away and became independent, I argued, but today there was the danger that instead of the British Empire there would arise an Italian Empire. From a human point of view, was such an exchange really desirable?

England was using the Italian "bogey" for imperialist purposes, Philby asserted. Look at England's hypocrisy: at the very time that it was complaining about Italy's deeds in Ethiopia and threatening sanctions, it was doing just the same in southern Arabia. Had anyone invited England to rule in that country? It was Arab territory.

In accordance with his suggestion, Philby on May 26, 1937, submitted the following draft agreement to me:

"We, the undersigned, are agreed on the following points:

"1) During the Great War the British Government made certain promises to the Arabs in respect of the independence of all Arab territories and also promised to the Jews all necessary assistance in their efforts to establish a National Home in Palestine.

"2) Logically these two sets of promises are incompatible with each other, and in practice they have resulted in the reduction of Palestine to the status of a British Colony peopled by two equally dissatisfied races.

"3) The existing impasse, resulting from the rebellion of 1936, is unlikely to be resolved by the recommendations of the Royal Commission, whose terms of reference debarred it from considering the Palestine problem from all angles.

"4) Nothing indeed but a freely negotiated agreement between Arabs and Jews can provide a satisfactory or permanent solution of the problem.

"5) The alternatives before the Jews are: a) to look to the West for support in the accomplishment of their dream; or b) to recognise their affinities with Arabia. From a) they have little to hope for, while b) is acceptable to them provided they can be guaranteed the position they seek in Palestine.

"6) The Arabs demand the abrogation of the Mandate and the withdrawal of the Balfour Declaration. The Jews would not oppose this demand in return for a suitable agreement with the Arabs.

"7) Both parties equally object to any partition of Palestine (as has been suggested) into Jewish, Arab and British spheres. Indeed, the Jews desire, and the Arabs favour, the extension of Palestine to form a single independent state with Transjordan, without internal religious barriers.

"8) The Jews demand the unrestricted right of immigration for all persons of

Jewish race who desire to become citizens of Palestine. The Arabs, subject to the acceptance of the principles stated in 6 and 7 above, would (or should) agree to allow immigration to all intending citizens of the Greater Palestine, without distinction of race or creed, subject only to the absorptive capacity of the country.

"9) a) The capacity of the country to accept the resulting influx of new citizens, greatly increased by the inclusion of Transjordan, would be determined by a mixed *ad hoc* permanent commission, subject to i) the Government, and ii) arbitration by the Permanent Court of International Justice, if necessary.

b) The Commission envisaged above might consist of a League of Nations President, two Jews nominated by the Jewish Agency, and two Arabs, together with a representative of the Arab State or States guaranteeing the agreement.

"10) a) The Jews would require guarantees for the faithful observance of any such agreement arrived at between them and the Arabs.

b) Assuming the union of Palestine and Transjordan to form a single political unit under an indigenous Government, the guarantee would be given by that Government. This guarantee would be confirmed by the countersignature i) of the League of Nations, ii) of one or all of the other independent Arab States, who would in the first instance be specially responsible to enforce the local Government's guarantee—a Commission representing these Arab States might in fact be the special immigration commission envisaged in 9. In the last resort, the League of Nations would be responsible to intervene.

c) A possible solution would be to place the Greater Palestine under the protection of Ibn Saud alone, as the most likely Power to be able to enforce the guarantee, in which case the League of Nations would have no actual responsibility in practice.

d) The form of the future Government of the Greater Palestine would be for a plebiscite to determine, e.g., monarchy under Emir Abdullah or some other monarch, or republic with a periodically elected President.

e) No Power, other than the various Arab States of the Peninsula, would be allowed any kind of preferential treatment, in the Greater Palestine— whether strategic, commercial or economic.

"11) The Jews would, of course, be guaranteed complete freedom to lead their religious and cultural lives according to their own principles."

On May 31, 1937, I wrote Philby as follows:

"Dear Mr. Philby,
"As promised when we met, I am sending you my own personal observations on your draft agreement.

"It seems that we are agreed that the recommendations of the Royal Commission may be expected to satisfy neither Jews nor Arabs, and that a satisfactory and enduring solution can best be reached by a free agreement between Jews and Arabs. There is also no difference of opinion between us with regard to the partition scheme: we both feel that we have to oppose not only the partition rumoured to be contemplated by the Royal Commission, but also to try and make good the mistake made by the separation of Palestine from Transjordan, and to re-unite the two halves of Palestine into a single economic and political unit. We are also agreed that Jewish immigration should be regulated in accordance with the economic absorptive capacity of the country, and that a guarantee of the League of Nations is necessary to ensure the rights of Jewish immigration. We agree, too, that Palestine should be completely independent, so far, at least, as her internal affairs are concerned. Jews and Arabs should be free to arrange for their cultural and religious needs in their own way.

"The central idea of our proposals is a free agreement between Jews and Arabs for a united Palestine. But I feel bound to point out that in your proposals the essential condition of such an agreement is missing. Your opposition to the probable findings of the Royal Commission is based—and here I agree with you—on the assumption that they will satisfy neither side; but if we want to reach any agreement between Jews and Arabs, this is impossible unless both parties obtain the satisfaction of their principal rights and claims. While your suggestion would, I think, give complete satisfaction to the Arabs—abolition of the Balfour Declaration, termination of the Mandate, independence of Palestine, it ignores completely the rights and claims of the Jews. You recognise in practice, it is true, the principle of immigration, but only in the form of general immigration; you do not discriminate against Jewish immigration, but you show no recognition of the fact that Jewish immigration to Palestine is as of right, and is a result of the Jewish people's rights in Palestine, and of their historical connection with Palestine. No agreement is conceivable which does not explicitly recognise the right of the Jewish people to establish themselves in Palestine. The Jews coming to Palestine do not regard themselves as immigrants: they are returning as of right to their own historic homeland. This right is limited only by the condition that the Palestine Arabs shall not be displaced. We are fully ready to admit this limitation; but you will not find a single Jew who would consent to the abolition of the Mandate in favour of an agreement with the Arabs which contained no clear recognition of the right of the Jews to enter Palestine and re-establish there their National Home. We are not intruders in Palestine, and our right to immigrate cannot be regarded as only a part of the general right of immigration into the country by all 'intending citizens.'

"Moreover, there is in fact no immigration problem for any of the Arab peoples. The territories held by independent and semi-independent Arab States would provide for a much larger population than they at present possess. Palestine is not, essentially, a country of immigration; before the war thousands of Arabs emigrated annually from it. Palestine is not capable of absorbing large additional immigration except through the methods adopted by the Jews, i.e., the expenditure of large sums of capital and much enterprise on the improvement of the soil, irrigation, the creation of new industries, etc. It is unreasonable to expect this expenditure of capital and energy to continue if it is to provide for an immigration from all over the world—Italian, Slav, Arab, Turkish—in which possibly a few Jews may be included.

"Thus, without this basis of recognition of the Jewish right to enter Palestine, there can be no agreement. And it is not only an abstract recognition of the principle which is necessary, but practical and effective guarantees that our immigration will not be interfered with so long as it does not exceed the economic absorptive capacity of the country.

"In my view, this can only be done by the regulation of Jewish immigration by the Jewish Agency itself, subject to the supervision of the Palestine Government, and to the submission of any disputes arising between the Agency and the Government to arbitration and decision by the League of Nations. It will be for the Government to see that Jewish immigration does not exceed the absorptive capacity of the country, but the final decision must rest with the League of Nations, either through a special representative for this purpose in Palestine, or through some other suitable means.

"Your proposal in para. 9 would in practice hand over the control of immigration to the Arabs, more especially since the Government itself, particularly after the re-integration of Transjordan into Palestine, will consist, in the great majority, of Arabs.

"Another problem which is of vital importance for us is the question of the constitutional regime in Palestine itself. At our first meeting, you expressed apprehension that the continuation of Jewish immigration would in a short time make Palestine into a Jewish State, since the Jews would, in 10 or 12 years, become a majority there. I quite understand this apprehension. The Arabs are entitled to be guaranteed against domination by the Jews. But the Jews are also entitled to be guaranteed against domination by the Arabs. In my view, the only way to achieve these guarantees is the establishment of complete parity, as between Jews and Arabs, irrespective of their numbers, in all central organs of the Palestine Government. I hope that this agreement will not be necessary for ever, because I believe that the time will come when Arabs and Jews will work together in mutual confidence, and the lines of division will become other than racial ones. This consciousness of a common citizenship will develop gradually as a result of economic cooperation, but until it has developed, and until the present racial suspiciousness has disappeared, it is necessary to have some arrangement which will prevent either race from being dominated by the other.

"It now remains for me to add a few secondary observations.

"a) The statement in para. 1 of your memorandum is not wholly in agreement with the facts, so far as they are known to me. The promises made to the Arabs did not include the independence of all Arab territories. Palestine and part of Syria were expressly excluded. I also do not believe that the promises made to the Arabs were incompatible with the promise made to the Jews. On the other hand, the Mandate expressly recognises the historical connection of the Jewish people with Palestine, and whatever may be our different views on this point, I think it is unnecessary to include these controversial questions, which have a mainly historical value, in an agreement of this kind.

"b) I cannot subscribe to para. 3 as it stands, although I too believe that the Commission will not succeed in satisfying either party, though my reasons may perhaps not be the same as your own.

"c) In the phrasing of para. 5 I think 'Jewish dream' is hardly the right word. There are now in Palestine more than 400,000 Jews, and with our achievements in the country, and a population of this size, it is hardly possible to speak of Zionism as a 'dream.'

"d) As regards para. 10, I would observe that, if and when the Mandate is abolished, it will be necessary to replace it not only by a guarantee from the Arab peoples, but also by a guarantee from the League of Nations. I do not place too high hopes in the latter institution, but so far, there is no better instrument of organised world opinion. The League of Nations includes among its members two Arab states.

"Finally, I also doubt whether the complete exclusion of Gt. Britain from this agreement would be desirable or feasible. The Jews will certainly do nothing behind the back of Gt. Britain. Palestine should be independent; but in my view, a Jewish-Arab agreement is in practice impossible without the consent and approval of Gt. Britain. And such consent is hardly imaginable without due recognition of the vital interests of Gt. Britain in Palestine—of course without prejudice to the real independence of the Palestinian State."

I never received a reply from Philby.
On May 31, 1937, I received the following letter from Captain Armstrong:

"Dear Mr. Ben-Gurion,
"After having had several long talks with those responsible I am at last reluctantly convinced that at this moment I should only do harm (and certainly no good) if I persisted in trying, in any little way, to put you and either the Saudi Legation here, or King Ibn Saud, into touch with each other, so as to discuss the future of Palestine.

"I have done all I can. It may be that the seeds I have sown will grow into plants: it may be that they will just wither up: I find the soil very stony and barren. I had better for the minute stand back, but if at any time in the future I can help in any way to bring the two sides closer together, you can count on me to do everything I can."

22 THE HYAMSON-NEWCOMBE PROPOSALS—1937-1938

The Report of the Royal Commission was published on July 7, 1937, and the British Government announced that it accepted the Commission's conclusions: the partition of Palestine and the establishment of a Jewish State and an Arab State in parts of the country. This led, once again, to an attempt to bring about a Jewish-Arab agreement, the initiative this time coming from the Arabs, although not directly.

On July 18, 1937, Dr. Chaim Weizmann cabled Moshe Sharett in Jerusalem, as follows:

"FELIX WARBURG STEPHEN WISE REQUESTING JOINT ARAB JEWISH INTERVENTION ENABLE POSTPONEMENT MANDATES COMMISSION MEETING AS RESULT CONVERSATIONS WITH TANNOUS SHATTARA RIHANI WHO PROPOSE TEN YEARS AGREEMENT AT END WHICH JEWISH POPULATION NOT EXCEED 40% STOP HAVE REPLIED NOT PREPARED INTERVENE MANDATES COMMISSION MEETING NO FINAL DECISION POSSIBLE GENEVA UNTIL COUNCIL OF THE LEAGUE OF NATIONS MEETING END OF SEPTEMBER THIS GIVES TIME FOR NEGOTIATIONS WHICH CAN ONLY BE LONDON OR JERUSALEM WITH FULLY AUTHORISED REPRESENTATIVES STOP IN ANY CASE ZIONIST MOVEMENT REJECT ANY PROPOSAL CONDEMNING JEWS MINORITY POSITION"

Sharett replied the next day:

"IN ADDITION TO REPLY GIVEN WITH WHICH FULLY AGREE SUGGEST CABLING WE ARE PREPARED ENTER INTO NEGOTIATIONS AT ONCE WITHOUT ANY PRELIMINARY CONDITIONS WOULD THEY PROCURE AGREEMENT PALESTINE ARAB LEADERS NEGOTIATE"

On August 3, Mr. Kalvarisky informed Dr. Dov Joseph that an Arab notable of Haifa, who had sought to meet with Mr. Sharett and had promised to give an answer regarding his authority to speak in the name of the Arabs, had taken sick and would not be able to leave his bed before the next Sunday. Kalvarisky also said that an Arab engineer by the name of Rafif Tuqan had approached him and suggested that he make contact with Dr. Khalidi, the mayor of Jerusalem, who wished to speak to him on behalf of the Mufti and his associates.

Kalvarisky telephoned Khalidi and asked whether he wished to meet him. The answer was affirmative, and he went to see Khalidi and told him that another step had been taken to bring about talks between the Jews and Arabs. Kalvarisky asked Khalidi whether his proposal came from the same source, and received an affirmative answer. Kalvarisky asked what basis the Arabs were prepared to propose for these talks. Dr. Khalidi answered that it would be best if the Jews submitted a proposal. Kalvarisky replied that he had proposed cooperation as far back as six years before. Dr. Khalidi commented that that plan had involved a federation, which was a broader and more general question. That problem would be deliberated between Arabs outside of Palestine and representatives of the Jews outside of Palestine. What they wished to discuss now was a problem pertaining to Palestine alone. Kalvarisky replied that he was considering the question and would propose a plan for discussion after a while.

Dov Joseph told Kalvarisky that he believed he had made a mistake in seeking out Dr. Khalidi the way he had. The impression created was that it was he who was anxious to see Khalidi, instead of waiting until Khalidi approached him. Secondly, Joseph said, Dr. Khalidi was personally acquainted with the members of the Zionist Executive and knew how to contact them. He also knew him, Joseph. He had met him only the week before. It was clear that he was not proposing a meeting with the elected representatives of the Jewish people or with anyone connected with the Jewish Agency. There was no point in talks on cooperation and peace between Jews and Arabs before the Arab leaders evinced an attitude of serious respect toward the elected Jewish representatives.

Kalvarisky tried to explain his error by saying that it was obvious that the purpose of Dr. Khalidi's talk with him was to meet representatives of the Jewish Agency. Joseph remarked that this was not so obvious from his story. If the Arabs were prepared to reach an agreement with us, they should propose a basis for the discussion. The members of the Executive had never published a statement implying that there could not be any discussion with us. The Arab leaders had done so, e.g., the declaration by Auni Abdul Hadi in Geneva a few days before that the Arabs insisted that this was an Arab country and nothing else. Obviously, there was no basis for discussions before they abandoned that declared policy. Kalvarisky agreed with Dov Joseph.

On November 4, 1937, Mr. A.M. Hyamson, who had been director of the Immigration Department when Sir Herbert Samuel was High Commissioner, wrote to Dr Weizmann, in his own name and that of Col. S.F. Newcombe:

> "I have excellent reasons for believing that responsible and representative Arabs are prepared to meet representative Jews to discuss the possibility of a settlement of the Palestinian question and I give below heads of a scheme that would be acceptable to them as a basis of discussion . . .

"a) A sovereign independent Palestinian state to be created on 1 Jan. 19—provided that the League of Nations certifies that the population of Palestine is then fit for self-government.

"b) Every Palestinian, independent of race, religion and nationality, shall have equal and complete political and civil rights.

"c) In the meanwhile Great Britain shall continue to be responsible for the government of the country, the Palestine Government giving members of the population, Arab and Jewish, an ever increasing share in the administration.

"d) Complete autonomy shall be granted to all communities in communal matters in the widest sense as soon as possible, provided that no community has jurisdiction over members of another community in those matters. A Jewish National Home but not a Jewish State would thereby be provided.

"e) Complete municipal autonomy should be granted as soon as possible to all-Jewish and all-Arab towns, villages and districts.

"f) The maximum Jewish population of Palestine, and later of Transjordan, shall not exceed an agreed figure which shall be less than fifty per cent of the total population.

"g) The interests of the different communities in Palestine after the creation of the independent state, shall be watched over by the British Government.

"h) Great Britain shall retain special rights at Haifa.

"i) This agreement shall hold for a term of   years from   and shall be renewable."

The secretary of the Zionist Executive in London, Mr. Arthur Lourie, sent the following letter to Mr. Hyamson on November 5, 1937:

"Dear Mr. Hyamson,

"In the absence abroad of Dr. Weizmann, I write to acknowledge with thanks the receipt of your letter of November 4th in which you mentioned that you have reason to believe that responsible and representative Arabs would be prepared to meet representative Jews to discuss the possibility of a settlement in Palestine. I notice that one of the conditions of the proposed scheme appended to your note is that the Jewish population of the new Palestinian State should remain a permanent minority. I feel it is only right to point out at once that there is very little likelihood of such a proposal being considered by any responsible Zionist, but before sending on your letter to the Executive in Jerusalem, I should be glad if you would let me know the names of the representative Arabs whom you have in mind. Hitherto any approaches which we have made to leading Arabs in Palestine—and, as you probably know, there have been a considerable number of such approaches—have revealed no desire at all on the Arab side for any agreement which would take into account the objects of the Balfour Declaration."

Mr. Hyamson did not hasten to answer this note. But on November 8, he wrote to Neville Laski, as follows:

"Dear Mr. Laski,
"I have had your letter of the 7th instant and send you herewith twelve copies of my letter to the Chairman of the Executive of the Jewish Agency for distribution to the members of the Political Committee.

"I have had a reply from Mr. Lourie of the Jewish Agency a) pointing out that it is impossible that the Executive would agree to any scheme that limits the Jewish population of Palestine to a minority, and b) enquiring who are the Arabs to whom I refer. My reply to a) was that the settlement proposed was for a limited period, and that it is most improbable that during that period immigration into Palestine and Transjordan of Jews capable of self-support could equal the non-Jewish population of the two countries. The point did not therefore seem to me to be a practical one.

"The reply to the second question was the members, or at any rate several of them, of the dissolved Arab Higher Committee were the persons I had in mind. I did not mention the Mufti by name, but could have done so.

"This morning I received a letter from Magnes to whom I sent a copy of the memorandum I drew up for you. He showed it, with my knowledge, to Hexter. They both accept the scheme laid down therein. They ask for the names of my Arabs, which I shall give them. Magnes who has consulted some other friends says they want to know whether a statement signed by four Jews, four Arabs and four English here would do any good. I am inclined to answer yes, provided the twelve people have some standing, and the statement is based on something definite, not merely on some pious aspiration. I should like your opinion—after tomorrow's meeting—if you think you are at liberty to give me one.

"Did I tell you that I have been in communication with Lords Samuel and Bearsted and have gained their sympathy?"

On November 10, Lourie wrote to Neville Laski:

"Dear Neville,
"I thought it would be useful to circulate Hyamson's letter to you of the 8th (assuming you have no objection) together with his letter of the 4th to the Chairman of the Jewish Agency.

"I should like to add, however, that I would not like you to think that my objection to Hyamson's scheme is limited to the provision that the Jews should agree to remain a minority. The proposal for the creation of a 'sovereign independent Palestinian State' in which 'every Palestinian . . . . shall have equal and complete political and civil rights' clearly implies a legislature in which the Arabs will, so long as the agreement lasts, have a majority voice. Whatever one's feelings about the Legislative Council scheme (in which at least an attempt was made to provide a variety of safeguards against the abuse of power by the Arab majority), I can see very few Jews willingly accepting a minority position in what would become an independent

Arab State. Perhaps it is unnecessary to refer to what has happened to the minorities in other Arab States, and—in the case of Iraq—despite the most explicit undertakings on the part of Great Britain, and the most careful safeguards that the League could devise.

"I believe you were present in Zurich at Shertok's exposé of the various discussions which had taken place between himself and his friends and responsible representatives of Arab opinion. I am quite certain that our people in Palestine are still keenly anxious to arrive at an agreement with the Arabs, if that is at all possible, but I do not believe that Mr. Hyamson's proposal carries the matter any further, nor have we any reason to place confidence in his powers as a mediator.

"I am, however, passing on his letter to the Executive in Jerusalem, while of course further action will be taken here in accordance with the Committee's decision last night. I felt, however, that I could not but let you know how I felt with regard to the whole matter."

The Hyamson plan was brought up for discussion at a meeting of the Zionist Executive only on November 21, 1937. On that day Sharett said he had something to report on negotiations with the Arabs. The information came from three sources, but it transpired that two of the sources were the same. A few days before, Sharett had talked with Mr. Kalvarisky, who told him of a conversation with Arabs who, even in Kalvarisky's opinion, should not be regarded as representing the country's Arabs but only as indicating the mood prevailing in certain circles. A Jewish-Arab agreement was discussed, and the talk centered on Jewish immigration in particular. Mr. Kalvarisky brought his interlocutors to accept in principle that the basis of the agreement should be equality in the number of Jews and Arabs in the country. It was not yet clear what the Arab viewpoint was on the constitutional system in the country, security, and the rate of immigration. Sharett advised that Kalvarisky be permitted to continue with these talks and also to visit the neighboring countries for this purpose, but he must inform his interlocutors that he was speaking as a private individual.

The second source was Dr. Magnes. Ussishkin reported on his talk with Magnes, who saw a possibility of an agreement with the Arabs. Magnes, too, had discussed with Arabs the equality of numbers. The Arabs had agreed, but they added a proviso: the entry of Erez Israel into an Arab Confederation. On November 29 Sharett spoke to Magnes. The same day he received material from London, including Hyamson's letter to Lourie. This was the third source. Hyamson's draft agreement contained nine paragraphs (as above), and in the letter to Laski it was stated that the persons conducting the negotiations were members of the Arab Higher Committee, and the Mufti's name might also have been mentioned.

Dr. Magnes reported to Sharett that he had recently spoken to two groups of Arabs and that he had found a readiness for an agreement among both. The talks were concluded with the preparation of a proposal in writing. There were, then, two versions of a draft agreement. One was that of Hyamson. The second version laid down only fundamentals, and the emphasis was on an Arab Confederation. This group proposed a plan based on four points:

1) Palestine is an integral part of an Arab Confederation;
2) The federal parliament will establish a Palestinian legislative assembly with political parity for the Jews and Arabs for an agreed period, on condition that agreement is reached beforehand between the Jews and Arabs on immigration and land sales during that period;
3) If the trial indicated above is successful in the opinion of all parties concerned, all the temporary arrangements will be abolished, and all citizens will have equal rights and equal obligations on the basis of a new agreement that will be concluded;
4) Britain will have a mandate over the new state for a limited period, and on its expiry treaty relations will be established with Great Britain.

Dr. Magnes attached importance to Hyamson's plan, since it emphasized that the number of Jews would be less than 50 percent, which meant that it could even be 49 percent. When Magnes was asked who the initiator of this plan was, he said it was difficult to answer.

The discussion had already been going on for months, and he had heard from Hyamson that the plan had originated from people who were backed by the Mufti. The second plan, based on four points, had come from another circle, less influential than that of the Mufti. Magnes asked whether he should continue the negotiations—he was not interested in talks but in an agreement. Sharett promised to submit the matter to the Executive.

At a meeting of the Executive, Ussishkin had advised that the negotiations be continued, though he was pessimistic as to the results. He suggested that we discuss the next decade. In that period the government would remain in the hands of the English, and therefore we should not talk about a confederation. We should not discuss percentages with the other side, but absolute numbers. In Transjordan and Erez Israel there were now 1,200,000 Arabs. Taking into account that the natural increase during the ten years would be 400,000, this meant that at the end of ten years there would be 1,600,000 Arabs on both sides of the Jordan. If, during this period, we wished to attain even 40 percent of the population, we would need an immigration of 80,000–90,000 a year. Negotiations should be conducted on that basis.

Having recently returned from abroad, I too recommended that the negotiations continue, though not in the manner proposed by Ussishkin. There was no assurance that any competent Arab body, or even the Mufti, was behind the negotiations. I was afraid that the whole plan was a plot to sabotage the proposal to establish a Jewish State. If it was evident that this was an Arab plan, then of course we should not adopt a negative attitude in advance, for from the Arab point of view it constituted a considerable advance in seeking a compromise with the Jews; obviously if it were not for the fact that a proposal had appeared on the basis of a Jewish State, influential Arabs would not even have put forward a compromise such as this. If this was indeed an Arab proposal the discussion should be continued for two reasons. As a matter of principle we must always try to reach mutual understanding with the Arabs if this did not interfere with the fulfillment of Zionism. To my regret, I did not see much chance of success, but we should try all the same. There was also a political reason: we had always claimed we were prepared to meet with the Arabs, and we should not give our enemies, particularly in England, a pretext for saying that the Jews refused to negotiate with the Arabs. We did not yet have a state, and we had no assurance that the British Government would keep its word and establish a Jewish State in the near future. As no one knew how much longer our confrontation with the British would continue, we ought to protect our position on that front.

But we should first of all find out who was conducting the negotiations. Negotiations on an agreement with Arabs should not be conducted with Jews. For negotiations with Jews the only place was the Zionist Congress. If Dr. Magnes approached the Executive on this subject he must inform us who the Arab was who wanted to negotiate. I was not at all certain that there really was such a group. Magnes was not the representative of the Arabs, and we were not obliged to respond to proposals that came from Jews. Before giving Magnes an answer we should ask him in whose name he was speaking. When we knew who the Arabs were we would discuss the proposal itself. And we should ask a second question: in Hyamson's draft agreement it was stated that in Erez Israel there was to be a Jewish national home, but not a Jewish State. Would the Arabs who were offering this proposal agree that the state would not be an Arab State. Hyamson's proposal was cleverly drafted in a way that might mislead the public. The formulation concealed the intention of its authors to establish an Arab State in Erez Israel, with a Jewish minority. We should expose this act of cunning. The whole world would understand us if we refused to remain forever a minority within an Arab State. If the proponents of the plan did not have an Arab State in mind let them say so explicitly.

Sharett asked: "What if the Arabs agree to strike out the words 'but not a Jewish State'?"

I replied that even such a deletion would be an achievement of sorts, if it were made by the Mufti. If the Arabs agreed to add "and not an Arab State" or delete the words "but not a Jewish State," then negotiations should be continued on the other points. But only on condition that it was not a Jewish proposal. It seemed to me that the whole thing was meant simply to frustrate the plan of the British Government to establish a Jewish State in the country. I would acquiesce in the dropping of the plan for a Jewish State (in part of the country) if this was due to opposition from Zionists like Ussishkin and Tabenkin. But I did not want to fall into the trap of those who opposed the state for non-Zionist reasons. After the plan for a Jewish State failed, I was sure that the same Arabs who were now approaching us with this offer — if Hyamson was in fact speaking in the name of Arabs — would talk in quite a different tone.

I was for the continuation of negotiations, but we should first make sure there was no trap. Who were the proponents? When it became clear that it was not being proposed that we remain a minority in the country permanently, we should discuss the plan. I was not opposed in advance to setting a maximum to the number of immigrants, if the limitation applied only for a number of years. In my opinion we should not go beyond five years, and furthermore the maximum should not be less than the immigration of 1935. But we had not yet arrived at that stage in the negotiations, and only after the two previous questions were clarified would there be room for its discussion.

Meanwhile, we must make all preparations to submit to the next Zionist Congress an agreed motion on the establishment of a Jewish State, and the Congress would decide on the matter.

Yizhak Greenbaum was of the opinion that the intent of the Hyamson plan was to establish an Arab State in Palestine. Even if the Arabs should agree to add a clause stating that an Arab State would not arise in Erez Israel, it would have no real value. There was another aim to the plan, namely to fix immigration quotas that would ensure that the Jews remained a minority permanently. The entire plan was anti-Zionist, and he preferred a Jewish State, even if only stretching from Tel Aviv to Haifa. We were prepared to negotiate with the Arabs, but we could not agree to remain a minority in an Arab State.

Rabbi Fishman thought the proposal was significant. There was no doubt in his mind that it was the recommendation of a Jewish State by the Royal Commission that had given rise to the draft, if it emanated from the Arab side.

Senator disagreed with my insistence that the draft itself be signed by Arab leaders. In all negotiations in the world there were different stages, and the first stage was not conducted by official bodies.

Dr. Rotenstreich supported my demand that we be informed who the Arabs were that were conducting negotiations with Magnes. The Executive could not give an answer until it knew exactly who was negotiating on behalf of the Arabs.

Kaplan favored the continuation of negotiations, although we should first establish the identity of the Arab representatives who were prepared to negotiate with us. He was inclined to favor negotiations on immigration in the next few years, but not to fix the political status for the future.

Ussishkin, as an out-and-out opponent of partition, set great store by the tactical side. He wanted to know whether there was a possibility of an agreement with the Arabs for a specific period. He thought I was right in insisting on knowing who was conducting negotiations on the part of the Arabs, but we should not demand written documents. Dr. Magnes' statement would suffice. He tended to support a ten-year agreement. In that period we would not become a majority, and it would assuage the Arabs.

Sharett agreed to both my questions, and he added a third: what was the intent of the proposal that the Jews would be less than 50 percent—did it apply only during the term of the agreement or permanently? If permanently, we would reject the agreement. He proposed that I too take part in the talk with Magnes. I proposed that Ussishkin also participate. Both motions were adopted by the Executive.

It was only on December 20, 1937, that we received an answer from Hyamson as to who the Arabs were. He wrote as follows to Arthur Lourie in London:

"Dear Mr. Lourie,

"I am now able to reply to your letter of the 1st. inst. The answers to your three questions are as follows.

"1) Who are the Arabs mentioned as ready to subscribe to the scheme? I have been given a list comprising practically all of the prominent Arabs of Palestine who would be prepared to meet representative Jews for a discussion on the basis of the scheme I submitted to you. The list is too long for all appearing in it usefully to take part in such a meeting and if it is agreed that there should be five or six members a side the following names have been suggested: Nagi Pasha Suedi (President of the Bludan Conference), the Amir Adil Arslan, Auni Abd el Hadi, Jamal Husseini and Moghanam Elias Moghannam. It is said that Haj Amin could not attend an unofficial gathering and moreover it might be undesirable for him to leave Syria if the gathering is to remain secret. The inclusion of Nagi Pasha has been suggested because Jewish settlement in the Arab states will also probably come under consideration. The Amir Adil as you know is a Syrian, in fact a Druze. The other three are prominent Palestinian Arabs, Moghannam being both a Christian and a member of the Opposition party. I think that if an agreement is made it should be with all parties in Palestine, not with one no matter how large or influential it may be. Similarly I think the Jewish side should not consist of avowed Zionists only, but of Non-Zionists also.

"2) It is not intended that the future Palestine state should be either an Arab State or a Jewish State. The sentence in par. d) of the scheme 'A Jewish National Home but not a Jewish State would thereby be provided' is not essential, since paragraphs a) and b) speak of a sovereign independent Palestinian state in which all Palestinians will be equal. Your point will I think be met by the omission of the sentence. The Arabs I know will agree to this and the omission will not alter in any respect the proposed scheme.

"3) I know of no objection to the amendment of paragraph f) to read 'The maximum Jewish population . . . . . . Transjordan, shall not, within the period of this agreement, exceed' etc. This is the intention.

"A few days after the receipt of your letter I heard from Jerusalem that your friends, who had put in effect the same questions as you and had received replies similar to the foregoing, were apparently satisfied with them and were prepared to meet 'appropriate Arabs who are ready for negociations', but that the first meetings would 'be unofficial and solely for the purpose of determining if there is hope for the success of real negociations or not'. I presume that this statement can be endorsed by you. This brings me to the questions of locale and date. Personnel is of course a matter for the Jews and Arabs respectively, although as I have said I think it is desirable that the participants should be limited to five or six a side. The Near East is far too much of a sounding-board for secrecy to be observed. The freedom of the consultations might be restricted by an English environment. The suitable place of meeting seems therefore to be France, preferably not Paris which is too much in the limelight but a convenient provincial town. The date should be as close as possible, some time next month. Each delegation will of course take with it its secretary and any other staff it may require. The Conference itself must have its own secretary or secretaries, who if it is so desired need not attend the meetings, but who at any rate would have to make arrangements for them and invite the members to attend. At the present stage neither side can issue the invitations. Since Colonel S.F. Newcombe and myself have hitherto been active in the matter it has been suggested that he and I should act as secretaries and conveners, but of course neither of us wishes to press any claims we may be supposed to have. Finally there is the question of a chairman. I suppose one is essential, not to take part in the discussions as much as to preside and smooth out any little difficulties that may arise. I have not consulted anybody on this point, but two possibilities occur to me. The chairman should be a man of standing, preferably with some knowledge of Palestine problems but not committed to either side and not even being suspected of being committed to either side. The names of Lord Snell and Lord Allen of Hurtwood occur to me. What do you think of them? And do any alternatives occur to you? Of course I do not know whether either of these would be acceptable to both Jews and Arabs or whether if so either would accept.

"I hope to hear from you shortly."

At a meeting of the Executive in Jerusalem on December 19, 1937, before Hyamson sent his letter, Sharett announced that in accordance with the decision of the Executive we had informed Dr. Magnes of our willingness to meet with Arab leaders, in complete secrecy, in order to clarify the possibility of Jewish-Arab negotiations. However, no reply had been received.

Sharett said that Kalvarisky had attended a number of meetings with Arabs. There seemed to have been some initial progress in the negotiations, and immediately afterwards a retrogression. In the course of the negotiations agreement was said to have been reached on equality of the number of Jews and Arabs during a certain period, the assumption being that after the expiry of the agreement the Arabs might possibly agree that the Jews become a majority in the country. The negotiations were based on an Arab Confederation and on agreement that the Jews would constitute a majority in the country as compensation for our entering the federation. The Political Department of the Jewish Agency thought it well to examine immediately how serious these negotiations were, and it suggested that a meeting be arranged with the Arabs, in which Dov Joseph would participate. When Kalvarisky proposed this to the Arabs, they made the counter-proposal that four Jews and four Arabs take part in the meeting. When Kalvarisky asked for the names of the four Arabs who would participate, and whether they accepted the point about numerical equality on which agreement had been reached, he was told that even those who had conducted the negotiations found it difficult to agree to numerical equality. To this Kalvarisky replied that the Jews would never agree to the status of a minority in the country, and if the Arabs would not yield on this point there was no sense in continuing the talks. The Arabs said they would consider the question further, but no answer had yet been received from them.

23 SHARETT CORRESPONDS WITH MAGNES—1937-38

When Hyamson submitted the proposals for Jewish-Arab negotiations to the Jewish Agency Executive in London at the beginning of November 1937 (they were dated October 9, 1937), he said these were Arab proposals. Dr. Magnes said the same thing in Jerusalem, apparently relying on the word of Hyamson and Newcombe. Eventually doubt arose as to the underlying truth of that assumption.

As early as November 19, 1937, Sharett wrote the following letter to Dr. Magnes:

"Dear Dr. Magnes,
"Permit me to put two further questions to you in addition to those I asked you orally:
a) Did the other side mention a number of years which could give an idea of what they had in mind as to the period of the agreement or as to the date mentioned in Clause I?*
b) Which side took the initiative in these talks—the Jewish, the Arab or the English?
"Pardon me troubling you on Shabbath, but the matter is important for hastening the clarification of the matter. If not convenient to you to write, please telephone."

Dr. Magnes replied by telephone, and recorded his answer as follows:

"November 19, 1937
"My answer over the telephone was as follows:
"1) I have always spoken of a period of 10 to 15 years. Some have agreed, some thought this too long, but there has never been great opposition.
"2) As to the longer document (Hyamson-Newcombe), that is the result of conversations begun last summer. It is difficult for me to say who began the conversations. But the present formulation is of recent date.
"3) As to the shorter document** the initiative was taken by the other side."

On December 3, 1937 Magnes wrote a letter on this subject to Sharett:

"Dear Mr. Shertok,
"I am writing in English because my correspondence with London is in English. Perhaps it would be as well if you could address your reply to me in English, so that I might send a copy of it to London.

---

* Of the Hyamson-Newcombe plan, p. 143.
** Summarized on p. 146.

"I wrote to London the day of our meeting at Mr. Ussishkin's office together with Messrs. Ussishkin and Ben-Gurion.

"I received an answer yesterday, under date of November 27th, as follows:

"1) *Question:* Is the 'suggested basis for discussion between Jewish and Arab representatives' a basis to which some influential Arabs have agreed?
Answer: Yes.

"2) *Question:* Who are these Arabs?
Answer: Members of the suppressed Arab Higher Committee, including the Mufti and Jamal Husseini, are, it is said, willing to accept the plan as a basis of discussion. These names may be given in confidence, but Mr. Shertok and the others should be asked to be careful they are not published.

"3) *Question:* Are the dates in paragraphs 'a' and 'i' necessarily the same and which date would have to be fixed first?
Answer: The two dates should not be identical. The question as to which date should be settled first might be settled by the two parties if they meet.

"4) *Question:* Is the maximum Jewish population to be fixed for all time or only for the period of the agreement? Mr. Ussishkin thought the procedure might be to have an agreed schedule over the period of the agreement, based upon the economic absorptive capacity of the country, it being understood that these figures will not bring the maximum Jewish population beyond the agreed percentage.
Answer: For the period of the agreement. M. Ussishkin's suggestion is excellent.

"5) *Question:* It is stated that a 'Jewish National Home but not a Jewish State would thereby be provided'. Does this mean that an Arab State would thereby be provided? If not, why is this mentioned at all?
Answer: It means a bi-national State, neither a Jewish State nor an Arab State. The sentence is put in order to show that the Arabs are ready to recognize the the idea of the Jewish National Home."

Sharett hastened to reply to Dr. Magnes, in Hebrew, on December 6:

"Dear Dr. Magnes,

"I received your letter of December 3, 1937, which purports to answer the questions we put to you at our meeting in Mr. Ussishkin's office on 22.11.37.

"As you see, I cannot adopt your suggestion to answer your letter in English and just for the very reason you propose this: so that you can send a copy of my letter to those with whom you are in correspondence in London. I assume that not all of them are known to me. Among those who are there is at least one name in which I cannot have complete confidence. Under the circumstances, I cannot agree that a letter signed by me serve as a document in the hands of some one, for purposes which are not sufficiently clear to me.

"My letter is therefore private and sent to you alone. But you are free to communicate its contents to those with whom you are in touch in London.

"I must say that the questions which we put to you were not formulated in your letter to London with complete exactitude. As to the two open dates (Question 3 of your letter) we did not mean to ask which of these two should be fixed first, but which of these two dates was actually the prior and which the later. There is something inexact also in the formulation of Mr. Ussishkin's suggestion in relation to immigration. Mr. Ussishkin said nothing about an agreed *percentage* of immigration, but rather about definite figures that would express our idea of economic absorptive capacity. But the most serious inexactitude is to be found in the cardinal question we put to you as to the nature of the independent state whose creation the text of the agreement makes obligatory (Question 5). The purpose of our question was not merely to have the correct interpretation of this clause—whether this intended state was to be Arab or not—but rather if the other side, which, according to your statement, accepts the text of the agreement as a basis for negotiations, would agree that it be expressly recorded that the state to be established in Palestine should not be an Arab State or—taking Mr. Ussishkin's suggestion—they would agree to delete the words 'and not a Jewish State'.

"It is not the purpose of this letter again to place before you the correct formulation of our questions and to ask you kindly to get the answers. First, this would be apt to drag out unnecessarily the preliminary clarification between us. Second, and this is the main point, we doubt the practical value of elucidating this. It is clear to us that the answers given to our questions from London are those of the Jewish-English group that drafted the text of the agreement and not the answers of the Arabs who, according to the statement of this group, are prepared to accept the text as a basis for negotiations. Your letter was sent to London on November 22, 1937, and the answer bore the date of the 27th. There was therefore not sufficient time for those who answered the letter to get in touch with any of the members of the former Arab Higher Committee before sending their reply. These answers are therefore the opinion of the intermediaries and do not express the attitude of the other side.

"The whole consent of the Arabs of the circle mentioned in your letter to the proposed agreement is really brought into question by the wording of the answer to Question 2. In accordance with this wording it transpires that even the members of the English-Jewish group in London are not completely certain of the agreement of the Arabs, but report this from rumor or, in any event, at second or third hand.

"Under the circumstances, we think that the only way to bring out the facts as they are and to arrive at real negotiations, in case such are possible, is to arrange a meeting between us and the Arabs who may be ready for negotiations. If you can propose such a meeting with Arabs of appropriate status, I herewith inform you that we are ready for that. It is self-understood that the first meeting should be only an unofficial meeting for the purpose of clarification, upon whose results it would be possible to determine if there be room for negotiations or not. For our part, we can promise not to give any publicity to this meeting, either before or after it is held, except that the two sides agree to this.

"I therefore propose to you to find out if a meeting is possible, and to inform us as soon as possible."

Dr. Magnes replied on December 9, 1937, as follows:

"Dear Mr. Shertok,
"I received your letter of December 6th yesterday.
"I am taking steps to find out if a preliminary conference of the kind you mention can take place.
"Enclosed please find a copy of an abstract of your letter such as I am sending to London.
"On your comments upon the questions and answers, as formulated in my letter of December 3rd, permit me to say:
"*Question 3:* The answer was in two parts: a) that the two dates are not identical; and b) that the question as to which date is to come first should be determined through negotiation. I think that answers your comment, if I understand it.
"*Question 4:* My use of the word 'schedule' indicates that I understood Mr. Ussishkin just as you did. The word 'schedule' in its accepted sense here, means—so I understand—that definite figures are to be worked out for the half-yearly or yearly Jewish immigration. I understood Mr. Ussishkin also to mean that these figures, when added up for the period of the agreement, will not bring the maximum Jewish population beyond an agreed percentage.
"*Question 5:* As I understand it, your formulation would be: Do the Arabs agree that it should be specifically stated that the sovereign independent Palestinian state to be created would not be an Arab State or a Jewish State: or would they agree that the words in the formulation as presented 'but not a Jewish State' can be stricken out?
"I shall send this formulation of the question to London and request an answer.
"I shall send to London also a copy of my present letter to you."

Magnes also sent his friends in London a synopsis of his letter to Sharett, and particularly noted the fact that in the opinion of the Jewish Agency the only way to clarify the feasibility of negotiations was to arrange a meeting between the Jewish Agency people and suitable Arabs who were willing to participate in such talks. The first meeting would be unofficial and secret.

Four days later, on December 13, 1937, Sharett sent the following letter to Magnes:

"Dear Dr. Magnes,

"I received your letter to me of December 9th and the attached copy of your letter to London of the same date, and I thank you for both.

"Meanwhile, you surely have seen all that has appeared in 'Falastin' the past several days and copied by other papers about 'negotiations'. This publicity makes an impression that the purpose of the Arab side, and maybe also other sides, is not to arrive at real negotiations which might result in prospects of a Jewish-Arab peace, but rather to create an impression of the possibility of such negotiations in order to defeat the idea of the Jewish State.

"If this impression be correct, one must regard the publicity given the matter as an intentional and deliberate step taken by the Arab side. But even if this impression be not correct, the fact of the publicity is testimony that the matter is not being kept secret by the Arabs but is being used as publicity material.

"That the matter is not being kept secret by the other side is shown by the note attached to this letter. This note contains what one of my assistants heard from one of our Arab informants. The author of this note knew nothing of the whole affair until he heard the account of it from his informant.

"I shall not deny that all these things are calculated only to increase our doubts as to the sincerity of the 'peace proposal' communicated to us and our suspicions that this is only a manoeuvre with a negative aim—the defeat of the State idea— and not with the positive aim of Jewish-Arab peace.

"In any event, if it becomes clear that there is the possibility of a meeting face to face such as I proposed in my previous letter, we shall have to make the prior condition that the meeting be kept secret by the other side. In my previous letter I contented myself with the statement that we, for our part, would keep the matter secret, thinking that the other side would naturally be interested in not having it made public. The facts of these last days, however, have completely upset this assumption. On the contrary, it seems as though the other side were interested only in publicity and not in real results. It must therefore be clear that if we do not have sufficient assurance that the other side would keep its word concerning the secrecy of the meeting, it is doubtful if the meeting can take place."

On December 14, 1937, L. Bakstansky, Secretary of the Zionist Federation in London, met with Musa Husseini, an Arab Leftist, at the latter's invitation. The following is an account of this meeting:

"I have met Mr. Husseini on several occasions during the past eighteen months, at meetings on Palestine. A few months ago he told me that he wanted to meet me in order to discuss the possibility of peaceful negotiations, and he hinted that he was in touch with a number of leading non-Zionists in this country and that he was rather hopeful that something might be done. He telephoned me yesterday afternoon and suggested that we might meet, and it was in these circumstances that he came to see me yesterday at 5 p.m.

"Mr. Husseini began by stating that he had heard from Colonel Newcombe, who told him on behalf of Mr. Hyamson, that the Jewish Agency in Palestine have in principle agreed to the Hyamson proposals, although they have addressed a number of questions to Mr. Hyamson, especially in regard to the title of the future Palestinian entity. Mr. Husseini said that both Colonel Newcombe and he decided that the information conveyed by Mr. Hyamson was so important that a special letter had been sent last Saturday to the Mufti to advise him of this development.

"He went on to suggest, however, that at least in two respects he did not agree with the Hyamson Memorandum and would prefer to rely upon Dr. Magnes' proposals:

a) That the Palestinian entity should be an independent state, subject to an agreement with Great Britain, similar to that of Iraq, but neither a British Mandate nor a Dominion; that the Palestinian state should form part of a larger Arab Confederation.

b) That whilst Mr. Hyamson envisaged the proportion of Jews in Palestine as under fifty percent of the Arabs, he and his friends could not, at any rate for the moment, agree to very much above thirty-five percent; ten or fifteen years hence, when Arab-Jewish relations improved, it should not be difficult to consider a higher percentage of Jews in Palestine, but they must never form a majority in the country nor even approximate to parity.

"He went on to elaborate the great advantages which the Jews could derive from the acceptance of his scheme:

a) Whilst the Jews would form a minority in Palestine, they would nevertheless have Hebrew recognised as one of the official languages, and would participate in the legislature of the country; the latter should consist of two chambers: the lower chamber to reflect the numerical proportions of the population; the upper chamber to consist of an equal number of Jews and Arabs.

b) That a considerable number of Jews could immigrate into the neighbouring Arab countries, especially Iraq, Syria and Trans-Jordan. Accepting Dr. Weizmann's figure that the urgency of the Jewish problem in Europe related primarily to two million young who must be saved in our generation, he thought that by the acceptance of his scheme, Palestine could accommodate a further million Jews—the other million would be accommodated in the neighbouring Arab territories, possibly even on the Eastern shores of Arabia, although not, of course, in Hedjaz itself. As to the million to be absorbed in Palestine, that could only be envisaged in the distant future, when the Arabs of Palestine would number not less than two million.

"He suggested that in the interests of the masses of Jews and Arabs, industry and land in Palestine should be nationalised; that of course included the present Electric and Potash Concessions.

"In reply to my question as to whether this view represented his own opinion, or whether he was authorised to speak on behalf of other Arabs, he pointed out that at the present time it was impossible for Arabs to make any official public proposals. He had, however, been in Palestine during the summer and had discussed these proposals with Jamal el Husseini, Izzet el Darwazi, Dr. Khalidi and Auni Bey, and he had found that they all concurred with his proposals. As to the Rulers of the neighbouring Arab territories, he had had conversations with the Iraqi Minister in London and he rather felt that providing the Palestine quarrel was amicably settled, it would not be too difficult to arrange for the immigration of numbers of Jews into the surrounding Arab states.

"Mr. Husseini then proceeded to elaborate the advantages of such an agreement, coupled with the great work which an Arab Confederation could discharge in the Near East with the co-operation of Jewish brains and Jewish intellect, and whilst he admitted that serious differences existed between Ibn Saud and the Government of Iraq, he felt hopeful that the inclusion of Palestine and Syria in an Arab Confederation would tend to relieve the tension between those two governments.

"He went on to tell me that he had been in touch with leading non-Zionists in this country whom he had found to be deadly opposed to the idea of a Jewish State, and he said that he shared their view that the establishment of a Jewish State would militate against their interests as British citizens, and that a conflict of loyalties would arise.

"Mr. Husseini suggested that Zionism consisted of three elements:
a) The desire to found in Palestine a cultural and spiritual centre;
b) that Palestine should be a refuge for homeless Jews; and
c) foundation of a Jewish National State in Palestine.

"He suggested that the Arabs would agree to the first, and partly to the second, aim of Zionism as he understood it, but in the interests of peace, the Zionists must forego the third.

"He was anxious to find out whether the Zionists would view with favour his scheme, and was a little disappointed to hear from me that as between his scheme and Partition, even most of the Zionist anti-Partitionists would prefer Partition.

"I explained our attitude in regard to a minority status in Palestine, and also pointed out to him the difficulties which he must continue to encounter so long as any proposals emanating from the Arab side are put forward by individual Arabs on their own responsibility and not as an official offer properly backed and one which set out to satisfy the essential Zionist thesis. I pointed out to him that his proposal did not represent any very great advance on the statement made by the Mufti to the Royal Commission, and it could in no sense be regarded as a compromise proposal, and therefore there was little hope that it could serve as a basis for satisfactory negotiations.

"Before he left, Mr. Husseini indicated that he would not be violently opposed to a Jewish State if both Haifa and Galilee were excluded, but he was not very definite as to whether the Negev or part of it might or might not be included within the Jewish State.

"He said that he was leaving for Paris, where he would stay for three weeks and that on his return he would like to meet me again for a more fundamental discussion."

Bakstansky reported the content of this conversation to the Jewish Agency Executive in Jerusalem.

On December 28, 1937 Sharett wrote the following letter to Dr. Magnes:

"Dear Dr. Magnes,

"I wish to inform you of developments in the matter that has served as the subject of meetings and an exchange of letters between us.

"Parallel to the answers you gave to our questions here, Mr. Hyamson sent answers to the same questions to our Political Secretary in London, Mr. Lourie. I assume that you have read a copy of the letter of Mr. Hyamson to Mr. Lourie dated December 20th. I was astonished to see that Mr. Hyamson writes that the members of the Executive in Jerusalem with whom you have been in touch in Jerusalem were satisfied with the replies they received from you. As is known to you from our letter of December 6th, 1937, the matter is not so and Mr. Lourie properly called Mr. Hyamson's attention to this in his letter to him of December 21st. As to the further details of the letter, insofar as it is not a repetition of the answers received from you, it seems to me that Mr. Hyamson is somewhat too hasty in talking about the details of the place of meeting, its secretaries and its chairman. First of all it must become clear if the meeting itself can take place at all and at present it is premature to talk about its sessions.

"Within the next few days we shall have a conference on this matter.

"Meanwhile, I must say that the more we hear of this chapter of negotiations and the proposals involved in it, the less I believe in the sincerity of the other side and in their readiness for an agreement. I enclose an extract of the Minute of a conversation between Mr. M. Husseini now in London and Mr. Bakstansky, Secretary of the English Zionist Federation. From this extract you will be convinced, first, that the impression was conveyed to the other side or the other side received the impression that the Jewish Agency had given its assent in principle to the proposals of Mr. Hyamson. You will know that that never was so, and this should have been known to Mr. Hyamson as well. Second, and this is the important point, Husseini declares explicitly that his friends would under no circumstances be able to agree to the volume of Jewish immigration mentioned in the text of the agreement of Mr. Hyamson and that this would have to remain at 35 percent or somewhat more during the period of the agreement. Third, it is not to be gathered from Mr. Husseini's words that even apart from this serious difference in the matter of immigration, there is Arab consent on the text of Mr. Hyamson's

agreement. On the contrary Husseini speaks of a far-reaching proposal as to an Arab Federation, which is not mentioned in the agreement handed to us.
"I communicate these things to you for your information."

Dr. Magnes' reply came quickly. On December 30 he wrote:

"Dear Mr. Shertok,
"I have just received your letter of December 28, 1937. I hope that you may hear from me in the course of the next week. May I add that I am responsible only for such things as come direct from me—not for Mr. Hyamson's letters and not for anything else."

At a meeting of the Jewish Agency Executive on January 16, 1938, Sharett stated (as recorded in the minutes):

"In accordance with the decision taken by the Executive we informed Dr. Magnes here and Hyamson in London that the Executive sees no point in negotiations between it and Jewish mediators, but that it is prepared to meet with Arabs for a preliminary and secret talk in order to clarify whether there are prospects for a Jewish-Arab agreement. We transmitted this statement to Dr. Magnes on December 6; a number of weeks passed without an answer. On January 12 Shertok met with Dr. Magnes at his invitation. Dr. Magnes said that he had not been in touch with Hyamson recently but that he had succeeded in contacting the Arab leaders staying in Beirut, through their friends in Jerusalem. Apparently, Dr. Magnes held two meetings with the Arabs. In any case, the last meeting was supposed to take place before publication of the letter of the Colonial Secretary, but it was postponed because the Arabs first wished to see the latter. Dr. Magnes said that it became clear to him at that meeting that Hyamson's report was not accurate, and that Colonel Newcombe, Hyamson's partner in drawing up the document known as the Jewish-Arab draft agreement, had exceeded the authority given to him by the Arabs and included points in the draft to which the Arabs had not agreed. By no means could it be regarded as binding them. It is the document of some third party, and they have no part in it. In general, they object, in the matter of these negotiations, to submitting any written document from their side.

"Dr. Magnes informed the Arabs that the Jewish Agency had stated its willingness to meet with the Arab leaders and he mentioned the name of Shertok. In reply to that, the Arabs asked Dr. Magnes to clarify privately whether it was Shertok's intention to reach an agreement on the basis of the terms Dr. Magnes had transmitted to Shertok orally, since Dr. Magnes had promised the Arabs not to submit any written document on these matters. The Arabs took as a basis the document of Colonel Newcombe and indicated on it those paragraphs they were prepared to accept, those they rejected and those in which they proposed changes. The changes, as recorded by Dr. Magnes, were: In Para. a) 'provided that the League of Nations certifies that the population of Palestine is then fit for self-government' are deleted.

in Para. b)—which talks about rights—the word 'nationality' is deleted. Para. c) remains as it was. In Para. d) the words 'A Jewish National Home but not a Jewish State' are deleted. In Para. e)—which talks about autonomy for Jewish and Arab towns and districts—the words 'and districts' are deleted. Para. f)—which talks about Jewish immigration—is deleted, and instead there is a new wording which says that 'the maximum Jewish population of Palestine should be the present population. All Jews now living in Palestine will be able to acquire Palestinian citizenship.' It is likewise stated that 'during the interim period envisaged, the Arab leaders have not been authorized by a congress or by the Arab Kings to agree to either Jewish immigration or to further land sales. Para. g) remains as it was. Para. i) is deleted entirely.

"So that the version which the Arabs are prepared to discuss is as follows:

"1) A sovereign independent Palestinian State to be created on 1st January. . . .

"2) Every Palestinian independent of race and religion shall have equal and complete political and civil rights.

"3) In the meanwhile Gt. Britain shall continue to be responsible for the Government of the Country, the Palestine Government giving members of the population, Arabs and Jews, an ever-increasing share in the administration.

"4) Complete autonomy shall be granted to all communities in communal matters in the widest sense as soon as possible, provided that no community has jurisdiction over members of another community in those matters.

"5) Complete municipal autonomy should be granted as soon as possible to all-Jewish and all-Arab towns and villages.

"6) The maximum Jewish population of Palestine should be the present population. All Jews in Palestine on 1st . . . shall be entitled to apply for and receive Palestinian citizenship. During the interim period, the Arab leaders have not been authorized to agree to further Jewish immigration or land sales.

"7) The interests of the different communities of Palestine after the creation of the independent State shall be guaranteed by the British Government.

"8) The legitimate interests of Gt. Britain shall be safeguarded."

"The Arabs had asked Magnes whether Shertok saw prospects of an agreement on this basis. And a second question was posed: whether the Jewish Agency would be prepared to meet with the Arabs after it knew that this was their stand. Shertok had answered the first question with an emphatic negative. To the second he had replied that the Agency definitely rejected such a basis and would not enter into discussion on it; however, if the Arabs, knowing that this was the attitude of the Agency, still wanted to meet, the Agency was willing. Shertok stated the same thing in a letter to Dr. Magnes on January 13.

"On January 14 Shertok received a letter from Dr. Magnes informing him that the Arabs saw prospects of a meeting only on their basis; nevertheless, Magnes recommended that the Jewish Agency express its willingness to meet on the basis of

Newcombe's draft, while announcing that the Agency did not agree to certain paragraphs in that draft.

"Ben-Gurion commented that there obviously was some monkey business afoot here. A proposal formulated in writing had been submitted to us and we were told that it had been agreed to by Arab leaders. On the basis of those proposals Hyamson and Magnes conducted negotiations with us orally and in writing. Now the Arabs inform us that they did not agree to that proposal. Only one out of two explanations was possible: either the mediators had deceived us by drawing up a proposal of their own and presenting it to us purportedly in the name of the Arabs, who had not authorized them; or the Arabs were now backing out of their previous proposal and claiming: 'Absolutely untrue!' Who here was the deceiver?

"Ben-Gurion was inclined to think that the Arabs were now having regrets, after the publication of the letter of the Colonial Secretary concerning immigration, from which it was clear that the plan of the Jewish State was no longer being considered by England. He did not suspect Magnes of evil intentions or of deliberate deceit. He did not know of the intentions of Hyamson and Newcombe. If they really had in their hands an Arab proposal, they should make that fact known and announce that the Arabs had changed their minds. We must not permit these men to continue their damaging and harmful game . . . and it was hard to understand how even a man like Magnes could advise us to meet with the Arabs on the basis of this proposal. We must denounce the deceit of 'the peace-mongers' who submitted that proposal to us at the beginning of the negotiations.

"It was decided by the Executive to demand explanations from Magnes and Hyamson as to how the document that they submitted to us as coming from the Arabs had reached them."

24 MAGNES ANSWERS CRITICISMS—FEBRUARY, 1938

At a meeting of the Jewish Agency Executive on February 6, 1938, Sharett submitted a report on Tufiq Ghussein, an Arab notable of the old school, who had been much respected in the days of the Turks and who occasionally invited Sharett for talks. In this period he was wont to put forward proposals for peace on the basis of the halting of immigration, which Sharett of course would reject. After the disturbances of 1936, Ghussein again approached Sharett on the subject of Jewish-Arab peace based on Jewish agreement to remain a minority. He explained that if there were peace between the Jews and Arabs and immigration would be discontinued, the bitterness on both sides would disappear and it might well be that in the course of time, after the Arabs overcame their fear of the Jews, they would even agree to a Jewish majority in the country.

A week before that, at the end of January, Sharett had been invited to meet the same personage, who discussed the question of partition. While he was not particularly keen on partition, neither did he object to it, Ghussein said, adding that there were important Arabs who were in favor of it. However, in order to implement partition a transition period was needed, during which there would be an armistice between Jews and Arabs. Sharett asked whether anyone backed him on this question. Ghussein replied that there was a group whom he was prepared to organize, and that he would no doubt have to visit Beirut to meet the leaders who had fled there. A few days later, when Sharett met the High Commissioner, the latter told him that the same Arab notable had come to him and told him about the proposal of an armistice between the Jews and Arabs. The High Commissioner asked Sharett if there was any chance of an armistice for two or three years. Sharett answered that the Jews would be willing to negotiate on the subject provided that it was absolutely clear that meanwhile the Mandate would remain in force and that immigration to Erez Israel would continue in accordance with economic absorptive capacity. In the meantime Ghussein visited the Emir Abdullah and on his return to Jerusalem told Sharett that the Emir supported partition. He again brought up his armistice proposal, and said he planned to go to Beirut to obtain the consent of the Arab Higher Committee. The Mufti might object, perhaps, but in that case he would remain isolated. Sharett told him that the Jewish Agency Executive was in favor of Jewish-Arab peace. The crux of the matter was the fate of immigration during the armistice. Ghussein said the figure would be set at 12,000 a year. Sharett declared that the Agency would not agree to that. Ghussein said that while he himself was agreeable to a larger number, there was not the slightest chance that the Arabs would agree. Sharett commented that his position on the immigration issue had not changed.

Sharett also reported to the Executive that contact had been made with members of the National Bloc in Syria, who were now the principal force in that country and whose leader was Jamil Mardam. They were interested in peace in Palestine, since they feared that terrorism in that country would delay ratification of the Syrian-French treaty, and our people had received a written invitation to meet the Deputy President of the Syrian parliament, who belonged to the National Bloc. At the meeting, the representative of the Bloc told our people that in their view no solution to the Palestine question was conceivable without the consent of the Jews, the Arabs and the English; but an agreement with the Arabs meant an agreement with the Mufti, for he was the representative of the Palestine Arabs, and they were in touch with him.

The Jewish Agency had established close relations with the National Bloc before it came to power, and its leaders wished to show that they had remained loyal. This was the only Arab group that made it a point to deal solely with the Jewish Agency on the subject of a Jewish-Arab agreement, but they were aware of the internal situation of the Arab national movement in Palestine and they knew that the Mufti was the principal power. For that reason they were not so optimistic about the prospects for an agreement, even though on their own part they evinced goodwill.

On the same day that Sharett made this report to the Executive, Dr. Weizmann arrived in Cairo. Among the people he visited there was Qatawi Pasha, the head of the Jewish community in Egypt. He informed Weizmann that he had invited Dr. Shahbander, an important Syrian personage, who had been offered the presidency of Syria after the negotiations between Syria and France on Syrian independence, so that he and Weizmann could discuss a Jewish-Arab agreement. After a while, Shahbander appeared. Dr. Weizmann told him that any agreement that was intended to fix the status of the Jews as a minority in Palestine was out of the question. Dr. Shahbander said he understood that the question of a minority status was not open for discussion, but what was needed at the moment was some arrangement that would ensure quiet for five years, during which time a permanent settlement could be discussed. Dr. Weizmann asked him about the fate of Jewish immigration during these five years. Shahbander at first tried to evade the question, but when Weizmann persisted, he asked Weizmann how many immigrants the Jews intended to bring in during that period. A quarter of a million, Weizmann said. Shahbander observed that the question was a complicated one and that he could not venture an opinion then and there. Weizmann thereupon asked him what solution he saw to the Palestine problem. An Arab Federation, he replied. Weizmann said that the Jews did not object to an Arab Federation, but that was not something that depended on the Jews, but on the Arabs themselves, and they were divided on this question, as were England and France. However, the Jews would agree to an Arab Confederation if a Jewish State were established in Palestine, and it would join the confederation. Dr. Shahbander stated that he was prepared to start working seriously for the attainment of Jewish-Arab peace and that for this purpose he was willing to travel to Syria, Iraq and Saudi Arabia. However, he greatly feared that if the Mufti were not excluded from the whole matter it would be difficult to arrive at an agreement.

Meanwhile reports reached the Jewish Agency concerning negotiations between Dr. Magnes and Nuri Pasha. At a meeting of the Executive on

February 20, 1938, Sharett reported that he had learned from a reliable Arab source that Nuri Pasha had informed the representative of the British Government in Baghdad about the results of his meeting with Dr. Magnes and the Anglican Bishop, in which the three of them had discussed the possibility of a Jewish-Arab agreement that would be based on a minority status for the Jews in Palestine and on fixing a ratio for the Jewish population in relation to the other inhabitants. Nuri Pasha reported that Dr. Magnes had expressed the hope that he would succeed in persuading the Jewish Agency Executive to authorize him to conduct negotiations along these lines, but that if the Executive refused he hoped that English, American and German Jews, as well as some Jews in Palestine, would quit the Executive and enter into direct negotiations with the Arabs. Nuri had been waiting for information from Magnes for two or three weeks. He further reported that he would still have to persuade the Mufti to agree to the proposal—which would certainly not be easy, but he hoped to succeed.

Sharett did not know whether everything that Nuri Pasha had reported in the name of Dr. Magnes was correct, but there was no doubt that the matter was serious and should be looked into. He requested authority from the Executive to seek clarification from Dr. Magnes. The chairman of the Executive was then in London.

In accordance with the decision of the Executive, Sharett had already written to Magnes requesting an explanation of his negotiations with the Arabs, of which the Government had knowledge. No answer had yet been received. Of course, he could write to him again, but if the second letter also went unanswered we should have to draw our own conclusions. If it transpired that Dr. Magnes had negotiated with Nuri Pasha, he, Sharett, would propose to the Executive that Dr. Magnes be asked to end all his political activities. For years now Dr. Magnes had been dabbling in politics of his own accord, without the slightest indication of success. On the contrary, he had only done damage. The contents of Dr. Magnes' conversations were reported to the Foreign Office by interested Arabs, and we did not know what spirit prevailed there regarding our affairs. The Foreign Ministry saw that a man who heads the Hebrew University in Jerusalem seriously suggests that the Jews of England, America and Germany as well as some Jews from Erez Israel should quit the Executive and make peace with the Arabs. It was obvious what damage such talk could cause us. Sharett had written to Professor Brodetzky about Dr. Magnes' activities and had used the expression "a self-appointed emissary." Dr. Hexter and Mrs. Jacobs had corresponded with Sharett about this matter and commented that inasmuch as Dr. Magnes had received authorization from us to clarify the possibility of a Jewish-Arab agreement he was not a self-appointed emissary. Sharett replied to Mrs. Jacobs that the fact was that Dr. Magnes had conducted negotiations with the Arabs even before he approached the Executive with his well-known proposal and before we requested details of the proposal. Even after he transmitted to us a proposal entirely different from the one we received from him the first time, and to which we replied with an absolute refusal to meet on the basis of the draft he had brought to us in the name of the Arabs, he tried to persuade us to agree to meet with the Arabs on the basis of the first proposal, which was now known to be nothing but the concoction of Hyamson and Newcombe. Our information about Magnes' talk with Nuri Pasha had come from two different sources. If it emerged that Dr. Magnes had conducted negotiations with Nuri Pasha on the basis of a Jewish minority in Erez Israel, we would have to draw the necessary conclusions.

Ussishkin related that eleven days before, Dr. Magnes had telephoned him to say that he and Gad Frumkin wished to visit him on an urgent matter. The meeting took place at Ussishkin's home. Frumkin was silent practically all of the time. Dr. Magnes reported that he had received Sharett's letter of January 25 but that he would not reply, since he found its contents to be insulting. Ussishkin commented that he had read the letter and saw no insult in it. He advised Dr. Magnes to answer it. Dr. Magnes told him that the Anglican Bishop [Dr. Brown] had spoken to him about the serious situation in the country and said that something must be done to calm things down. They had both gone to Beirut to meet with Nuri Pasha. Ussishkin immediately asked whether he had informed Sharett of this trip. His reply was negative. Ussishkin remarked that Dr. Magnes had made a mistake in going to Beirut without first requesting the opinion of the director of the Political Department of the Jewish Agency. Dr. Magnes made no comment, and went on to say that in Beirut they had met with Nuri Pasha and had discussed the situation in Palestine with him. The basis of the conversation was a temporary agreement, for five or ten years, on a Jewish minority in the country. Nuri expressed his opinion that on that basis it would be possible to reach an agreement, and he proposed that the permanent percentage of Jews in the country in proportion to the other inhabitants be fixed immediately. Dr. Magnes had replied that the Jews would not agree, and he suggested that they talk about immigration during the next five or ten years. Nuri Pasha also mentioned the matter of the confederation, and Dr. Magnes commented that that was a topic for the future. The Anglican Bishop was happy to hear Magnes' words. Nuri Pasha said that he would still have to consult on the matter with his friends. He himself agreed to Dr. Magnes' proposal and they might have to meet again soon, perhaps even in Jerusalem. Ussishkin had asked Dr. Magnes to report the matter to Sharett. Dr. Magnes refused, and authorized Ussishkin to report in his name. Ussishkin informed him that he refused to accept that task. Since then he had not spoken to Magnes on the subject. He proposed that Dr. Hexter be charged with arranging a meeting between Dr. Magnes and Sharett. He, Ussishkin, was prepared to take part in that meeting. Only after the meeting would it be possible to reach a conclusion.

Dr. Hexter said that Sharett knew the reason for Dr. Magnes' failure to answer. He, Hexter, had tried to reconcile them, without success. Sharett had sought a way of approaching Dr. Magnes again, but Dr. Hexter had told him that there was no need for that, since Dr. Magnes was about to reply to his letter. Instead of a meeting with Dr. Magnes, as suggested by Ussishkin, Dr. Hexter proposed that Dr. Magnes be invited to a plenary meeting of the Executive to present his side of the story. That should be done after his reply to Sharett's letter of January 25, 1938, was received. He added that Dr. Magnes could be believed when he said that he had never proposed a permanent minority status in Palestine as a basis for a Jewish-Arab agreement.

Rabbi Fishman said that Dr. Magnes' relations with the Zionist movement were a disheartening chapter. Down the years he had done us damage. But he agreed to Dr. Hexter's proposal that he be invited to a meeting of the Executive, so that we could tell him explicitly that he was not to engage in political activity or to interfere in matters in which he was not competent. We must demand explanations from him and request him to continue his work at the university and not interfere in politics.

The motion to invite Dr. Magnes to a meeting of the Executive was put to a vote. Four voted in favor, and three against. Dr. Rotenstreich asked that the question be submitted to Messrs. Ben-Gurion and Brodetsky in London. Greenbaum asked Sharett to discuss the question with me on the telephone and to inform the Executive of my opinion.

The next day Sharett and the other members of the Executive received a letter from Dr. Magnes, dated February 21, 1938, which read as follows:

"As you are aware, I have been engaged in an attempt to bring about a meeting between Jews and Arabs. This was undertaken at the request of the Executive of the Jewish Agency in letters, dated December 6th, 1937, December 13th, 1937, and January 13th, 1938.

"I herewith present a report.

"This report has taken on a form other than that I had planned, because of the need also of answering Mr. Shertok's letter of January 25, 1938, with the contents of which I presume you are familiar.

"I would suggest that, at the present juncture, I meet with the Executive to discuss Jewish-Arab relations.

"The Hebrew text of this report will follow."

"1) Towards the end of October 1937 I received from Mr. Hyamson of London the text of a 'Suggested Basis for Discussion Between Jewish and Arab Representatives' (Appendix I, text 1). Mr. Hyamson also communicated this text to the Jewish Agency in London on November 4, 1937.

"This text had been drawn up by Mr. Hyamson and Colonel Newcombe in London.

"Col. Newcombe was one of the founders and later the Treasurer of the Palestine Information Bureau, which was the accredited representative in London of the Arab Higher Committee until the suppression of that Committee.

"Mr. Hyamson reported that this text had behind it some influential Arabs, and that it was the precipitate of many discussions that had taken place between Jews, Arabs and Englishmen during the summer of 1937 in America, England and Geneva.

"You are probably aware of the tenour of some of these discussions.

"2) This text seemed to me worthy of particular attention, both because of the participation of Col. Newcombe in its authorship as also because of its form and contents.

"It had been drawn up with each word carefully weighed. It was not in legal form. It was not a draft of a peace agreement or formal treaty, but merely what it purported to be: 'A suggested basis for discussion'. Some important points, for example land sales, were omitted. The dates in the first and last paragraphs were left open. The immigration clause was intentionally broad and vague. The term 'minority' did not appear. The term 'Jewish National Home', but not the term 'Arab State' appeared. Transjordan was mentioned. Thus this text was meant to serve, like many another of this genre, not as a legal and binding agreement, but as a means of preparing the way for bringing about a first meeting of opposing sides.

"3) I brought this text to the attention of Messrs. Hexter and Ussischkin of the Jewish Agency, with the result that first Mr. Shertok and I, on November 22, 1937, had talks together for the purpose of clarifying the meaning of the text.

"I gave answers to their detailed questions, as best I could, seeing I had had nothing to do with the drafting of this text. I also, at their request, wrote to Mr. Hyamson for more formal answers and I communicated these to Mr. Shertok on December 3, 1937 and December 9, 1937, I enclose copies of this correspondence with Mr. Shertok on these questions (Appendix II, IV, V).

"Questions as to the meaning of the text were put simultaneously by the Agency to Mr. Hyamson in London and answers were given by him to the Agency there.

"4) In a letter of Mr. Shertok to me, dated December 6, 1937 (Appendix IV) I received an authorisation from the Agency to endeavour to bring about a meeting between the Agency and Arabs of appropriate standing, this meeting to be secret, unofficial and preliminary. This authorisation was repeated in letters dated December 13, 1937 and January 13, 1938 (Appendix VI, IX).

"The authorisation in the letter of December 6th, 1937, reads as follows:

'Under the circumstances we think that the only way to bring out the facts as they are and to arrive at real negotiations, in case such are possible, is to arrange a meeting between us and the Arabs who may be ready for negotiations. If you can propose such a meeting with Arabs of appropriate status, I herewith inform you that we are ready for that. It is self understood that the first meeting should be only an unofficial meeting for purposes of clarification, upon whose results it would be possible to determine if there be room for negotiation or not. For our part we can promise not to give any publicity to this meeting, either before or after it is held except that the two sides agree to do this. I therefore propose to you to find out if a meeting such as this is possible and to inform us as soon as possible.'

"The letter of December 13, 1937, said:

'In any event, if it become clear that there is the possibility of a meeting face to face such as I proposed in my previous letter, we shall have to make the prior conditions that the meeting be kept secret by the other side. In my previous letter I contented myself with the statement that we, for our part, would keep the matter secret, thinking that the other side would naturally be interested in not having it made public. The facts of these last days, however, have completely upset this assumption. On the contrary, it seems as though the other side were interested only in publicity and not in real results. It must therefore be clear that if we do not have sufficient assurance that the other side would keep its word concerning the secrecy of the meeting, it is doubtful if the meeting can take place.'

"The above is not correct, as shown on page 9 para. 30 of this Report.

"At about the same date, I became uncertain as to the actual extent to which one of the Arabs mentioned by Mr. Hyamson was behind the text for a suggested basis of discussion.

"5) As a consequence I at once took such steps as would ensure the receipt of direct information from the Palestine Arab leadership in Beyrouth.

"To this end I met on December 16th, 1937 with an Englishman of note and an Arab. The latter is the authorised representative of the former Arab Higher Committee. I have had a number of meetings with these two gentlemen, both of whom have spared no effort to bring about the secret, unofficial, preliminary meeting as proposed by Mr. Shertok.

"I shall have something to say about these meetings later on. Suffice it to say here that the Hyamson-Newcombe text served throughout as the basis of our discussions and our efforts.

"6) On December 28th, 1937 (Appendix VII) Mr. Shertok wrote me, taking exception to a letter of Mr. Hyamson to Mr. Lourie, the political secretary of the Agency in London, dated December 20th. He also enclosed an extract of a Minute of an interview between Mr. Moussa Husseini and Mr. Bakstansky of the English Zionist Federation, on December 14, 1937.

"In my answer to Mr. Shertok on December 30th, the day I received his letter of December 28th (Appendix VIII) I said that I hoped that he might 'hear from me in the course of the next week. May I add that I am responsible only for such things as come direct from me—not for Mr. Hyamson's letters, and not for anything else.'

"7) On January 6, 1938 I requested one of Mr. Shertok's colleagues in the Executive of the Jewish Agency to tell Mr. Shertok the following:

"That I had been in touch with Arabs in Beyrouth through intermediaries, with whom I had had three meetings; that the fourth meeting was to have taken place on January 4, but that it had been postponed at the last minute, probably because the Ormsby-Gore despatch appeared on that day.

"8) On January 11th, 1938, at one of these meetings with the Englishman and the Arab whom I have mentioned, I was handed a text (Appendix I, text 2) giving the basis upon which the Palestine Arab leadership in Beyrouth would be willing to meet with the Jewish Agency in a secret, unofficial, preliminary meeting as proposed by Mr. Shertok.

"This text used the form and some of the paragraphs of the Hyamson-Newcombe text. But it contained radical changes as to the crucial points of immigration and land sales, and also as to the possibility of a provisional agreement which might be renewable after a period of years.

"9) On January 12th, Mr. Shertok met with me and I communicated these changes to him, and at the same time asked him, as I had been requested to do, to give me his personal opinion as to whether the Jewish Agency would meet upon the basis of this amended text.

"He said it would not.

"I had already expressed this same opinion to those with whom I was meeting. I later communicated Mr. Shertok's oral answer to them.

"10) On January 13, 1938 Mr. Shertok wrote me (Appendix IX)—
   a) analysing at length the differences between the original Hyamson-Newcombe text and the text as amended in the name of the Beyrouth Arab leadership;
   b) stating that: 'The Jewish Agency rejects the text of the other side as the basis for negotiations and declares that it will not enter into a consideration of it;'
   c) yet 'if the other side wishes a meeting with the Agency after it knows that this is the Agency's attitude, the Agency is ready for a meeting. In relation to this meeting all the conditions are to remain in force as given in my letter to you of December 6, 1937. I am sure that you will without delay communicate to me the other side's answer to our declaration.'

"11) On the same day I translated the whole letter of January 13, word for word, to those with whom I was meeting. Yet despite the unsatisfactory stage the conversation had reached they were anxious that our meetings be continued.

"12) On January 14, (Appendix IX) I wrote to Mr. Shertok, as follows:

'At the meeting yesterday I received the declaration that there were chances of a meeting only if their (Beyrouth Arabs—J.L.M.) text served as a basis for discussion.

'Nevertheless we agreed to meet again next Thursday (January 20th) upon my return from Nathania.

'In my opinion it would be worth while to consider the possibility of a further answer from you—perhaps in this sense that you repeat the readiness of the Agency to meet upon the London text as a basis of discussion, despite the provisions which are unsatisfactory to the Agency.

'And then, if this be possible, to prepare a text giving expression to the attitude of the Agency towards all the paragraphs of the text prepared by them (Beyrouth Arabs—J.L.M.).'

"13) As an answer to this, Mr. Shertok sent me his letter, dated January 25, 1938 (Appendix X).

"He asks for an explanation of the alleged discrepancy between my representations to the Executive in November 1937, concerning the Arabs behind the Hyamson-Newcombe text and the fact that in January 1938 the Beyrouth Arab leadership had accepted only some parts of that text, and as to other parts had made radical changes.

"14) I shall answer this question as to this alleged discrepancy.

"But before doing so I wish to point out that in his letter of January 25, 1938, Mr. Shertok himself finds the explanation of the alleged discrepancy in 'lying statements', 'deceit', 'false impressions', 'baseless rumours', 'wilful misrepresentation'.

"It is not entirely clear from Mr. Shertok's letter to whom all of this refers. Inasmuch as he has not exempted me from these charges, although full opportunity was given him to do so, I presume he includes me as being also guilty of the above.

"I waited for a considerable time for Mr. Shertok to avail himself of the opportunity given him through a member of the Executive of changing some of these expressions. But in vain; and this explains largely why my reply to his letter is belated.

"Should any documents on this question have been circularized, I wish to call attention to the fact that these documents did not await my answer to Mr. Shertok's letter of January 15, 1938 (received on January 26th) and that these documents were not shown to me for possible correction and answer.

"15) I have confined myself scrupulously to the terms of reference given me by the Executive. I have been carrying on not 'negotiations' for a final and legal 'agreement' between Jews and Arabs, but conversations and soundings that might lead to the preparation of a basis upon which the secret, unofficial, preliminary meeting proposed by Mr. Shertok might take place. I have been careful to emphasize that the Hyamson-Newcombe text was not prepared by the Jewish Agency and that the Jewish Agency did not agree to all of its provisions. Nevertheless, despite this, the Jewish Agency was ready to regard this text as a preliminary basis for an informal secret discussion, if the Arab leaders would also so regard it. If the preliminary meeting were to take place, either side would be at liberty to accept or reject or amend the provisions of this draft, or to make proposals not contained in this draft.

"What I have just said is confirmed by a Minute, prepared by the Englishman to whom I have referred above, and which I quote with his consent:

> 'Dr. Magnes translated extracts from two official letters, dated 6th and 13th December, from a leading member of the Executive of the Jewish Agency, in which the writer stated that the Jewish Agency was willing to meet representative Arabs upon the basis of this document . . . with no promise of the consequent opening up of negotiations. As these two official letters were marked "private and confidential" he did not give us copies of them, but translated relevant paragraphs from Hebrew into English.'

"This Minute goes on to say:

> 'It was pointed out (to the Arab leadership in Beyrouth—J.L.M.) that the Jewish Agency itself only accepted the document as a basis for discussion and could not commit itself to the whole of it, but were prepared to meet on it; and that this might well be the attitude of the members of the Arab Higher Committee.'

"A few of my friends have met with this eminent Englishman, who has indicated to them a number of details which, of course, for reasons that must be obvious to you, I cannot commit to paper. If the Executive is interested, I shall be glad to give the names of these friends.

"16) Now as to the alleged discrepancy referred to by Mr. Shertok in his letter of January 25, 1938.

"My letters to Mr. Shertok of December 3rd and December 9th, 1937, (Appendix III, V) contain questions and answers that, at the request of the Agency, were intended to explain the meaning of a number of points in the Hyamson-Newcombe text.

"The following occurs in my letter of December 3, 1937:

> '1. *Question:* Is the "Suggested Basis for Discussion between Jewish and Arab representatives" a basis to which some influential Arabs have agreed?
> *Answer:* Yes.
>
> '2. *Question:* Who are these Arabs?
> *Answer:* Members of the suppressed Arab Higher Committee, including

X and Y, are, it is said, willing to accept the plan as the basis for discussion.'

"17) I call your attention to the caution with which this sentence was drawn up. The words 'it is said', as above, are the words used by Mr. Hyamson in his letter to me. Mr. Shertok in his letter of December 6th and elsewhere calls attention to this very caution and draws the conclusion from it that 'even the members of the English-Jewish group in London are not completely certain of the agreement of the Arabs, but report this from rumour, or at any event at second or third hand.'

"18) But my answer to the alleged discrepancy is that there *was no* discrepancy in the base sense in which it is meant by Mr. Shertok.

"There *were* 'some influential Arabs' behind this document as a suggested basis for discussion.

"Mr. Hyamson was informed of this by Colonel Newcombe in the summer and early autumn, and Colonel Newcombe confirms this to me in a statement under date of February 4, 1938, as follows:

'I discussed possibilities with X and Y (one of whom was a member of the former Arab Higher Committee and the other in close touch with the Committee— J.L.M.) and though they left England in July and Hyamson drafted the scheme with me in August or September, I feel quite justified in saying that they would have accepted it *in general*, and as a *basis of discussion*. That was the sense of the draft. It was not intended that the actual wording would be accepted by both parties; it was hoped only to be wide enough to embrace both sides and so form the basis of discussion.

'Clearly, the phrase in para. 6 "The Jewish population shall not exceed an agreed figure" is inconclusive and meant to be so, until both parties agree to terms. The Mufti, for example, had never, to my knowledge, mentioned Transjordan: it is outside his province: but other leading Arabs have suggested that Transjordan would become open reasonably if a settlement is reached.

'Similarly one or two other passages are more vague than the Mufti could have accepted: but they still form a basis of discussion and include *in general* the views given to me.

'Therefore, it seems to me clear that the Mufti could not have agreed to the wording as it stood, nor could I have had his authority in detail: but the general outline did approximate to the views of the Mufti's advisers.'

"Col. Newcombe adds that he had sent this draft to the Mufti after consulting two other 'influential Arabs' whom he names.

"It is clear, therefore, that Mr. Hyamson had good authority for replying definitely and briefly in the affirmative to Question 1, put by the Agency representatives: 'Is the suggested basis for discussion between Jewish and Arab representatives a basis to which some influential Arabs have agreed?'

"19) In the unseemly haste to find base motives for the alleged discrepancy between the earlier Arab attitude and the Arab attitude later on, Mr. Shertok has overlooked a significant explanation.

"This is made clear in the following statement which the two gentlemen with whom I have been meeting have authorized me to make:

> 'Despite the fact that Col. Newcombe had not been authorised to formulate the immigration paragraph in the vague way in which it appears in that document (Hyamson-Newcombe), there was nevertheless a willingness on the part of some members there (Beyrouth—J.L.M.) to arrange for a secret, preliminary meeting for the purpose of discovering whether or not any formal negotiations were possible.
>
> 'Any hope of such a meeting faded upon the appearance in the Arab press of summaries of Mr. Ben Gurion's speech on December 21st, 1937. This speech gave rise to the impression of bad faith on the part of the Jewish Agency.
>
> 'It was pointed out (to the Arabs in Beyrouth—J.L.M.) that Mr. Ben Gurion in his speech had opposed a *permanent* minority status for the Jews, whereas the document in question (Hyamson-Newcombe—J.L.M.) provided for an agreement for a given period. The indignation caused by Mr. Ben Gurion's speech, however, was so great that even those who were willing to consider the preliminary meeting were now opposed to it.'

"I venture to direct your attention to the fact, here explicitly recorded, that it was pointed out to the Arab leadership in Beyrouth that Mr. Ben Gurion's statement was not necessarily in conflict with or in contradiction to my conversations, as that speech opposes only *permanent* minority status. In all of my discussions, everywhere I have emphasized that the Jews would not be prepared to accept permanent minority status as a basis of discussion. I have emphasized, however, that an agreement for a period of years, at the end of which the Jews would still be a minority, had a fighting chance of acceptance among the Jews, and, as I was convinced, among the Arabs as well.

"I may add that Mr. Ben Gurion's statement which was given wide currency in many languages, including Arabic, was regarded as 'a strongly worded challenge' and as 'an outward ultimatum', and it was construed by the Arabs 'into meaning a final rejection of any possible terms of negotiations or conciliation', and it was recorded in the Minute to which I have referred, 'that the Arab Higher Committee could not in the light of this even accept the terms of the Hyamson-Newcombe document as the basis of discussion. It seemed to undermine even this basis of discussion.'

"I have expressed the conviction to those with whom I have been meeting that Mr. Ben Gurion's statement was not intended to 'torpedo' the conversations that were going on or to disavow these efforts. Rightly or wrongly, however, his speech was so interpreted, at the time it appeared in the Hebrew, English and Arabic press. I consider certain expressions in Mr. Ben Gurion's speech as most unfortunate and while doubtless not intended to make a preliminary meeting difficult or impossible they had that effect.

"20) A further very patent reason which Mr. Shertok seems to have overlooked and that will help explain the differences in the attitude of the Arab leaders in October, November and early December, and their attitude later in December and in January, is the following:

"There were wide-spread newspaper rumours, which may also have given rise to Mr. Ben Gurion's speech, that a strong party within the British Cabinet desired to 'crystallize' the percentage of the Jewish population in Palestine. These rumours so far as I know still remain rumours. But they were followed by the despatch of Mr. Ormsby-Gore to the High Commissioner on January 4, 1938. This despatch was interpreted in Beyrouth as being not unfavourable to the Arab position.

"21) Yet even after all this, there were 'some influential Arabs' who wanted to make the attempt to convene the secret, unofficial, preliminary meeting proposed by Mr. Shertok.

"To this end there was handed to me on January 12, 1938, as a suggested basis for discussion at a first meeting, the 'Beyrouth text' (Appendix I, text 2) to which I have already referred.

"Permit me again to cite the Minute which I have already quoted:

> 'These changes Dr. Magnes promised to convey to Mr. Shertok, the secretary of the Jewish Agency (The head of the Political Department is meant—J.L.M.); but he pointed out that they seemed completely to alter the basis of the document, and from that point of view the changes were such that he felt the Jewish Agency could not agree.'

"22) Though the attempt to arrange a first meeting had thus broken down for the reasons I have given, I nevertheless sent to Mr. Shertok the letter which I have quoted above on page 5 (Appendix IX) and which suggested that:

  a) the Agency renew their willingness to meet with the Arabs, with the original Newcombe-Hyamson document as a basis for discussion, despite the Agency's lack of accord with provisions of this text, and/or
  b) the Agency prepare their own text, using the Hyamson-Newcombe document as a basis in some such way as was done by Arab leaders or by third parties acting for them.

"23) This seems to have pained Mr. Shertok, and he asks how I could make such proposals to the Agency under the circumstances.

"24) My answer is as follows:

"First, I have already stated (page 5 above) that the two gentlemen with whom I had been meeting thought our effort should not be permitted to end.

"25) Second, I think, as I am sure do many others, that it would strengthen the Agency's position to have it known that it was ready to meet for preliminary discussion, even upon the basis of a text with some of whose provisions the Agency was not in accord. If the Jewish Agency keeps reaffirming publicly its desire to meet with the Arabs and publicly points with pride to its efforts 'with an outstretched hand', it should be ready to meet on the basis of even a partially satisfactory text or to state its peace aims. I hold it to be a mark of strength and of conviction in the justice of one's cause, if one is ready to meet for discussion with one's opponents.

"26) Third, the two gentlemen with whom I have been meeting were also canvassing the possibility of a meeting between the Jews and the Arabs, either upon the basis of no written text at all, or in order to record such points as Jews and Arabs were in agreement upon, leaving the disputed points for future consideration in the reverse order of their difficulty, that is, leaving immigration to the last. This took place between January 21st and 26th at the very time Mr. Shertok was penning his letter to me of January 25th, ascribing in the name of the Executive base motives to everyone concerned in this effort.

"The Minute from which I have been quoting recites that it was stated to the Beyrouth Arab leadership, that:

> 'It would be of definite value to record together at a preliminary meeting for discussion between representatives of Arabs and representatives of Jews those points on which there was agreement concerning the situation and future of Palestine. The representatives might come together without any formal basis or on the basis put forward for discussion by Col. Newcombe. It was expressed as a "firm conviction that such a meeting would prepare the way for the dawn of a happier day in Palestine."'

"27) Fourth, if finally, the efforts to arrange for a first meeting upon some basis or other were to break down, I thought it would advance the informal discussion one small step further (perhaps it is only through slight advances that we can progress in the difficult matter) if the Agency were to consent to have done what the Arab leadership had consented to have done: on the one hand use as much as possible of the wording of the Hyamson-Newcombe text, and on the other hand make its own amendments and changes—conveying an indication, if you will, of the Agency's peace terms.

"28) I might end this report here. But there is a further important step which I have taken and which I would like to describe.

"Before doing this, however, I shall want to deal with a number of futher points in Mr. Shertok's letters. I cannot answer all the inexactitudes his letters contain. I shall try to deal with a few of them.

"29) Mr. Shertok's letter of January 25, 1938, contains the following:

> 'In our first conversation on 19.XI.37 you handed me two texts of an agreement and said the two of them were brought to you by groups of Arabs ... At the second meeting on 22.XI.37 with Messrs. Ussishkin and Ben-Gurion you declared in answer to the question of Mr. Ben-Gurion, that, to be sure, the text had not been drafted by Arabs but by a Jew and an Englishman.'

"As a matter of fact, in my first conversation I told Mr. Shertok the text had been drafted by Messrs. Hyamson and Newcombe. This is indicated in Mr. Shertok's note to me of the same day (Appendix II). He asks:

'Which side took the initiative in these talks—the Jewish, the Arab, or the English?'

"How does he come to mention 'the English' if I had not mentioned an Englishman as one of the authors of the text?

"Moreover, Mr. Shertok told me that very day, November 19th, that he had received the same text from the Agency in London to whom it had been communicated by Mr. Hyamson on November 4, 1937, but that he had not had time to go over it. In his letter to me of January 13, 1938 (Appendix IX) Mr. Shertok refers to this letter of Mr. Hyamson of November 4th.

"30) Mr. Shertok's letters of December 13, and December 28, 1937, charge 'the other side' with insincerity and with the sole desire of gaining illegitimate publicity which they could use with the public and with the British Government to the embarrassment and harm of the Jewish Agency.

"I have been assured from competent sources that not one single word has up to this moment appeared in the Arab press about the Hyamson-Newcombe document or about the Beyrouth document or about the conversations connected with these efforts. This fact in itself shows with what seriousness the Arab leadership has taken this whole effort. It is to be hoped that even Mr. Shertok and his informants now recognise that the articles in the Arab press that prompted his letters to me of December 13 and December 28, 1937, had nothing whatsoever to do with the action we are here concerned with.

"31) Mr. Shertok further says in his letter of December 28, 1937, 'that the members of the Executive in Jerusalem with whom you have been in touch were not satisfied with the replies (to the questions about the Hyamson-Newcombe document contained in my letter of December 3rd—J.L.M.) they received from you. As is known to you from our letter of 6:12:37 the matter is not so, and Mr. Lourie properly calls Mr. Hyamson's attention to this in his letter of December 21.'

"But I wrote a second letter to Mr. Shertok under date of December 9, 1937, (Appendix V) in which I gave him further answers to the questions which had been put to me concerning the Hyamson-Newcombe text. Mr. Shertok never refers to the answers I gave in my letter of December 9, 1937. This was an indication to me that they were satisfactory. On December 13, 1937, he acknowledged to me receipt of this letter and made no reference whatsoever to my replies to these questions. On December 28th, however, he says that the answers in my letter of December *3rd* were not satisfactory, without referring to my answers of December 9th. Between December 9th and his letter of December 28th which reached me on December 30th, three weeks of silence on his part, he permitted me to believe that my answers had been satisfactory and permitted me to carry on my efforts to arrange

for a meeting with the Hyamson-Newcombe text as the basis for discussion.
"32) Mr. Shertok's letter of December 28, 1937, says:
'From this extract (of an unconfirmed conversation in London—J.L.M.) you will see, first, that the other side was told, or that it received the impression, that the Jewish Agency had agreed in principle to Mr. Hyamson's proposals. You will know that such was never the case and this should have been known also to Mr. Hyamson.'
"The statement was never made to me nor was the impression conveyed nor did 'the other side' receive 'the impression that the Jewish Agency had agreed in principle to Mr. Hyamson's proposals'. 'The other side' knew, as I have already stated and proved by the Minutes I have quoted, that the Jewish Agency was *not* in accord with some points of the Hyamson-Newcombe document, but that, nevertheless, the Agency would regard this document as sufficient for a suggested basis for discussion, provided the Arab side also agreed to this.
"33) But more startling is Mr. Shertok's statement in his letter of January 25, 1938 (Appendix X):
'As is known to you, we never accepted the Hyamson-Newcombe text as the basis for any negotiations whatsoever.'
"This was not known to me. The contrary was known to me. The text was to serve as the basis for discussion.
"If persisted in Mr. Shertok's statement would compel a reasonable man to draw the most damaging conclusions as to the political morality of the Jewish Agency.
"Mr. Shertok also says in this letter that this text had not been accepted even as a basis for discussion. This is the only letter in which Mr. Shertok uses the term *basis for discussion*. There is throughout Mr. Shertok's letters confusion and looseness' in the use of the terms 'negotiations', 'agreement', 'basis of agreement', 'basis for negotiations', 'basis for discussion'. If this text was not accepted by the Agency even as the basis of discussion, how then did Mr. Shertok expect to get the secret, unofficial, preliminary meeting he proposed?
"His letter of January 25, 1938, is the first and only time such a statement was made. It does not appear in any other letter of Mr. Shertok nor was that statement ever made to me orally. I was permitted to believe that the Agency was ready to meet the Arabs with that text as a basis for discussion, in the manner I have described above.
"No other basis for the meeting proposed by Mr. Shertok had been suggested to me by him. There was no other basis, and this was known to Mr. Shertok.
"If this text has never been accepted even as a basis for discussion, why is it that from first to last this text was the subject of our letters and talks? It was the assumption on which everything else was based. Our original meetings, our whole correspondence, the authorisation thrice repeated, would otherwise be completely unintelligible.
"The London text was subjected to searching scrutiny. In his letter of January 13,

1938 (Appendix IX) Mr. Shertok compares the London text in its minutest details with the Beyrouth text, and praises the London text.

"The political secretary of the Agency in London, Mr. Lourie, in a letter to Mr. Hyamson proposed that paragraph 6 of the Hyamson-Newcombe text be amended to read 'the maximum Jewish population... Transjordan, shall not, within the period of this agreement, exceed, etc.'. Mr. Lourie was therefore also given to understand that this text was to be taken seriously as a basis for discussion.

"Mr. Shertok's letter of December 6th, says: 'The important point' is not the meaning of this word or that paragraph of the text, but the convening of a meeting with the Arabs. In his letter of December 28th he says that 'the important point' is not the interpretations that have been given to various expressions of the text, but the immigration paragraph of that text, concerning which Mr. Lourie made certain suggestions, as pointed out in the preceding paragraph.

"Mr. Shertok contradicts himself in the very same letter of January 25, 1938. He says:

'The question of a meeting with these Arabs is no longer on the Agenda, not even upon the basis of the London text.'

"That means that such a meeting upon the basis of the London text *was* on the Agenda before January 25, 1938.

"34) Mr. Shertok's letter of January 25, 1938, says further:

'nor did we express approval of any of its paragraphs.'

"But in his letter of January 13, 1938, he says with reference to certain of the paragraphs:

'This change (in the immigration clause—J.L.M.) together with other amendments completely alters the picture of the agreement which one had from the first draft (of the Hyamson-Newcombe text—J.L.M.) that was handed to us and removes from it all those elements in which it might have been possible to see some advance on the Arab side toward an agreement with us. These elements were three: the recognition, even though only outwardly and with the lips, of the Jewish National Home; the extension of the framework of the agreement (that is Hyamson-Newcombe text—J.L.M.) to Transjordan, with the possibility of Jewish settlement there; bringing Jewish immigration close to 50 percent of all the inhabitants in the course of a definite period.'

"He also regretted the elimination by the Beyrouth document of paragraph 9 of the Hyamson-Newcombe draft.

"Moreover, in the conversation in Mr. Ussishkin's presence on November 22, 1937, Mr. Ben Gurion stated that the autonomy paragraphs (3 and 4) of the Hyamson-Newcombe draft marked an advance on what had been hitherto conceded by the Arab leaders.

"35) Mr. Shertok says further in his letter of January 25, 1938:

'We only sought to know if this text (Hyamson-Newcombe—J.L.M.) was proposed to us by the Arabs or if, in any event, there were Arab circles of weight which approve of this text.'

"'We *only* sought to know'. Is it possible that the move was in contemplation to make 'the other side' believe through me that the Agency was ready to meet for discussion on that basis and in the event that the other side had declared their willingness so to meet then for the Agency calmly to announce that it had never accepted this as a basis of discussion at all?

"Everyone observing the methods of politicians knows that they are ready all too often to disavow mediators and peacemakers. When preliminary feelers meet with obstacles, 'strategic retreats' and jockeying for tactical position and political advantage are a time-worn custom. It comes hard, however, to realise that at such a critical hour we seem to be 'like all the nations', making the end justify whatever means we think it necessary to employ.

"36) I do not wish to criticise Mr. Shertok unduly. I have no heart for criticism at this moment when we face a turning point in the history of Palestine. I realise the difficulties which confront every leader of public opinion, and particularly those entrusted with responsibility for the Political Department of the Jewish Agency. I must, however, confess that I do not grasp Mr. Shertok's attitude. Perhaps he can make it clear to me. I am sure there are others here and elsewhere who would be equally perplexed if they had knowledge of this attitude.

"I sincerely hope Mr. Shertok did not mean here what his words seem to indicate.

"37) I come now to the further point of importance to which I referred above. This point will, I think, prove that I was right in not letting the effort I was making come to an end because of Mr. Shertok's intemperate letter of January 25, 1938.

"38) Together with the two gentlemen I have mentioned several times, I had a long talk with a prominent non-Palestinian Arab on February 6th, 1938.

"The upshot of this talk was that this Arab said that he was prepared to emphasise to the Arab leadership the distinction between a text drafted as 'a suggested basis for discussion' whose purpose it is only to bring about a first meeting and the text of a formal agreement which is arrived at only after discussions are once begun.

"He was prepared also to advocate the following modifications in the Hyamson-Newcombe draft as amended by Beyrouth, provided he could know that the Jewish Agency were in accord, or provided the Jewish Agency were to make proposals of its own with which he found himself in accord (Appendix I, Text 3).

"*Para (1)* For the eliminated words ' . . . provided that the League . . . ' to substitute the words ' . . . in accordance with procedure adopted by the League for other Mandated territories such as Iraq and Syria.'

"*Para (2)* The retention of the word 'nationality' so that this paragraph would remain as it was in the original draft.

"*Para (3)* The same as in the original draft.

"*Para (4)* The same as in the original draft, with the elimination of the words 'a

Jewish National Home . . . provided'. Whereas paras 2, 3, 4, and 5 provide in substance for a Jewish National Home, this contentious phrase itself and all others should be avoided in drafting a possible basis for the first discussion.

"*Para (5)* The word 'district' to be re-instated, so that the paragraph would remain as it was in the original draft.

"*Para (6)* and *Para (9)* to be combined to read as follows:

'The maximum Jewish population of Palestine shall be X percent until there be a further agreement between the two peoples.'

Transjordan not to be included, because the Palestine Arabs have nothing to do with Transjordan. It is believed by the gentlemen who proposed the above formulation that if an agreement is achieved in Palestine, not only would Transjordan come within the sphere of Jewish settlement, but other Arab lands as well.

"*Para (7)* Both the words 'watched over' and 'guaranteed' to be used, so that the paragraph remains substantially as it was in the original draft.

"*Para (8)* 'The legitimate interests of Great Britain shall be safeguarded' is doubtless a better formulation than that of the original draft.

"The situation would therefore be that seven of the nine paragraphs of the Hyamson-Newcombe text remain the same or largely as they were in the original draft, and that as to the crucial paragraphs 6 and 9 the situation would be as follows:

a) As to immigration, no figure is used in order that the chief obstacle to the first meeting might be removed. Both sides were then left free to bring forward whatever immigration figures they chose.

b) The idea of an agreement on immigration for a limited period is envisaged, although vaguely and in unsatisfactory terms.

"39) I am aware of many objections to these further proposals as thus formulated. A better formulation can, I am convinced, be found through a direct exchange of views or through intermediaries, if there be the will. The important point is that the above formulation indicates a serious attempt on the part of one important factor to bring the discussion another step forward.

"In my opinion, the search for a formula that would enable the calling of the first preliminary meeting should be continued in every possible way and, I cannot repeat too often, with good will. The formulation should not be sought if it is tinctured with a desire to achieve merely a tactical victory. It should not be sought if it is merely an effort to gauge the temper of the other side in this conflict. It should only be sought if the Jewish Agency has an honest desire to sit down and to discuss terms. It is the more necessary to try to meet with the Arabs, seeing that the resolution to this end adopted by the Agency at Zurich in 1937 seems to have met some strange end about which the public, so far as I am aware, has not been informed.

"40) It may be that an agreement can be arrived at with the Palestine Arabs other than those represented by the former Arab Higher Committee. I, for one, do not know who such Arabs are. If we are to make peace, it must be with those of our opponents who have influence and power. But if an agreement is to be come to with the Beyrouth Arab leadership it would seem to be clear that in questions of immigration and land sales they are looking for some kind of 'authorisation' from an Arab Congress or the Arab Kings, i.e. the neighbouring Arab States.

"Even in the Beyrouth version of the Hyamson-Newcombe proposals two facts stand out: 1) that members of the former Arab Higher Committee were ready to meet with the Jewish Agency, a fact of no mean importance; and 2) that conversations on immigration and land sales were envisaged if proper 'authorisation' for this is given them from without.

"It would therefore seem to be part of wisdom for the Jewish Agency to take the initiative and endeavour to bring about this 'authorisation' to these leaders of the Palestine Arabs. The Jewish Agency should, so I think, take the initiative because, if such an 'authorisation' is to be useful, it should be such as would bring about results which the Jews also could accept.

"41) At so critical a juncture in our affairs I think it the duty of everyone of us to offer to be of service in every possible way, and I hope it may be possible for me to meet with the Executive and to be of further service to it. Any further questions that may be put to me I shall be only too glad to answer, if I can."

25 MEETING WITH MUSA ḤUSSEINI—FEBRUARY, 1938

I was in London at the time. I happened to meet Musa Ḥusseini and he said he would like to have a talk with me. We met on February 23, 1938. He opened with a lecture on Zionism. There were three types of Zionism: a spiritual center, a haven for persecuted Jews, and a Jewish State. To the first the Arabs would not object. The second was impossible for objective reasons. Weizmann spoke of six million (in his testimony before the Royal Commission). Palestine could not absorb that number of Jews, and there was thus no solution for Jewish refugees in Palestine. As for a Jewish State—the Arabs would fight it. A Jewish State, just like Lebanon, would only serve as a base for foreign imperialism, and a Jewish Palestine would constitute a wedge between the Arab countries and would interfere with their unification. An agreement should therefore be reached on the percentage of Jews in the country. This percentage could only be one-third, but in order to help Jewish refugees the other Arab countries— Syria, Iraq, Saudi Arabia—would also accept Jewish immigrants. Not all

Arabs would agree even to this—for this was recognition of a Jewish right in the country—but if the Jews accepted, perhaps the Arab leaders would also agree. However, the condition was the elimination of all foreign rule. Palestine would be an independent Arab State, and afterwards, when an Arab Federation or Confederation was established, Palestine would be part of it. That federation would include not only the Arab countries in Asia, but also those in North Africa (Egypt, Tunisia, Algeria, Morocco). And if it should be asked what guarantee there was that the Arabs would act fairly toward the Jewish third, Arab history had already furnished the answer. Never had an Arab state persecuted Jews or oppressed them. What had happened in Palestine was only a defensive war. But if there were an agreement, the riots would end and the Jews would be free to develop their language and culture and would build their spiritual center. There were Jews who agreed to this. Magnes had been in Beirut and met with Nuri Pasha, Jamal and the Mufti. Nuri proved to him that no agreement was conceivable other than on the basis of a Jewish one-third. Magnes was convinced and undertook to persuade the Jewish Agency.

The draft proposed by Hyamson and Newcombe in London and by Magnes in Jerusalem was not and never had been an Arab proposal. He and Tannous had told Newcombe that the Arabs would agree only to a maximum of one-third, on condition the agreement was signed for a given period, and if at the end of that period there was no other agreement then this agreement would remain in force. Hyamson's statement in his letter to the Jewish Agency Executive that the Arab Committee and the Mufti agreed to Newcombe's draft did not contain a grain of truth. They had never agreed to Newcombe's proposal.

I asked: "Would the Arabs have agreed to one-third ten years ago?"

"By no means," Musa Ḥusseini answered. "The Mufti doesn't agree to it even now. He insists on 7 percent, as it was at the end of the World War."

Did that mean that the rest would be driven out? I asked.

No, they did not want to drive anyone out. Four hundred thousand was a fact that must be accepted.

"And if there will be two million Jews in the Jewish State that is now being offered us, will they accept the fact?"

They would accept the fact, he said, but if the state would be unable to absorb a single Jew more and the Jews would then wish to make an agreement with the Arabs, the Arabs would insist that not a single additional Jew enter. I should also know, he said, that if a Jewish State arose, the Arabs would declare war against it and fight.

Wouldn't they care about England and the League of Nations?

If they could not declare war they would organize a boycott, he answered. The Jewish State would have to be industrial, otherwise it would be unable to absorb even two million. The Arabs would boycott our products.

"But in effect you are doing that even now, when there is no Jewish State, aren't you?"

Of course they were fighting, he said, because the Jews were supported by England and were hindering Arab independence.

I asked whether the Arabs were not suffering more from that war than were the Jews.

In what respect? he asked.

Hadn't Jaffa been ruined and Tel Aviv built up?

He admitted the truth of that, but said that Jaffa would rise again.

But meanwhile it was being ruined? I retorted.

That was why he was proposing peace, he answered.

I explained to him what Zionism was, and I advised him not to waste his time in negotiations with Jews who carried no weight among the Jewish people, and not to make proposals which no one would accept.

"Then there is no hope for peace?" he asked.

I told him how I saw the possibility of an alliance between the two peoples. Erez Israel as a Jewish State, open without restriction to every Jew who wished to come there or was forced to do so, would be willing to join an Arab Federation as a free state. But I feared that the time had not yet come for such an alliance, for no Arab leader wished to hear of it. But when a Jewish State was established, and its strength and ability increased, we would find a common language.

Musa Ḥusseini had studied at al-Azhar, and he said he was the only sheikh in the Ḥusseini family. He was now studying Hebrew. He declared himself to be a left-wing socialist, the kind that was between socialism and communism. He wanted to see a socialist government in the Arab State, even though he saw no chance of that. He planned to return to Palestine in the summer.

Out of personal esteem for Magnes, I felt it my duty to write to him about this conversation, and on February 24, 1938 I sent him the following letter from London:

"Dear Dr. Magnes,

"Yesterday Musa Husseini visited me to talk about a Jewish-Arab agreement. His proposal is undoubtedly known to you: fixing the Jewish community in the country at one-third the total population, and arranging Jewish immigration accordingly. Palestine would become an Arab State and would join an Arab Federation or Confederation, which would eventually include all the Arab countries in

Asia and Africa. Naturally, I advised him not to waste his time with such proposals. However, he assured me that he had been told there were important Jewish circles that were prepared to discuss it, and he said that you had gone to Beirut and met with Nuri Sa'id Pasha after his return from London. The Mufti and Jamal Husseini were also present on that occasion and Nuri proved to you that the only possibility of a Jewish-Arab agreement was consent to Jewish immigration in such a way that the Jews would not attain more than one-third of the country's population, and you agreed to this and undertook to persuade the Jewish Agency or other Jewish circles to accept that plan.

"I don't know whether all that Husseini told me is entirely accurate, nor am I aware whether you saw fit to report the content of that talk to the Jewish Agency. But I do know that Nuri Sa'id and the Mufti saw to it that this agreement that was allegedly reached between you and Nuri Sa'id in Beirut was reported immediately to the British Government, and that the Government here received a report that a number of Jews, headed by you, agree to an arrangement with the Arabs whereby the Jews will remain a minority in the country.

"When I asked Musa about the plan which you and Hyamson submitted to us in November 1937 in the name of a group of the Arab Higher Committee, he told me that there was no basis for Hyamson's statement that that draft had been approved by the Arabs. On the contrary, he and Tannous had told Newcombe explicitly that they did not agree to any proposal that would enable the Jews to become more than one-third of the population, and that there was not a grain of truth in Hyamson's letter to the Executive alleging that someone among the Arabs was prepared to enter discussions on the basis of such a plan. The Mufti did not even agree to one-third, for in his opinion the Jews should not exceed 7 percent, but other leaders were prepared to make a concession and agree to one-third. According to his information, there are many Jews who are willing to accept this basis, and when you were in Beirut recently you undertook to recommend this plan to the Jews.

"When I first heard of the proposal submitted to the Executive on behalf of a group of representative and important Arabs, I had a premonition that this was a trick designed to weaken our political position in London. At our meeting in Ussishkin's office on November 22, I expressed that apprehension to you. In the course of time it was made clear by you yourself that the negotiations were neither frank nor authorized. I do not know whether I should rely on Musa Husseini's words and join him in saying that Newcombe and Hyamson have misled us, or whether I am to think that the Arabs deceived Newcombe or that they later changed their minds and are now backing out of their initial proposal. In any event, our caution saved us from the trap that someone laid for us.

"Now there is no doubt, however, that a report has been submitted to the Government in London, on the basis of the information supplied to the British rulers by Nuri Sa'id and the Mufti, to the effect that you agreed to a plan which lays down the rate of Jewish immigration in such a way that the Jews will not exceed one-third of the country's population. According to the report, in agreeing to this plan you relied on an entire Jewish group.

"I would not be fulfilling my duty to you, as a man I have always honored and esteemed for his moral courage and fidelity to Jewish and human ideals, as you understand them, if I did not tell you that I regard this action as a serious and dangerous assault on our political position. As an individual you have a complete right to freedom of opinion, even if you disagree with the most precious aspirations of the Jewish people. We have differed more than once on fundamental Zionist issues, and I have not ceased honoring and esteeming you, but it is impossible not to distinguish between opinion and action. You stand at the head of the supreme cultural institution of the Jewish people, and political circles do not regard you as an individual but as a representative. After the 'error' in the proposals of Hyamson-Newcombe became clear to you, and the representatives of the Mufti stated that they were prepared to hold discussions with us only on a minority status, the Executive informed you that it could not even enter discussions with anyone on the basis of such proposals. You were not unaware that not only the Executive but the whole Zionist movement would regard the entire proposal designed to keep us a minority in the country as undermining the Jewish people and its historic hope. In fact, Nuri Sa'id and the Mufti have already exploited your consent (if they are to be believed in saying you consented) in order to influence the British Government to liquidate the whole policy of the National Home.

"I am forwarding a copy of this letter to the Jewish Agency Executive together with the suggestion that they summon you and demand that you discontinue this activity that is jeopardizing our entire future."

26 BEN-GURION REPLIES TO MAGNES—MARCH, 1938

While in London, I received a copy of Dr. Magnes' long and detailed letter of February 21, 1938, to the Executive. I replied on March 3, 1938, one day after his letter reached me:

"I regret that from your letter to the Executive, one gains the impression that there is a quarrel between you and Shertok. The letters that Shertok sent you were of course written and drafted by him, but Shertok acted in this matter, as in all the political matters with which he deals, as a representative of the Executive. The entire discussion between you and him, as well as your letters and those of Hyamson, were submitted to a meeting of the Executive and that body discussed them and took a decision on them. Shertok acted entirely in accordance with the instructions of the Executive, and I, as a member and chairman of the Executive, take full share of that responsibility.

"I cannot accept your view that Shertok's letter to you of January 25 contains a personal insult. I do not find a single word in it that would justify such an interpretation. He did not attribute any distortions *to you*, but expressed the view of the entire Executive that the proposals which were submitted to it as having been agreed to by members of the Arab Higher Committee turned out, according to your own words, not to have been agreed to at all, so that it was clear that some distortion had been made here by someone.

"Anyone reading the correspondence closely cannot but gain the depressing impression that there was a distortion here, but no one will think that you were the man who knowingly misled the Executive, for the information that you transmitted to us in the middle of January was based on reports that you received from London.

"However, I cannot accept your explanation that there was no deception whatsoever of the Executive, since the proposal which you call 'the Hyamson-Newcombe draft' was submitted to us in London not as a 'suggested basis for discussion between Jewish and Arab representatives,' as you now say in your letter, but as a plan that is 'acceptable' to 'responsible and representative Arabs' (Hyamson's letter to us on November 4, 1937). In reply to Mr. Lourie's question, Hyamson (in his letter of November 8) stated that the Arabs who had agreed to this proposal as a basis of discussion were members of the Arab Higher Committee. The question that still remains to be answered is: was that statement of Hyamson's true or not? At the time, the proposal was sent to us not as that of Hyamson-Newcombe but as a plan agreed to by Arabs. In Hyamson's letter it is stated clearly that the main points in this draft are agreed to by 'representative' Arabs. And in his second letter—that these Arabs are members of the former Arab Higher Committee. Was that statement correct or not? Was Arab approval given to the 'Hyamson-Newcombe Draft,' as Hyamson informed us in his letters, or was it only the proposal of Hyamson-Newcombe, without having obtained Arab approval, as you tell us now? Did the Arabs see the 'Hyamson-Newcombe Draft,' as you now call it, before it was sent to us, or not? If so, did they agree to it or not? If they saw it and did not agree, on what basis did Hyamson write what he did? And if they did not see it at all, the same question can be asked even more pointedly.

"It is surprising that you ignore these questions. On November 19 you met with Shertok and informed him that you had held talks with two groups of Arabs and had found among both a willingness for an agreement. The conversation with each group ended with the formulation of a written proposal, and you submitted the two proposals to Shertok. Since you did not ascribe much importance to the second proposal, I will not deal with it. But Proposal A, which in your last letter you call the 'Hyamson-Newcombe Draft' (and which I believe you called the 'Hyamson

Plan' even then), was recommended by you, since an important Arab group supported it. Did you then think that this plan was agreed to by influential Arabs—or that it was really a proposal of Hyamson-Newcombe directed to both sides? Did you then hear from Arabs that they regarded this plan as a basis for discussion—or not? And if you yourself did not hear this from Arabs, did Hyamson then not inform you that the plan had been agreed to by Arabs as 'a basis for discussion'? Is this true or false? And can it now be said—or can it not—that those who are dealing with this proposal then misled the Executive?

"In your letter, you emphasize again and again that the 'Hyamson-Newcombe Draft' was 'a suggested basis for discussion.' I have already noted above that it was not in this form that the proposal was originally submitted to us. But the main point you ignore in the clarification of the question of whether there was deception here or not is this: Who was the party that 'suggested' the basis for discussion: Hyamson-Newcombe or the Arabs? From all the early letters it would appear that the suggestion, if not originating from Arabs, was agreed to by them. We raised this question more than once in conversations and in letters. We asked for the names of those who had agreed, and we were given names. We were assured that members of the Arab Higher Committee had expressed this agreement. In the middle of January you informed us that these Arabs claimed that they had not agreed. Who, then, deceived us: Hyamson-Newcombe or the Arabs, who for some reason changed their minds? That is the main question, and that question you ignore.

"You dwell in your letter on clarifications of the content of the proposal. It is true that we wished to clarify the true interpretation of the proposal before discussing it and deciding whether it was likely to serve as a basis for discussion or not; but while we were desirous of determining the correct meaning of the draft proposal, we were no less interested in finding out who were its sponsors, if not its drafters. I must say that the answers given to us originally by Hyamson and then by you to this second question contradict the reply we later received from you.

"In your letter of December 3 to Shertok, you write: '*Question:* Is the suggested basis for discussion . . . a basis to which some influential Arabs have agreed? *Answer:* Yes.'

"That answer was supplied to you from London in a letter of November 27. Was it true or not? Are we entitled to say, since you told Shertok on January 12 that the Arabs did not agree to this plan, that there was deception in that 'Yes' or not? Don't you yourself see that your informant in London either deliberately misled you, or that the Arabs first said yes to him and afterwards no to you?

"You yourself admit that in the course of time (paragraph 4 of your letter) you were no longer confident that there was Arab agreement to the plan. Does this fact not prove that there was deception here? We all along had no confidence in Arab agreement to the plan, and our doubt increased after we read, in Answer 2 (your letter of December 3) to the question, 'Who are the Arabs?' the words, 'it is said.'

"This doubt about the authenticity of the answer from London was expressed in Shertok's letter to you on December 6, and for that reason we came to the conclusion that only in a direct meeting with influential Arabs would it be possible to find out *whether there was a basis for discussion or not.* You were requested to 'clarify whether such a meeting is feasible' or, as you phrase it, you 'received authorization from the Jewish Agency to bring about such a meeting.'

"After certain efforts you received a second draft which even in your opinion, as you expressed it to the persons concerned, could not have served as a basis for a meeting with the Jewish Agency. Shertok, of course, confirmed that view, and after the matter was submitted to the Executive it was decided to ask you for an explanation of the contradictions between the first draft ('Hyamson-Newcombe') and the second ('the Beirut draft'). Shertok requested this in his letter to you on January 25, 1938.

"In Para. 15 of your letter it seems to me that you do not present matters in the proper light. You say that you confined yourself scrupulously 'to the terms of reference given to you by the Executive.' The only 'term of reference' (if that is the right term for a request) was 'to clarify the possibility of a meeting with influential Arabs,' and not as you say in this paragraph of your letter 'conversations and soundings that might lead to the preparation of a basis upon which the secret, unofficial, preliminary meeting might take place.' Neither orally nor in writing were you given by the Executive or by Shertok any 'term of reference' to discuss and clarify on what basis a meeting would be possible, but only to ascertain whether the Arabs were willing to meet us for a preliminary, non-binding talk so that we ourselves could determine, in a direct manner, whether or not there was a basis for discussion.

"In the excerpt from the Minute written by the anonymous Englishman, it is stated in Para. 15 of your letter that 'Dr. Magnes translated extracts from two official letters dated 6th and 13th December ... in which the writer stated that *the Jewish Agency was willing to meet representative Arabs upon the basis of this document ...*'

"I have before me the two letters in question, *and they make no mention of the passage I have marked.* I must emphasize this fact, since the Executive has not yet reached the point of discussing whether or not to accept the proposal (the 'Hyamson-Newcombe Draft') as a basis for discussion. It has not yet said yes, and it has not said no, for it is not at all clear to us, and our doubt increases from day to day, that there was any proposal on the part of the Arabs. The entire correspondence between you and Shertok, and all the conversations, were devoted to a clarification of the following points: 1) What is the meaning of the draft? 2) Who are its sponsors? Our stand has been that only if this is an Arab proposal—that is, a proposal that originated with Arabs or was agreed to by them—and not a Jewish or an English proposal, are we interested in considering it as a basis of discussion. We have not yet even discussed among ourselves whether this proposal serves as a basis for discussion or not, and you had no grounds for informing the Arabs that the Executive had accepted the 'Hyamson-Newcombe Draft' as a basis for discussion, as this was certainly not implied in Shertok's letters to you of December 6 and 13. Not a word in these letters says that we regard this draft as a basis for discussion. I do not say that we declared that there was no basis for discussion in this proposal. There was no need for that. For we had our doubts about the authenticity of the proposal. What we decided, and what Shertok passed on to you in his letters of the aforesaid dates, was only that we were prepared to meet with Arabs to clarify whether there was a possibility of negotiations or not, but we did not decide, and we did not inform you, what would be the basis for these negotiations. And an error was made either by you or by the anonymous Englishman when 'It was pointed out that the Jewish Agency itself only accepted the document as a basis for discussion . . .'

"I see no point in the attempts of Hyamson-Newcombe to 'explain' the contradictions between the November-December statements and the later ones. Anyone who has read the letters from Hyamson and yourself and the draft of the 'Beirut' proposal and your remarks about the later talks can judge for himself. Newcombe's statement to you of February 4 and Hyamson's letter to us of November 4 contradict each other too strikingly. After all the new explanations I don't know who misled whom—whether it was the anonymous Arabs that misled Hyamson-Newcombe or Hyamson-Newcombe that misled us, or a combination of both of these. The fact remains that Hyamson's words to us, and your own words to us on the basis of Hyamson's letter, were not in accord with the truth. Who had a greater part in this deception—Hyamson-Newcombe or the anonymous Arabs—is of no interest.

"Apparently certain Arabs agreed to something—to what is not clear—and they later changed their minds. Instead of explaining the reason for the change in the proposals of these Arabs with regard to the basis of the agreement, you try in Para. 19 of your letter to explain why the Arabs changed their minds with regard to *a willingness to meet*. And the reason allegedly is my speech of December 21. This entire explanation is amazing:

1) On January 12, you informed Shertok that the Arabs were prepared to meet with us, but only on the basis of 'the Beirut Plan.' We refused to meet on such a basis. For what purpose do you state that the possibility of the meeting was ruled out by the Arabs after they read my speech?

2) No one asked why the Arabs did not wish to meet us. The question was, and it remains after all of Newcombe's explanations, why another proposal was made to us. It was about *this contradiction* in the Arab position—as it was reported to us by you and by Hyamson—that we asked, and instead of an answer to this question you explain why the Arabs changed their minds about their willingness to meet with us. What has one thing to do with the other?

"I see no need to apologize for my speech. It was not an expression of my personal opinion but of the position of the Zionist movement and that of the Jewish Agency. However, since the gentlemen from Beirut (or from any other place) saw fit to say that they regarded my speech as bad faith on the part of the Jewish Agency, I must ask: Were these gentlemen ever told that the Jewish Agency was prepared to discuss a minority situation? I do not imagine even for a moment that you could have told them such a thing, and it is difficult for me to conceive that anyone else could have told them that. What then is the basis for the claim of these 'knights in shining armor'? When did these gentlemen hear from us that we were prepared to discuss with them our permanent status as a minority in the country?

"You were present on a number of occasions during my conversations with Arabs. Did I not say each time that what we want is millions of Jews in the country, and that the only limitation we accept on Jewish immigration is the objective restriction of the possibility of economic absorption?

"With these gentlemen, of whom you hint, we held no negotiations on this occasion. Hyamson and you brought us a proposal, and we said we were prepared to meet with the Arabs. We did not even manage to meet and talk to them, and these gentlemen already accuse us of bad faith. Bad faith toward whom?

"I note that you defended me, and I am sure that you did so with the best intentions. But I see no need for coming to my defense. I stand by every single word in my statement of December 21. Neither I nor my colleagues submitted proposals to anyone which we later repudiated, and the Arabs who did so (if we are to believe Hyamson-Newcombe) are the last ones to assume a pose of righteous indignation.

"If the Arabs did back out of proposals they had agreed to, there is no doubt that the reason for their repudiation was the White Paper and the rumors that preceded it. This was clear to me as soon as I heard from Shertok about your talk with him on January 12, and what you state in Para. 20 of your letter verifies that assumption. You are simply wrong when you say that Shertok ignored this. Shertok, like me, understood the reason for the change in the position of the Arabs, if indeed there had been a change in position. From the first moment we suspected that the entire 'plan' was simply meant to thwart the establishment of the Jewish State, and that it was only fear of the Jewish State that had impelled the Arabs to propose or to agree to some understanding with Jews. As soon as it was apparent to them that this fear had disappeared, they reconsidered for their own reasons.

"One can only wonder why, after this became evident even to you, you continued to maintain contact with these gentlemen.

"In Paras. 21–27 of your letter, you explain your reasons in favor of a meeting between Arabs and the Jewish Agency. And the impression might be gained that the Jewish Agency was opposed to a meeting. You know as well as I do that this is not the case. The Jewish Agency was opposed to a meeting on the basis of the 'Beirut' draft. But it agreed unconditionally to a meeting if the other side, knowing the attitude of the Jewish Agency, would also agree to one. Shertok informed you of this in the most explicit language in his letter to you of January 13, when he said: 'The Jewish Agency rejects the draft of the other side as a basis for negotiations, and it states that it will not enter into any discussion of it. If the other side wishes a meeting with the Jewish Agency after knowing that this is its attitude, then the Jewish Agency is willing to meet.'

"It seems to me that it was your duty to point out that it was not the fault of the Jewish Agency that the meeting did not take place. The only 'charge' that can be laid against the Jewish Agency—and I assume full responsibility for it—is that it absolutely refused to enter into any discussion whatsoever on the basis of 'the Beirut draft.' However, it expressed its willingness to meet—without presenting to the other side any plan as a precondition or as a necessary basis for discussion. There was no need or grounds for explaining, as you do in your letter, the value of a meeting. Our willingness to meet without prior conditions still holds good. Naturally, that does not mean that we do not have *a priori* views and demands from which we will not budge under any circumstances. The other side also surely has views and demands from which it will not budge. Nevertheless, we were and are willing to meet with the other side to clarify whether there is or is not a basis for an understanding and an agreement, permanent or temporary. That has been our stand throughout the years, and it has not changed.

"I will not discuss here a number of details at the end of your letter. I am sure that insofar as they pertain to Shertok personally he will deal with them himself. Perhaps I have no right to pass in silence over your startling assertion in Para. 33 of your letter. You state that you knew, contrary to what Shertok had told you in his letter of January 25, that the Executive had accepted the Hyamson plan as a basis for discussion, and you go on to say that if that was not the case one must arrive at damaging conclusions about the political morality of the Jewish Agency. I identify myself completely with what Shertok wrote to you in that letter, and I ask you: When did we announce that we accepted the Hyamson plan as a basis for discussion? When did we inform you even that we had in anyway discussed the proposals as such? When did we authorize you to inform the other side that we accepted any basis whatsoever for discussion?

"It is true that 'the London draft' was thoroughly examined by us, because we had grounds for doubting the honesty of its intentions, its authenticity and its political meaning (and not without reason, as it later transpired), but never did we reach the stage of discussion on the draft itself. Read carefully all of Shertok's letters to you, recall the questions which Shertok, Ussishkin and I put to you at our meeting on November 22—all of these were designed to clarify the two questions which I have already mentioned several times in this letter: 1) What is the intention of the proposal? 2) Who are its sponsors? As soon as we became aware that this would not be clarified by means of talks and correspondence with you, we said that we would do so at a direct meeting, for 'the only way to bring out the facts as they are and arrive at real negotiations, in case such are possible, is to arrange a meeting between ourselves and the Arabs.'

"That meeting did not materialize, and the Executive never even got down to a discussion of any basis whatsoever, neither did it decide affirmatively or negatively on Hyamson's draft, for it neither wishes nor is obliged to discuss the proposal of a Jew or an Englishman. It would discuss the proposal of an Arab if it believed that Arab to be a man of stature. Such a document we did not have before us, and the only decision reached by the Executive was that it was willing to meet. No less or more than that. You ask: 'If this text has never been accepted even as a basis for discussion, why is it that from first to last this text was the subject of our letters and talks?' For a simple reason: we wanted to know if this draft was something meriting consideration. The Jewish Agency does not latch onto every proposal it receives. What was the content of the 'letters and talks' that you rely on? Only questions and examinations of the content of the proposal and of the authority of its sponsors, and nothing more. If you bring me a proposal and I ask you, 'In whose name does this proposal come, and what does it mean?' does that constitute acceptance of the proposal as a basis? I do not say that we rejected the proposal as a basis, but I claim that we did not even arrive at a discussion of the proposal as such, and we never informed you, explicitly or implicitly, that we accepted the plan as a basis.

"Each of us could have evaluated this or that paragraph in 'the plan' positively or negatively. Personally, if I believed that this proposal really came from Arabs who carry weight I would regard it as a big step toward an understanding, even though I would not accept the proposal as it stands. Other members of the Executive might think otherwise. However, none of us was even asked to express an opinion on the proposal, because we did not know whether this was in any way an authorized proposal.

"From what you say in Para. 35 of your letter it would appear that at first the Executive authorized you to mediate and later repudiated you. I emphatically deny this charge. It was not we who approached you to mediate between us and Arabs. You and your friends or acquaintances in London conducted negotiations with Arabs, and a proposal was submitted to us by you. We said that instead of correspondence and conversations with you we preferred to meet with the Arabs themselves, if there were such, in order to clarify on what basis they were prepared, and whether they were prepared at all, to hold discussions with us. It is not your fault that the meeting did not come about. But you have no grounds for thinking and writing that we repudiated the authorization that we gave you. You were asked to clarify whether the Arabs were prepared to meet with us—neither more nor less. And I don't know why you speak of 'strategic retreats' and 'jockeying for . . . political advantage.'

"If someone misled you or withdrew his approval of the proposal you submitted to us, it was not Shertok or any other member of the Jewish Agency. It is very strange that after you defend Newcombe and Hyamson and the Arab parties, you accuse the Jewish Agency of having resorted to unfair tactics.

"Permit me to say, finally, that neither I nor my colleagues in the Executive ever suspected you of having deliberately supplied us with incorrect information. However, after carefully reading your letter, it is clear to me that we were deceived from beginning to end in this whole wretched business. It is difficult for me to say how much of this deception is to be attributed to bad will and how much to irresponsibility. I know that Newcombe is a blatant anti-Zionist. But that alone is not sufficient reason to charge him with deception. A person can be an anti-Zionist and honest too. But I regret to say that his role, and that of Hyamson, in this 'opera' was not above suspicion. As for the Mufti and his people, I have no need to suspect. I am familiar with their machinations. In the very days when they purportedly sought a way to peace they organized acts of murder and terror in the country. You did not fully appreciate the fact that we were willing to meet even with these murderers, if there was only the faintest hope that we could arrive at an understanding that would enable us to continue our enterprise peacefully.

"But we will not lend a hand to the stratagems and plots of the Mufti and his supporters in England. While we do not resort to stratagems ourselves, we will not fall victims to those of the other side. We will examine seven times every plan and every proposal that is supported by these deadly enemies of ours. We are not afraid and we do not refuse to meet with them, but we will not rush to fall into their trap. In this entire matter you acted out of good intentions; of that I have no doubt. But intention alone is not enough. It is clear to me that your honest striving for peace is being exploited in order to undermine our position. In fact, your activity, against your will, only widens the breach between us and the Arabs. I do not complain about your views, though I disagree with them, but I regret your lack of caution and your discussions with the other side without the prior knowledge and consent of the Jewish Agency Executive.

"With respect and esteem,
"David Ben-Gurion

"P.S. After finishing my letter, I received your cable in reply to my letter to you of February 24. I am glad to see your denial and await your letter. I must tell you that I have information from a totally reliable source that Nuri Pasha informed the British Government as follows: That he met in Beirut with you and the Anglican Bishop of Jerusalem and discussed a settlement of the Palestine question on the basis of *a perpetual Jewish minority*. According to him, you said you hoped to persuade the Jewish Agency Executive to authorize you to negotiate with the Arabs on this basis, and if the Jewish Agency did not accept the proposal then Jews of America, England and Germany would break away from the Jewish Agency and make an agreement with the Arabs on their own.

"I am not responsible for the veracity of Nuri's words, but the source from which

I received this information leaves no doubt in my mind that this report was transmitted by Nuri in your name to a representative of the British Government. "These things speak for themselves.

"I am sending a copy of this letter to the Jewish Agency Executive."

27 TALK WITH SAUDI AMBASSADOR—AUGUST, 1938

At a meeting of the Executive held with Dr. Magnes on April 24, 1938, to clarify the development of the various proposals for a Jewish-Arab agreement, the identity of the sponsors, and the meaning of the contradictions that had come to light in the course of time, Magnes said that talks had been held in America, England and Geneva. In the talks in America, the participants on the Arab side were Dr. Tannous, Amin al-'Attawna and Shattara, who heads the Arab organization in the United States. The Jewish representatives were non-Zionists and several members of the American-Jewish Committee. These talks took place in the months of May and June, 1937. In England talks were held in July and August. The participants on the Arab side were Dr. Tannous, Jamal Husseini, Arslan, and a few others. On the part of the English there were Newcombe and a few Members of Parliament whose names Dr. Magnes did not know. Hyamson also took part in these talks, and he submitted a report on them to Neville Laski, Lord Samuel and a few others.

In Geneva, talks were held with Auni Abdul Hadi, Dr. Tannous and others. On the Jewish side there were Messrs. Becker and Orlinsky. The two reported on the talks to Dr. Magnes.

The talks in America, England and Geneva were connected with one another. The plan called the Hyamson-Newcombe draft was received by Dr. Magnes direct from Hyamson. The second proposal, which is mentioned above, was received by Dr. Magnes direct from Arabs. From the questions and answers at the meeting of the Executive three points were clarified:

1) Dr. Magnes was misled as to the agreement of the Mufti to a Jewish-Arab agreement.

2) Newcombe was not authorized, according to what Magnes said in the name of Jamal Husseini and his colleagues, to include a paragraph on Jewish immigration in his proposal.

3) Jamal Husseini and his colleagues after a certain time changed their minds about their willingness to meet with representatives of the Jewish Agency, either because I in one of my speeches said that the Jewish Agency was not prepared

to discuss with any party the idea that the Jews should permanently remain a minority in Ereẓ Israel, or, more likely, because they saw in the Ormsby-Gore despatch published at the beginning of 1938 a sign that the Jewish State plan was no longer favored by the British Government. From what Magnes said at the meeting it was clear that he too was not prepared to propose a plan to turn the Jews in Ereẓ Israel into a permanent minority. Dr. Magnes emphatically denied that in talks with Nuri Pasha he had agreed to a Jewish minority.

The Government in the course of 1938 withdrew its endorsement of the recommendations of the Peel Commission. After the Commission submitted its Report there was a two-day debate in the House of Lords (July 19–20, 1937), and immediately thereafter a debate in the House of Commons. In both houses, sharp criticism was leveled at the conclusions of the Commission and at the Government's decision to accept them. The critics included Winston Churchill, Lloyd George and Labour members. Three shortcomings were stressed: the small size of the area proposed for the Jewish State, the exclusion of new Jerusalem from the jurisdiction of the Jewish State, and the failure to allocate the Negev to the Jewish State. As a result of this criticism, or taking advantage of it, the Government withdrew its approval of the conclusions of the Royal Commission and appointed a new body, the Woodhead Commission, to examine the partition plan. In November 1938 this commission submitted a new proposal, which neither the Jews nor the Arabs could possibly accept, for in effect it was not a plan of partition between Jews and Arabs but one for the abolition of the Mandate and maintenance of British rule in the country without any obligations, either to the Jews or to the Arabs.

On August 24, 1938, a German Jew by the name of Richard Altmann called on me to say that the Ambassador of King Ibn Saud in London wished to meet me. The meeting took place the next day, on August 25, 1938, at the Ambassador's home.

Ḥafiz Wahbah received me cordially, and when he offered me a cup of coffee he explained that according to Arab custom a guest's refusal to have a cup of coffee is a sign of unfriendliness, whereas drinking the coffee is a sign of peaceful and friendly relations between guest and host.

At first we spoke of the position of the Jews in the Arab countries: Iraq, Yemen, Egypt, and others. Ḥafiz Wahbah asked why the relations between Arabs and Jews were amicable in all these countries, and why the situation was different in Palestine. In his opinion, the Jews who came to Palestine from Poland and Rumania were apparently different from the veteran inhabitants of Palestine, who had always lived as good neighbors with the Arabs.

I commented that he had undoubtedly heard of the riots that had broken out nine years before, in 1929. The most serious rioting had actually occurred in Hebron and Safad, where the Jews had been living for hundreds of years, and it was precisely they who were murdered by their Arab neighbors. I asked him whether the report in the London *Evening Standard* of August 23, 1938, about his Government's support of a ten-year truce plan between the Jews and Arabs in Palestine was correct. He believed that there was no foundation to the report. It was true that six months before there had been such proposals, but they had had no substance, and nothing new had taken place recently. He had heard that Lord Samuel had proposed the fixing of certain ratios between the two peoples, and such a proposal had also come from Nuri Pasha and from British Foreign Office sources. He had heard that Dr. Weizmann was inclined to consider Nuri Pasha's proposal. I said that it was well-known that Lord Samuel was interested in such an arrangement and that he had even spoken about it in the House of Lords the year before, after the publication of the Report of the Royal Commission, but that there was no foundation for saying that the Jewish Agency or Dr. Weizmann as its head were prepared even to consider such a proposal, which from our point of view was quite out of the question. We would never accept limitation of Jewish immigration to a certain percentage of the total population. We were only willing to agree that the immigration would not rise above the country's economic absorptive capacity—that it be neither higher or lower.

A discussion on the Arabs in Palestine ensued. Ḥafiz Wahbah insisted that there was a difficulty in getting Palestinian Arabs to meet with Jewish representatives. They were afraid to be seen talking to Jews, for those who had met with Jews were said to be in their pay. He told me of his own experience. A few years before he had said in a newspaper interview, inter alia, that Jerusalem was a holy city, not only to the Moslems but also to the Jews and Christians, and that it was only proper that peace and quiet should prevail in the Holy City. Two days after the interview appeared in print he received stacks of cables protesting against that statement, and in one he was asked: "How many thousands of pounds did you get from the Jews?"

I told him that I myself had conferred with a few Arab leaders, including Auni Abdul Hadi, and that at first we had tried to find a foundation for mutual understanding based on a Jewish Ereẓ Israel in an Arab Federation, but when the riots began in 1936 he came out against any Jewish immigration and I feared that there was now no basis for an agreement. Ḥafiz concurred, saying: "Yes, everyone is now afraid he may be accused of treason."

I said that for that reason I had come to the conclusion that the only personality in the Arab world who was sufficiently strong and independent to do something was King Ibn Saud, and that we would be happy to meet with him in order to consider the situation. Ḥafiz Wahbah replied that it would be helpful to have a discussion with him. It would be worth writing to him on the subject. The difficulty in arranging such a meeting was that Ibn Saud had gone to Jedda for the beginning of the pilgrimage to Mecca, and that would take four months. Ibn Saud did not like to receive visitors at Riadh; the only place for a meeting was Jedda, and that was impossible now. He (Ḥafiz Wahbah) was prepared to write to Ibn Saud, and he himself might be going to Mecca that year.

I asked Wahbah whether, since the King himself could not meet with us at Jedda then, but only in four months' time, there was no possibility that he would delegate someone to discuss the situation with us on his behalf. Ḥafiz Wahbah believed that no one could take the place of the King, and that the only effective intervention conceivable would be that of the King himself. He added that the Emir Saud (Ibn Saud's son) was living not far from Wahbah's own house during his stay in London, but that this was a strictly private visit (he had come for dental treatment), and he did not interfere in political matters. He, Ḥafiz Wahbah, would accompany the Emir Saud when he went to Paris, and perhaps also to Saudi Arabia. The Emir would sail from Marseilles on September 10 and return to Arabia. But he, Ḥafiz Wahbah, would write to the King. He asked me where I could be found in London, and we exchanged addresses and telephone numbers.

He asked—in the event that the Arabs and Jews reached an agreement—whether the British Government would be willing to accept it. I expressed my opinion, based on my talks with the High Commissioner, in the affirmative, and Ḥafiz Wahbah agreed with me.

In general, he seemed to be a pleasant man, without resentment or hatred and ready to be of help. He was cautious, but wise. I recalled what Armstrong had told me about Ibn Saud's ways at our meeting in May 1937, and I saw from Ḥafiz Wahbah's behavior that his evaluation was correct.

Meanwhile, the British Government for reasons of its own undertook to arrange a meeting of Jews and Arabs in London at the beginning of 1939.

Dr. Weizmann, as President of the Zionist Organization, and I, as Chairman of its Executive, met immediately with the Colonial Secretary, Malcolm MacDonald, and Dr. Weizmann asked him whether the Government intended to condemn the Jews to be a minority in Palestine. MacDonald assured us that there were no grounds for such an apprehension.

David Ben-Gurion in the thirties

Moshe Sharett (Shertok)

Judah Leib Magnes

Dov (Bernard) Joseph

Musa Alami

Ḥussein Khalidi

Haj Amin el-Ḥusseini, Mufti of Jerusalem

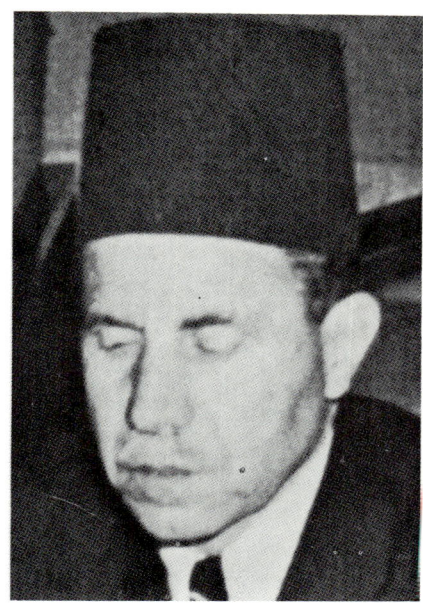
Jamal el-Ḥusseini

Pinhas Rutenberg

Moshe Smilansky

Justice Gad Frumkin

Moshe Novomeysky

Chaim Weizmann

Menahem Ussishkin

Sir Arthur Wauchope

H. St. John Philby

The Arab Delegation at the St. James' Palace Conferences, 1939. *Front row (starting 2nd from left)*: Ragheb Nashashibi, Jamal Husseini, Auni Abdel Hadi; *(at end)*: Hikmat el-Masri. *Left-hand table (left to right)*: Azzam Pasha, Abdel-Haleq Sarwat, Ali Maher Pasha, Amir Abdul Moneim; Yemenite delegation—Amir Saif ul-Islam al-Husain *(in center)*. *Right-hand table (2nd from right)*: Nuri el-Sa'id; *(at end)*: Emir Faisal (Saudi Arabia). *Center back*: Neville Chamberlain; *on his right*: Lord Halifax; *on his left*: Malcolm MacDonald

The Jewish Delegation at the St. James' Palace Conferences, 1939. *Front row (left to right)*: Maurice Perlzweig, Nahum Goldmann, Selig Brodetsky, Chaim Weizmann, David Ben-Gurion, Mrs. Rose Jacobs, Moshe Sharett, Arthur Lourie. *Left-hand table (outside—from middle)*: Leonard Stein, Lord Reading, Lord Bearsted; *(inside)*: Lavi Bakstansky, Israel Feldman, Rabbi Moshe Blau, Jacob Rosenheim, Chief Rabbi J.H. Hertz. *Right-hand table (inside)*: Rabbi J.K. Glodbloom, Berl Katznelson; *(last)*: Izhak Ben-Zvi; *(outside)*: Berl Locker; Harry Sacher; Sholem Asch

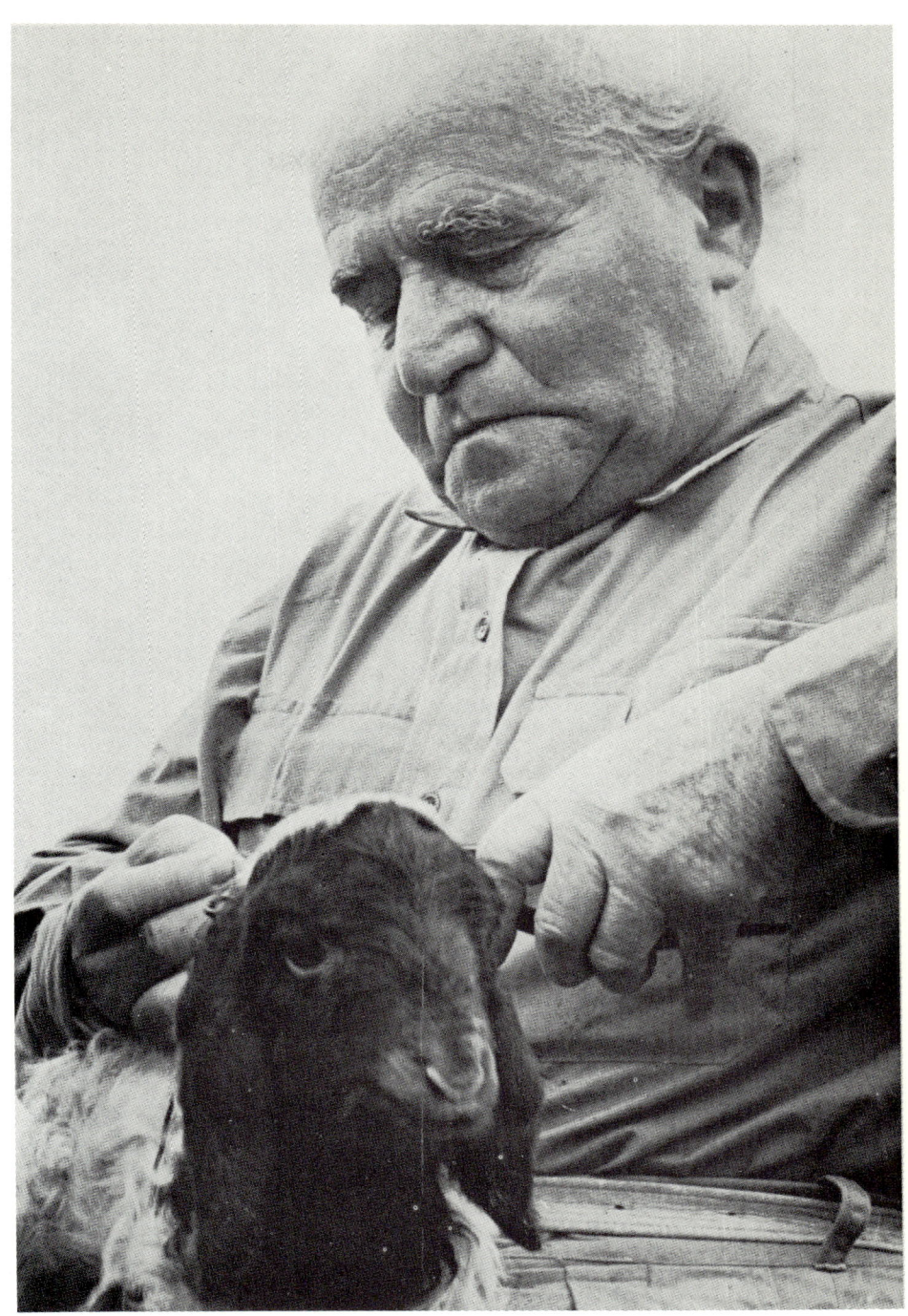

David Ben-Gurion at his kibbutz home in Sdeh Boker, 1954

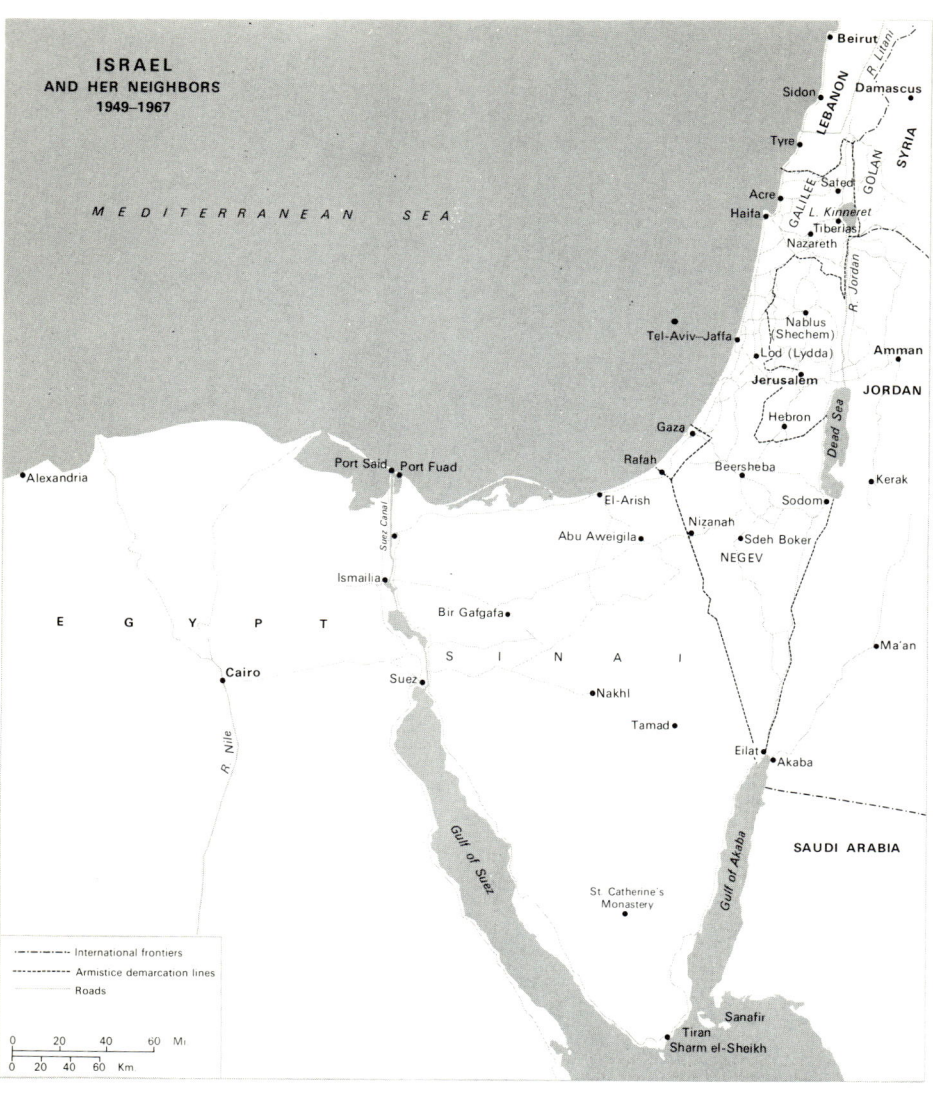

28 LONDON CONFERENCE OPENS—FEB. 2, 1939

Not only delegates of the Jewish Agency were invited to the London talks from the Jewish side, but also representatives of Agudat Israel from England and America, of the Jews of Britain, America and Poland, of the Vaad Leumi (National Council) of the Jews of Palestine, of the Mizrahi, and of the English Zionists.

On the Arab side, representatives of all the Arab parties in Palestine were invited: Jamal Husseini, Musa Alami, Dr. Hussein Khalidi, Auni Abdul Hadi, George Antonius, Amin Tamimi, Alfred Roch, Jacob Ghussein, Fuad Saba and Ragheb Nashashibi. Nashashibi, however, did not take part in the talks, since the Mufti's people would not sit down together with him.

Also invited were delegates from Egypt, Saudi Arabia, Iraq, Yemen and Transjordan. The Arabs refused to sit together with the Jews, and the British Government arranged for separate meetings.

At the first meeting with the Jews, on February 7, 1939, the British Government was represented by the Prime Minister, Neville Chamberlain, the Foreign Minister, Lord Halifax, the Colonial Secretary, Malcolm MacDonald, the Under Secretary of State, R. A. Butler, and Lord Dufferin and a number of officials.

The Jews who participated in this meeting were: Dr. Chaim Weizmann, David Ben-Gurion, Prof. Selig Brodetsky, Dr. Nahum Goldmann, Mrs. Rose Jacobs, Rev. M. L. Perlzweig, and Moshe Sharett—members of the Zionist Executive; Sholem Asch, Viscount Bearsted, Izhak Ben-Zvi (Chairman, Vaad Leumi), Rabbi Meyer Berlin (President of the World Mizrahi Organization), Rabbi M. Blau (Chairman of Agudat Israel, Jerusalem), Rabbi J. K. Goldbloom (Chairman of the English Zionist Federation), Harry A. Goodman (Agudat Israel, England), Rabbi Joseph H. Hertz (Chief Rabbi of the British Empire), Berl Katznelson, Berl Locker, Dr. J. M. Machover, Dr. B. Mossinsohn, Lord Reading, J. Rosenheim (President of Agudat Israel, England), Harry Sacher, Leonard J. Stein (Counsel to the Jewish Agency), Robert Szold (representative of the American Zionists), Dr. B. Weill-Halle, and Dr. Stephen S. Wise.

Chamberlain opened the meeting with the following address:

"This is not the occasion for any detailed discussion of the matters which will form the subject of our future deliberations, and I do not propose to enter upon a long speech. When His Majesty's Government first announced their intention to invite representatives of the Jews and the Arabs to separate discussions, they made it clear that opportunity would be given to both peoples to state their views and proposals without any reservations. Mr. MacDonald informed the House of Commons last November that the Government would enter the discussions bound by their obligations under the Mandate—obligations to both Jews and Arabs—and bound by their duty to Parliament and to the other members of the League of Nations and to the United States of America; but that the Government would not seek to prevent either the Arab or the Jewish representatives from presenting arguments, if they were so disposed, as to why the Mandate should be changed. These discussions are to be full, frank and free. In conformity with this undertaking, the representatives of the United Kingdom will not commence the proceedings by laying down any basis of discussion, nor will they offer their own views until both Jews and Arabs, in our separate discussions with them, have been given a full opportunity of putting their case.

"Those of you who have followed the course of international affairs during the past few years—and surely everyone must do that in these days when events in one place may affect us all in every part of the world—those of you who follow these affairs will, I hope, need no assurance that the object underlying the policy of the Government of which I am the head is the promotion of peace; peace in our relations with the European countries with which our interests and destinies are so closely interlocked; and peace in the lands for whose administration we bear a special responsibility. I need hardly say how deeply His Majesty's Government deplore the unhappy events in Palestine, which have brought severe material loss, and distraction of mind, and insecurity to every community there. I would here pay tribute to the discipline and restraint which have been shown generally by the Jewish community during a period of extreme difficulty and danger in Palestine. We all have a deep attachment, a special attachment, to Palestine, and surely we all carry in our hearts a fervent hope that peace and prosperity will soon be restored.

"I have said that our policy is one of peace. You will be aware that my particular method of approach to peace is through understanding, and the first essential step to understanding is personal contact.

"The problem before us is a difficult one; it has sometimes been called insoluble. But the more difficult the problem the more I am convinced of the importance of personal contact between men of influence concerned. During your stay in London I shall hope to deepen my personal acquaintance with you and, so far as my other duties permit, to participate in your deliberations. You will appreciate that the pressure on a Prime Minister's time is such that I must leave it to my colleagues in the United Kingdom Delegation to bear the main brunt of the discussions, but I shall follow their progress with the closest attention and do all that is in my power to promote their success.

"It is the task of statesmanship when faced by what may appear to be a deadlock between two peoples to achieve a compromise on the basis of justice. This is the task before us—difficult, no doubt, but surely not beyond the capacity of our united powers. We are meeting in a Royal Palace which His Majesty the King has graciously placed at our disposal. The history of these stately rooms stretches back 400 years, and is intimately connected with our national story during those centuries. Your people no less than ours have cherished traditions and a history which stretch far back into the past, but, while not unmindful of what lies behind us, let us concentrate on the realities of the present situation, giving due weight to all essential facts and endeavouring to appreciate each other's point of view. In this spirit lies our best hope of achieving a settlement of our present problem which will provide a foundation on which mutual understanding may grow, and peace in Palestine be at last secured."

Dr. Weizmann, in his reply, began by thanking the Prime Minister for his welcome and the King for enabling the Conference to meet in "these auspicious surroundings." He continued:

"One historical association which occurs to me is that it was in this very Palace, maybe in this very room, that the Palestine Mandate was finally approved by the Council of the League of Nations on July 24th, 1922, at a session at which the late Lord Balfour represented His Majesty's Government.
"It gives me special pleasure to be able to address myself to you, Mr. Prime Minister, in view of the deep sympathy which your illustrious father and you yourself have shown for the lot of the Jewish people.
"We have responded to the invitation extended to us by His Majesty's Government, and appear before you here, to state the Jewish case in regard to Palestine, and to hear the views of His Majesty's Government on that subject, with a view to reaching an agreed policy. Our aspiration has always been for peace in Palestine which is I am sure compatible with the maintenance of our fundamental rights. Peace—Shalom—is our watchword in Palestine. I sincerely hope that the discussions which you and your colleagues will be conducting with the Arab representatives will also contribute to the achievement of the same object.
"Our delegation here comprises representatives of the Jewish Agency—the body recognised by the Mandate as the official mouthpiece of the Jewish people in relation to Palestine—and of Jewish circles and organisations who are lending it their co-operation at the present juncture—representatives of the Jewish communities in various countries, the Agudath Israel Organisation, and gentlemen like Lord Reading and Lord Bearsted, who appear here in their individual capacities.
"We meet you at a dark hour in our history; it is no exaggeration to say that the hopes and prayers of millions of Jews, scattered throughout the world, are now centered, with unshaken confidence in British good faith, on these deliberations.

We believe that all our work in Palestine has been the result of a grim necessity to face realities, and I would submit that no reality is today more bitter than that which the Jewish people is called upon to face. Your own kind reference to the stand made by Palestine Jewry during the present hour of trial would also appear to testify to the capacity of the Jews to face realities. We have endeavoured through all these difficult years to maintain the co-operation with the British Government which has always been the corner-stone of our policy, and we are approaching our present task in the same spirit."

Izhak Ben-Zvi then spoke in Hebrew. His remarks were as follows:

"On behalf of the Jewish population of Palestine I would like to thank you, Sir, most cordially for the kind words of appreciation which you were good enough to devote to us. The line of conduct of the Palestine Jewish community in the hard trial of the past three years is that enjoined upon us by the ideals of peace, justice and human brotherhood preached by our prophets, and by the unshaken will of our people to rebuild the ruins of its native land, even under attack.

"Palestine Jewry, although consisting largely of newcomers, is really the most ancient Jewish community in the world. In spite of repeated destructions which we have sustained during our long history, by Babylon, Greece, Rome, Persia and other invaders, the remnant of Israel has clung to the Land. It kept alive the connection between the whole people and Palestine, and our hope of return to Zion. This hope has not been deceived. Through all the centuries of the dispersion, and from all parts of the Diaspora, Jews have been coming back to Palestine. When Lord Allenby's armies conquered the country, they contained a Jewish Legion from Palestine, together with Jewish Legions from the United Kingdom and America.

"On behalf of this Jewish Community may I say that, just as we shall continue in all circumstances to devote our energy to our work of reconstruction, so shall we do our utmost to preserve peace and justice in that country. And this is in accordance with the prophet's words: 'For Zion's sake will I not hold my peace, and for Jerusalem's sake I will not rest, until the righteousness thereof go forth as brightness and the salvation thereof as a lamp that burneth'."

29 WEIZMANN'S ADDRESS—FEB. 8, 1939

The second session, on February 8, was devoted to Dr. Weizmann's statement. While recognizing the very great difficulties in which the British Government found itself, he declared:

"There are certain vital interests which it is our duty to safeguard, and certain rights which we cannot surrender, particularly at a time when the Jewish position in the world is more tragic than when I had the honour of appearing two years ago, in November, 1936, before the Royal Commission. This is the third time in the course of two years that it has fallen to my lot to open a discussion leading up to a close scrutiny of the affairs of Palestine. Sometimes it seems to me that we are like an impatient gardener who pulls a plant out of the soil, looks at the roots, and puts it in again, in the hope that the plant may grow."

Since he had dealt with the Jewish problem as a whole in his address before the Royal Commission, he felt that he need not go over the same ground again. Summarizing the situation at the present time, he went on:

"A Commission was sent to Palestine. It was invested with great authority and dignity. It consisted of people of great experience in administration and in English political life. They worked extremely hard; they went all over the country; they had a great many witnesses before them, Jews, Arabs, and British, and they presented a unanimous Report. The central point of that Report was a suggestion that, in order to satisfy the legitimate claims of both sides, and at the same time ease the task of the Mandatory Power, a partition of Palestine into two States, one Jewish and one Arab, should be effected. His Majesty's Government announced in July, 1937, their adoption in principle of this solution, and one of their main reasons for adopting it was that, among other things, it would secure the establishment of a Jewish National Home on proper foundations, and relieve it of any danger or possibility of being subjected in future to Arab rule; it would convert the Home into a State with full control of immigration.

"I need not hide from you that the proposal of the Royal Commission was a shock to Jewish public opinion. It divided historic Palestine after it had been divided once already. Grave doubts arose in our midst, and this policy was not regarded by many in the Zionist Movement and outside it, as equivalent to what had been promised in the Balfour Declaration and subsequently embodied in the Mandate. It became a matter of first class controversy in our own ranks; but, after a good deal of heart-searching, at the Congress at Zurich we decided by a considerable majority (something like 60% or over) to explore this possibility and to see how we could co-operate with His Majesty's Government even on a proposal of that kind.

"It was perfectly clear that two guiding principles had been laid down by the Royal Commission, and accepted by the Government: namely, that the Jews should, within the territory allotted to them, be in sole control of immigration without outside interference, and they should be guaranteed against becoming a minority or leading a minority life—the sort of life which we have to lead all over the world. I believe that whatever may have been the fate of the partition proposal, these two main principles still have their full moral binding force...

"May I remind you of the debate in the House of Commons and also in the Lords, on the Report? I think I am not exaggerating or overstating if I say that the general sense of the debate was that the Jews were not getting a square deal, and that the proposal was not an equivalent to the promise given, but was something much less.

"There was another important point which was made clear in the Royal Commission's Report. The Royal Commission was satisfied, after having investigated the matter thoroughly, that the Balfour Declaration *did* mean that eventually a Jewish State might arise in the whole of Palestine. In the words of the Royal Commission, it would depend mainly on the zeal and enterprise of the Jews whether the 'Home' would become large enough to be a State. As a necessary corollary of this very important statement, I venture to submit that it would seem to rule out any artificial restriction on Jewish immigration and again any relegation to minority status. . . .

"I cannot conceive that the Government, after twenty years, should be retreating from its moral and political position, and seeking an interpretation of the Mandate which might lead to a further curtailing of our fundamental rights. I, for one, consider it impossible, and impossible not only from a purely Jewish point of view but because there are legally binding documents; and, if I may say so with the utmost possible respect, I believe it to be inconceivable from a British point of view. I believe that the whole structure of the British Empire is such that a retreat from a great moral position such as that embodied in this policy, would mean such a departure from tradition as would shake its very moral foundation. . . .

"This is why I cannot believe that even political expediency may possibly lead to fundamental changes in the principles of a policy on the basis of which we have worked, expended our energy, our blood, our efforts, for almost a generation. But you can imagine that in these difficult times for us—and if I say 'difficult' I err on the side of understatement—certainty about these fundamentals is essential. I think that the two above-mentioned underlying principles in the Report of the Royal Commission are valid, even if the actual Report has not been carried into effect."

Dr. Weizmann went on to survey developments since the publication of the Royal Commission's report, and continued:

"Let us see the net result. The Mandate has been declared unworkable; the Peel Report has been destroyed; the Woodhead Report is going the way of the Peel Report; and all we are left with, at the present stage, is the so-called 'political high level' for immigration—one of the palliatives which the Peel Report suggested as an alternative in case their project should not be adopted. Three years have elapsed, a time during which the artificial restriction of immigration has caused us great suffering, suffering which, I submit with respect, was avoidable. I do not want to be offensive, or to harp on the matter, or appear to you as a carping critic, but it has led to the refusal of admission into Palestine of young children and old people from Germany. I do not want to harass your feelings by picturing to you, even if I could, what it means in reality. In order to bring it a little more into relief, perhaps you will permit me to mention something which I saw a few days ago in the press. Some correspondents describing the floods in the Fen District wrote that one of the most tragic things which happened there was that children were separated from their parents for almost three hours. Thousands and thousands, tens of thousands, of children in Germany today would be happy to be separated for ever from their parents, if they could only find the slightest chance of getting out of that hell upon earth.

"Do you realise that even if I were so bold as to ask for a very large figure of immigration—let me say 70,000–80,000 a year for the next five years—it would scarcely affect five per cent of the people who are doomed to destruction—people like all of us here who sit in these magnificent surroundings—doomed to destruction? One cannot help speaking feelingly about this artificial restriction of immigration, however great the political expediency of the moment may appear to His Majesty's Government.

"And what has been happening in these last two years, since I had the opportunity of speaking for the Jewish community before the Royal Commission? At that time, two years ago, we still hoped against hope that, to use the words of Goethe, 'Even hell has its laws'—that somehow the position of Jewry in the Reich would be stabilised—at a low level perhaps as an ostracised and disfranchised community—but it would be stabilised. The contrary has happened. With a ferocity which can only be compared with the actions of Genghiz Khan or Tamerlane, community after community is being destroyed. The Reich proper; Austria; Czechoslovakia; now Hungary. And behind it all, there looms the spectre of a still greater tragedy—Poland and Roumania. Out of this centre of evil, death and destruction is spreading over a community which has made its contribution, morally, intellectually and materially, to the countries which are now destroying it—by mass arrests, destruction and confiscation of property, and literal physical annihilation. Sir John Simpson in his recent report sums up by saying that the fate of six millions of people—six millions whom we represent before you here—hangs in the balance; they will have to go—whither nobody can answer.

"It is erroneous to suppose, as is sometimes suggested, that at the time of the Balfour Declaration, a large scale immigration into Palestine was not taken into consideration, that the Balfour Declaration was, so to say, not related to the needs of the Jewish victims of persecution. It is true that in Russia—whence I come—where I had the opportunity of seeing and living through anti-Semitism at its worst, owing to the fact that they were incapable of evolving a system of scientific torture the position of our community then was not so parlous as the position of the Jews today, but it was not far from it. During the years before the war, from, I believe, 1905 to 1914 an annual average of about one hundred and twenty thousand Jews migrated from Russia alone. The modern American Jewish community is built up largely from immigrants from Eastern Europe, as it existed before the war and before the Balfour Declaration.

"The whole Zionist movement is built up on the conception of the homelessness of the Jews, and in saying 'homelessness' I do not mean to contend for one moment that the Jews in England or in France or in Switzerland or in Holland have not a home in those countries and are not related internally, morally, politically, socially to those countries, as to their home. It has nothing to do with loyalty to those countries. As I said before the Royal Commission, it is extremely easy to be a Jew in England. There is no conflict of loyalties. We ourselves demand even from the Jews of Poland, of Roumania, loyalty to their country. Individual groups of Jews may have homes but as a people we are homeless, and it is this homelessness which has produced what is commonly called the Jewish problem. We stalk through world history like disembodied ghosts. We are of the people with whom we live, and at the same time we are not; therefore we are accepted, integrated into the peoples, in small quantities and as soon as the quantity exceeds a certain limit, reaction sets in. This reaction is vulgarly known as anti-Semitism. I am not accusing the peoples. It is perhaps our fault that we have not been completely dissolved, without leaving a residue, in the peoples among whom it is our fortune to live.

"It is essential that there should be one place in the world where we should not be a fraction, or a part—an appendix or an adjunct to something else, which is merely accepted and tolerated—but where we should be ourselves, where we should be masters of our own destinies. That is the essence of the Zionist conception, and it is the tragic confirmation of this very conception which we are witnessing today. Jews had lived in Germany for a thousand years. The community lived in peace. One day they are uprooted and destroyed, cruelly and wickedly.

"There are, therefore, two conceptions in the Zionist movement: one a positive conception, which is to normalise the existence of the people in the country of its origin; and the other, a negative one, which is really the basis of the first—to find a home for those who are persecuted, or may be persecuted tomorrow.

"Every great movement is thus built up of two factors, a positive and a negative. The Socialist movement would never have assumed its breadth or importance if the position of the workman as a component in modern society had been perfectly normal. The adjunct is a desire, and a positive desire, to build up a new society. It is therefore wrong, fundamentally wrong, historically wrong, and wrong in principle, to say that when all these discussions leading up to the Balfour Declaration were going on—and they were going on for years—the quantitative factor, the factor that you must find a place where you could absorb an appreciable quantity of Jews, was not taken into consideration. It was. In fact at that time the notion of Palestine was much larger in scope than it is now. Palestine and Trans-Jordan were at that time indivisible."

Dr. Weizmann went on to discuss various "well-intentioned projects" that were being sponsored as schemes which might, even temporarily, take the place of immigration to Palestine:

"If the test of these projects is immediate relief, I am afraid that none of the 'territorial' projects, whether it be British Guiana (which I am quite sure was a most generous suggestion on the part of the Government) or whether it be parts of Africa—or Paraguay, or countries of South America all of which are mentioned as possible countries of absorption—I believe none of them answers the test of immediate relief. No primitive country can absorb quickly large numbers of people. I can imagine that if a great deal of money and effort is expended, then at some time you may here and there be able to place 1,000, or 2,000, or 3,000 immigrants, and it is all to the good to save so many people. But curiously enough, small Palestine to-day does answer certain demands. You can absorb people quickly, particularly Jews, in a country where there is a Jewish community ready to play its part. It is difficult to imagine Jews who are town-dwellers finding themselves among Indian natives or other primitive, backward people, and making themselves at home quickly there."

"All the experience which is required for the renaissance of a country Palestine has already gone through. It has gone through a process, a painful process, of trial and error. Three generations of pioneers have given their sweat and blood to fertilise the soil of Palestine. Palestine has a Jewish agriculture; it has a Jewish industry; it has a normal stratification of Jewish society rooted in the soil. It could therefore to-day relieve quite an appreciable number. One meets with this rather curious argument. It is said: You cannot absorb in Palestine *all* the Jews who need a home, so *because* you cannot absorb all you had better not absorb any. I think the logical reply is that if you cannot absorb all you must make the best of what is possible, and what is possible is more than the 'political high level' which prevails at present.

"I humbly submit that it is a great mistake to think that because Palestine has been agriculturally, and perhaps otherwise, a success, that success is to be guaranteed in another country. Palestine has been a success because it is Palestine; because the Jew in Palestine is prepared to go through all the hardships involved in adaptation to a new country, and I am afraid he would not show the same fervour, the same apostolic devotion, in any other country. It is not any particular properties of the soil in Palestine, or any particular inventions that the Jews have made as regards agriculture in Palestine. Not at all; Palestine was a hard country, and it *is* a hard country.

"Agriculturally and climatically, perhaps, there are many better countries in which Jewish settlement has been tried, and it has not been a signal success. If Moses had chosen to bring us to America, our problem would have been easy, but he did not choose to do so, and he is not here to discuss it."

After reviewing the progress made in Palestine during the past three years, "under the bullets and bombs of Arab terrorism," Dr. Weizmann continued:

"Perhaps you, Sir, and the Rabbis who are sitting here, will forgive me if I bring in a text which I discovered yesterday in the fourth chapter of Nehemiah, vv.7–8: 'BUT it came to pass that when Sanballat, and Tobiah, and the Arabians and the Ammonites and the Ashdodites heard that the walls of Jerusalem were made up, and that the breaches began to be stopped, then they were very wroth, and conspired all of them together to come and to fight against Jerusalem, and to hinder it.'

"So it seems that a united front against Jewish endeavour to build up Palestine is no new thing in our history. One comfort which one always derives from reading Jewish history is that, whatever trouble we may be in, we can always say 'it has happened before.'

"I hope you do not think this quotation inappropriate; I do not for one second underrate the fundamental importance of good Arab-Jewish relations, and I say for my colleagues and myself that we have been gravely concerned about them throughout these years of tribulation. We have tried to bring about an agreement. We have repeatedly urged the Mandatory Government to assist us in these efforts. . . .

"The history of Jewish-Arab understanding, or attempts to come to a Jewish-Arab understanding, is as old as the Balfour Declaration. Soon after the Declaration was issued, still during the War, when I paid my first visit to Palestine, I set out to meet the spokesman of the Arabs, with the knowledge and encouragement of the late Lord Allenby. Together with Lord Harlech, then Mr. Ofmsby Gore, we went to Akaba, and from Akaba we went part of the way, as my ancestors did, to speak to the peoples to find a right of way into Palestine. I met Feisal and Lawrence, and a great many of the British officers who had then been instrumental in bringing about the appearance of the Arab people in the theatre of war. Frankly and honestly we explained to Feisal, the only spokesman of the Arabs at that time, our intentions and our aims, and it may be not unknown to the members of the Government that this beginning of a contact with the Arab leader developed into a life-long friendship, and produced a definite agreement between Feisal and myself, as representing the then Zionist organisation, because the Jewish Agency did not exist at that time in its present form. . . . It is true that some of my Arab friends have tried to impress upon the world at large that this agreement is a forgery; but it is a genuine document, which incidentally had some caveat which had nothing to do with the substance of the agreement, written by Feisal in Arabic and translated into English by Lawrence, who had been instrumental in bringing it about.

"Since this first attempt, which was by no means abortive, we have invariably tried to meet the Arabs, not only in Palestine, not only in Jerusalem, but in Damascus, in Beirut, in Baghdad, in Cairo, in London, in Paris, and in Geneva, and wherever we had an opportunity of meeting them. Either myself or my friends or our representatives in various Arab centres have tried to get in touch with the Arabs, and have tried to explain to them, and to understand them. All these meetings, if I may say so—and it involves no disrespect to the Arabs—are always characterised by one particular feature: each Arab representative is perfectly reasonable and friendly if you talk to him privately, but somehow it has never happened yet, with the exception of Feisal, that they live up in public to what they are prepared to concede in private conversations.

"But I do believe, and I am saying something which may possibly strike you as hazardous, that if the Arab masses in Palestine today could be consulted, and their authentic views heard at this Conference, you would find much less antagonism than is generally supposed to exist. It is the leaders in Palestine, particularly, who refuse to admit the peculiar historical connection of the Jews with Palestine, although in their own Holy Books they might find some guidance in this direction... and I may say that sometimes this attitude of the Arabs, that we have not got even as much right to come to Palestine as, say, to come to Kent, is emulated even by British people.

"We have been thrown out of Palestine by force. We have not acquired any other territory. We have carried this idea of Palestine with us on our long road, and our connection, even after this great lapse of time, has been maintained not only morally but from time to time physically. For example, if you look at the history of Tiberias, you will find that the Arabs destroyed it and we have rebuilt it.

"It is perfectly true that Palestine is a holy place for the Moslems. It is also a holy place for the Christians, which the Arabs sometimes do not sufficiently acknowledge; but it has never been a national centre for the Arabs. Jerusalem cannot be compared from a national point of view with Damascus, for instance.

"At the present moment, Arab intransigence towards the Jews is being strengthened by two factors: first of all the indifferent attitude of the British Administration. I shall not use one more word on the attitude of the British Administration; they are not here to answer me, and it is perhaps not relevant to the main subject which we are discussing. Secondly, there is the intervention of powerful and hostile forces from outside. Our implacable enemies who persecute the Jews today in the south and centre of Europe continue their persecution in Palestine, using the Arabs as their instruments. I do not want to meddle in international politics, and I would not presume to do so in the presence of a distinguished Foreign Secretary; but it is not too much to say that these implacable enemies are not altogether the best friends of this country. Great Britain is not arming against France or the United States or Switzerland or Holland. I shall say no more.

"Whenever the subject of Palestine is on the tapis there is always a great deal of argument about conflicting promises. It may be true that conflicting promises have been made as far as Trans-Jordan is concerned, but what is certain is that the conflict has been solved, not by way of compromise but by a settlement one hundred per cent in favour of the Arabs. The so-called McMahon letters are constantly being quoted; I had believed that the ghost of those letters had been laid; but it still appears from time to time, and perhaps in this connection it is right to remind you of a letter from Lawrence which has just been published. He says, speaking of the settlement for which Mr. Winston Churchill was responsible, that he placed 'honesty before expediency in order to fulfil our promises in the letter and the spirit.' Sir Henry McMahon himself gave what I thought was a final explanation of this matter. But, if I may say so with respect, the Secretary of State for the Colonies stated only recently that the Arabs were not consulted when the Balfour Declaration and the Mandate were in preparation. I believe, with the utmost possible respect, that the Secretary of State did not perhaps take into consideration all the facts of the case when he spoke on this subject. Sir Mark Sykes, who was one of the Secretaries of the Cabinet at the period previous to the Balfour Declaration—and again I am sure that the Records of the Colonial Office and the archives of the Foreign Office will prove this—and who was intimately concerned with the negotiations connected with the Balfour Declaration, was in close touch with King Feisal, who again was the only available representative of the Arab people. The Arabs of Palestine were then in the enemy camp.

"Now the Arabs of Palestine and of the neighbouring countries are here. . . . I think it is proper to say that the appearance of these Arab States may possibly be interpreted as giving the impression that there is equality of status between the Arabs and the Jews as far as Palestine is concerned. That would be wholly erroneous. There is an essential difference between what Palestine means to the Jews and what Palestine means to the outside Arabs. I think it is true to say that a great many Jews, even those who do not share the Zionist approach to the problem, are vitally interested in Palestine, to say the least, as a place where the Jewish immigrants—tormented, driven from pillar to post—can have some slight chance of beginning a new life, and leading a dignified existence. That is not the case with the Arabs. The permanent Mandates Commission underlines this particular point by saying: 'It should also be remembered that the collective sufferings of Arabs and Jews are not comparable, since vast spaces in the Near East, formerly the abode of a numerous population and the home of a brilliant civilisation, are open to the former, whereas the world is increasingly being closed to settlement by the latter.'

"Full comparisons, in my submission, should be made as to how far His Majesty's Government's promises to the Jews, and their promises to the Arabs, have been fulfilled; and now when, for the first time, His Majesty's Government has an opportunity of meeting—unfortunately separately—Jews and Arabs, those comparisons are particularly indicated.

"I think the Arabs emerged from the War with something like four Kingdoms. This position has been achieved primarily through the expenditure of British blood and effort. They have contributed something themselves, but nothing in any way proportionate to the results that they have obtained. Nor is it irrelevant to the question to compare what the Arabs have made out of the extraordinary opportunities offered them—opportunities which are still there—and what the Jews have made of the chance—small or large, I am not going to discuss it—which was given to them in a part of Palestine. I do not want to be disparaging as far as my opponents are concerned, but I may be permitted, as one who knows the East and tries to understand his opponent (in the hope that one day he may become a friend), to say that I think the Arabs are trying to run before they can walk.

"The boon of statehood has come to them with very little trouble, and has produced a nationalist movement which I am afraid is hollow, which has fashioned itself on the totalitarian pattern. The affinity between the modern totalitarian states and some of the Arab States is no mere accident. The Arab States have a great many difficulties. They will have still greater difficulties in time to come. A country becomes *your* country only when you have overcome great difficulties; I believe that as long as the Arabs are intransigent they are cutting into their own flesh. Those vast countries will stand empty, may become anybody's prey. Any adventurer will consider them as something to covet. I truly believe—and I am speaking with the utmost possible sincerity—that the Arabs and Jews can find a meeting-ground beneficial to both. We can give them what they need badly to-day. They need advice, they need guidance, they need technical help, they need financial help, they need loyal allies. All these we can give them.

"Many Arabs—for instance the present Government of Syria—have repeatedly made approaches to us. Representatives of former Governments of Iraq spoke to us, of their respect for our work, and of the desirability of exchange of experience and of co-operation. But a barren and destructive nationalism appears for the moment to hold sway amongst the Arabs and the rise of the Totalitarian States serves only to encourage their opposition. The Arabs are blinded by what I believe to be a mirage of brute force. They have all got their problems, very difficult problems, problems which may threaten the very existence of the State, but somehow the only principle on which they have found it possible to unite was a purely negative one, opposition to us. Repeatedly it has been said that the Palestine Arabs fear 'the domination of the Jews.' I believe that this is little more than a catch phrase. In Iraq they did not fear domination by the Assyrians; the Yemen need not fear domination by the few thousands of Jews who are there. The fate of the Assyrians in Iraq is known; and the Jews in the Yemen are suffering, though as long as they are willing to remain the under-dogs they have something of a tolerable existence.

"The desire to run before they can walk has produced a spirit of intolerance amongst the Arabs. It is not that they are frightened of *our* domination; it is their desire to dominate which is the true root of the trouble. I have submitted repeatedly to the Secretary of State, and have found him receptive on this point, that a road to an understanding—perhaps a narrow path and not a royal road—may be found in the principle of mutual non-domination. We do not want to dominate the Arabs but we do not wish to be—we cannot be—dominated by them. Once that fundamental principle has been inculcated into the Arab mind, as the result of a considerable educational process, I am not without hope that some day we shall find a way to each other.

"Today the whole perspective in Palestine has been thrown out of focus; unfortunately we are trying to arrive at a solution at a time when the British Government and the world at large are oppressed by war clouds on the horizon, and when in Palestine itself there is a minor war going on all the time. . . . The Arabs sit on Britain's lines of communication. If they choose to turn Nazi you may find yourself in a difficult position. I am not a strategist but I do know this country and I have never suffered from the disability of underrating one's enemy—or let me say, opponent.

"I think as a scientist, I am not incapable of weighing evidence, and I verily believe (and I think that soldiers who know the circumstances will bear me out) that there is a grotesque exaggeration of what may be called the military nuisance value of the Arabs; the more *that* is brought into the picture, and the more that certain Arab leaders stress it, as they do openly, the less am I convinced of the importance of this factor. . . .

"There is another unreality in the position of the Arabs. If I may say so, the Arabs have borrowed from European political terminologies all the shibboleths and clichés. They try to push Arab life into these clichés. They speak easily. 'We are a majority in Palestine; there should be an Arab National Government.' It seems to me somewhat unreal that a country which has a one-third Jewish population (and that one-third is responsible for two-thirds or more of the actual economic, cultural, intellectual activity of the country), which has all Palestine's great Christian traditions, should suddenly be made, by order of the Mufti, into an Arab country. It seems to me unreal, just as I think the bringing in of the military element has vitiated this Conference from the very beginning.

"May I turn to something else which weighs heavily on me and I think on my friends. I hear, and I am sure it is true, that responsible British statesmen tend to weigh up the position in somewhat the following way: We must look to the Arabs; they are the important factor; it is they who will tip the scale; the Jews we have anyhow. There is truth in this. I believe it is true to say you have the Jews unconditionally. For us Jews loyalty to Great Britain is almost an unconditional thing. I shall not discuss the ethics or even the sportsmanship of this particular statement, as I would beware of doing its authors an injustice. But this affinity of Jews and Britons is not only based on the Balfour Declaration; it is based—and I hope again that I am not venturing too far—on a moral and ethical affinity between what made us what we are and what made the British a symbol, in this destructive world, of what is just and fair.

"I believe that you have become great because your work and your policy has been inspired by the Book which we have produced in Palestine. This is the secret of why the Balfour Declaration came as a natural expression of British conscience in a time of great trial for the British nation. It is written in the stars that you should be the sponsors, just as it is written in the stars that Palestine will be the Jewish National Home. I may seem to you to be somewhat of a romantic, but I verily believe that these things are the realities, and not guns, not torpedoes, not even aeroplanes. Therefore, I would submit respectfully that if we want to come to a fair solution, we should for the purposes of this Conference disregard the war cloud about which so much is being said to-day.

"To finish on a positive note, I believe that a far-sighted programme for the development of Palestine, as has already been advocated many times, would be the first basis for peace. It is infinitely more urgent to-day, because the Arab economy in Palestine is destroyed, and I see no way of recuperation for the Arabs unless, as an outcome of this Conference, the Government find it possible, without help and co-operation, to initiate a policy of development which would serve both sides equally. This, in my humble opinion, would be the safest bridge. Perhaps both sides will at the beginning tread it with great caution and suspicion, but this caution and suspicion will in time be overcome. . . .

"I am sure that it is not beyond the great experience of His Majesty's Government in constitutional problems to create in and for Palestine a political structure guaranteeing political equality to both sides and removing Arab fears, so far as they are genuine, at any rate from those Arabs who wish to have them removed. I believe that then Palestine could be opened to a large immigration of people endowed with the capacity of reclaiming its ancient soil and making it into what it was thousands of years ago. It is for this creative task that I invoke the help of His Majesty's Government. From you, who have carried the ideals of justice, fairness, and good government into the remote corners of the globe, from you who have taken upon yourselves the white man's burden, I claim—and I believe I have the right to claim, with all respect and humility—that you should do justice to my people in this dark hour."

Malcolm MacDonald responded with a few compliments to Weizmann, and he proposed that they meet again on Friday morning, February 10. The Jewish Delegation agreed.

30 BRITISH MEET ARAB DELEGATIONS—FEB. 9, 1939

On February 9 the first working session of the British Government representatives and the Arab Delegations took place. The Government was represented by Lord Halifax, Malcolm MacDonald, R. A. Butler, Lord Dufferin and a number of officials.

The Palestinian Arabs present were Jamal Husseini, Amin Tamimi, George Antonius, Auni Abdul Hadi, Musa Alami, Alfred Roch, Dr. Hussein Khalidi, Jacob Ghussein and Fuad Saba. Egypt was represented by: Prince Mohamad Abdul Moneim, Hassan Nashat Pasha (the Egyptian Ambassador in London), Ali Maher Pasha (Prime Minister), and Abdul Rahman Azzam (Egyptian Minister to Iraq and Saudi Arabia). Iraq was represented by its Prime Minister, Nuri Sa'id. The Saudi Arabian delegates were Emir Faisal (the Foreign Minister), Hafiz Wahba (Saudi Arabian Minister in London), Fuad Hamza (Deputy Foreign Minister), and Ibrahim al-Suliman (Secretary). Transjordan was represented by Taufiq Pasha Abdul-Huda (Prime Minister) and Sheikh Najib Alumuddin (Secretary). Yemen was represented by Prince Saif ul-Islam al-Husain, Al Qadhi Muhammed, Abdullah al-Shami, Al Qadhi Ali ibn Husain al-Amri, Sayed Ali ibn Akiel, Mahmoud el Soud, and Prof. Ibrahim el Mougy.

MacDonald asked the Arabs to open the discussion. George Antonius reported that all members of the Palestinian Delegation were present, with the exception of Ragheb Nashashibi, who was prevented from coming owing to ill health. The actual discussion was opened by Jamal Husseini.

The Arabs, he said, believed that their case was one of self-evident justice. It rested on the natural right of a people to remain in undisturbed possession of their country, and on their natural desire to safeguard their national existence and ensure that it would be secured and developed in freedom and in harmony with their tradition and their ideals. The Arab case had nothing in common with anti-Semitism. It was not inspired by any hostility to the British people or to any other people. It was the case of a population, by nature peaceful and hospitable, trying to preserve the integrity of their country and to prevent the land to which they were deeply attached from being forcibly converted into a national home for another people.

Arab opposition to the policy initiated in Palestine manifested itself soon after the issue of the Balfour Declaration in November 1917. Until then, the Arabs had always lived at peace and on friendly terms with the numerous Jews who were in Palestine from devotional motives. It was only after the issue of the

Balfour Declaration, when the Zionist Jews began to exhibit political pretensions and to reveal their real intentions, that Arab fears and opposition were aroused.

The policy pursued by Great Britain in Palestine since 1918 had shown that Arab fears were far from groundless. The Arabs had been denied the independence which had been promised to them in the British Government's pledge of October 24, 1915, and confirmed in several subsequent pledges, in return for their share in the Allied victory. A Mandate was imposed upon them, whose terms were a flagrant violation not only of the promises made to them and of their own natural rights, but also of the right to political independence which was specifically recognized to them in the Covenant of the League of Nations. An administration had been set up in Palestine which, for the last twenty years, had exercised unfettered power equivalent to an absolute dictatorship in all the domains of government—legislature, executive and judiciary—thereby denying the Arabs of Palestine, who before the War had enjoyed the privileges of parliamentary representation and ministerial responsibility, the most elementary rights of self-government.

The terms of the Mandate were the product of close consultation between the British Government and the Zionist Jews, from which the Arabs whose country was at stake were deliberately excluded. In virtue of its provisions, and in spite of constant Arab protests, the Mandatory Power had enacted legislation to enable the Zionist Jews to pour their immigrants into the country and buy up all the land they could. In twenty years, the percentage of Jews in Palestine had risen from about 7 to about 29, that is to say from a Jewish population of about 53,000 to one of over 400,000 in a country whose total population was approximately 1,400,000 inhabitants and whose resources had long been overtaxed by that abnormal increase of population. In the same period, the Jews who in 1918 owned some 150,000 acres of land were now in possession of 333,000 acres out of a total available area of 1,750,000 acres. These purchases which were made in the most fertile tracts of cultivable land in the country had resulted in the steady dispossession of an increasing number of Arab cultivators who had been driven to seek a makeshift livelihood elsewhere than on the soil which they had been cultivating for centuries. Arab villages had been razed to the ground, their homes and mosques and cemeteries entirely wiped out, and their names (which in some cases had historical associations) officially erased from the map and replaced by the Hebrew name of some new Zionist colony. Moreover, the acquisition of land by Jews had led to such congestion in the rural districts that the present average holding in Arab hands was, as every British Commission of Inquiry had ascertained, no longer sufficient to provide the holder with even the barest means of subsistence.

The Arabs had never recognized and never would recognize the Balfour Declaration or the Mandate. The first contained a promise which Great Britain was not entitled to make without Arab consent and which was, in any case, invalid since it conflicted with a previous and binding British pledge. The second was an illegal document. The terms of the Mandate which could only have derived their sanction from the Covenant of the League of Nations were demonstrably in conflict with the letter and the spirit of the relevant article (namely Article XXII) of the Covenant. The Palestine Arab Delegation were prepared to present an argument to prove conclusively the invalidity of the Balfour Declaration and the basic illegality of the Mandate. They considered that the measures taken in virtue of the provisions of the Mandate, such as facilities given to Jews to enter Palestine, acquire land, and enjoy other exceptional privileges—to say nothing of the great number of Jews who had been smuggled into Palestine with the knowledge and connivance of Jewish organizations—must be regarded as null and void and as deserving to be abrogated.

It was beside the point to argue that Jewish immigration had benefited the Arabs materially. The argument was demonstrably false, for, when account was taken of all the changes brought into the economic and social structure of the country by the influx of Jewish money and immigrants, the result was found to be on balance dangerously detrimental to the material interests of the Arab population. But even if it were true, the argument was beside the point. In the eyes of the Arabs, the point was not primarily one of material consequences but first and foremost one of moral and political values. Was it right that the Arabs, who had been in continuous occupation of Palestine for over 1,300 years and whose life was deeply rooted in its soil and its countryside, should be forcibly evicted or squeezed in order to enable the Zionist Jews to establish the Jewish National Home in their midst? That was the real issue. Palestine could not provide a solution of the Jewish problem, and in any case, the country already had a far larger population than it could support.

The demand of the Palestine Arabs, Jamal Husseini said, could be summarized under four headings:

1) the recognition of the right of the Arabs to complete independence in their country;

2) the abandonment of the attempt to establish a Jewish National Home in Palestine;

3) the abrogation of the Mandate and of the illegalities resulting from it, and its

replacement by a treaty similar to that concluded between Great Britain and Iraq, creating in Palestine a sovereign Arab State;

4) the immediate cessation of all Jewish immigration and of sales of land to Jews.

The Arabs were prepared to negotiate, in a conciliatory spirit, the conditions under which reasonable British interests would be safeguarded; to approve the necessary guarantees for the preservation of, and right to access to, all Holy Places, and for the protection of all legitimate rights of the Jewish and other minorities in Palestine.

MacDonald said that Jamal Husseini had made a very concise and clear statement of his Delegation's case, and that he assumed that this was the basis of future discussions. He proposed that they meet again on Saturday, Febuary 11, and after a brief discussion about the publicity to be given to the speeches, that proposal was accepted.

31 MALCOLM MACDONALD'S PROPOSALS—FEB. 10, 1939

At the session of February 10, the Government was represented only by MacDonald and Butler. MacDonald's reply to Weizmann revealed much about the Government's intentions. After complimenting Weizmann on his comprehensive statement at the previous session, he said he would confine himself to two or three aspects of the question which might be regarded as fundamental.

MacDonald said that he might have begun by stressing points in favor of the Jewish case which would no doubt have pleased his audience: he might have mentioned the horrors of persecution and the anxiety of the British people to do all they could to help the victims: he might have referred to the binding nature of the pledges of His Majesty's Government to the Jews and to the remarkable achievement of the Jews in Palestine. It was, however, unnecessary for him to take time at this stage to make a statement of that nature, though all these points would no doubt be mentioned in future discussion. He would prefer to dwell on certain opposite considerations which had to be discussed if we were to get to the roots of the matter.

He would like first to say something about the Arab point of view and he hoped that he would not be misunderstood if, on this occasion, he confined himself more or less to that aspect of the question. The British Government was not pro-Arab. It was their duty to be neither pro-Jew nor pro-Arab, but pro-Mandate. All would, of course, agree that much difficulty would be overcome if there were a country where the Jews could have a state of their own. Dr.

Weizmann had said that Palestine was the natural place for such a state, and up to a point that was true. If Palestine were empty, Dr. Weizmann's statement would not only be true, but it would be simple to bring the Jewish State into being.

But there were over one million Arabs whose ancestors had been settled in Palestine for many generations. It was as much their country as any country belonged to a people who had inhabited it for centuries, and we had to recognize that the Arabs had certain rights in that country. The Mandate enjoined protection of Arab rights and, speaking for himself, MacDonald found it quite impossible to say that the Arabs had not a political or natural right to be consulted with regard to the disposition of their country. The fact that the Arabs were a weak people and could be suppressed, if they rose, by a force of eighteen battalions, did not mean that they had not this right.

It was true that these rights might have been influenced and perhaps modified by the Balfour Declaration, which was endorsed by fifty nations at Geneva and by the United States of America. The British Government did not seek to avoid the obligations which it had undertaken to the Jews in Palestine, but he thought that he was correct in saying that the promise was a somewhat vague one. The term "Jewish National Home," for example, was ill-defined. The Balfour Declaration appeared to have been deliberately left vague by the authors, whose attitude seemed to have been "let us make a start and see what happens." Some of the authors, Lloyd George for example, expressed hopes with regard to the establishment of a Jewish state in the whole of Palestine. We could not ignore the statements of individual public men concerned with the Balfour Declaration, but we must not overestimate the significance of such statements. We must recognize that the authors made certain assumptions which have been falsified by events. For example:

1) Some Ministers responsible for the Balfour Declaration did not seem to have appreciated that there were at the time 600,000 Arabs in Palestine. MacDonald was certain that he was right in saying that the authors of the Balfour Declaration did not anticipate that the Arab population would grow by natural increase from 600,000 in 1917 to just over 1,000,000 in 1939, and that it would increase greatly again in the following two decades.

2) The authors of the Balfour Declaration also appeared to have assumed that it was possible to obtain the acquiescence of the Arabs in the establishment of the Jewish National Home. That assumption had been falsified. So far from it being possible to say that the Arabs were prepared to acquiesce, we had to confess that Arab hostility had become stronger and more bitter.

The immigration of Jews had helped the Arabs economically, but despite that the political and moral opposition of the Arabs was widespread and deep-seated. We had also to reckon with the opposition of the Arab countries outside Palestine. It might be true that these countries had no legal standing in the business, but it was impossible to deal with the question on the basis of legality. 3) The terms of the promise to the Jews had not been clearly defined. What did a "Jewish National Home" in Palestine mean? Such an expression was open to all kinds of interpretations. Lloyd George had contemplated, at some future date a Jewish state covering the whole of Palestine. He had said that if, when the time came for the establishment of self-governing institutions, the Jews had a majority in Palestine, then Palestine would be theirs. The Arab would say, "Very well, if the Arabs have a majority of the population when the time is ripe for these institutions, then Palestine should be an Arab state with a Jewish minority." The force of the Arab argument must be admitted. We must do justice to the Arab point of view.

MacDonald went on to say that under the Mandate, they were required to establish, in due course, "self-governing institutions." In the opinion of the Arabs the time had already arrived for that step, and the Arabs were in a considerable majority. Arabs in the countries surrounding Palestine had been given self-government over vast areas. It must, however, be remembered that this fact only increased in the eyes of the Arabs of Palestine their claim for self-government in Palestine.

He referred to Dr. Weizmann's question whether the British Government stood by the pledges which had been given to the Jews during and after the War, or whether subsequent developments had made the British Government wish to withdraw from those promises: whether, in short, their policy was one of expediency?

A case could no doubt be made out for the view that the British Government were acting from motives of pure political expediency. There was rebellion in Palestine and a state of potential hostility in surrounding Arab States. The whole Moslem world, including India, might be affected.

These facts could not be ignored, and the Jews surely ought not to wish that such facts should be ignored by the British Government. They must, to use an unpopular word, be "realists." If peace were assured in Europe for ten years ahead, the position would be different, but in present circumstances, they could not be and ought not to be indifferent. If the British Empire were to go down, the Jews would go down also; they and the United States were our most powerful friends.

It was true then that a case could be made out for the view that the policy of the British Government was based on expediency, but such a conclusion would be entirely false. Their obligations under the Mandate were to both Jews and Arabs. One of these obligations was that of safeguarding the rights of the Arab population, and he could not doubt that the term "rights" must cover the political rights of the Arabs. The present troubled state of Palestine was an illustration of how deeply the Arab population resented their policy. If they pushed their Jewish policy through against such strongly expressed opposition, they were ignoring Arab rights and infringing the Mandate. Their policy was not one of expediency; they were endeavoring to carry out the principles of the Mandate.

(At this point the proceedings were suspended and the representatives of the British Government withdrew for 20 minutes in order to enable the Jewish Delegation to confer in private. Weizmann asked me to reply to MacDonald when the British representatives returned.)

When the meeting was resumed, Weizmann called on me to reply to some of the more important points which had been raised.

I said that the Colonial Secretary had put the case as a quarrel between the Jews and the Arabs. In the Jewish view, this gave a false perspective of the case, which was one between the Jewish people and the whole world. The Arabs of Palestine and surrounding countries were only a small fraction of the non-Jewish half of this antithesis, though an important one because of their geographical position. If the issue were not one between the Jewish people and the whole world, the Jewish Agency Delegation would not be present here in discussion with His Majesty's Government as the Mandatory Power on behalf of fifty nations.

The Secretary of State had asked us to put ourselves in the shoes of the Arabs. This was a fair request only if the other side were prepared to reciprocate. But this was the one thing which the Arabs would not consider doing; they would not even sit at the same table with the Jews.

MacDonald had argued that many of the authors of the Balfour Declaration had been ill-informed about Palestine, which they had thought was a relatively empty country. I could not but believe that British statesmen and public opinion had been tolerably well-informed as to the real state of Palestine prior to the Balfour Declaration.

The Jewish connection with Palestine had not begun with the Balfour Declaration or the Mandate, which were simply the recognition by the whole civilized world of a pre-existing historical connection. Hence the Jews were in Palestine by right and not of sufferance, and had indeed been there before the present Arab population. They were sixteen million people whose only rightful home was in Palestine.

I expressed doubts as to the accuracy of describing the Balfour Declaration and the Mandate as vague. Admittedly, these documents did not say that there should be a Jewish State; they could not do this because it was not for the nations who ratified the Mandate to compel the Jews to go to Palestine. What was intended was that if Jewish enterprise and settlement there were successful, then the natural result would be a Jewish State.

The saving clause in the Balfour Declaration regarding the civil and religious rights of the existing non-Jewish communities both proved that the authors of the Declaration knew Palestine not to be empty, and at the same time disposed of the accusation of vagueness. It was rather the Secretary of State's reference to Arab "natural rights" which was ill-defined. This saving clause was the only limitation on the promise to the Jews and, needless to say, they had no intention of infringing it.

The Secretary of State had made two assumptions. The first was that the consent, or at least acquiescence, of the Arabs was in some way an essential to the carrying out of the Balfour Declaration and the Mandate. But such consent or acquiescence was not mentioned in either document, in which Great Britain undertook obligations to the whole world by recognizing the prior rights of the Jews in Palestine. As against these rights those of the Arab population of Palestine were secondary.

In the second place, the Secretary of State had assumed that it was the intention that when the country was ripe for self-government, whichever side had a numerical majority would be entitled to exercise the normal democratic rights of a majority. It was hardly fair to bring this up as an argument against the Jews. If there was not a Jewish majority in Palestine by now, it was due not to natural limitations but to restrictions imposed by the Mandatory Power. A fundamental assumption underlying the Balfour Declaration was that the existing population in Palestine was only a small fraction of the population which, when fully developed, Palestine would contain. The increase which had taken place in the Arab and the Jewish populations only verified this assumption. Since the Balfour Declaration the total population had more than doubled, mainly as the result of Jewish development. It could be doubled again and even more than that. It was a question not between the 900,000 Arabs in Palestine and the 400,000 Jews there now, but between the present population there and the millions of Jews who might come there—not by displacing the existing population but by creating new resources for their settlement.

The Jews were peculiarly fitted to understand the argument of a people threatened, as the Arabs said they were, with loss of independence and homeland. But surely the Arabs were one of the few peoples of the earth who were concentrated almost entirely in their own countries and almost entirely under the rule of their own people. Palestine was a foreign land which they had once forcibly conquered for a short time, and the Jews were its original inhabitants. It was sometimes said that if the political philosophy in the Balfour Declaration were generally applied, the Italians, for example, would have a right to reoccupy Britain. But surely if the parties now conferring did not recognize the special historical connection of the Jews with Palestine, and their unique homelessness, that this was a case sui generis, there was no case to be argued at all.

The Arabs of Palestine could not have it both ways. If they considered themselves to be part of the Arab world, they must take the larger view, in which Arab national aspirations had been in general satisfied and would not be threatened by a relatively small Jewish State, even if this State comprised the whole of historic Palestine.

Arab opposition to Jewish settlement was familiar to us and we did not underrate its seriousness. But I doubted if this so-called rebellion was in fact a rebellion of the whole or even of a large part of the Arab people of Palestine. The fact could not be ignored that the terror was directed perhaps as much against Arabs as against Jews, and many prominent Arab leaders in purely Arab towns like Jaffa, Hebron, Nablus, had been assassinated.

With the reference to self-governing institutions in Article 2 of the Mandate, I said that if "the self-government of Palestine" had been meant, the Mandate would have said so. The reference to the development of self-governing institutions came after, and was therefore subordinate to, the clause referring to the establishment of the Jewish National Home; if the former were to be interpreted as applying to the State of Palestine as a whole, it would vitiate the whole intention of the Mandate. It was the Jewish contention that the civil and religious rights of the Arabs could be fully safeguarded while the primary object of the establishment of the National Home was carried on. We saw no conflict of rights.

Dr. Weizmann then said he would like to ask one or two fundamental questions.

Was or was not the establishment of the National Home a question of reconstitution? The word "reconstitute" was used in the Mandate, and he believed he was right in saying that the prefix had been the subject of much discussion while the Mandate was being drafted. Was it the return of an ancient people to its ancient home? If the conscience of the civilized world which had expressed itself in the Balfour Declaration had now ceased to exist, then it was useless to continue these discussions. Was it still His Majesty's Government's opinion that these Jews had a right to return to Palestine?

MacDonald said that there was no question but that the Jews have special rights in relation to Palestine. But that did not mean that the whole of Jewry possessed those rights. It was also the case that the Jews were not the only people with special rights in relation to Palestine, for a similar claim could obviously be made on behalf of the Arabs who had lived in the country for centuries.

It would be admitted that the rights of the Jews were limited in two ways:
1) By the physical smallness of the country. The Jewish population of the world could have no right to go to a country which would not hold them;
2) By the rights of the Arabs.

In mentioning the question of the consent of the Arabs, MacDonald said that I had really gone to the root of the matter. I had said that there was no mention in the Mandate that the consent of the Arabs was to be sought before it would be possible to set up the Jewish National Home. That was agreed. But it could not be denied that the authors of the Mandate had assumed that the acquiescence of the Arabs in the facilities to be allowed for the development of the Jewish National Home would be secured in the course of time.

Did the Jewish Delegation think that the Jewish right was so great, and the obligations of His Majesty's Government under the Mandate such, that the policy of establishing the Jewish National Home should be pursued without the acquiescence of the Arabs and in face of the hostility of the non-Jewish peoples who had rights in Palestine?

Dr. Weizmann said that he would answer fully at the next meeting.

After some discussion it was agreed that our next session would take place on Tuesday, February 14.

32 MACDONALD ANSWERS THE ARABS—FEB. 11, 1939

At the meeting with the Arabs on Saturday, February 11, 1939, MacDonald and Halifax and their two deputies were present. MacDonald praised the concise statement made by Jamal Husseini at the previous meeting, and said he would attempt to follow suit. He thanked the Palestinian Arab Delegation for their statement that if an independent Arab Government were established in Palestine that Government would be prepared to safeguard legitimate British interests in the country. But he wished to contest some of Jamal Husseini's statements, which he thought were not entirely just.

The Palestinian Arabs' statement had virtually ignored the existence of any obligations to the Jews. His Majesty's Government appreciated the position of the Palestinian Arab leaders in this matter and their consistency in refusing to recognize the Balfour Declaration or the Mandate or any of their derivatives. But His Majesty's Government were differently situated in this regard.

Jamal Husseini had also referred to the pledges of Arab independence given by Sir Henry McMahon in 1915. The Palestinian Arabs were entitled to maintain their own interpretation of those pledges; but His Majesty's Government had never accepted that interpretation and were convinced that they had fulfilled both in the letter and in the spirit their obligations to the Arabs. The question was one of intention, and surely His Majesty's Government as the authors of the pledges must be the best judges of what they had had in mind.

His Majesty's Government, unlike the Palestinian Arabs, were bound in honor to recognize the Balfour Declaration and the Mandate. These documents had been endorsed not only by themselves but by other powers, the members of the League of Nations and the United States of America, and it was therefore all the more impossible for these obligations to be ignored. Under these documents, His Majesty's Government had assumed obligations to both Arabs and Jews. He could understand the feeling of the Palestinian Arabs that the promises made to them had not always been so much emphasized as those made to the Jews. Frankly he agreed that this had sometimes been the case.

These obligations were twofold: to facilitate under suitable conditions the establishment of a Jewish National Home, and to safeguard the rights and position of the existing population. He thought that the policy which the Mandatory Administration had pursued had carried out both these obligations. Jewish immigration had taken place on a considerable scale. Three hundred thousand immigrants had come into the country, and they were still entering, though under restrictions which His Majesty's Government were under considerable pressure from various quarters to remove, in order to contribute more fully to the rescue of Jewish refugees from Central Europe. But Palestine alone could never solve the Jewish refugee problem, and other homes for the refugees must also be found. The United Kingdom was itself contributing in this way, as were the United States and the British dominions and colonies.

Moreover, while this large number of new settlers had been entering Palestine, the well-being of the Arab population had not been prejudiced and their numbers had in fact remarkably increased. In spite of this, there was no abnormal unemployment problem. Under British rule, and with the increased revenue resulting from the development of the country, there had been a considerable expansion of social services in Palestine from which the Arab population had benefited. These, he thought, were in brief the facts of the position which they now had to face.

But the Palestinian Arab Delegation had made one point which was of first rate importance. They had said that it was not a question of material advantage or disadvantage but of moral and political values. His Majesty's Government understood that. The Arabs of Palestine had seen the steady and at times large Jewish immigration, to which there was no definite limit under any existing agreement, and they wondered when, if ever, it was to stop. Hence they feared eventual political domination by an alien people. Against this there was no guarantee today, and the Palestinian Arabs declared that no mere material advantage could compensate them if it were to take place.

The British people understood these sentiments because they shared them and, in similar circumstances, would themselves make material sacrifices in defense of their freedom. He wished it to be understood that His Majesty's Government accepted the principle that there should be no domination of Arabs by Jews in Palestine. One of the subjects of their detailed discussion would be to work out effective means of securing this end. He would like at the same time to repeat his statement to the House of Commons that there should similarly be no domination of Jews by Arabs, but this again could be discussed when specific proposals were under review.

Palestine had for many centuries been different from any other land. It was unique in containing the Holy Places of the three religions, and was a country dear to millions of people scattered all over the earth. The protection of the Moslem Holy Places was, he felt sure, a matter of supreme concern to every delegate present. He wished to say in conclusion that His Majesty's Government regarded their part in this duty as a high honor and a sacred trust which they would faithfully fulfill for as long as they might be associated with the government of Palestine.

Jamal Husseini thanked the Colonial Secretary for his kind remarks on the statement of the Arab delegations. The Palestine Delegation hoped to submit detailed comments on the points which the Colonial Secretary had made.

However, the Colonial Secretary had made an important remark about the McMahon correspondence. He asked whether the United Kingdom Delegation would put the McMahon documents on the table for discussion. A question of contract was at issue, and such a question could not be discussed on the basis of the intentions of the parties but the text of the documents. Furthermore, the Arab case did not depend only on the interpretation of pledges, but also on the basis of the natural rights of the Arabs.

MacDonald replied that he was prepared to consider with his colleagues the question of the publication of the McMahon correspondence. He feared, however, that the decision would almost certainly be adverse. These were secret documents and subject to the rules applicable to other such documents.

This led to a lengthy discussion, in which Auni Abdul Hadi, Nuri Sa'id, Fuad Ḥamza and Antonius participated. MacDonald said that documents emanating from the British Government could not be made public without authority, but that the United Kingdom Delegation would do all that it could to assist the Conference. Jamal Husseini proposed that the question of the British Government's pledges be discussed first and that the Conference should then proceed to discuss the Arab claims for independence, the stoppage of immigration, and the prohibition of land sales.

It was agreed that at the next meeting attention would be centered on the McMahon pledges, but that any Delegation would be free to make any kind of statement. It was decided that the next meeting would be held on February 13.

33 NURI SA'ID'S SPEECH—FEB. 13, 1939

The meeting of February 13, 1939, was devoted almost entirely to the statement of Nuri Sa'id, Prime Minister of Iraq.

He expressed regret that the Conference was meeting at a time when world Jewry was suffering such an unparalleled misfortune. It was particularly unfortunate that at such a time the Arabs should feel compelled to resist the free entry of Jews into Palestine.

The position of Jews under Islam had always been guaranteed since the days of the Arab Empire, and they had given shelter to the Jews when Christendom rejected them. As the representative of a State where Jews were equal citizens with Arabs, Nuri hoped that the unfortunate position of the Jews in Europe would not be used as an argument for denying justice to the Arabs of Palestine.

Palestine, like Iraq, had been part of the Ottoman Empire, and until the postwar policy was initiated the two countries had been similar in population and institutions. Both had contained Jewish minorities. There had been eight hundred thousand Jews in the Ottoman Empire. Within the Ottoman Empire there had been no movement of Jews toward Palestine. They were content to remain in the provinces which had sheltered them for centuries, and identified themselves more with the local Arab populations than with Jews in the rest of the Empire.

In Iraq this state of affairs had continued. There were two hundred thousand Jews in Iraq, half of them in Baghdad alone, forming a wealthy and contented community which played an important part in the national life. In affairs of personal status they were subject to the courts of their own community.

The habitual tolerance of the Arabs had only been threatened in recent years, and it was Zionism which had caused the change. Hostility in Iraq to political Zionism showed itself soon after the war, when Sir Henry Dodds asked the Iraqi Jews to accept a branch of the Jewish Agency in Baghdad, and the latter refused on the grounds that they did not wish to be associated with Zionism. As Prime Minister, General Nuri felt assured that he was representing not only the Arabs but the Jews of Iraq, whose interests were identical.

The situation had deteriorated rapidly in the last few years. At the time of the 1929 Wailing Wall disturbances in Palestine the Iraqi Government had frustrated attempts at anti-Jewish demonstrations in Iraq, where public interest was increasingly focussed on Palestine affairs. Since then, there had followed in Palestine a repressive policy, Jewish bomb outrages, and the resulting Arab rebellion which had profoundly moved Iraqi public opinion. There had been abortive attacks on the Jewish quarter of Baghdad. The Iraqi Government, needless to say, would not tolerate any kind of pogrom, but they were alarmed at these circumstances outside their country and beyond their control, which were seriously affecting relations between two groups of Iraqi citizens.

Representatives of Syria were unfortunately not present, but their views were widely known and the evidence from Syria was similar to that from Iraq. Nuri cited the demonstrations against Zionism which were provoked by Lord Balfour's visit to Damascus in 1925.

The Iraqi Government was compelled to take a lively interest in the situation in Palestine, since it affected the maintenance of law and order in Iraq itself.

Nuri then turned to the non-fulfillment of the McMahon pledges. He asserted that from the Arabic text of the letters it was evident that Palestine was included in the area of Arab independence which was promised to King Hussein. The Arabic text was the original and should therefore be considered the authoritative one. During the many discussions which took place during the Great War between British military and political officers and those of the Sherifian forces, it was never suggested on either side that Palestine was to be excluded from the area of Arab independence. Since the Arabic text was already published, the difficulties with regard to publishing a secret document to which MacDonald had referred at the previous meeting did not arise.

The reason for the non-fulfillment of the specific promise with regard to Palestine was the Balfour Declaration. In the Arab view the Balfour Declaration could not be permitted to delay the execution or to affect the interpretation of the prior pledge to the Arabs. All British officers then serving in the Middle East had shared the view that the Jewish National Home was to be no more than a cultural and spiritual center and that Palestine would enjoy self-government as part of an Arab state.

Meanwhile, Zionist propaganda was giving an entirely different interpretation to the Balfour Declaration, as the Arabs discovered for the first time at the Peace Conference. But even the 1922 (Churchill) White Paper had implied that the National Home was to be simply a center in which the Jewish people as a whole might on grounds of race take an interest and pride. It was not to be a political center. But nevertheless His Majesty's Government accepted from the League of Nations a Mandate of vastly different implications, which had been drafted jointly with the Jews.

The Palestinian Arabs had been told to restrain their protests until the decision of the League of Nations was published. But their worst fears were justified by the Mandate. Feeling that they were betrayed, they refused to cooperate with the British Administration and could not but reject all palliatives, such as the Legislative Council. Jewish immigration had been encouraged in every way, even to the extent of illegal immigration connived at by the Jewish Agency. Meanwhile the obligation to the Arabs had been almost entirely ignored, in spite of the emphasis laid in the Passfield White Paper on the urgency of developing self-governing institutions. Since then the Palestinian Arabs had been in despair and could no longer cooperate with the Mandatory. In conclusion Nuri said that he had been speaking throughout as a friend of Great Britain.

The Colonial Secretary announced that Butler would make a statement on the question of pledges the following day.

34 THE MCMAHON LETTERS—FEB. 14, 1939

The next day, February 14, the Arab Delegations again met with MacDonald and Butler at 11 a.m.

Emir Faisal, son of Ibn Saud and Foreign Minister of Saudi Arabia, said that his Government was motivated by two main considerations:

1) that the maintenance of friendly relations between the Arabs and the British called for cooperation on all points of difference which might arise between them;

2) that unless the unhappy controversy which had risen in Palestine was satisfactorily settled, relations between the two parties might be prejudiced.

Butler said that the request of the Arab Delegations for the publication of the McMahon correspondence had been carefully considered. Publication had been refused hitherto on grounds which had nothing whatever to do with the controversy relating to the inclusion or otherwise of Palestine in the undertaking given by Sir Henry McMahon. Certain passages which had a bearing on that controversy had been published already in Churchill's White Paper of 1922 and in the Report of the Peel Commission. His Majesty's Government had now decided to place before the Conference all the letters comprising the so-called McMahon correspondence. The British Government, he said, had consistently held that Palestine was excluded from the area in which Great Britain was stated to be prepared to recognize and support the independence of the Arabs. That remained their view today. His Majesty's Government had never been in any doubt that the whole area of Palestine between the Jordan Valley and the Mediterranean was excepted from the pledge. Moreover, it was scarcely conceivable that, if the pledge was intended to include Palestine, the letter should have made no reservation about access to the Christian Holy Places. The British Government's view had always been definite and had never wavered. One of the questions in dispute had been what was the intention of British Government. Of that the British Government must know more than any one else.

Sir Henry McMahon, the actual author of the correspondence who was acting on instructions from the Foreign Office, was the greatest authority on this point, and he had repeated recently in public and again in private that the area of Palestine was meant to be excluded.

Butler went on to quote the following passage from a letter dated April 12, 1923, written by Sir Gilbert Clayton which had been read out in the House of Lords:

> "I was in daily touch with Sir Henry McMahon throughout the negotiations with King Hussein and made the preliminary drafts of all the letters. I can bear out the statement that it was never the intention that Palestine should be included in the general pledge given to the Sherif; the introductory words in the letter to the Sherif were thought, perhaps erroneously, clearly to cover that point. It was I think, obvious that the peculiar interests involved in Palestine precluded any pledge with regard to its future at so early a stage."

Copies of the English translation of the McMahon correspondence were then handed to delegates.

MacDonald emphasized the importance, on grounds of Parliamentary privilege, of keeping the fact of the distribution of these documents confidential. Leakage of this fact to the Press might, he believed, render Butler and himself liable to imprisonment in the Tower.

It was agreed that the next meeting would take place on February 15.

35 DISCUSSION ON STRATEGY—FEB. 14, 1939

That same afternoon, February 14, at 4:30, MacDonald, Halifax and Butler met with the Jewish Delegation. MacDonald opened the proceedings by remarking that the subject for discussion at this meeting, which was the strategic issue, arose out of his own reference at a previous meeting to the importance of maintaining generally friendly relations with the Arab States of the Middle East. He therefore thought it would perhaps be preferable for him to open this afternoon's discussion, which was unfortunately by no means an academic question. The security of British forces in the Middle East and lines of communication with India and the Far East depended to a considerable extent on their being able to persuade the Egyptian and other Governments in that part of the world to fulfill their treaty engagements where these were in existence, or otherwise to maintain a friendly neutrality. For example, Egypt commanded the air and sea route to the East and the air and land route to the Sudan and Africa, and contained the land base for the defense of the Suez Canal and the only naval base (Alexandria) suitable for the defense of the Eastern Mediterranean.

Iraq commanded the air and land routes to the East and was the center of important oil interests there and in Iran.

A hostile Saudi Arabia could threaten lines of communication through Transjordan to Iraq, and the Aden Protectorate. His Majesty's Government's advice was that in the event of war Ibn Saud could cause great embarrassment if he so desired. It was necessary not to exaggerate, and he wished to maintain a detached view, but he must emphasize that a great deal depended in the event of war on the active support of Britain's allies in the Middle East and the friendship of the remaining States.

The strength of the British forces in the Middle East and their dispositions were all made on this assumption. If this assumption were incorrect, and if they must contemplate even the risk that one or more of these States might be neutral or, at the worst, hostile, British land, air and naval forces in the Middle East would have to be greatly increased as soon as possible.

According to His Majesty's Government's estimate, it would be necessary to reckon with this potential hostility, and to make this readjustment, if the States of the Middle East were tried too hard in the matter of British policy in Palestine.

There was also the question of Northern Africa. In the event of war with a Mediterranean Power, valuable support could be looked for from the Moslem populations of Northern Africa, only if British-Moslem relations generally were good. Similarly, it would be necessary to postulate a good deal of unrest among the Moslems of India which could be exploited by parties interested in preventing Indian cooperation with the rest of the British Empire in a crisis.

His Majesty's Government had received strong and unanimous warnings from all their sources of information in the Near and Middle East and in India as to the probable effects on public opinion in those countries of the pursuance of certain policies in Palestine. The military advisers had in turn given a strong warning to the Cabinet.

He was well aware that there were other considerations. In the event of war, American feeling toward Great Britain was of great importance, and policy in Palestine was a considerable factor in the formation of that opinion. His Majesty's Government certainly kept this fact in mind. But it might be that the crucial moment would be in the early stages of a possible war, in which the theater of war in the Near and Middle East would be as important, perhaps more important, than any. In certain circumstances this area might be the "Achilles' Heel." He had emphasized at an earlier meeting that the defeat of the British Empire would be, at least for a time, an equal disaster for the Jews.

Dr. Weizmann in reply said that he fully realized the weight of the Colonial Secretary's remarks. He accepted all that MacDonald had said as to the strategic importance of Egypt. But he thought that the interests of Egypt, materially if not morally, were as much bound up with Great Britain's interests as were those of the Jews. There might be certain elements in Egypt who had dealings with the potential enemies of Great Britain; but the Egyptians knew what to expect from an Italian occupation. Their loyalty would be conditional on the military success of Great Britain and would only be strained if that was not forthcoming.

Dr. Weizmann visualized the strategic problem in the Middle East in two circles; the real value of the inner circle, which comprised the Arab territories, depended almost entirely on the outer circle which consisted of Turkey, Iran and Afghanistan. If there was no alienation of these States, the rest of the Arab world would follow their lead. In his view the key to the position was Turkey.

MacDonald asked whether some other delegate wished to speak on this subject.

Sharett said that so far as he could see, there were three factors which were rallying the Arab or Arabic-speaking countries to the Palestinian Arabs. They were:

1) The "noblesse oblige" created throughout the Arab world by the feeling that the Palestinian Arabs needed assistance.

2) The interplay of the Government and opposition forces in Arab countries. The opposition parties used the Palestine Arab question to stir up feeling against the Governments by accusing them of turning a deaf ear to the plight of the Arabs in Palestine.

3) The Arab Governments had come to realize the "nuisance value" they had in assisting the Palestine Arabs. Egypt, Iraq and Saudi Arabia had claims of one sort and another, in matters of territory and money, against the British Government, and they felt that they could bring pressure to bear on Great Britain by putting themselves on the map as far as Palestine was concerned. The satisfaction of the Arab claims in Palestine might help the British Government temporarily in dealing with the claims of the Arab Governments, but they would be pressed on other grounds when the Palestine question was settled.

Continuing, Sharett said that he did not think that the policy of the British Government could rest content with securing the general loyalty of the Arab countries for the time being. He wondered how stable that loyalty was and whether it could withstand temptations. He would advocate the exploration of the possibility of creating a second line of defense which would consist of reliance in the military sense on Jewish Palestine. He admitted that this course would not solve British strategic problems in the East, but he submitted that it would constitute an important factor in their solution.

This raised the question of Jewish loyalty and whether it could be relied on. He would remark that seven of the ten Jewish delegates present were British; their loyalty as individuals was that of subjects, but as representatives of the Jewish cause their loyalty was that of allies. He submitted that if there was one thing that was certain in the present state of flux, it was that Jewish loyalty in any serious emergency which might come to the British Empire was a solid reality which could be built upon.

There were technical and geographical conditions to be taken into account in considering Palestine as a line of defense. Palestine was further than Egypt from Italian air bases, it formed the bridgehead to Aqaba and the Persian Gulf for use in case of the closing of the Suez Canal. Palestine had much greater industrial possibilities than Egypt if plans of industrial development for defense purposes were under consideration. It contained certain raw materials and an invaluable store of technical skill and scientific knowledge and talent which would be enthusiastically applied in the interests of the British Empire. As soldiers in the Zionist Army, the Jews would be capable of unlimited devotion.

It was a matter of common knowledge that the British Military reserves in the Near East at present were not what they should be, whereas the overseas commitments of Great Britain had greatly increased since 1914. It would possibly be difficult to bring over reinforcements from India or Australia in view of the dangers to British positions in the Far East. Their naval bases in the Mediterranean and elsewhere were in a more vulnerable position than formerly and would tie up larger military resources. The use of the Mediterranean route might become difficult and the despatch of reinforcements by the Cape route would involve delay. In such circumstances the value of reinforcements from Palestine would be considerable, but in order that such reinforcements might be available, it would be necessary 1) to train a Jewish force in Palestine; 2) to admit more Jews into Palestine in order to meet the possible drain on industry and agriculture which the formation of a local Jewish military force might involve.

I suggested that there was an optical error in the picture which the Colonial Secretary had drawn of the Palestine situation in relation to the strategic needs of the British Empire. The forces of moral and religious sympathy which actuated the people of Egypt and of the Arab countries surrounding Palestine were at present operating on the plane of peace and I doubted whether these forces could be projected onto the plane of war. It was easy to understand the sympathy felt by Egypt and the neighboring states with the Arabs of Palestine; it was natural that they should send representations to His Majesty's Government and that they should have sent delegations to London to defend the Arab cause; but it was fallacious to suppose that the attitude of these countries in the event of war would be decided by their concern for the Palestine Arabs, and not by their own vital interests. In such an event Egypt, Iraq and Saudi Arabia would have to consider the preservation of their position as independent states, and I thought that it was unlikely that their sympathy for the cause of the Arabs of Palestine would then be a determining factor. There were other matters besides Palestine in which these countries had a common interest. And yet they quarrelled among themselves because each country wished to preserve any advantages which it might have against the others.

I ventured seriously to doubt whether the question of Palestine would play any considerable part in the attitude of the Arab states in the event of war. Each country would have to decide whether it was to its interest to stand by the British Empire or by Germany. If one or other Arab state did take sides against the British Empire in time of war, she would do so in any case even if the British Government were to decide to expel all the Jews from Palestine.

Lord Reading asked two questions:

1) It was commonly said that the policy of Great Britain in the event of hostilities with any Mediterranean Powers would be to abandon the Mediterranean basin and concentrate on bottling the two ends of that sea. Was this so? If so, it would have an important effect on the position of Palestine.

2) There had been much talk of a confederation of Arab states. Was that still a live proposal, or had it been abandoned? Were the Arab states considering such a plan amongst themselves?

Replying to Lord Reading, MacDonald said that question 1) was hypothetical and that British plans would of course depend on the circumstances existing at the time when trouble broke out. It might be that his own reference to Alexandria as an important naval base in time of war was a sufficient indication that they should not in all circumstances confine their attention to closing both ends of the Mediterranean. As regards question 2), MacDonald said that he was not certain of the present attitude of the Arab states toward the proposal for a confederation. There were many considerations and interests working against it.

Dealing with the remarks of previous speakers, MacDonald said that in the first place he agreed with me that, if it came to a supreme emergency, other considerations besides Palestine would enter the Arab mind. But they could not possibly dismiss Palestine completely from their minds. The Arab world had been in a ferment for two years over the Palestine question, and while he did not wish to exaggerate its importance, it would be a vital mistake to underestimate it. Stories of British atrocities—propaganda not against the Jews but against the British—were rife in Arab countries.

Dr. Weizmann had spoken of the "outer circle" and the "inner circle," and his thesis had been that if we could hold the "outer circle" that hoop would keep the "inner circle" under control. As to this, MacDonald would say in the first place that the "outer circle" was not entirely indifferent to what was happening in Palestine. Dr. Weizmann had referred to the existence of a fairly strong pro-German sentiment in Afghanistan, but undoubtedly one of the most potent forces at the disposal of German propaganda in Afghanistan was their alleged outrage of Moslem religious susceptibilities in Palestine. He had received many reports indicating that Palestine might well affect at least one part (Afghanistan) of the "outer circle."

As for Turkey, the Jewish Agency Delegation were aware that a great deal had been done recently to maintain friendship with that country.

But apart from this, the Colonial Secretary was not sure that he would place so much confidence in the "outer circle" being able to control the "inner circle." If things went badly in the "inner circle," as at present, His Majesty's Government were bound to feel anxious.

He did not dispute that it was to the interest of Egypt and the other countries to be on Britain's side in the event of war; nor did he dispute the fact that intelligent people of these countries (except for certain interested politicians) were well aware that such was their interest. But public opinion in those countries was not so well informed and the leaders depended on public opinion. Anti-British propaganda was already active in the Arab countries, and it was too much to hope that a certain amount of mud would not stick.

Sharett had stressed the unreliable nature of the Arabs in contrast with the unquestionable loyalty of the Jews. His Majesty's Government did not undervalue the industrial and technical resources and manpower of Palestine Jewry. Nevertheless, if it came to a choice between Jewish or Arab support, he did not believe that, valuable as Jewish assistance would be, it would make up for what would have been lost by the lack of the vital support of the Arab and Moslem world. But there was no such blunt choice before the Conference; His Majesty's Government were not arguing that the whole Arab case must be granted at once; but they did argue that there was serious reason for the British and Jewish representatives to consider together whether there were not ways and means, without sacrificing the Jewish cause more than they thought proper, of meeting the Arabs and getting their consent and goodwill for what was going on in Palestine. In this way all three would be united in a common interest.

Rabbi Wise spoke of the reactions of Jews in America to the general strategic question. In 1915 and 1916 the Jewish leaders had done more than their share to move the President and American public opinion generally to throw in their lot with the Allies. The Balfour Declaration was not a bribe to sway the American Jews, but a recognition of the special rights of the Jewish people in any territorial redistribution which might result from the war.

In September, 1938, the American Jewish leaders had begun exploratory talks in the same direction. They found the young Jews of America anxious to form a Jewish legion to reinforce the democratic Powers in the West and the Jewish community in Palestine. Unless His Majesty's Government took such action as would needlessly estrange the American Jews, this help would be available in any future crisis long before the United States itself came in.

Moreover, in the event of war in Europe, American public opinion would be strongly divided, and the President and those who supported him would not find it easy to persuade their fellow citizens into active military support of the democracies. In this sphere also the Jews of America could give the President most valuable support unless, he must repeat, any action were taken to cool their ardor.

Dr. Weizmann said that he differed from the general opinion that the critical period of a war was necessarily at its commencement. There were fifty to seventy thousand young Jews who could be brought in and trained today and would form an army of devoted people; there was technical skill available in abundance. There was no need to discuss the question of loyalty.

He felt that Jewish shares had gone down in the world in recent years mainly because the Germans had shown that a Jewish community was in fact destructible. He would only say that on the long view God's will was man's law. From the point of view of pure British self-interest, he thought that it was a great advantage that there should be a powerful community of Jews who were not working against Great Britain. They could organize a regiment of scientists and technicians entirely at the disposal of Great Britain, and all this quite unconditionally.

I said that we were handicapped in discussions of strategy by the fact that we were private persons, but as a layman I queried the danger of an early and decisive blow being inflicted in the deserts of Arabia. A knock-out blow might be aimed at large centers of population in Western Europe but I doubted whether it would be possible in, say, Iraq.

I wondered what were the political conclusions of the strategic premises. Suppose the Arabs wished to expel the Jews altogether from Palestine. What was to happen if the Arabs were not satisfied? In my view they should bring the largest possible number of young Jews into Palestine in the shortest possible time. It was possible to train Jews for defense of this character today. Some were already being trained. This would offset to a very great degree the danger of which they had spoken.

MacDonald agreed that there was really no question of a knock-out blow being delivered in the deserts of Arabia, but events might take place there from which they would never recover and which, whilst they might not of themselves end in Britain's defeat, might certainly cramp her throughout the struggle.

He knew that it was held in some quarters that the immigration of large numbers of Jews into Palestine would counteract Arab hostility if it arose, but he thought that such a policy would have very serious results. It would lose Britain not only the friendship of the Arab world, but also that of the wider

Moslem world. His Majesty's Government would be bound to attach considerable importance to the susceptibilities of the Arab states.

Sharett said that in the crisis of September, 1938, the Egyptian press was full of articles stressing the loyalty of Egypt to Great Britain. The Jews in Palestine today could do as much as Egypt or Iraq to assist Great Britain. There were fifty thousand Jews now in Palestine available for military duties, half of whom could be used locally and half placed at the disposal of Great Britain for action around Palestine.

Lord Halifax, who joined the discussion for the first time, said that no one could have listened without being greatly moved by much that had been said and without being profoundly conscious of what appeared to be a clash of thought, but was not really so. No one could assess with any precision the potential "nuisance value" of the Arabs. In such a matter there was much room for error, exaggeration and underestimate. He himself was disposed to set his estimate of the anxiety he felt if the British Empire should confront itself with Arab ill-will more high than Dr. Weizmann. This was because the Jewish community was more intelligent than the Arab and more capable of weighing the real issues. There was great force in what MacDonald had said about the Arabs being prepared to take the worst possible view of any knocks which might fall upon the British if they got into trouble. The fact that the Arabs were less intelligent would add weight to their feelings. In this connection he would allude to the feeling in India, with which he had had first-hand acquaintance [he had been Viceroy of India] and which he had found to run like fire and be very difficult to control. For these reasons he did not feel able to underestimate the danger to which MacDonald had referred.

Lord Halifax said that he had been struck by Rabbi Wise's remarks on the reality of the challenge to the world today. The issues were plain to the world; there was a contest between the profoundest philosophies of human life. If this diagnosis were correct, their discussions would lead them to see lucidly how necessary it was for them to reconcile administrative necessity and fundamental and eternal spiritual claims and rights. He recalled a meeting with Gandhi in which was apparent the same clash between administrative necessity and spiritual rights. He had had to admit Gandhi's claim, but had successfully pleaded administrative necessity.

He would suggest that the Jews should, of their own free will, dispose of their rights by offering terms of conciliation, and on the long view of their own problem and also of the problems which confronted the world, he was satisfied that all parties must give freely in order to reach a solution.

MacDonald said that he hoped to put forward one or two ideas at the next meeting, which might form a practical basis for discussion.

The next meeting was fixed for February 15, at 8:30 p.m. The Government had already arranged to meet the Arab delegations the same day at 4:00 p.m.

36 JORDANIAN AND YEMENITE SPEECHES—FEB. 15, 1939

All the Arab delegations were present at that meeting and, on the British side, MacDonald, Lord Dufferin, and Butler. The discussion was opened by the Prime Minister of Transjordan, Taufiq Abdul-Huda. He spoke in Arabic and his remarks were translated into English by his colleagues.

He said he would have thought it unnecessary for him to add anything to the statement of the Palestinian Delegation, which had set out so clearly the logical basis of their just claims, but for the fact that Transjordan was of all the Arab states the closest to Palestine and that it was ruled by the Emir Abdullah, son of the late King Hussein and his intermediary in the war-time negotiations with the British, which had already come under discussion.

The danger of trouble in Palestine spreading across the frontier could not be overlooked. Hence Transjordan was concerned in the fate of Palestine not only from common Arab sentiment, but in the interests of public security at home.

The Emir had foreseen the dangers of the Palestine situation long ago. In 1933 and again in 1934 he had warned the High Commissioner of the disastrous results which would follow from pushing forward Jewish immigration and land purchases. We had now reached the future which the Emir had predicted. Had it not been for his influence, things might have been worse still.

Taufiq Pasha then turned to the subject of the McMahon correspondence. The British Government's case was based on their interpretation of the fourth and fifth paragraphs of Sir Henry McMahon's letter of October 24, 1915. But King Hussein in a subsequent letter expressly reserved the right to raise the question of "Beirut and its coasts" at a later stage. Butler had said in the statement at the previous meeting that it was made clear to King Hussein at the time that Palestine was excluded from the area of Arab independence, and that Sir Henry McMahon, in his letter to *The Times* two years before, had reinforced this view. But the Emir Abdullah, who was peculiarly fitted to know the real circumstances on the Arab side, repudiated this in a letter to the High Commissioner, which he regretted had not been published in spite of a request for this to be done. Butler had said that the most important factor was the intentions of the British

Government in making their promises. But in a contract binding on two parties the intentions of one of them were irrelevant. The Emir Abdullah, he said, was convinced that the Arab peoples were the most loyal friends of Great Britain, and he implored His Majesty's Government not to squander the valuable assets of their friendship.

MacDonald observed that there was room for various opinions in regard to the McMahon correspondence. Butler and he had had a long discussion over the week-end with Sir Henry McMahon, who was a very honorable man and whose recollection of the events was perfectly clear. Furthermore, Butler had quoted a statement by Sir Gilbert Clayton, whose integrity was beyond reproach, and in that statement Sir Gilbert had said that it was perfectly clear that Palestine was excluded from the area of eventual Arab rule. That statement had been made in 1923 and Sir Gilbert was not suffering from any loss of memory. Another authority, whose integrity had never been questioned, Colonel T.E. Lawrence, wrote after the Cairo Conference that that Conference had carried out the intentions of the McMahon correspondence. All these authorities had placed on record that the area known as Palestine was excluded.

Prince Saif ul-Islam of Yemen said that Yemen had a long interest in the question by reason of the large number of Jews within its borders who enjoyed perfect justice under Moslem rule. His country was deeply affected by the troubles and disturbances in Palestine, and he had taken measures to prevent the influx of Jews from the Yemen into Palestine. The King of the Yemen had asked the British Government to solve the Palestine question justly. He disagreed with Mr. Butler's remarks with regard to the McMahon promises. Prince Saif ul-Islam praised the statement made by MacDonald in the House of Commons on November 24, 1938, to the effect that the British people ought to be the last people in the world not to understand the feelings of the Arabs in this matter. Yemen had not, like Iraq, taken part in the Great War with the Allies; but although in those days the Yemen was on the opposite side to the British, it was only on that side out of loyalty to pledges. Today the Yemen and Great Britain had common interests.

Ali Maher Pasha, the Egyptian Prime Minister, said that the Egyptian Delegation fully shared the views of the Palestinian and other delegations on the subject of the McMahon pledges, and he hoped that the United Kingdom Delegation would give satisfaction to the Arab representations in this matter.

An argument arose with regard to a sub-committee to examine the true content of the McMahon pledges. The question was deferred to the following meeting, on February 16.

37 DISCUSSION ON IMMIGRATION—FEB. 15, 1939

The same evening at 8:30 the Jewish Delegation met with the representatives of the Government—MacDonald, Butler and Dufferin.

Chief Rabbi Herzog opened the discussion. He said that he spoke not as a leader of a political party but as the spiritual head of Palestine Jewry. The Jewish title to Palestine was infinitely older than the Balfour Declaration and was founded on Divine assurance delivered through a succession of men of God beginning with Abraham. By issuing the Declaration, Great Britain had made herself an instrument of Divine Providence, and Jewry regarded it as the beginning of the promise of the restoration of Israel. He recalled that King George the Fifth had on one occasion given thanks that Great Britain had been given the opportunity of playing the part of a second and greater Cyrus.

MacDonald then called on Rabbi Blau, of Agudat Israel, who spoke in Hebrew. Rabbi Blau associated himself with Rabbi Herzog's statement regarding the religious aspect of the Jewish rights in Palestine. Continuing, he said that in a recent statement the Colonial Secretary had alluded to the far-reaching character of Arab resistance to the policy of the Balfour Declaration, which he said had not been foreseen.

As regards Arab resistance, Rabbi Blau recalled that in 1920 and 1921 there were on two occasions riots and disturbances in Palestine. Relying fully on the Mandatory regime, he together with thousands of other Jews lived at that time in the Arab quarter, and he and members of his family had only been saved by a miracle from a cruel death. When the British Mandate was confirmed by the League of Nations in 1922, it was already well known that the Arabs did not consent to the establishment of the Jewish National Home. As to the alleged right of the present Arab majority in Palestine to self-government, Rabbi Blau was doubtful whether such a proposal could be seriously considered. He referred to the recent brutal massacre at Tiberias and asked whether it was conceivable that His Majesty's Government should entrust to Arab administration and arbitrary discretion the lives and property of 400,000 Jews. Moreover, for the sake of the personal ambitions of one man the Arab nation had murdered hundreds of the best and most respected of its own members.

Certain countries might exist today which were prepared to reward those engaging in murder and cruelty to Jews, but it was clear that His Majesty's Government was not to be found amongst them. Providence had chosen in His Majesty's Government a trustee for the Holy Land, a trustee for the return of the

Jewish people to the land of its inheritance and for the establishment of a home for the Jewish people in their Holy Land until the time of full redemption. He prayed that His Majesty's Government might remain faithful to their trust and to the confidence placed in them.

Sholem Asch said that he was there to present before His Majesty's Government the cause of the poorest of the Jewish masses in Eastern Europe. Palestine had been a light to the Jewish masses in their darkest night and had never ceased to be a supreme factor in Jewish life. With the Messianic hope of Palestine, the Jews had power and courage to endure pain, suffering and martyrdom. What they had attained in Palestine had been accomplished by the hands of the poor with the moral and physical assistance given to them by their fellows on both sides of the Atlantic, and he could testify to the willing sacrifices which had been made in order to rebuild their historic homeland.

Hundreds of thousands of young people were training themselves in order that they might have the privilege and the happiness of giving their experience and their devoted efforts to the only country which had a meaning for them. He was certain that disillusion in regard to Great Britain would be the greatest blow sustained by his unfortunate people. Palestine was their right, and just as they could not escape from their destiny, so were His Majesty's Government unable to renounce the great and holy task which God had placed in their hands.

MacDonald, having ascertained that no other delegate wished to contribute to the general discussions, said that it was necessary to move on to details and practical proposals, and he proposed to start discussion by opening the question of the policy which should be adopted in regard to immigration. At this point he urged on the delegates the confidential nature of their discussions. If there was to be free and frank discussion it was imperative that the various suggestions made should not be able to be misconstrued, for example, in the Press as definite proposals.

As he understood the Jewish proposal, it was that immigration should continue indefinitely on the basis of the economic absorptive capacity of Palestine. The formula of economic absorptive capacity obviously set no limits. The Arabs would remember the large figures of past years and would think that it would mean the continuation of Jewish immigration until there was a Jewish majority. No Arab fears would be allayed and they would be afraid, if that were the result of this Conference, that the last opportunity of checking their domination by the Jews would be gone. This fear of the Arabs was one of the most important factors in the whole problem, and if it continued they would have to face the consequences of resulting Arab hostility. Rabbi Blau had said that Arab terrorism had occurred before the Mandate was drawn up; that was true, but at that time the League of Nations and the United States of America had only witnessed one series of violent acts, bad though they were, and they had hoped that with time the Arabs would acquiesce in the presence of the Jews. His Majesty's Government had always hoped that prosperity would reconcile the Arabs to the idea of the Jewish National Home.

It was only when revolt had followed revolt that they had come to the conclusion that that policy could not lead to reconciliation. He himself was certain that Arab hostility would persist whilst the Arabs were possessed by the fear of Jewish domination. Moreover, it was certain that external hostility would also grow. In those circumstances, they might have to develop the Jewish National Home by force.

It would be right for His Majesty's Government to change the policy and to gain Arab consent by removing the Arab fear of Jewish domination. He suggested tentatively that Jewish immigration should continue for a period of years (not necessarily with Arab consent) calculated on the formula of economic absorptive capacity, provided that within that period the yearly quotas should be such that immigration should not exceed a certain figure, a figure which would maintain the position of the Jews definitely as a minority in Palestine. At the end of this period there would be no further Jewish immigration except with Arab consent. This would remove the genuine Arab fear of numerical domination by the Jews. Only then could a psychological change take place which would enable them to appreciate the argument that Jewish immigration brought material advantages.

They were faced now with deciding policy for (say) the next quarter century, and it seemed to him that the suggestion he had just made was more hopeful than that of obstinate retention of the full doctrine of economic absorptive capacity.

Dr. Weizmann said that he did not feel able to enter into a discussion of MacDonald's suggestions now. He would only say that it appeared to place the Jews in a minority in Palestine, a course which seemed to him inconceivable.

After a brief exchange between MacDonald and Weizmann, I said that, speaking as a Palestinian Jew, I felt certain that I was voicing the feelings of at least 90 percent of the Jews of Palestine. The Colonial Secretary had proposed:
1) That after a period of x years Jewish immigration should be stopped. True, it was to depend upon Arab consent at the end of x years, but who could say what the attitude of the Arabs would then be? The Colonial Secretary had suggested that the Arabs should have the right to stop immigration.

2) That as far as it depended on His Majesty's Government, the Jews should be a permanent minority in Palestine.
3) That for x years Jewish immigration should be subjected to an arbitrary "high level."

I went on to say that the Jews had begun to return to Palestine long before the British occupation. The Jews had come to Palestine (and I was one of them) as their National Home; they came there as of right. MacDonald's suggestion meant that the Jews must renounce their title to be in Palestine as of right. The suggestion meant that after x years they were to be at the mercy of non-Jews, under the government of those who had always opposed the National Home by violence and murder. Could it possibly be believed that the 400,000 human beings who came to Palestine, not by chance, but because that country had a deep historic significance for them and at the word of one of the greatest Empires endorsed by fifty other nations, could it be believed that they would accept the suggestion that they should renounce their National Home and live in bondage —the kind of life they were leading in all countries of the Diaspora? If the Jews were to accept this suggestion, their situation in Palestine would be as it was now in Germany, if not worse.

The Jews felt a deep attachment to Great Britain, I said, but even stronger was our faith in our redemption in our ancient homeland. Great Britain could say "The Jewish National Home was a dream; it is no more." It was beyond the power of the Jews to waive our right to our National Home, to renounce Erez Israel. We could not consider accepting in Palestine the position of a minority in a foreign state, to live in bondage in Palestine with our right of entry dependent on Arab consent. Under the Turks there had been a law in Palestine which provided that a Jew entering the country could remain there only for three months. The Jews had been compelled to break that law for the sake of a higher law. I myself was one of those who had remained in the country illegally. I arrived in Palestine in 1906, at a time when this law was still in force, and was issued a permit for three month's residence—I had stayed on illegally up to this day. The Jews in Palestine could not recognize the moral validity of a law which denied the right of Jews to enter Palestine unless the Mufti permitted. It was not for this that I had come to Palestine 33 years ago. It was not for this that I went to plow Jewish land in a remote village in the Galilee 32 years ago, with a rifle on my shoulder. And it was not for this that my eighteen-year-old son had now gone to guard the same village, he, too, with a rifle on his shoulder. It was not possible to turn Erez Israel into a new exile.

MacDonald said that he was grateful to me for saying clearly and firmly how

I felt about his suggestion, and how the Jews in Palestine would feel. I had made it clear, he said, that with all their anxiety to help, the Jews might find it impossible. For his part he assured us that His Majesty's Government were anxious to to help the Jews. Continuing, he said that he had merely stated a principle of policy for consideration and that he had not made a decisive proposal. No period of years was stated, that was a matter for discussion. As for the statement that the Jews could not accept the position of a minority in a foreign state, he had not made any suggestion of the kind. He had only made a suggestion about immigration. Supposing that the minority was not in a foreign state but in a territory under British Mandate, or in an independent state with a constitution on a basis of parity giving the Jews complete security. He suggested that the Jewish Delegation had, perhaps naturally, taken too rigid a view as to the permanence of the scheme which he had suggested. It was plain that policy for all time could not be settled now, and His Majesty's Government did not intend to try to do so. Supposing there were a Jewish minority at the end of, say, five years, in a United Palestine, that was not necessarily permanent. Supposing that after five years Palestine were partitioned into an Arab Area and a Jewish Area, the latter with a large measure of Jewish control. That was not an impossible evolution. The Jewish Delegation should not assume that his suggestion had complete permanence; if it were adopted, it might merely be the means of working to another eventual solution. The Government's task was to create conditions in Palestine in the near future which would give peace and the condition for calm constructive planning and not close the door to what might be the eventual solution.

Professor Namier said that the Colonial Secretary had stressed the day before the importance of the Arab states surrounding Palestine—Egypt, Saudi Arabia, Iraq, etc.—and that the British Empire itself had to take account of them. He had also stressed that these states were deeply interested in Palestine. If, in spite of all these friends surrounding Palestine the Palestine Arabs feared to find themselves in a minority against the Jews, how much more justified would be Jewish fears. If the setting up of a constitution on the basis of parity was the answer to their fears, that could be applied to the Arabs as well.

MacDonald said that they were trying to deal with facts as they were today. He believed that a few years ago it would have been possible to get agreement on a basis of parity by itself. But the situation had changed, and such a solution was very doubtful now. He himself had never suggested that His Majesty's Government should not pay heed to the fears of the Jews.

Professor Namier said that as it was not possible to keep the Mandatory machine forever; it was evident that the Arabs would in time become the rulers.

MacDonald denied this interpretation of what he had said. His Majesty's Government understood perfectly the fears which the Jews had of becoming a minority in a foreign state. There were at least two ways in which the Jews might form a minority in Palestine without being a minority in a foreign state: 1) by the maintenance of the Mandate system, perhaps with some measure of partition; 2) by the creation of an independent State with a constitution on the basis of parity, the Jews being equal partners in power.

Dr. Weizmann said that the Arabs refused to say how far they were prepared to live with the Jews. For them the Jews did not exist. He feared that MacDonald's hopes of peace were built on sand. The Arabs knew that His Majesty's Government was in a difficult position. He was sure that the British Government would soon find itself in a better position. He thought that if 300,000 Jews more were today settled in Palestine the discussion would have been simpler. Why did the Arabs not come to the table? Their absence made him sceptical that MacDonald would achieve his purpose.

MacDonald replied that the Government was concerned at the fact that their policy in Palestine in face of the bitter opposition of the Arabs was arousing the hostility of the neighboring Arab states. This was, of course, a consideration of the greatest importance. Speaking personally, however, he would base the British attitude on a more important consideration. He did not believe that it was right to put the Arabs of Palestine against their will under the domination of another people, even if this were good for them. He knew that the Jews did not wish to dominate the Arabs, but he wished that he could convey to the Jewish Delegation his conviction that British policy was based not only on expediency but on the principles underlying the Mandate, which could not be held to justify the imposition of a dominating Jewish National Home on the Arabs of Palestine in face of their strong opposition.

Dr. Weizmann had asked whether MacDonald's suggestion with regard to immigration would bring peace in Palestine. MacDonald said he was unable to answer this question. In the talks with the Arabs the stage of discussion of practical proposals had not yet been reached. The Arabs were holding out for the complete stoppage of immigration and an independent Arab State with safeguards for British interests and for the Jewish minority. At the present moment the Government was merely exploring every kind of suggestion.

Referring to the Arab demand for complete stoppage of immigration, I said that it was physically impossible for the Arabs to stop Jewish immigration without the aid of British bayonets. The Arabs could not prevent Jews from immigrating to Tel Aviv or to Haifa or to other parts of the coastal plain which were in Jewish hands. For that matter, it was also impossible to establish an Arab State in the teeth of Jewish opposition unless with the aid of British bayonets. Such demands by the Arabs were merely bluff.

MacDonald observed that some Arabs were only longing for the British Government to withdraw in order that they might deal with the Jews. If the Jewish attitude were really as pictured by me, British withdrawal would mean a bloody civil war, the outcome of which he would not venture to prophesy.

Dr. Weizmann suggested that the discussion should be adjourned. MacDonald agreed, and asked whether any members of the Delegation had any questions. Dr. Weizmann asked whether the United Kingdom Delegation could give an indication of their proposals regarding the two other main issues, namely, land and the constitutional question. The Jewish Delegation would like to see the whole picture.

MacDonald said that the only reason why he hesitated to do this was that if he were to present proposals covering the whole field, the Jewish Delegation might interpret these proposals as the decisions of His Majesty's Government, which they certainly were not. Dr. Weizmann said that he quite understood the position. MacDonald agreed to put forward suggestions in outline regarding land and the constitutional question purely as a basis of discussion. As regards the constitutional question, the suggestion was that British Mandatory control should continue and that constitutional organs should be created on a basis of parity as between Jews and Arabs. As regards land sales, the British authorities should be given power to restrict sales of land from Arabs to Jews. In some districts there might be prohibition; in others restriction. The essential feature was the principle of restriction.

Dr. Weizmann said that this gave the Jewish Delegation sufficient material for consideration. He suggested that the next meeting might be postponed until Monday (February 20). MacDonald suggested that this might give the impression that the Government had broken off their discussions with the Jewish Delegation. After discussion, it was agreed that the next meeting should be held at 11 a.m. on Friday, February 17.

Before the meeting adjourned, Butler referred to the need for the greatest caution in dealing with representatives of the Press, since the value of the discussions depended on their privacy. MacDonald proposed that he inform the Press that the general discussion was concluded and that discussion was begun on more detailed points, chiefly immigration. He would add that the Jewish Delegation had maintained their demand that economic absorptive capacity should continue to be the guiding principle in connection with immigration.

At the conclusion of the meeting, Butler came over to Sharett and told him that he well understood that there could be no talk of a Jewish minority in an Arab State.

38 MEETING WITH CHAMBERLAIN—FEB. 16, 1939

MacDonald's hostile intentions were now obvious, and the Jewish Agency Executive met the next day to discuss the situation.

I proposed that we inform the Government that we were willing to make an agreement with the Arabs on the basis of give and take, provided that our basic rights were ensured and that no arrangement would be made that involved, explicitly or implicitly, the fixing of a minority status. We would not insist on a direct meeting with the Arabs; if the Government wished, it could mediate between us. However, if the Arabs refused to compromise and stuck to their extreme demands, we would insist on the granting of our demands to the full and would make no concessions to the Government. Furthermore, we should explain that in that case there was no way to ensure peace in the country and protect England's lines of communication other than by large-scale immigration and the rapid increase of the Jews in the shortest possible time. Only such a policy would reduce the period of the disturbances and bring the Arabs to grasp the necessity of reaching an inderstanding with us. Any concession we made to the Government, even the most minor, without an agreement with the Arabs, would only serve as an additional cause for hardening the opposition of the Arabs, and both we and the Government would only lose.

In the middle of the meeting three members were compelled to leave: Dr. Weizmann, Dr. Stephen S. Wise, and I. The day before Dr. Weizmann had received an invitation from the Prime Minister to meet him at 11:30, and to bring along two of his colleagues. Dr. Weizmann had asked Dr. Wise and me to accompany him.

Chamberlain received us at 10 Downing Street, in the Cabinet room. He sat at the middle of the table, with Malcolm MacDonald next to him. The three of us sat opposite them.

After some friendly remarks on both sides, Dr. Weizmann opened by saying that we were anxious to assist the Government in securing peace in Palestine, and that we were preparing to negotiate with the Arabs to that end either directly or through the good offices of H.M. Government, though without, of course, surrendering our essential rights, or accepting minority status. He ventured to submit that in case the Arabs should remain intransigent, there was really no reason why we should make any concessions at all, since if a policy were to be imposed by H. M. Government, the Arabs would continue to make trouble, and next year the Government would again come to us and say: "There is trouble in Palestine; the whole Arab world is supporting the Palestine Arabs; you must make yet further concessions." It was not his intention here to go over all the details of the discussions now in progress at St. James's but he would like to say one word about a question the Colonial Secretary had raised there the day before: the land question. Land was the basis of the National Home; we were not coming to Palestine to remain town-dwellers, but were striving to return to the soil. Land was thus fundamental to our work. More than this, agricultural settlement was the main basis of our work in Palestine, and had a direct bearing on immigration. Every agricultural settler created a possibility of additional settlers in other occupations; industry and commerce depended upon it. Restrictions on land and on agricultural settlement were bound to act as restrictions on immigration. This was why we were so disturbed by the Colonial Secretary's remarks the previous evening with regard to restrictions on land settlement.

The Jewish Agency was anxious to cooperate with H. M. Government in a scheme of development. Such development was necessary not only in Jewish interests, but perhaps even more in Arab interests. As a result of three years of disturbances, there was terrible distress in Palestine, especially among the Arabs. The rich Arabs had left the country, for fear of extortion or even assassination; the poor Arabs had become still poorer, especially the fellaheen. The country needed capital for development. We were anxious, together with the Government, to work out a plan of development which would both assist our immigration and at the same time improve the lot of the fellaheen. Poverty was really one of the main causes of the unrest in Palestine, because the less people felt they had to lose, the more likely they were to make trouble.

The Prime Minister said that Dr. Weizmann was as always very reasonable, so reasonable as to disarm people. He was even alarmed to find how disarmed he was. He had been specially glad to hear what Dr. Weizmann had said with regard to development in the interests both of Arabs and Jews. He entirely agreed with the view that concessions were not the way. As an honest man, however, he must admit that he did not know what the Government would be doing in a few years' time; first of all he might not be in that Government; secondly he did not know what the circumstances would be in two or three years' time. But he believed that if there were some measure of appeasement achieved now, then the chances of satisfactory development in future would be much improved. He would like to know whether the Jews would be prepared to help, not only the Palestine Arabs, but the neighboring countries, for instance Egypt?

Dr. Weizmann said that so far as he knew, Egypt did not need our help.

MacDonald mentioned Saudi Arabia, and Dr. Weizmann said he thought perhaps something might be done there.

Chamberlain resumed and said that he had followed the discussions at St. James' with close attention and had read the minutes. He knew, therefore, that the strategic aspect had been discussed. In this connection he thought he had to make it clear that there had been a moment when they were only an inch from war. At that time they had been quite unprepared, both in England, and also in the Mediterranean. Even if they had had to fight then, he was sure they should have won through in the end, but since then they had become much stronger, and the relative strengths of the parties had changed in favor of Great Britain. He believed they could now face any situation that might arise without undue worry. He remembered that his father [Joseph Chamberlain] had always advised him not to "kick against the pricks." It was well-known that his father had always been much interested in Jewish work, and that he himself had great sympathy for it. He knew that the Jews in Palestine had had many disappointments, but he believed that once peace was achieved, progress would be easier. Finally, he asked whether we had anything to add.

Dr. Wise said that Dr. Weizmann spoke for a large constituency in the United States—where there were about five million Jews. A few of them might be against Zionism, but there were at least four and a half million American Jews who were firmly behind Dr. Weizmann. And not only Jews, there were millions of Christians who took a similar view. All the nonconformist churches, with their twenty million adherents, believed deeply in the prophecies of the Jewish return to Palestine. The American Christians could not imagine that the land promised to the Jewish people should be handed over to the Arabs, who for them were "pagans." American Jewry was at the moment engaged in the collection of a fund of four million pounds for the refugees. The first line of settlement for them was Palestine; they needed land for settlement in Palestine, and without land they would be able to do nothing. He would therefore associate himself with Dr. Weizmann in his anxiety over the land restrictions suggested by the Colonial Secretary.

I followed Dr. Wise, and said that I could speak for the nearly half a million Jews of Palestine. The Prime Minister had himself mentioned disappointments. It was true that we had sometimes had to bear very bitter disappointments, and not seldom at the hands of the British Administration itself. But although we had often had to criticize the Administration, and criticize it severely, and I feared we might have to go on doing so, I wished to assure the Prime Minister, on behalf of the whole Jewish community in Palestine, that if—God forbid—Great Britain should ever have to fight, the Jews of Palestine would stand as one man behind her. I also wished to say that in spite of the many difficulties experienced in the last sixty years of our resettlement in Palestine, and especially in the last three years, the Jewish community in Palestine had complete confidence in its strength, its work, and its future. We believed that we should achieve our aim, and that when we had done so, England would not be ashamed of having helped us.

I also thought it desirable to say that although the achievement of an agreement with the Arabs seemed at the present moment very doubtful, with the growth of our work and the increase of our numbers in Palestine more favorable conditions would be created for such an agreement, so that a strong Jewish Palestine would be able to establish peace not only in Palestine itself, but also contribute largely to peace and security in the neighboring Arab countries.

Chamberlain said that he was very glad to hear this statement from me as one who was familiar with conditions in Palestine. He thanked me for my reference to the attitude of Palestinian Jewry toward Great Britain.

Dr. Weizmann asked if he might add a few words in conclusion. He said the Arabs were making a great deal of fuss about Palestine. It was curious when one recalled that Alexandretta had been torn away from Syria without anybody taking any notice to speak of, or doing anything about it. He firmly believed that the recent disturbances were not rooted only in Palestine. There was unrest in Palestine, but there were powerful external forces who were interested in fomenting trouble there, and for which Palestine and the Jews were only very small considerations. He need not specify against whom these forces were really directed. The Prime Minister said he knew this; we were now facing grave difficulties, but he hoped that better times would come, in which both they and we would be able to get on with our constructive work.

39 PROPOSALS TO THE ARABS—FEB. 16, 1939

On February 16, the United Kingdom Delegation had a meeting with the Arab Delegations.

MacDonald recalled the purpose of the Conferences, which was to promote a frank exchange of views and, if possible, some kind of understanding; but if unfortunately agreement should not be possible, His Majesty's Government would at least be able to formulate their future policy with the fullest knowledge of all sides of the case.

So far as the present meeting was concerned, they had now reached the stage when detailed proposals could be examined. There were three factors to be borne in mind; first, that the Arab Delegations did not recognize the Balfour Declaration or the Mandate; secondly, that His Majesty's Government entered the discussions bound by their existing obligations, as well as by their interpretation of the MacMahon correspondence; and thirdly, the facts of the situation today. He was sure that all parties desired a practical settlement. He then set out what were, in his view, factors militating against the proposal which Jamal Husseini had made for the immediate setting up of an independent Arab State in Palestine. Recent events, he said, had shaken the confidence of those Governments which were interested in Palestine affairs in the ability of an Arab Government to give adequate security to the substantial Jewish minority in Palestine. He accepted Jamal Husseini's statement that the Arabs of Palestine were not anti-Semitic. But it was, nevertheless, a fact that circumstances in Palestine during the last twenty years, culminating in the events since 1936, had created a very strong feeling against the Jews in Palestine. Jamal Husseini had assured the Conference of the desire of the Arabs of Palestine to safeguard the rights of this Jewish minority; but, while accepting this assurance, it was also a fact that the political leaders of the Palestine Arabs had often confessed themselves unable to restrain the actions of the more violent of their countrymen. Therefore, even if constitutional safeguards were given, he thought that the interested Governments would not be reassured that the Jewish minority would be secure from attack under an independent Arab Government in Palestine.

He was anxious to be fair, and it was a fact that there were violent elements among the Jews of Palestine as well as among the Arabs. But world opinion would regard this as, if anything, increasing the danger of uncontrolled outbursts by both sides leading to retaliation, and to a situation approaching a state of civil war, unless the Mandatory Power with its police and military forces were to remain in the country. He did not assert that the record of the Mandatory Government in matters of public security was beyond criticism, but it was at least fair to say that without it things might be much worse.

Thus, one of the facts which they had to face was that many of those Governments which had an interest in Palestine affairs might not be willing to see an Arab State established. The Palestinian Arabs should remember that they had not to deal with the British Government alone, and that the ratification of the

League of Nations was necessary for any changes in the constitution of Palestine. It would be a blunder from which not only His Majesty's Government but the Arabs themselves would suffer, if the Conference were to reach an agreement which would be rejected at Geneva, or which the pressure of American public opinion would make inoperative. He saw little prospect of the Jewish minority feeling sufficiently secure in Palestine unless the Mandatory Administration were to continue for some time to come.

They might think that he had so far placed undue emphasis on Jewish rights to the exclusion of the rights of the Arab majority which were threatened today. The meaning of the National Home promise in the Balfour Declaration had never been properly defined. Certain of its authors (for example Lloyd George and President Wilson) had, however, expressed the view that it was intended to lead up to a Jewish commonwealth; so far this had always been a possibility, and a possibility most threatening to the Palestine Arabs. His Majesty's Government did not think it right that this uncertainty should continue any longer, and would propose to make a public announcement to the effect that they did not contemplate that Palestine should become a Jewish State—unless of course the Arabs should wish it.

Antonius asked whether this assurance would cover all parts of Palestine.

MacDonald referred to the rejection of the Partition Commission's proposals and said that His Majesty's Government would not contemplate a sovereign Jewish State in any part of Palestine. This definite interpretation of the Balfour Declaration would, he thought, bring some measure of reassurance to the Arabs of Palestine. Moreover, His Majesty's Government thought that the time was overdue when self-governing institutions should be begun in Palestine. The efforts they had previously made indicated the Government's anxiety to achieve this. In their view one of the principles of the future government of Palestine should be that neither community should be in a position to dominate the other. He did not think the time was appropriate, while they were discussing the Arab demand for an independent state, to go into details of means for securing this object, but he thought it right to give a general sketch of the conclusions to which, in the Government's view, the facts of the present situation led.

His Majesty's Government retained an open mind, and the suggestions he had just made were intended to go no further at the moment than putting before the Conference alternatives to an independent Arab State in Palestine.

Husseini in reply referred to MacDonald's statement that the various interested Governments were not confident in the ability of the Palestine Arab leaders to control communal feeling unaided. The Arabs had lived with the Jews before the War for centuries and there had been no pogroms or collisions. Collisions had only started after His Majesty's Government had introduced a policy for which the Arabs were not responsible. During the twenty years preceding 1935 the Arabs had been more or less self-controlled. He agreed that small uprisings had occurred from time to time, but as everyone knew, these uprisings represented an attempt to draw the attention of the British Government to wrongs and calamities, and in no case had Commissions of Enquiry laid the blame on the Arabs. These Commissions had stated that the fundamental cause of the trouble was the policy of His Majesty's Government; they had recommended certain remedial measures which had not so far been put into effect. Therefore the prime responsibility for the uprisings rested on the British Government.

Husseini went on to say, as regards the ability of the Arab leaders in Palestine to quell disorder, that if the leaders could tell the people that their demands would be met, they could put an immediate end to the revolt just as they had put an end to the general strike in 1936. But unless these demands could be met, neither the Palestinian Arab leaders nor the whole of the Arab Delegations would be able to pacify the people of Palestine after all their sacrifice.

MacDonald had referred to the possibility that the United States or other countries interested in Palestine would not allow the British Government to accede to the Arab demands because they would not feel confident as to the future security of the Jewish minority. Husseini made two suggestions: 1) that if the United States adopted this attitude, she should be asked to take over the Mandate: 2) that if, as Dr. Weizmann was alleged to have said, the Jews could raise 50,000 men to defend themselves in Palestine, their safety was assured and British troops could withdraw.

The Arabs were usually peaceful; they were anxious to have the goodwill of the world, especially as the greater part of their resources was derived from the tourist and pilgrim traffic and its associate industries. The Arab countries would guarantee to the Jews any rights which they enjoyed as minorities, for example, in the United States or in England. The guarantee of these countries and of Great Britain should give them a sufficient assurance.

The Arabs did not wish to get rid of the Jews, but if the Jews wished to leave Palestine, so much the better. If they wished to remain, the Jews would be given the same status as others.

Husseini then referred to Lloyd George and to Churchill, who had laid down in 1922 that there was no question of a Jewish State and had since given evidence before the Royal Commission that the Balfour Declaration contemplated the ultimate creation of such a state. It was such tactics as these that had robbed the

Arabs of Palestine of all confidence in the British Government. MacDonald had now given them another assurance. Who could guarantee that another Government would not reverse policy? No one except the Arabs themselves could convince them that their rights were guaranteed.

Antonius referred to MacDonald's remark that the British Government desired a state of affairs in which the Jews would not dominate the Arabs and the Arabs would not dominate the Jews. He suggested that no such state of affairs was conceivable in any country. In any country, whatever the composition of its population, it was inevitable that the majority should in some way or other prevail over the minority.

MacDonald replied that it was a general but by no means universal rule of democratic governments that the will of a numerical majority should prevail. For example, the populations of the States which composed the Australian Commonwealth were not equal, but each had the same representation on the constitutional body dealing with inter-State affairs. The majority always had the last word in countries which had a homogeneous population, but in countries which contained different nationalities it was not undemocratic to make special arrangements in order to avoid one nationality dominating the other.

Dr. Khalidi said that the Palestinian Arabs had come to the Conference in the company of representatives of all the Arab countries to ask whether His Majesty's Government were willing to make a fundamental change in the international status of Palestine. If His Majesty's Government were willing to accept a solution based on a fundamental change by admitting Arab independence at the outset, questions such as methods of safeguarding Jewish rights, and the transition period, could then be examined.

Jamal Husseini asked MacDonald whether he seriously supposed that the Arabs of Palestine would accept the humiliation of being placed no more than on an equality with a Jewish minority.

Auni Abdul Hadi said that in the discussions of 1922, when the Palestinian Arabs faced His Majesty's Government without outside support, they had been offered better terms than they were being offered now.

Emir Faisal asked whether the principle of an independent Arab State had actually been accepted as a basis. If so, the whole discussion should proceed on that basis.

MacDonald replied that the British Government had accepted the following principles:
1) that there should be no Jewish State;
2) that the Mandate should not last for ever;

3) that the establishment of an independent *Palestinian* State was contemplated. The British Delegation had not yet, however, been persuaded to accept the view that Palestine should be an independent Arab State.

Ḥassan Nashat Pasha (the Egyptian Ambassador in London) proposed that as the subject was of such importance, especially after the statement which MacDonald had made, the Arab Delegations should meet together the next day for private discussion.

Ragheb Nashashibi, who made his appearance at this meeting, asked whether the people of Palestine had a prospect of independence or not. MacDonald had said that the Mandate would be terminated some time and that independence would be given to Palestine, in spite of the Balfour Declaration and the pledges to the Jews. Therefore the only obstacle now standing in the way of independence was that of guaranteeing the rights of minorities. He believed that when independence was given to Iraq, the minority question was not regarded as an obstacle, though it had come under discussion. (He apparently forgot that in independent Iraq the Assyrians were practically wiped out.)

MacDonald asked the Delegations not to make public what he had said, and announced that they would meet again on Saturday, February 18.

40 BRITISH PROPOSALS REJECTED—FEB. 17, 1939

The next day, February 17, 1939, at 10 a.m., the Jewish Delegation met with the United Kingdom Delegation—MacDonald, Halifax and Butler.

Dr. Weizmann spoke first. He said that the Jewish Delegation could not possibly accept MacDonald's suggestion that at the end of a certain period the Arabs should have the power to fix the size of Jewish immigration, or to terminate it altogether. He also emphasized that the problem of immigration could not be dissociated from that of land purchase. The fact was that we had drained and cultivated disease-ridden swamp land, had increased land productivity, and had also benefited the Arab community.

Perhaps the Jews were more amenable to pressure than the Arabs, Weizmann said; but there was a limit to the "compressibility" of the Jews. They would not submit to Arab rule, and they would not run the risk of suffering the fate that had befallen the Assyrians in Iraq. If such a surrender were imposed on us, those of us who had made cooperation with the Mandatory Power the cornerstone of their policy would not be able to carry on.

Ussishkin then spoke. His address was in Hebrew, and Sharett translated into

English. He was opposed to MacDonald's suggestion, which meant the division of Palestine into three zones—the first in which Jews could freely acquire land, the second in which they could do so under restrictions, and the third in which they would be prohibited from doing so. The Jews could not consent to a system of "pales of settlement" with which they were familiar from Czarist Russia. The Jews had not acquired the best land in Palestine, but by their efforts had made the land they had bought into the best. As to immigration, we were not merely immigrants, but Returners to Zion. We would never acquiesce in a minority position in Erez Israel. Nor did he agree that the constitutional principle of parity would be an effective safeguard.

MacDonald had appealed to us to face realities, Ussishkin said. He recalled the story of the meeting between Kaiser Wilhelm II and Theodor Herzl in 1898, when the Kaiser dismissed Herzl's appeal to assist in the restoration of the Jews to Palestine as a fantasy. But what was the position now? Herzl's "fantasy" had become a powerful living force in the world, while the Kaiser was a forgotten man.

Sharett, Stein, Brodetsky, Professor Namier and I also spoke.

41 EXECUTIVE DISCUSSES POLICY—MAR. 7, 1939

On Tuesday morning, March 7, 1939, a meeting of the Jewish Agency Executive was held at which I analyzed in bitter words the development of the negotiations, the unstableness of the Government's attitude, each of its changes being worse than the previous, and the deterioration of our position in the negotiations which we had continued after refusing to treat on the basis of the Government proposals. All the Government meant to do now was to find an expedient to protect the four hundred thousand Jews already in Palestine. We should thank them for their goodwill, but reject their favors. We did not need them; we could come to terms with the Arabs ourselves. Zionism meant *aliyah* [Jewish immigration to Erez Israel], and without *aliyah* we had nothing to discuss. I proposed that we should immediately break off negotiations and publish a statement on our attitude.

In the debate, opinion was divided. Suprasky and Rabbi Berlin were opposed to the immediate breaking off of negotiations. According to the former, there was a certain flexibility in the Government's attitude, especially in what they had stated to the Arabs. We had to be armed with patience and demand a definite reply from the Government within the next two days as to the possibilities of immigration and work in Palestine. After the answer was received, we would be able to decide. Rabbi Berlin was of the opinion that much importance was to be attached to the statement that had been elicited that no Palestine State was feasible without cooperation between the two peoples. He agreed that the Advisory Panel (the group of participants in the Conference, Zionists and non-Zionists, from among whom were selected the individuals who would meet with the representatives of the British Government at St. James' Palace at each particular session) should disperse. The Executive, however, had to continue the negotiations until the very end.

Dr. Mossinsohn supported my opinion.

Dr. Weizmann agreed with my analysis of the situation, but disagreed with my conclusions. We should be prepared for a breakdown toward the end of the negotiations, and we should draw up a statement on the lines of "*J'accuse*" for that eventuality. But for the time being we should continue. If we succeeded in bringing the Government to admit that a Palestine State was dependent on the agreement of both parties, it would be an important achievement. It was also necessary to explore the possibilities of a Federal State. It was not clear whether the Government had any definite plan. The subject of an independent state was still liable to be dropped. However, as long as there were no other conclusions, we should not quit the talks.

Dr. Goldmann, Prof. Brodetsky and Ben-Zvi were also opposed to breaking off the negotiations immediately. Dr. Goldman suggested that a letter be addressed to the Government stating that in our opinion there were two bases for negotiations: the Mandate and the Peel Commission Report. We should demand an answer—was it prepared to discuss either one of them? If the Government replied by proposing a Federation of States, we would look into the matter. Ben-Zvi demanded that we should go on exerting pressure for mutual consent as a condition of independence. Dr. Goldmann agreed with the proposal to disband the Advisory Panel, while Brodetsky had his doubts: at all events a small panel should be retained. Ben-Zvi was of the opinion that even if the Panel were dissolved the Erez Israel Delegation should stay on, in accordance with the cable received from Jerusalem.

Sharett agreed to the dissolution of the Panel and to Goldmann's proposal about sending a letter to the Government. The dissolution of the Panel would be an act. A brief statement would be published: since the Government were not changing their basis for the negotiations, the delegations from the various countries were disbanding. We would tell the press to write where the sting was: a state in which we were doomed to a minority status. My proposal was unfeasible, because even if we terminated the negotiations we would maintain relations with His Majesty's Government and would not be able to commit a breach of faith and publish our proposals before they published them. The Government could also issue a denial and announce that these had only been trial proposals and not final conclusions.

Fishman was in favor of dissolving the Panel, but he thought that the Executive had no right to break contact with the Government without a resolution by the Zionist General Council or the Congress to that effect.

Berl Katznelson was opposed to the dispersal of the Panel. If negotiations continued the Panel should remain. He himself was in favor of breaking off negotiations. That step should have been taken when we first heard the Governments' proposals regarding immigration and land transfer.

Finally there was a vote. For immediate termination: Szold, Mossinsohn, and myself; against: Ben-Zvi, Suprasky, Berlin, Locker, Brodetsky, Fishman, Goldmann and Sharett. For sending a letter: Lipsky, Locker, Ben-Zvi, Berlin, Suprasky, Fishman, Brodetsky, Goldmann and Sharett: against: one—myself. Mrs. Jacobs and Berl Katznelson abstained. Dr. Weizmann was not present at the voting. It was decided that we would not meet with the Government until a reply to the letter was received.

In the middle of the meeting a question came from MacDonald by telephone: would we come to a meeting with the Arab States at 9:30 that evening? I suggested that we answer in the affirmative, but that we stipulate that MacDonald would serve only as the chairman and not intervene. This would be a talk between us and the Arabs. Dr. Weizmann undertook to present this condition.

42 BRITISH, JEWS AND ARABS MEET—MAR. 7, 1939

Accordingly, a tripartite meeting was held that evening, March 7, 1939, between representatives of the Jews, the Arab States, and the British Government.

For this meeting there is an official British Government transcript, which is in glaring contradiction to what was recorded by Moshe Sharett and myself. I give here Sharett's version, as written in his diary. Only toward the end do I add something from a letter of mine.

> "The time came to set out for St. James'. Each successive trip to St. James' was marked by greater anxiety and tribulation. What had impelled His Majesty's Government to summon us this time together with representatives of the Arab Governments? What trap had been set for us this evening?
>
> "When we arrived, we saw that Halifax was also present. This was called for out

of respect for their Arab Highnesses. There were three Arabs: Ali Maher, Tewfik Suweidi, and Fuad Ḥamza. We were four: Weizmann, Ben-Gurion, Bearsted, and myself [Sharett].

"Who would open? Weizmann and Ali Maher [the Egyptian Prime Minister] with considerable politeness tried to honor each other with the opening. Ali Maher's politeness won, and Weizmann opened.

"His remarks were designed to create a spirit of peace and cordiality rather than to outline a political program. But he stressed two main principles: agreement on the régime and possibilities for the expansion of the Jewish National Home. The first implied mutual non-domination, while the second meant immigration.

"He was followed by Ben-Gurion, who made some supplementary remarks. The Government had discussed with us questions regarding the political system and was undoubtedly conducting the same negotiations with the Arabs. At the meetings with us the Government spoke as though it were a faithful representative of the Arabs. He assumed that in the talks with the Arabs the Government was defending the stand of the Jews. What was being discussed was an independent state with safeguards for the Jews therein. Our answer was: for *such* safeguards we have no need; the Yishuv would hold its own by virtue of its own strength even without constitutional safeguards. The main point was not the fate of the Jews in Palestine, but the fate of those who were not yet in the country and who had to settle there. Such Jews were entitled to enter Palestine because it was their home, and if the Arabs recognized that right, then there was a basis for peace. It was possible that the expansion of the basis for negotiations and the inclusion of the neighboring countries would help. The intention was not the settlement of Jews in Iraq or in some other neighboring country—this was not what we aspired to. But in a broader scope, it was possible that a way would be found to meet the national aspirations of both the Arabs and the Jews.

"Ali Maher replied. He spoke softly, either from cunning or from a humane feeling. He appreciated the Zionist ideal—it was a very exalted ideal. The Jews deserved a state of their own. If Palestine were unpopulated, Egypt would have welcomed Jewish immigration to that country, and even the creation of a Jewish State therein. But the trouble was that the country was not empty, but populated. This was the country of the Arabs who had lived there from time immemorial. Already, 400,000 Jews had been brought into the country. It was not feasible to continue immigration despite Arab opposition. They would not permit it. They would fight, and were prepared for sacrifices. One had to face realities and not persevere in the realization of a dream that some visionary had seen.

"I asked to be permitted to reply to Ali Maher. I said that we were a small and unique people, and we could not expect that everyone should be acquainted with our history. But for us, our history was a powerful reality, it was the basis of our being. Zionism was the outcome of that history, and not the dream of an individual.

The dream of the Return to Zion was as old as the exile from Zion. In every generation Jews had striven to return to Palestine and to settle there. Present-day Zionism was only a new expression to an old movement. The fact that Palestine was today settled by Arabs was a physical reality, which could not be overlooked; but our bond with the country and our striving to return were also a reality, psychological perhaps, but a reality no less decisive with respect to the fate of the country than that of the Arab community. The strength of this reality was testified to by the sacrifices the Jews were making in order to return to the country and to hold their own therein: a war against nature, inner conflicts, the revolution they were effecting in their lives and the blood they were prepared to spill in defense of their lives and the fruits of their labor. They would not be deterred; we must strive not for domination by one element over the other, but for their mutual adjustment. Perhaps such a possibility of adjustment might be found if the framework of the negotiations could be extended beyond the confines of Palestine.
"Here Halifax interjected that both Ben-Gurion and I had used the same expression —expansion of the framework. What did we mean?
"Ben-Gurion replied: Supposing that Western Palestine was recognized as a Jewish State, that State could nevertheless become part of a greater body embracing the neighboring countries. The Arabs in Palestine would then not feel themselves a helpless minority, for they would constitute part of the great Arab people with an overwhelming majority within this wide framework. On the other hand, the Jewish State could pour benefits not only on the Arab inhabitants but also on the neighboring Arab countries, which would be its allies within the confederation.
"Halifax made no comment. Among the three Arabs there was some stirring upon hearing these words. Tewfik Suweidi was particularly affected. He exchanged glances and even whispered to Ali Maher to his left and Fuad Ḥamza to his right.
"From this point on I don't remember the course of the conversation precisely. The nature of the talk was such that it was absolutely impossible to take notes. We were sitting at very close quarters, supposedly very intimately—Halifax, MacDonald and their assistants with their backs to the fireplace, Ben-Gurion, Bearsted and I opposite them, the three Arabs to our right, and Weizmann to our left.
"Ali Maher again questioned our rights in Palestine and repeated the argument that if the historical past were considered then the Arabs had a right to Spain.
"Weizmann replied: 'Yes, really, why don't you claim Spain?'
"Tewfik Suweidi interjected: 'Maybe you'll help us in this matter with the British Government?'
"Weizmann countered that it was nevertheless a fact that they were not going to Spain and were not demanding it, whereas we were returning to Palestine. That was the answer. After all, we had once been offered Uganda and had not accepted it.
"Ali Maher: 'It was a great sin to have rejected Uganda.'

"Weizmann here recounted his historic conversation with Balfour in Manchester in 1906 on the question of Zion and Uganda. Balfour refused to understand how it was possible to reject such an offer. Whereupon Weizmann had asked him: 'Mr. Balfour, supposing I were to offer you Paris instead of London, would you take it?' To which Balfour replied: 'But we have London.' Weizmann: 'But we had Jerusalem when London was a swamp.' Only then did Balfour grasp the crux of the matter, and he asked: 'Are there many Jews who think like you?' Weizmann replied: 'In Eastern Europe you can pave the streets with them.' Balfour: 'The Jews I meet are quite different.' Weizmann: 'Mr. Balfour, unfortunately you meet the wrong kind of Jews.'

"In the course of the conversation our work in Palestine was touched upon. We stressed that we had done no harm to the Arabs; on the contrary. Ali Maher conceded that we had wrought wonders in the country. Finally, he turned to us, as though speaking from his heart. For three years now the bloodshed had continued in the country and if we insisted on our rights to the full the bloodshed would continue in the future as well. We must take a step forward toward peace, and concede something in order to buy Arab friendship. We should ourselves announce that for the sake of peace we were prepared to suspend immigration or at least restrict it. That would create a different spirit in the country. Afterwards we could even renew our immigration.

"Suddenly the atmosphere around us thickened. Lord Dufferin nodded at Maher's remarks. Halifax and MacDonald were silent, but their expressions were serious and concentrated. The Englishmen and the Arabs had united into a single front. Ben-Gurion whispered to me: 'This is why this meeting was arranged—to appeal to us for this concession.'"

(The rest of this chapter is taken from a letter I wrote to my wife the very same day.)

"The eyes of all the Englishmen were fixed on us. It was felt that the Arabs and the Englishmen constituted one side, and without a word having been spoken Ali Maher's comments had been greeted with sympathy. The Englishmen looked at us with censorious glances and a kind of satisfaction at our discomfiture: the Jewish Shylock was demanding his pound of flesh without considering the consequences.

"I said to Ali Maher: 'I appreciate the spirit of peace with which you made your appeal. We regret no less than anyone else what has happened in Palestine. It is not we who have disturbed the peace, and its restoration does not depend on us. But the appeal to us to stop our work for a time is like the appeals from happy families, blessed with many children and living in affluence, to a woman who after years of barrenness has become pregnant, and when she cries out in her birth pangs her neighbors rebuke her and shout: "Stop the noise and don't be in such a hurry to give birth so that we can sleep in quiet!" The mother cannot stop. You can kill the child or kill the mother, but you cannot demand that she stop giving birth. Our work in Palestine is an organic creation, vital forces are throbbing in it, and you cannot demand of us that we stop it. The appeal for peace should be directed to another quarter.'

"After Fuad Ḥamza's intervention, Weizmann said that he had listened to Ali Maher's remarks with satisfaction. For the first time in twenty years he had heard words of friendship and appreciation from a Moslem. In that spirit we could talk to one another. We were prepared for negotiations with the Palestinian Arabs in order to give and take. Fifty to sixty thousand persons could enter Palestine each year. If it is suggested that we make an agreement and slow down a bit, we can find a common basis.

(Moshe Sharett wrote here in his diary: "When I heard this I thought my hair was turning white. I felt as though an abyss had opened at our feet." The continuation of this account is also from my letter to my wife.)

"Malcolm, who had been silent all along, finally opened his mouth. The meeting had not been in vain, he said. Finally a common language had been found. And it seemed that there was common ground for slowing down immigration for a certain time. It looked as though there was a need to continue the talk the next evening.
"I immediately asked permission to make a comment. I was sorry to disturb the rejoicing, but I did not yet see that there was 'common ground'; we did not agree to 'slowing down.' Dr. Weizmann had spoken about mutual concessions, and each of us was prepared for negotiations on the basis of give and take, but slowing down could not be discussed; that was a one-sided concession.
"Malcolm (with great dissatisfaction): 'We'll continue the discussion tomorrow.'
"I asked: 'Will it be possible in the continuation of the discussion also to put speeding-up on the agenda?'
"Malcolm (firmly): 'No!'
"I: 'Why?'
"Malcolm: 'Because on the basis of 'speeding-up' there will be no agreement.'
"I: 'I'm afraid that on the basis of slowing-down there won't be an agreement either.'
"Malcolm (turning to Weizmann): 'Shall we meet again tomorrow?'
"Weizmann said that he would be able to give an answer only the next day.
"Before the end, Halifax made a cutting remark. In the absence of the Palestinian Delegation it was difficult to make an agreement, he said. With all due respect to me, he would suggest that the question of 'war guilt' should not be raised. Making peace called for understanding the other side.
"When the talk was over we went into the anteroom, where tea was served. I spoke

to Ali Maher and invited him to visit Palestine. He had passed through the country only once, by car, on his way from Egypt to Lebanon. He invited me to visit him in Cairo.

"Malcolm MacDonald told me that every time he heard me speak he was reminded of Snowden (who had been Chancellor of the Exchequer in the Cabinet of his father, Ramsay MacDonald). My forehead also reminded him of Snowden's forehead. (Snowden had been one of his father's sharpest and bitterest opponents.)"

The negotiations with the Arab States were not renewed.

43 BRITAIN'S FINAL PROPOSALS—MAR. 15, 1939

After meetings which introduced nothing new and changed nothing, Malcolm MacDonald brought to the final meeting, on March 15 (neither Weizmann nor I were present at this meeting), the final draft of his Government's policy on the question of the Constitution.

The members of the Jewish Delegation did not enter into a discussion with MacDonald.

The same draft was submitted by MacDonald to the Arab Delegations on March 15.

"1) His Majesty's Government's ultimate objective is the establishment of an independent Palestine State, possibly of a federal nature, in such treaty relations with Great Britain as would provide satisfactorily for the commercial and strategic interests of both countries. This would involve the termination of the Mandate.

"2) It is not the objective of His Majesty's Government that Palestine should become a Jewish State or an Arab State; nor do they regard their pledges to either Jews or Arabs as requiring them to promote either of these alternatives. It should be a State in which Arabs and Jews share in government in such a way as to ensure that the essential interests of each are safeguarded.

"3) The constitution of the independent State would be drafted in due course by a National Assembly of the people of Palestine, either elected or nominated as may be agreed. His Majesty's Government to be represented on the Assembly and to be satisfied as to the provisions of the constitution, and in particular as regards:
   a) the security of and access to the Holy Places;
   b) the protection of the different communities in Palestine in accordance with the obligations of His Majesty's Government to both Arabs and Jews, and as regards securing the special position in Palestine of the Jewish National Home.

"His Majesty's Government would also require to be satisfied that the interests of certain foreign countries in Palestine, for the preservation of which the Government are at present responsible, were adequately safeguarded.

"4) The establishment of the independent State to be preceded by a transitional period throughout which His Majesty's Government, as the Mandatory Power, would retain responsibility for the government of the country.

"5) As soon as peace and order are sufficiently restored, the first steps are to be taken towards giving the people of Palestine, during the transitional period, an increasing part in the government of the country.

"The first stage of this process would be as follows: In the *legislative* sphere—the addition of a certain number of Palestinians, by nomination, to the Advisory Council; the numbers of Arab and Jewish representatives being fixed approximately in proportion to their respective populations, and so as to give a majority of Palestinian members.

"In the *executive* sphere—the selection of Palestinian members of the Advisory Council to sit on the Executive Council; the numbers of Arab and Jewish representatives being fixed approximately in proportion to their respective populations, and so that half the members of the Council would be Palestinians.

"The second stage would be: In the *legislative* sphere—the conversion of the Advisory Council into a Legislative Council with an elected Palestinian element and with certain powers reserved to the High Commissioner; in the *executive* sphere—certain Departments would be placed in charge of Palestinian members of the Executive Council.

"Then a third stage: further advances towards self-government in the transitional period might be in the direction of increasing the powers of the Legislative Council and placing more Departments under the charge of Palestinian members of the Executive Council.

"6) His Majesty's Government would be prepared, if conditions in Palestine permit, to hold elections for a Legislative Council within two years. The composition and powers of the Council would be a matter for consultation between the different parties. Beyond this no time limit can be fixed now for the advance from stage to stage of constitutional development in the transitional period; nor can a date be fixed for the end of the transitional period and the establishment of the independent State. His Majesty's Government would hope that the whole process could be completed in ten years, but this must depend upon the situation in Palestine and upon the success of the various constitutional changes during the transitional period, and the likelihood of effective co-operation in government by the people of Palestine. His Majesty's Government could not contemplate relinquishing all responsibility for the government of Palestine unless they were assured that the measure of agreement between the communities in Palestine was such as to make good government possible.

"As regards immigration:

"1) Immigration during the next five years would be at a rate which, if economic absorptive capacity permits, would bring the Jewish population up to approximately one-third of the population. Taking into account the expected natural increase of the Arab and Jewish populations, and the number of illegal Jewish immigrants (estimated at 40,000) now in the country, this would entail the admission of some 75,000 immigrants over the next five years, who would be admitted as follows: 10,000 per year, and in addition 25,000 Jewish refugees (special consideration being given to refugee children and dependents). The refugees to be admitted as soon as the High Commissioner is satisfied that adequate provision is secured for them.

"2) The existing machinery for ascertaining economic absorptive capacity would be retained, and the High Commissioner would have the ultimate responsibility for deciding what the economic capacity allowed. Before a decision was reached, appropriate Jewish and Arab representatives would be consulted.

"3) After the period of five years further Jewish immigration would only be permitted subject to the acquiescence of the Arabs as well as of the Jews and the British authorities. The question to be discussed and settled through the medium of the appropriate constitutional organs functioning during the transitional period, or by means of consultation between His Majesty's Government and representatives of the Arabs and the Jews.

"4) His Majesty's Government are determined to check illegal immigration, and further preventive measures are being adopted and will be strictly enforced. The numbers of any Jewish illegal immigrants who, despite these measures, succeed in coming into the country and who cannot be deported would be deducted from the yearly quotas.

"Finally, with regard to land sales, the High Commissioner would be given general powers to prohibit and regulate transfers of land. The High Commissioner would be instructed to fix areas in which transfer was to be permitted freely, regulated or prohibited, in the light of the findings of the Peel and Woodhead Reports. He would retain this power throughout the transitional period.

44 JEWISH AGENCY SAYS "NO"—MAR. 17, 1939

On March 17, 1939, Dr. Chaim Weizmann sent the following letter to MacDonald.

"Sir,
"I have the honour to inform you that a plenary session of the Jewish Agency Delegation held yesterday at this office, after hearing a full report on the informal conversations between members of the British and Jewish Delegations, and con-

sidering the proposals submitted by His Majesty's Government on March 15th, unanimously adopted the following resolution:

" 'The Jewish Delegation, having carefully considered the proposals communicated to them by His Majesty's Government on March 15th, 1939, regret that they are unable to accept them as a basis for agreement, and decide, accordingly, to dissolve.' "

The British Government and the Arab Delegations could not have envisaged that in less than ten years an independent Jewish State would be established in 77 percent of the area of Palestine west of the Jordan, and that the invading armies of Egypt, Jordan, Iraq, Syria and Lebanon would be routed by an Israeli army created overnight after the proclamation of a Jewish State called Israel—despite the fact that the population of the invading countries numbered 30 million, and that of the renewed State of Israel only 650,000.

45 THE ARAB WAR AGAINST ISRAEL—1947-53

As we have seen in the previous chapters, the attempts to reach an agreement, which would have prevented so much grievous suffering and bloodshed for both peoples, were unsuccessful. After a temporary halt during World War II, the conflict in Palestine broke out afresh and the problem was submitted to the United Nations. On November 27, 1947, acting on the report of the UN Special Committee on Palestine, the General Assembly adopted its historic resolution calling for the establishment of Jewish and Arab states, with an economic union between them. Although the area proposed for the Jewish State was only a small part of the Land of Israel in which, according to the League of Nations Mandate, the Jewish National Home was to be established, the Jews accepted the resolution and pledged their cooperation in implementing it. They were ready to forgo a large part of their cherished aims and their just demands in the hope of achieving a peaceful agreement with the Arabs.

The Arab leaders, however, showed no such conciliatory spirit. On the morrow of the Assembly resolution Arab attacks on Jews started in Jerusalem and elsewhere, and on May 15, 1948, on the departure of the British, when the Jews proclaimed Israel's independence in conformity with the UN decision, the armies of the neighboring Arab countries invaded the new state with the declared purpose of strangling it at birth.

From the outset, the State of Israel emphasized its sincere desire for peace and cooperation with the Arabs. In two important paragraphs, the Proclamation of Independence declared:

"Even amidst the violent attacks launched against us for months past, we call upon the sons of the Arab people dwelling in Israel to keep the peace and to play their part in building the State on the basis of full and equal citizenship and due representation in all its institutions, provisional and permanent.

"We extend the hand of peace and good-neighborliness to all the States around us and to their peoples, and we call upon them to cooperate in mutual helpfulness with the independent Jewish nation in its Land. The State of Israel is prepared to make its contribution in a concerted effort for the advancement of the entire Middle East."

The outstretched hand was not accepted, and the newborn state was compelled to embark on a desperate struggle for survival against superior numbers and equipment. The cost was heavy—over five thousand of our finest young men and women paid for victory with their lives—but the Arab rulers did not succeed in destroying the Jewish State. They did, however, prevent the establishment of the Arab State envisaged in the UN resolution. The Egyptians occupied the Gaza Strip, while King Abdullah of Transjordan occupied the Arab-inhabited areas of Samaria and Judea, as well as the Old City of Jerusalem, and later annexed them to his kingdom, which he renamed "Jordan." The Arabs who had fled during the tension and fighting at their leaders' call were kept in refugee camps by their Arab brethren.

When the fighting ended, Israel again set her face toward peace. The preamble of each of the armistice agreements signed by Egypt, Jordan, Lebanon and Syria between February and July 1949 began with these words: "With a view to promoting the return of permanent peace in Palestine, . . . the following principles . . . are hereby affirmed; . . ." and the principles were formulated in Articles I and II:

"No aggressive action by the armed forces—land, sea or air—of either Party shall be undertaken, planned or threatened against the people or the armed forces of the other." (Art. I, 2)

"No element of the land, sea or air military or paramilitary forces of either party, including non-regular forces, shall commit any warlike or hostile act against the military or paramilitary forces of the other Party, or against civilians in territory under the control of that Party." (Art. II, 2)

My colleagues and I had hoped at first that our Arab neighbors, having failed in their attempt to crush Israel and having joined us in calling for the establishment of permanent peace, would negotiate with us in a spirit of compromise and conciliation. We offered to discuss the settlement of all outstanding problems, including that of the refugees, but all attempts at negotiation, including those through the UN Conciliation Commission (consisting of the United

States, France and Turkey), broke down. The Arab States made it clear that they had no intention of accepting the existence of independent Israel and making peace with her. They openly declared that their aim was the destruction of Israel, thus violating the Charter of the United Nations Organization, which obligates all its members to "settle their international disputes by peaceful means" and to "refrain in their international relations from the threat or use of force against the territorial integrity or political independence of any state" (Art. 2). The Arab League, which contained all the countries that took part in the invasion, organized an economic boycott against Israel and business concerns that traded with her.

Bands of murderers and saboteurs, mainly from Jordan, used to cross the border and attack from ambush anyone they came across. In the three years 1951–1953 they killed or wounded over 450 citizens of Israel. This terrorist warfare did not attract much attention in the outside world; the murder of an Israeli two or three times a week did not make headline news. The United Nations Truce Supervision Organization seldom even censured the aggressors and was unable to stop their incursions. The Government of Israel showed great patience in the face of these attacks on its people, but it was ultimately compelled to take measures of active defense, and the security forces were brought into operation against the bases of the terrorists across the border, with strict instructions to take every possible precaution to avoid injuring civilians.

Jordan also violated a special provision of her armistice agreement with Israel which referred, inter alia, to Jerusalem. Article 8 of the agreement called for the establishment of a special committee to formulate "agreed plans and arrangements" for "resumption of the normal functioning of the cultural and humanitarian institutions on Mount Scopus and free access thereto; free access to the Holy Places and cultural institutions and use of the cemetery on the Mount of Olives." The Jordan Government refused to cooperate in setting up the special committee. It denied the Jews access to the Holy Places and the historic Jewish cemetery on the Mount of Olives, and did not permit the resumption of the normal functioning of the Hebrew University and Hadassah Hospital buildings on Mount Scopus. The ancient synagogues and houses of learning in the Jewish Quarter of the Old City were almost totally destroyed. For the first time in a millennium and a half Jews were not permitted to approach their most sacred shrine, the Western ("Wailing") Wall of the Temple Court.

Egypt closed the Suez Canal to Israeli shipping in flagrant breach of the Constantinople Convention of 1888, to which she was a signatory. When Israel protested to the Security Council, Egypt justified her action on the ground that a state of belligerency existed between herself and Israel (though the Convention provides for free passage even in time of war). In 1951 the Security Council rejected this argument, ruling that a state of belligerency was incompatible with the Armistice Agreement, and that Egypt was therefore not entitled to deny Israel free passage in the Canal. But Egypt defied the Security Council, and the United Nations did nothing to make her respect the authority of international law and the Council's ruling.

In 1950, Egypt seized Tiran and Sanafir, two uninhabited islands in the Straits of Tiran at the southern end of the Gulf of Akaba, near Sharm el-Sheikh, which had never belonged to her. The Egyptian Government assured the United States that the occupation of these islands was not intended in any way to obstruct navigation in the Straits and that navigation would remain free in accordance with international practice and the recognized principles of international law. Despite this assurance, an Egyptian force was stationed at Sharm el-Sheikh to obstruct Israeli navigation, and neither the United States, which had received an express undertaking from the Egyptian Government, nor the United Nations did anything whatsoever to prevent or halt this violation of international law.

Israel repeatedly declared her readiness to conduct negotiations for a peace settlement with any or all of her Arab neighbors, without prior conditions on either side. As early as in the summer of 1950, she proposed to the Soviet Union that representatives of Egypt and herself should be invited to peace talks, but there was no reply. She offered to discuss specific problems, such as the question of the refugees, if the Arab Governments were not yet ready to talk peace. She proposed a non-aggression pact, or an agreement on the mutual limitation of armaments, to be followed by disarmament. Despite the unsatisfactory nature of the long and winding Armistice Demarcation Lines, she even offered to accept them as permanent boundaries, subject to minor rectifications by mutual consent. Such offers were repeated on innumerable occasions. All were rejected.

When a group of officers headed by Mohammed Nagib deposed King Farouk of Egypt in 1952, I made a gesture of conciliation to the new regime. I told the Knesset, the Israel Parliament, on August 18, 1952, that wherever positive tendencies toward reform and progress existed in the Middle East we regarded them with favor, and continued:

"The events that have taken place in Egypt during the past few weeks should be welcomed, and we may accept the evidence of Mohammed Nagib, the leader of the Egyptian military revolt, at this time, that he and most of his colleagues in the army were opposed to the invasion of Israel, and that it was Farouk, the deposed former king of Egypt, who was mainly responsible for the war against us.

"It may be that the reasons for Nagib's opposition to the invasion were purely military, but there is no doubt that there was not at the time, and there is not now, any reason or basis for strife between Egypt and Israel. The two countries are separated by a broad and extensive desert, and there is therefore no room for border disputes. There was not, nor is there now, any occasion for political, economic or territorial antagonism between the two neighbors.

"The State of Israel wishes to see a free, independent, progressive Egypt. We bear her no grudge for what she did to our forefathers in the days of Pharaoh, or even for what she did to us four years ago, but we cannot ignore the fact that even this Egypt shows no sign of goodwill to repair the grievous wrong committed by the deposed King Farouk, and none of us can say with any certainty in which direction Egypt's face is turned: toward peace or war."

Mohammed Nagib, however, did not last long as head of the revolution. In 1954 a young officer called Gamal Abdel Nasser deposed him and gained complete control over Egypt.

46 THE GROWING THREAT FROM EGYPT—1954-55

At the end of 1953 I found it necessary to leave the Government for a time. On December 7 I submitted my resignation to the President and broadcast my farewell to the nation.

My intention was to go to work in a small, young kibbutz in the Negev desert for at least two years. To my deep regret, in 1954, while I was at work in Sdeh Boker, there was a serious deterioration in the relations between the new Prime Minister, Moshe Sharett, and the new Minister of Defense, Pinhas Lavon. Mr. Sharett invited me to rejoin the Government under his premiership as Minister of Defense, as there was no other candidate for the post, and, since I always regarded defense and army matters as of overriding importance, I felt it my duty to respond to his call.

The last session of the Second Knesset ended on June 30, 1955. On July 26, 1955, new elections were held, and I was again called upon to take office as Prime Minister and Minister of Defense. The basic principles of the new Government's Program were not substantially different from those of Israel's first regularly appointed Government.

In my first statement to the Knesset I referred, in particular, to the unstable security position. I saw, to my regret, that there had been no improvement, and that our relations with our Arab neighbors had deteriorated. I was particularly disturbed by the "Czech arms deal," as it was called at the time. On September 27, 1955, the Egyptian Prime Minister, Gamal Abdel Nasser, stated over Cairo Radio: "Last week we signed a trade agreement with Czechoslovakia, according to which that country will supply us with arms in return for cotton and rice." Two days later it was announced that ships carrying heavy arms—tanks, artillery, jet planes and submarines—were reaching Egypt, and Cairo Radio declared: "The day of Israel's annihilation is approaching. There will be no peace on the border, for we demand revenge. This means death to Israel."

At the beginning of 1956, on January 2, reviewing the security position in the Knesset, I said:

"We did not want the first war in 1948 and it was forced upon us by the Arab rulers. We believe that the maintenance of peace is preferable even to victory in war. Our aspiration has been and always will be: the rebuilding of the ruins of our homeland, the ingathering of the sons of our scattered people, the building of a model State, the achievement of our Messianic aims in the redemption of the individual, the nation and mankind, cooperation with our neighbors in mutual friendship and the strengthening of world peace. We knew that any war, even if we had the upper hand, involves havoc and destruction for both sides and intensifies hatred between peoples. We knew that after a victory on our part in one war, there could be a second round, and even after our victory in the second round there could be a third, and there would be no end to it. A few days after the end of the fighting seven years ago, when our young army, which had not completed its first year, won brilliant victories over its enemies, I warned: 'Let us not be intoxicated with victory ... It is perfectly natural that many, not only in our own midst, should see it as a miracle: a small nation of seven hundred thousand souls fought for its life against six nations numbering some thirty million. But none of us knows whether the trial by battle is yet concluded.'

"Since then about seven years have passed and we have had to bear all the great and growing burdens involved in building and defending our country. The number of those who have returned to Zion in our day is fifteen times as many as in the days of Zerubbabel, Ezra and Nehemiah. We have been confronted with tremendous difficulties in absorbing penniless immigrants—and we have had to rebuild the ruins of the land and repair the damage done by conquerors and foreign rulers from the time of Rome until the period of the British Mandate. For these reasons, and others as well, our aim has been peace. We harbored no resentment against aggressors and invaders; we were ready for a covenant of peace with our neighbors and cooperation with them in order to make the lands of the Middle East flourish and strengthen world peace. But the trouble is that two sides are needed for peace, while one is sufficient for war.

"After the end of the fighting, armistice agreements were concluded with Egypt, Lebanon, Jordan and Syria, but they were violated by our neighbors, with the exception of Lebanon. . . . The agreement was first violated by the Government of Jordan, but the worst violations were committed by Egypt. In 1951, 137 citizens of Israel were killed or injured, mainly by gangs coming from Jordan. In 1952 the number of casualties rose to 147 and in 1953 to 182. In 1954 Egypt began to compete with Jordan in these criminal activities: the number of casualties rose to 180, 117 of which were caused by bands from Jordan and 50 by attacks from Egypt. In 1955 Egypt took first place: in that year only 37 casualties were caused by attacks from Jordan and 192 by murderous bands from Egypt, which were specially organized by the Egyptian dictator, Gamal Abdel Nasser.

"Egypt deliberately organized fedayeen—terrorist gangs, who had previously been meant to fight the British when they controlled the Suez Canal, and when that conflict was over were transferred to the Gaza Strip. These bands of fedayeen were also despatched by the Egyptian military junta to Jordan and Lebanon, although the authorities in these two countries did not favor such operations. The Egyptians also mined Israeli lines of communication and in 1955 alone 49 casualties were caused by these acts. During the past five years these armed bands, regular and irregular, have been responsible for 884 casualties, of which 258 were caused in the past year, 1955, alone.

"Egypt also blocked the passage of Israeli shipping in the Suez Canal and afterwards in the Straits of Tiran as well, in violation of international law and an express decision of the UN Security Council adopted on September 1, 1951, which specifically confirmed the right to free passage.

"Egypt's behavior after the deposal of Nagib, and especially during the past year (1955), has proved beyond any shadow of doubt that Nasser's Egypt is not intent on peace. The Egyptian dictator has published a pamphlet called *The Philosophy of the Revolution*. It is not my concern to discuss here the nature of the revolution and the philosophy presented in this pamphlet, but the author frankly describes the ambitions that guide his steps: 1) to become the head of the Arab countries; 2) to become the leader of the Moslem peoples; 3) to become the spokesman of the African continent. The internal reforms—elimination of disease, education for the people, development of the country, improvement of the position of the fellah— in the name of which the revolution was ostensibly made, have apparently been deferred to the distant future and replaced by foreign political ambitions. . . .

"And in order to gain hegemony over the Arab countries, the Egyptian dictator has apparently made up his mind that the easiest and cheapest method is an attack on Israel. The fedayeen gangs . . . have reached the outskirts of Tel Aviv in their murderous activities and have also been sent to Jordan and Lebanon in order to strike at our border villages in east, north and west. Recently, Egyptian units have been sent to occupy Israeli territory at Niẓanah. And Egypt's new ally—Syria—has also tried to take similar action to the north of Lake Kinneret [the Sea of Galilee]. In the light of these grave attacks, the new Government that presented itself to the Knesset on November 2, 1955, made the following statement:

'The Government of Israel is prepared, as before, faithfully to observe the armistice agreements in every detail, in the letter and spirit. But this duty applies equally to the other side. An agreement violated by the other side will not be binding on us either. If the armistice lines are open to saboteurs and murderers from across the border, they shall no longer be closed to defenders and fighters. If our rights are violated by acts of violence on land or at sea, we shall maintain freedom of action to defend our rights in the most effective manner available.'

"And I will only mention the two latest violations of our rights, on land and on the water: the invasion of the Niẓanah area by an Egyptian unit and the deliberate bombardment by Syrian units north of the Kinneret to prevent Jews fishing in the Lake, which is entirely within Israeli territory. All the warnings of the UN Observers were fruitless and our army had to be instructed to drive off the invaders on land and water in order to insure the integrity of our land and water frontiers.

"During the last few months, the 'Czech Deal' has radically transformed the situation in the gravest and most dangerous manner. It is my duty to inform the Knesset and the people of Israel—and also, as far as possible, impartial world public opinion (and there is such a thing)—of the terrible danger and the deadly purpose involved in the flow of Soviet arms to Egypt, which is also being reinforced continually by a flow of British arms for Cairo's armies. These weapons, both Soviet and British, are intended solely for aggression against Israel. No one in his right mind would imagine for a moment that Nasser and his colleagues would use the Soviet arms to make war against the West, and the British arms to fight the East. I have not the slightest interest on this occasion in the purposes and motives of the suppliers— all that concerns me is the unmistakable aims of the recipients.

"On June 4, 1955, Cairo Radio, which is under the Egyptian dictator's orders, declared: 'The Egyptian revolution was born on the soil of Palestine ... Egypt has established a strong army, backed by 22 million citizens, for the restoration of Palestine and the complete eradication of vile Zionism.' On October 16, 1955, Nasser himself told the editor of the *New York Post* that he was not fighting Israel alone, but also international Jewry and Jewish capital.

"The flow of Soviet and British arms to Egypt gives these threats an immediate and dangerous significance, and we shall imperil our very existence if we ignore it. I am perfectly confident that it will not be easy to subdue our small people. An Egyptian attack would undoubtedly cost us precious lives and do tremendous damage in town and village, but I am certain that they would not defeat us in the end ... But we shall only be able to hold our ground if from now onward we prepare for whatever is in store and muster all our strength—moral, economic and military—to forestall the blow. There is one reliable way to prevent war in the

Middle East, with all its grave consequences for the whole world, and that is the rapid supply of defensive arms to Israel.

"On December 5, 1955, I invited the head of the UN Observers, General Burns, to see me and handed him a statement of the Government's declared policy. I asked him to find out from the rulers of Egypt: 1) whether they are prepared to issue orders for a complete cease-fire, as we have done; 2) whether they are prepared to comply fully with the Armistice Agreement in all its clauses, as we undertake to do; 3) whether they accept the proposals of the UN Secretary-General which were submitted to them and to ourselves on November 2.

"General Burns went to Egypt and on December 11, 1955, visited me again—without having received from the Egyptians any undertaking to maintain a cease-fire, without any undertaking to comply with the Armistice Agreement, and without any agreement to the proposals of the UN Secretary-General, Dag Hammarskjöld.

"A single verse written by the Psalmist of Israel fully defines what is demanded of us in this fateful hour: 'The Lord will give strength to His people, the Lord will bless His people with peace' (Psalms 29:11). If through the valor of the State and the people we can increase and intensify the strength of Israel—moral, economic and military—we have it in our power to ensure peace for Israel as well. Let us dedicate all our might, all our will, all our efforts in this hour to these two things: strength and peace."

47 THE PRESIDENT'S EMISSARY ARRIVES—JANUARY 1956

At the beginning of January 1956, Dwight D. Eisenhower, the President of the United States, decided to send one of his most important aides to Egypt and Israel, to conduct talks on his behalf with the governments of the two countries. The emissary first visited Nasser, in early January, and reached Jerusalem only on the 23rd. Here he met myself, as Prime Minister, and Foreign Minister Moshe Sharett. Present at the talks were also Teddy Kollek (now Mayor of Jerusalem and then Director-General of the Prime Minister's Office) and Yaakov Herzog (now Director-General of the Prime Minister's Office and formerly Israeli Minister in Washington). The emissary was accompanied by the US Ambassador, Edward B. Lawson, and a representative of the American Intelligence. He brought with him the following letter from President Eisenhower dated January 9, 1956:*

* Translator's note: The letters exchanged by President Eisenhower and Prime Minister Ben-Gurion (except for the President's letter of February 27) and the discussions with the President's emissary have been re-translated from Mr. Ben-Gurion's Hebrew version.

"Dear Prime Minister,

"I hereby present to you Mr. X. L.—an excellent American, who was Assistant Secretary of State for Defense, a good friend of mine in whom I have complete confidence. I have asked him to discuss with you and others some of the serious problems of the area which concern Israel, her neighbors and the non-Communist world in general. Mr. X. L. is well acquainted with my personal concerns and hopes in this field, and I am confident that you and he will want to have a full discussion about these problems. I am hopeful that you and he can give each other and your countries valuable assistance in the effort to solve these problems.

"I take this opportunity of sending you my most cordial personal greetings."

The Emissary: I came here because I have the same aspiration as you, Mr. Prime Minister, for the achievement of peace in this area. I stayed in Cairo a few days. During those days Nasser was busy with the publication of the Egyptian constitution and appearances at demonstrations in honor of the event. He spoke about six times. All my talks with him took place at night. Before I tell you about these talks, I should like to hear from the Prime Minister an analysis of the situation and proposals for a solution.

Ben-Gurion: Even many of our own people did not accept the Zionist solution, because of three objections: 1) A people that had lived for centuries only in the towns could not live in the countryside; 2) In Palestine it would be necessary to accept a lower standard of living; 3) The land to which we were returning was desolate. And indeed, at the beginning the task seemed to be impossible, but spiritual strength overcame all difficulties.

There were also non-Jews who believed in the return to Zion. The second President of the United States, John Adams, wrote to a Jewish officer in America at the beginning of the 19th century that a day would come when the Jews would return to their land and revive the Jewish State. In Britain, too, there were several who shared in the vision of Zion even before the Balfour Declaration.

The UN decision of 1947 was the final international sanction for the renewal of the State of Israel. At that time we were prepared to accept the UN decision as it stood, although Jerusalem and Western Galilee were excluded from the Jewish State. The Arabs defied the UN decision and tried to destroy the Jewish State on the day of its establishment. We were attacked by five states, but although we were few—we triumphed. We were prepared to forget what our neighbors had done to us, hoping that the armistice agreements would bring

---

* Translator's note: From this point onward, the main points of the conversations are given in dialogue form.

peace. We were wrong. For the past eight years we have been living, working and bringing in hundreds of thousands of immigrants in a situation of neither peace nor war. There was one Arab ruler who wanted peace and was not afraid to say so in public—that was Abdullah of Jordan, and he was murdered.

The change of regime in Egypt aroused in our hearts a hope for peace. We were aware of Egypt's internal problems—widespread disease, mass illiteracy, poverty in the villages—and we were prepared to help. We contacted Nagib, but he asked us to wait. When Nasser succeeded Nagib, we renewed the contact with him—without results. The situation has deteriorated. First we suffered mainly from Jordan. In the past two years the attacks have come mainly from the Gaza Strip. Life has been almost unbearable for our people near the Strip. If there is any possibility whatsoever of achieving peace, not only we here, but the great majority of our people would willingly accept it, although there are a few amongst us who claim that our borders ought to be expanded. We have chosen peace, and that is the attitude of the majority of our people.

We have a large, desolate and empty desert, and it could absorb millions. We know it could be developed and populated, and some successful beginnings have already been made. Our success in the Negev would serve as an example to many countries in Asia and Africa. If we are to concentrate on this enterprise, as well as on the absorption of immigrants and the improvement of their educational and economic standards, we need peace—peace on the basis of the status quo—for ourselves and our neighbors.

If the rulers of Egypt consider it their function to supply their people's needs in economic development, education and health—there is hope for peace. If their aspirations go beyond the needs of their people and they believe that both East and West need them and would support them—it is hard to believe in peace. On our part there is full readinesss for peace, not only because of the value of peace itself and the aspirations of our Prophets in ancient days, but also because we need peace to devote all our efforts to making the land flourish and absorbing immigrants. There is nothing we will not do for the sake of peace, and we unreservedly offer our assistance to you and anyone who might come to continue your work for peace.

The Emissary: Your words have touched me deeply. My wife and I are Methodists and devoted to our faith; on our way to Jerusalem I told my wife: I am happy that my first visit to the Holy City should be on a mission of peace. No one can come here with greater devotion to peace than I, and that is the President's feeling too.

The problem is difficult. We all understand that in the deal with Czechoslovakia Egypt found a source of arms that introduces a new and dangerous element into the Middle East. The fact that the Arab side has forty million and on your side there are only a million and a half has far-reaching implications. If the Arabs will not have a little of your capacity for moral vision, the outlook is dark.

I met Nasser at night. Zacharia Muḥi el-Din was with him. I told Nasser that he needs peace to free Egypt from disease, to build schools, to raise the standards of education and living. Despite the Czech deal he could not at one and the same time maintain a large army and make a great economic effort. Nasser said he understood the economic problems and would call upon his people for austerity. I told him that, as a man with military experience, he must understand that all the expenditure on rearmament was a waste, and the best thing would be not to use the arms. I asked if he was prepared to express his opinion on this subject.

I found that his talk revolved around two axes: 1) the tension between Syria and Israel; 2) the political problems existing between his country and the other Arab states. He wanted to discuss his relations with the United States and the West. In his opinion, the Baghdad Pact was a British creation. It worked against the independence of the Arab countries and their partners. I pointed out that the United States had not joined this pact, despite approaches on the subject, and he must consider what had happened to the countries that had joined with the Soviet Union; he had no doubt discussed this with Tito.

Nasser is very much concerned with his activity in Egypt and the relations with the other Arab countries. He said he was ready and willing for peace. According to him, the refugees were the source of the border incidents and the tension. There were two problems—repatriation, and compensation for the refugees. Repatriation or the granting of freedom of choice was the most important issue.

I pointed out that Israel was a small country in a special position and therefore limited. Nasser said that he was interested not in numbers but in the principle of free choice.

I asked if he was thinking of a particular percentage of returnees. He said: No. But, he continued, he could not speak in the name of all the Arab countries. There might be difficulties with Syria and Jordan, for in those two countries there were no stable governments. He spoke of the problem of territorial continuity of the Arab countries, which would connect Africa with Asia.

It seemed to me that this is the major divergence between Egypt and Israel.

Nasser discussed this matter at great length, and I advised him to show more flexibility on the subject. But Nasser persistently refused to discuss any arrangement, except for Arab sovereignty, which would ensure this continuity. I told him that he should be flexible; I asked him to look at the map and compare the area of Israel with that of the Arab countries.

I asked Nasser about his views on the Holy Places. Nasser replied that this is mainly an issue between Jordan and Israel, and that, in his opinion, territorial division in Jerusalem is preferable to internationalization.

I asked him whether there were other territorial problems. Nasser replied that unification of villages with the agricultural areas that have been cut off from them was a problem that had to be solved, but this was of secondary importance. I said that the best way to good-neighborliness was free trade, and therefore we were interested in the questions of freedom of navigation in the Suez Canal and the economic boycott. Nasser said that these questions existed only because of the state of hostility, and did not constitute an obstacle to peace.

I must emphasize that during the conversation he returned to the question of his capacity. Where is there another Arab leader who is prepared to sit and talk to me?—he asked. I said that no one could solve the problems except the countries concerned. The task of a mediator was not to produce decisions but only to make proposals. Nasser said he understood what was the responsibility of the leaders, but he was faced with limitations. He said frankly that when he was confronted by the Baghdad Pact and its political implications he had to take up a position against Turkey and the Western powers. It would be necessary to calm down the emotions he had roused against Turkey, the United States and Britain, because of his conception of the Baghdad Pact. But he could not rectify in one speech what had been done during more than a year.

Nasser said, and repeated it more than once, that the circumstances were such that if the initiative he was now taking in these talks was known in public he would be faced not only with a political problem, but—possibly—with a bullet as well. There were undercover minorities in Egypt who were not realistic and did not want peace. It was impossible to get rid of these minorities, but with the support of the majority they could be controlled. If the majority was hesitant, it would be impossible to resist them. He had had experience with the majority during the Nagib crisis. He had overcome the difficulties, and he believed that the problem of peace could also be overcome with his own efforts. I told Nasser that now was the time for action and not for talk. He agreed to think about it and see what he could do.

I asked Nasser what were his hopes. He said that his greatest dream was to bring his people not taxes but fresh water from the Nile. Hence his great concern with the Aswan Dam. He also wanted to give his people civic centers and schools. I told him that these were praiseworthy aims, but every country ought to know that its total income was limited; and military operations imposed a heavy burden.

I must add that Nasser is interested in the secrecy of these talks. They are limited to himself and Zacharia Muḥi el-Din, since his people, especially the radical forces, are not yet ready for them. If they become known, he will have to deny the report.

I asked Nasser to explain his attitude and said that it was not enough if we just sat and talked and every side said it wanted peace. It was necessary to make progress toward peace. If we were not prepared to discuss the matters in dispute we must examine the readiness for a settlement and the methods of approaching it. Nasser said he could assure you that he did not want any more acts of hostility. I asked him if he would punish those responsible for such acts and publish the fact of punishment; he said that this was possible. I asked him if he would put a statement on paper on this subject and he agreed to think it over. He was very anxious that we should understand that he could discuss the matter only so long as secrecy was maintained.

I tell you that the main problem is territorial. I appreciate their sensitivity and the feelings of your people. My position is not that of an attorney—I only want to clarify the position.

Ben-Gurion: The main question is whether there is a will to peace. Nasser told you that he wants peace. I don't want to doubt it, but if there is any possibility of knowing, it will only be if the two sides meet together to discuss the issues that concern them. I see no other way. There are facts that are not consistent with the expression of the will to peace. There are major issues connected with the Baghdad Pact and East-West relations.

There are also small things. Two months ago we asked the Chief of Staff of the UN Observers, General Burns, to go to Egypt and try to get Nasser to commit himself to a cease-fire, just as we have issued strict orders that no one is to shoot; to undertake full compliance with the detailed provisions of the Armistice Agreement, and to accept UN Secretary-General Dag Hammarskjöld's proposals, which we have accepted. Burns met the Egyptian Foreign and Defense Ministers and the British and American Ambassadors. He came back and said, with great regret, that he could not promise Egyptian agreement to any of these three points.

I understand Nasser's difficulties in undertaking to observe the whole of the

Armistice Agreement, such as freedom of navigation in the Suez and so forth. But why does he not agree to a cease-fire? He has the authority for that. In his position as dictator he is afraid to make peace, but if he has the slightest desire to rectify the situation, why can he not accept Burns's demand for a cease-fire? It is difficult to reconcile this attitude with a will to peace. It was not we who concluded the Baghdad Pact; he is interested in destroying it, for through this pact Iraq is allied with Turkey, Pakistan, Britain and also the United States.

If he has a will to peace—the incidents on the borders should be stopped. After that, representatives should meet. I understand his desire for secrecy and on our part it will be maintained to the end. Even if there are no results, no one will know about the whole affair. But how can we make progress toward peace without a meeting? It does not have to be between Nasser and me. Sharett perhaps would be better. There has been contact before, too, and it has never been disclosed. But without contact, nothing will be achieved.

As for territorial continuity, that never existed, except for a short period when Ibrahim Pasha conquered Palestine and Syria—and he withdrew. If peace is established, there will be full cooperation between Israel and Egypt, and full freedom of passage on both sides. There will be full cooperation in the economic field and even political cooperation. Does the present regime in Egypt respect the dignity of man, and what is the meaning of democracy in that country? If, despite his being a dictator, Nasser respects human values (Ataturk was also a dictator), there can be full political cooperation, and Israel will serve not as a barrier but a bridge. Lebanon will follow in his footsteps and make peace too. And perhaps Jordan as well. As far as we know, Nuri Sa'id said that if Nasser makes peace he will not use it against him, but will do the same.

The great question is whether Nasser does not want to join up with the Eastern Bloc. Egypt could be the key to the conquest of Africa, which is more open to Communist penetration than any other continent. Communism has already conquered more than half of Asia and rules six hundred million people. If it also conquers Africa, through Egypt, it will not be far from its final goal. We are interested not as Israelis but as citizens of the free world; while Nasser thinks he is using the Soviet Union for his own aims, he is in fact only serving her.

To return to our affairs. Does Nasser want peace? I see no sign of it. And if he wants it—is he capable of it?

The Emissary: If each side makes a statement to someone like the President of the United States, promising observance of the cease-fire and punishment of violators; and if after that each side appoints a representative or representatives to meet in a neutral place to discuss the major problems, each according to its own initiative, is it to be understood that you will regard this as the first step toward peace?

Ben-Gurion: Our answer is yes. (*Sharett:* Decidedly. That would be a serious first step.) This does not mean that each side has to accept what the other side says.

The Emissary: It is my impression that if there is a hope of solving problems, it would be possible to ensure the maintenance of the cease-fire and, thus, the cessation of acts of hostility.

Ben-Gurion: You mean observance of the Armistice Agreement?

The Emissary: I deliberately tried not to refer to something specific.

Sharett: This is only a further confirmation, for Egypt is already a signatory to the Armistice Agreement.

The Emissary: The major issues will be decided by the people authorized to do so. But there can be no peace so long as fighting continues, and the first prerequisite is a suitable atmosphere. Nasser has taken the position that he wants peace, but he cannot speak in the names of all the allied states. I told him that a leader is essential, and that he is the man to lead. He said if that was so—the atmosphere was needed. What I am now trying to find out is whether I can get Egypt to declare a cease-fire, punishment of violators, and discussion on some other level than that of Nasser and the Prime Minister. I want to ask the Prime Minister: If an effort is made in this direction, will that bring peace nearer? And you, Mr. Prime Minister, have pointed out the difference between a democracy and totalitarian countries. I can understand a dictator's difficulties in arranging meetings.

Sharett: The difficulty is due not only to the totalitarian regime, but also to nationalist feeling. The leaders of Egypt are driving their people into a frenzy and terrifying them with specters. They denounce Israel and describe us as blacker than the devil. In this way they make their people slaves to hatred. There is a need not only for a physical cease-fire, but also a political cease-fire. To prepare the ground, Nasser must stop showering fire and brimstone on Israel in his speeches. If this policy of fanning the flames of hatred continues, it will be impossible to break the vicious circle.

The Emissary: I have emphasized to Nasser the need to replace the inflammatory speeches by a peaceful atmosphere. They have arms from Czechoslovakia and are conducting virulent propaganda against the West, emphasizing that the West is the real enemy. That should be stopped. Nasser replied in the affirmative, but said that it could not be done overnight. I said he should begin to discuss what he was prepared to do.

Ben-Gurion: There is one question I want to ask you: Is it your conclusion that all you can achieve is a cease-fire and readiness to send representatives—no more?

The Emissary: I do not say that there are absolute limitations; I prefer to put it in the opposite way. I do not believe that I can bring about at this moment a meeting of heads of state to discuss the major problem, but my feeling is that considerable progress can be made if we try to develop a flexible way of thinking and arrive at the conclusion that peace is possible. I doubt whether anyone can say more so long as there are no talks between the two parties. I hope it will be possible to determine principles even if the two sides do not agree and there are differences of opinion between them. The establishment of the principles will clarify the gap that has to be bridged. The main differences are over boundaries. I told Nasser that it would be important if he would initiate and maintain a position of discussion and flexibility.

Ben-Gurion: I want to explain the meaning of the question I asked. Let us assume that Nasser agrees to a cease-fire and the representatives meet. (If we obligate ourselves to secrecy, we shall keep our word, even if the meeting ends without success.) The talks will last months, and create an illusion in the minds of the United States Government. I should like to believe that what Nasser says about peace is true, and I will not venture to assert that he is lying. Besides the cease-fire there is an obligation in the Armistice Agreement that no side will be entitled to carry out acts of hostility against the other. Acts of hostility can continue even while Czech arms are flowing into Egypt.

I want you to understand the depth of our anxiety. We are facing a position which, so far as we are concerned, is one of life or death. If the Egyptian army invades our country and defeats our army, that is the end of our people. It is true that the power of the spirit is greater than physical might, but we have no means of stopping bombers, which could reach us and launch an attack within ten minutes. A large part of our population is concentrated in Tel Aviv and Haifa. These could easily be destroyed by a prolonged bombardment by planes with a speed of 900 kilometers an hour. We have nothing with which to confront the Egyptian planes.

With such a force at his disposal, the temptation to a military dictator to make war is very great. Nasser has rivals; he is eager to enhance his prestige in all the Arab countries. He has sent hundreds of fedayeen to Jordan and his agents are active in Morocco, Algeria and Tunisia. He undoubtedly believes that a defeat of Israel by him would increase his prestige in all the Arab countries more than anything else. If he has the power—or if he believes he has the power—to destroy us, it is hard to believe that he will not try to do it. You must see in what a position we are placed.

We cannot rely on what he tells you. He has said nothing in public. He is not prepared to observe the Armistice Agreement when that means stopping the blockade of our shipping in the Straits of Tiran and the Suez Canal. If he sends a statement to the President of the United States, I assume that he will observe the cease-fire and send representatives to a meeting, but in the present situation, when Soviet arms are piling up in Egypt, Nasser is under tremendous pressure to attack us. We are in terrible danger and if the United States continues the embargo on arms to Israel, while Egypt gets arms from Russia and Britain, you will understand our position. We can meet, but after six months we could be destroyed. He could send representatives—but all the political and military factors will not be altered.

He has a tremendous ambition; he wants to be the leader of the Arabs, the Moslems and the peoples of Africa. He is a clever man, and while he does not want to lose the goodwill of the United States, he does not want to be solely dependent on the United States, and that is why he is dealing with the Russians. We are ready to do anything for peace. But if we do not look to our security and our survival, that will be the greatest crime in our history. If he thinks he can destroy us in six or eight months' time, why should he make peace.

The President of the United States has done a great thing by sending you to Egypt and Israel for the sake of peace. Unless we have deterrent arms in our possession your labor will be in vain. For us this is a question of survival, and not only for our people living in this country. I do not know what is happening to the Jews of Morocco, Algeria, Tunisia and Egypt itself. We have the right to live no less than Korea. I cannot conceive that you should not understand our position. President Eisenhower as a general knows what war means. I have made the acquaintance of three British generals—Wauchope, Plumer and Gort —all three of them hated war. I met President Eisenhower when he was Supreme Commander of the Allied Armies in World War II. I believe he will understand our position.

48 THE ARAB REFUGEES

A second talk between the emissary and myself took place in the afternoon of January 23, 1956. Two subjects were discussed: flexibility and free choice for the Arab refugees.

Ben-Gurion: Demands are being addressed only to one side: Israel. We are being asked for territorial concessions, although Israel's area is only 20,000 square kilometers and the area of the Arab countries is 11,516,403 square kilometers; in Israel there are 75 persons to the square kilometer, in the Arab countries seven or eight. There is no moral justification for such an approach. Territorial changes are possible only on a reciprocal basis.

What Nasser said means that Israel is to be dislodged from the Red Sea and Eilat. That is out of the question. Israel's maritime trade started on the Red Sea three thousand years ago in the days of King Solomon. Eilat was the first Jewish port, in the time of the kings of Judah, and until the middle of the sixth century—that is, 1,400 years ago—there was Jewish independence on the island of Yotvat (Tiran) in the south of the Straits. Procopius, a sixth-century Greek historian born in Caesarea in Palestine, in his book on the wars between the Byzantines and the Persians, described the island, now called Tiran, and wrote: "There the Hebrews have been living since ancient times and governing themselves, and during the reign of the Justinian of our days they became subject to the Romans" (i.e., the Byzantines). This island remained desolate for centuries and it was only a few years ago that it was occupied by the Egyptians, who installed a garrison on it to interfere with Israeli shipping in the Straits.

Would it occur to anyone to tell Egypt to get out of Alexandria, although Alexandria was not founded by Arabs or Egyptians, but by Greeks in the days of Alexander the Great? Doesn't Saudi Arabia have direct access to Jordan? Doesn't Egypt have direct access to Akaba?

And as for the Arab refugees, the Arab States are using them as a political weapon to destroy Israel. During the first four or five years of the State, we took in about five hundred thousand Jewish refugees from Arab countries: Iraq, Yemen, Morocco, Tunisia, Libya, Algeria, and Egypt. Our position during those years was terrible. There were no houses, no work, no schools, but we welcomed the refugees like brothers. And although not all of them are completely settled as yet, the great majority have housing and work; their children go to school; they have set up scores of villages and towns of their own, and there is not the slightest doubt that very soon they will all be absorbed. The Arab refugees got no help from the Arab countries; they were not absorbed in these countries, although in Iraq and Syria there are enormous cultivable areas which are unpopulated.

But the main question is: Why did the refugees leave Palestine? Was it the Jews who caused this flight? First of all there is the simple fact: No refugees ran away from the State of Israel. All the Arab refugees who fled from the areas designated by the United Nations resolution to be part of the State of Israel did so during the days of Mandatory rule, when Britain alone governed in Palestine and did not permit the UN Implementation Committee to enter the country. The Mandatory Government had 100,000 British soldiers in Palestine at the time.

The first refugees started to leave a few days after the Assembly resolution on the partition of Western Palestine. At first the rich left. The prime reason was the renewal of the disturbances by the Arabs. On the morrow of the UN resolution of November 29, 1947, seven Jews were killed on their way from Haifa to Jerusalem. Then there was an attack on the Jewish commercial center in Jerusalem—and the British police prevented the Haganah, the Jewish defense force, from approaching the scene of the trouble. In April 1948 the British Command in Haifa, under General Stockwell, told both sides, for some reason, that the British army would remain neutral and would not intervene in the quarrels between Arabs and Jews.

Fighting started between the Haganah and the Arab bands in Galilee. The first decisive battle was in Tiberias, on the night of April 16–17. The Haganah won, and immediately the Government sent a fleet of buses, packed in all the Arab inhabitants of Tiberias, young and old, men and women, and evacuated them all from the town.

After Tiberias came Haifa's turn. Again the Haganah won. On April 23 the Arabs met representatives of the Haganah, in the presence of the British military commander and the Governor, Mr. Low. The Haganah stated that all the Arabs could stay where they were and would be treated as citizens with equal rights, but they must hand in their arms. The British authorities supported this demand. It was accepted as reasonable by the Arab representatives, but the Arab Higher Committee (which sat in Egypt at the time) ordered them to leave Haifa, because in two or three weeks an Arab army would enter the country and drive out all the Jews, and then they would be able to return not only to their own homes but also to those of the Jews. About four thousand Arabs did not obey—and remained in the city; the rest, some five thousand, left.

The same thing happened during the following days in Safed, where there was a large Arab majority, but the Haganah won—and all the Arabs of the town left. The same thing happened in Beit She'an (Beisan) and a few days before the proclamation of the State in Jaffa, where some three thousand Arabs remained and the rest left.

From the beginning of December 1947 until May 13, 1948, about 350,000 left the area designated by the UN resolution to be part of the State of Israel. About 100,000 persons remained in the towns and villages.

From the UN Assembly decision on November 29, 1947, until the invasion of the Arab armies on the night of May 15, 1948, about a thousand Jews were murdered. All the roads in the country were dangerous for Jewish travelers. Scores of Jewish villages were continually attacked and in the three main cities the violence did not stop for a single night. It was not only the Arabs of Palestine, but soldiers, officers and men, from Syria, Iraq and Transjordan, as well as a few from Egypt, disguised but well armed, who took part in these attacks. And the British Government and Army either took a neutral stand or prevented the Haganah from defending their people. Although the Government undertook to protect freedom of movement to Jerusalem, it did not keep its word, and the road to Jerusalem was severed and blocked by the Arab bands.

The State of Israel has made and is still making constant efforts to absorb the Jewish refugees and improve their economic and cultural conditions. The Arab countries have treated the Arab refugees like strangers and are exploiting them as a political weapon against Israel.

"Free choice" means the introduction of a fifth column to destroy the Jewish State from within. Israel is willing to contribute from her vast experience to help in the absorption of the Arab refugees in the unoccupied empty spaces in Syria and Iraq, and partly also in Sinai, if the Arab rulers are really concerned for the welfare of the refugees. The State of Israel is not responsible for the flight of the Arab refugees, but it has absorbed some forty thousand of them to facilitate the reunification of families.

Before the establishment of the State, during the period starting in 1936, and from the end of November 1947 until the day the State was established, Jewish life in this country was imperilled and hundreds were murdered, but not a single Jew fled the country. In the area designated by the UN Assembly for the State of Israel there were perhaps 450,000 Arabs—so how has the UN Relief and Works Agency counted about a million refugees?

The slogan of free choice for a million refugees, only about a third of whom came from the area of Israel, is only a cover for the plan to destroy Israel—and Israel has not the slightest intention of agreeing to commit suicide. If the Arab countries were really concerned for the fate of the refugees who fled from Palestine they could have been settled a long time ago in the Arab countries, among their brethren, and would not have had to be maintained at the expense of the UN as a weapon for the destruction of Israel.

49 CEASE-FIRE AND DIRECT TALKS—JAN. 24, 1956

In the morning of January 24, 1956, the emissary again met the Foreign Minister and myself. Sharett said he had been informed by the UN Secretary-General, Dag Hammarskjöld, that Nasser would not agree to give a cease-fire order: his units were in forward positions and his soldiers got nervous when they saw our patrols. As for the dispute at Niẓanah, which had been occupied by Nasser's soldiers, the Secretary-General had intervened and submitted proposals which we had accepted and the Egyptians had rejected, but now he stated that they were prepared to withdraw. This would rectify the situation in the Niẓanah area, but in the Gaza Strip the shooting was still going on.

With map in hand, I drew a picture of the Gaza Strip and the Israeli settlements. The Egyptians had posts some 500 meters from the border. Our men had to patrol close to the border to protect the villages and the fields, which extended up to the border itself. For that reason, Nasser said, he was unable to give an order for the cease-fire. I had told the UN Secretary-General that I had given a cease-fire order to our soldiers and they had been told not to reply to fire from the other side unless they were under serious attack. We could not give up the patrols without abandoning the villages and thousands of acres of land. The lives of our settlers were in danger from the shooting. In the Gaza Strip there were three battalions of Egyptian troops. If the shooting did not stop there was danger of a conflagration. Some of our settlers, including a young pioneer, a girl, from Australia, had been killed or injured.

The emissary asked if the building of fences had been discussed.

Sharett: We agreed to this, but it will be useful if both sides build fences and undertake to guard them.

The Emissary: Would it be practical for the patrols approaching the border to raise a flag as a sign that they have no intention of opening fire?

Ben-Gurion: I am prepared to consult the Army on this question. But it is obvious that if the order is given not to fire, the peace will be kept.

The Emissary: No doubt you have heard about the Mexican raids. I know veteran patrol men from Texas. I asked one of them how often he found it necessary to shoot. He told me that he could not exclude the possibility that he had killed Mexicans, for the guards shot first as soon as they saw a Mexican.

Ben-Gurion: How did it stop?

The Emissary: It was stopped by both sides.

Ben-Gurion: Let Nasser try to issue a cease-fire order and we shall see what will happen. Let them give an order for a week, and then, if there is quiet, for a second week. As for your proposal, since you will be here again in a few days, I shall consult my commanders in the meantime.

Sharett: Where the cease-fire is concerned, it is important that when he gives such an order, Nasser should include it in his letter to the President.

The Emissary: People are only human, and with the best possible efforts, something may go wrong. If an incident of this kind occurs, would it not be better for the other side to punish the violator rather than have reprisals?

Ben-Gurion: In principle, I agree, but there may be cases in which that is impossible. For instance, if they fire at one of our patrols and it cannot be extricated from danger, and the only way to save it is to take the post the shooting comes from. But in general, if the other side also agrees on a cease-fire, we shall give such an order, apart from exceptional cases. If Nasser gives such an order and notifies us that violators will be punished, your proposal is accepted. Previously, there was no shooting by soldiers, but now there are many in the Gaza Strip.

Ambassador Lawson: Has Hammarskjöld a general impression of the extent to which the Egyptians are worried about the internal situation?

Sharett: The only impression was that of Fawzi, who was more quiet and moderate than ever before. Hammarskjöld prepared a statement which he meant to publish at the end of his mission. He will show the statement to both parties. We said the wording was excellent and we would willingly sign it. We asked whether Cairo intended to lift the blockade on the Suez, which is a breach of the Armistice Agreement, and also whether Jordan would comply with Article 8 of the Armistice Agreement (about free access to the Holy Places, Mount Scopus, etc.). Hammarskjöld smiled and said that that would be like the Preamble to the UN Charter—everybody knew what it said, but it was not binding.

The Emissary: I want to tell your neighbors that I have found on the part of the Israel Government a will to arrive at a peace settlement, to ensure the best conditions for the peoples of the region and to contribute to the welfare of Egypt like one good neighbor to another. I will say that you want to examine the existing differences seriously and sincerely, on the highest level, in the light of the existing possibilities. On your side the main differences are in regard to refugees and borders, but there is a readiness to discuss them. You recognize that there are differences of a secondary importance, and you want to settle them too, perhaps in a series of steps. Small beginnings with goodwill might expand understanding. The main thing is to create an atmosphere in which differences can be removed.

Mr. Prime Minister, I should like to be authorized to say that in view of Hammarskjöld's proposal you are prepared to examine the question of patrols.

Ben-Gurion: I forgot to mention the issue of the fedayeen, who cross the border and hide during the day in order to strike at our villages in the dead of night. Nasser has admitted to Henry Byroade [the UN Ambassador in Cairo] that he sent fedayeen to Jordan.

The Emissary: I did not know that. But I want to note the things I will submit to the other side. I should like to convey to the other side a determination to examine all possibilities for a settlement and an atmosphere of hope that something will be done. I must tell you, and I shall say the same to Nasser, that I do not claim or believe that the problem is an easy one. But I should like to say that there is hope and there is goodwill and a decision on both sides to see the problems as they are and seek a way to solve them.

Ben-Gurion: I have been considering what you said about stages. You mentioned free choice for the refugees and border changes. It is easier to arrange small things than big things. But the opposite is also true. I have thought more deeply about what you said to me. I am convinced that if there is a possibility—and perhaps there is, thanks to the President's intervention—it will be realized only on the highest level, because of Nasser's psychological difficulties. If Nasser participates personally, and the entire scope of the problem is examined, it is possible that peace might be attained in ten days.

The Emissary: It is very important that we should all think about things that can be done. I agree that time is very important, and that no one wants to put all the chips on the table at the same time. At lunch time Mr. Sharett remarked that the numbers of those returning to their families should be increased.

Sharett: If the parties meet, it may be assumed that each side will make an effort to reach the bridge.

The Emissary: Perhaps this is a new era. The President has undertaken to bring about a settlement. This adds some reality to the idea that we are facing momentous decisions. I am at your disposal until I leave Jerusalem tomorrow.

Ben-Gurion: There are three issues here: one that occupies our minds—our relations with our neighbors and our participation in the revival of the region—and two that concern the other side: refugees and territory. These questions can only be discussed by the two sides. They are so complex that I doubt whether any progress is possible without direct contact. No matter how much I try to explain these problems to you, it seems to me that, with all your goodwill, you will not see them as we see them. But I believe I can see things as Nasser sees them, that I can convince him and he can convince me. Many of your people, including some of the best of them, will say, not without logic: for heavens' sake, since the peace of the region and perhaps the peace of the world are involved, what do so many kilometers matter? We know how much they matter and Nasser knows how much they matter. If we sit together we shall be able to understand one another. On questions decisive for our future and our survival and, on Nasser's part, for his duty to the Arab people, it seems to me that no one from the outside—even the best and noblest of men—could understand them as we understand them.

The Emissary: My intention is proposals—not for the solution of the fundamental problems, but proposals to create an atmosphere that would enable the two sides to meet.

50 CLARIFYING THE POSITIONS—JAN. 24, 1956

In the afternoon of January 24 the discussion continued at the home of Foreign Minister Sharett.

The Emissary: We must not ignore the psychological factors that underlie the attitude of your neighbors. They measure their possibilities according to their capacity as it appears to them. Whether they correctly evaluate their capacity has still to be examined. I am not an expert in psychology, and it cannot be done until we can start talks between the governments.

Sharett: We must not despair. We want to succeed.

The Emissary: After yesterday's conversation do you have more hope?

Sharett: We are more determined to utilize the present opportunity. Perhaps there may be factors in the situation that will deter the other side from sliding to disaster. We welcome the purpose which has brought you to us. We understand the decisive importance of a meeting, and it should be a meeting on the highest level, but we would agree even to less than that.

The meeting will be a decisive test of the seriousness of their goodwill. Without a meeting, we can only doubt Nasser's sincerity—whether he really aspires to peace. We believe that only a meeting can lead to clarification, to the advantage of both sides. You say that the territorial question is the most important one in Nasser's eyes. Let him try to convince us, let us have the opportunity to show him that the loss of territory is impossible, and we shall see what is the true interest involved in territorial continuity, and whether it is justified; perhaps we may be able to satisfy him without undermining our sovereign rights. Even if the meeting does not bring about substantial results, we shall not be sorry it was held, for contact will have been established and mistaken suspicions eradicated. I do not say that such a meeting is bound to lead to full agreement, but a partial agreement is of great value. There are four possibilities: 1) a full peace settlement; 2) partial settlements; 3) mutual understanding on a particular question; 4) the peaceful maintenance of the status quo.

The Emissary: May I ask whether Hammarskjöld's talk with Nasser has any relation to our problem?

Sharett: Hammarskjöld received a statement from the Government of Egypt which he regarded as an agreement to a cease-fire. I am not certain that this view is justified, but that is his impression.

The Emissary: I am interested to know whether he got that impression from the Egyptian Foreign Minister or from Nasser. The source is important. I understand from what Sharett said that you will consider that progress has been made if the cease-fire leads to secret talks in an agreed place. (*Sharett:* Also on an agreed level.) You want the highest possible level?

Sharett: Yes.

The Emissary: In my opinion it is also important to reduce the tension, that is, to avoid making provocative statements, to show caution as evidence of sincerity, and also to take an interest, as far as possible, in what interests the other side.

Ben-Gurion: There are two issues: the one is peace and the second is the prevention of war. Peace depends entirely on the will of the leaders. We want peace. We are prepared for peace at once or peace in stages. By stages I mean quiet on the border, observance of the Armistice Agreement and a non-aggression treaty. It is possible that Nasser can't do it. I am trying to understand his situation. It is possible that he can't do it because of the army, or because he is afraid of losing the friendship of other Arab countries. And perhaps there are other reasons. But war can be prevented, and there is a danger of war. Goodwill talks are important; and let us assume that Cairo Radio stops demanding the destruction of Israel. But other things are happening. Arms are flowing into Egypt, and we know what bombers and armor are needed for.

The danger in our view is great, and the prevention of war does not depend only on Egypt. War can be prevented if you and your Government act and do what has to be done. If Nasser wants to meet us he can come with the agenda you spoke of yesterday: refugees and territory. I hope that at such a meeting we could find a solution. If Nasser wants to join up with other Arab countries, we have no objection. We could even take part in a regional confederation which provides for joint action while its members keep their sovereignty. I don't know whether they are ready for it.

If Nasser was capable of convincing his colleagues that Israel is a fact which cannot be eliminated, it would be much easier to get peace. But even without that, the prevention of war is the most important thing in this part of the world. And not only here. The United States is capable of guaranteeing that no war should break out in this part of the world. If that is assured, it will be an important step toward peace. When you left the United States you did not know all the dangers. If the danger of war has been averted, your mission will be much easier. I don't want to discourage you, but you cannot ignore the danger of war after the "commercial transaction" [the arms deal between Egypt and Czechoslovakia]. We are a small people with a small country, and we don't want to lose thousands of our youth again as we did seven years ago.

The Emissary: I want to understand your thinking. There is apprehension on Israel's part because arms are flowing to Egypt. But there may be fear in Egypt. As I understood you, you want an external assurance that Egypt shall be in no danger from you, nor you from Egypt.

Ben-Gurion: An assurance not in words but in deeds. A nation whose very existence is in danger cannot rely on words. We can be attacked within minutes, and some time would pass—who knows how much?—in discussions between Governments before they were ready to act. We therefore see the need for the creation of *facts* for our security, and if necessary for the other side as well. They believe that we are superior to them in the military sense, but they had a serious dispute with Britain before they got the Soviet arms—and it did not enter our minds to attack them. Nevertheless they say that we might attack. Give them assurances as well, to remove all fear and all possibility of war. If these two factors are removed, I believe there is hope for peace.

The Emissary: I want to be sure that I have understood your intention: first of all, both sides should be assured of the existence of a force that will make war superfluous and undesirable; second, an assurance should also be given which, from a psychological point of view, will leave no room for fear.

Ben-Gurion: The first point is the most important. I should not like your mission to be postponed until steps are taken for the prevention of war. I should only like you to tell Washington that this is a burning question. In the meantime go back to Egypt and try to arrange a meeting: on our side it can be Mr. Sharett, who was Prime Minister until a few months ago. On their side it is desirable that it should be Nasser. If Nasser does not take part, there is little likelihood of progress, but we shall not refuse to have a meeting even on a different level.

The Emissary: Any level?

Sharett: It must be a responsible level.

The Emissary: Suppose the first meeting is not on the desired level. In your opinion that will not do much good. But perhaps, even if this meeting does not have conclusive political authority, it will establish the fact of contact, and after that we can make progress.

Sharett: Obviously, even that would be better than no meeting at all.

The Emissary: I can make an effort to arrange a meeting on the highest possible level. If not, then on a lower level in order to establish contact.

Ben-Gurion: Is it possible to arrange such a meeting in Cairo? That would facilitate contact with Nasser.

The Emissary: What do you think of unilateral statements by both countries addressed to the President of the United States? These statements could contain historical points and arguments of both sides but will include agreement to a cease-fire and an undertaking to punish violators.

Ben-Gurion: And observance of the Armistice Agreement.

The Emissary: Something like that, not exactly, but in that direction.

Ben-Gurion: Will that be the only thing?

Ambassador Lawson: You will regard that as only a start in the right direction.

Ben-Gurion: If measures are not taken to prevent war, we shall be unable to forget the danger.

The Emissary: I understand the depth of your feelings, and I shall inform my Government that this is your principal concern.

Sharett: If your talk with Nasser sheds light on the situation or if you discern progress, will you come to us again?

The Emissary: Yes.

This was the end of the meeting. On January 25 we had a brief session.

The Emissary: I wanted to clarify one point. On the other side only possibilities were mentioned and not the will to carry them out. The problems I raised are new and that has to be clear here.

Sharett: I believe they approached Arab notables in Israel to find out whether, in their opinion, our desire for peace is sincere. That happened in the last few days. They did not reveal to the people who were asked that something was under consideration.

The Emissary: It seems to me, from our discussions, that you here are moving much faster and have more definite ideas about what can be achieved. I am going to Egypt now for only two or three days. If the question of the meeting is raised during my talk with Nasser, I should not like to find myself in a position in which I would have to tell him that he must give a reply within a day or two, otherwise it would be interpreted as a mark of ill will. I would rather he said to me, "I must think about it." I don't want to be in a position of pressure, so that when I come back here in three days you will think I have failed.

Sharett: I understand your position, but on the other side they must know that the President of the United States and you believe that the situation is urgent and that you must know whether it is possible or not. The problem is not a new one for them. Nasser has undoubtedly thought a great deal about it. Since the new regime came to power he has made attempts to establish direct contact, not only between Ben-Gurion and Nagib or between Nasser and me. Letters have been exchanged through various channels. And in one case a reply was received.

There was an exchange of letters in April 1953, before the fall of Nagib. The reply came from Nasser. It was not sent directly to us, but a certain official handed it to us. (Sharett read out the Israeli letter and Nasser's reply.) In December 1954, a British Member of Parliament, a Jew, went to Nasser on behalf of the World Jewish Congress—an institution that defends Jewish rights all over the world; for example, they are active now in Morocco. He came to me before he went to Cairo. He visited Cairo on three occasions, and after seeing Nasser he was in contact with Ali Sabri.

At the same time there was a second contact in Paris. Nasser sent one of his men to Paris, where we had some of our people, and there was an exchange of letters. A number of Egyptian Jews were arrested in Cairo and we worked to save them from the scaffold.* We did not succeed: our operation in Gaza** at the beginning of 1955 had no connection with the death penalties in Cairo; it was a reply to fedayeen operations from the Gaza Strip. I approached Nasser several times through an emissary to get these operations stopped—but I received no response. If Nasser thinks that the Gaza operation was meant to start a war, he is mistaken, and he does not adequately evaluate all the damage done by the fedayeen. He must understand that we cannot endure penetrations across the border to strike at our people. We knew that these operations were organized by the Egyptian army. He must understand that our operation was not meant to bring about war or to get him removed from his position.

---

* Translator's note: Eleven Egyptian Jews were accused of spying for Israel and planting incendiary bombs at the US information center and other places in Cairo in July 1954 in order to disturb US-Egyptian relations. Six were sentenced to long terms of imprisonment and two were executed on January 31, 1955.

** Translator's note: Israeli troops attacked the Egyptian base near Gaza on February 28, 1955, in retaliation for Arab attacks on Israel. Thirty-eight Egyptians and two local Arabs were killed.

Since then there has been no more direct contact between us. A Quaker named Jackson came here in August or October, and he went to Egypt to bring about an exchange of prisoners. For a time it seemed that Nasser was interested in that.

The best thing would be if it was possible to arrange a meeting in Cairo. That would give Nasser complete confidence that he would control the talks. Either he would participate in them himself, or his representative, who could be in constant contact with him. This might appear surprising—but in Cairo it would be possible to maintain complete secrecy. If they are held in some other place—in Geneva, for instance—Nasser's presence would be known, and he would have to explain what he was doing there. On the other hand, in Cairo a meeting could be hermetically concealed. If they want a settlement, they must want a meeting, and the best place for a meeting of this kind is Cairo.

The Emissary: As I pointed out in my first talk, it seems unlikely that a meeting can be arranged on the highest possible level. I do not even know if I can arrange a meeting on a lower level, but I will try. I am certain that Nasser is concerned with his political problems. There is a second point: several times during our talks you referred to Nasser's control of the press and the radio. I admit I don't know the entire situation, but he said several times that there are forces in the press and the radio that he does not control. That no doubt refers to the press and radio in other countries.

Sharett: Yes, but in Egypt he is the undisputed ruler.

The Emissary: Can I say in Egypt that you promise secrecy and that I have heard that there have been contacts which have been kept secret?

Sharett: Yes, and one more remark about the things you said about an undertaking or letter to the President about the cease-fire. We do not demand that he should publicly proclaim a cease-fire, but, on the other hand, a letter to the President will be of no value unless a military order on the subject is issued. A Government is not obliged to publish military orders. We published them because the United Nations was involved. The main thing is that he should issue an order.

The Emissary: I do not know what the form of orders in Egypt is. But what we want to avoid is a deterioration, and therefore, since there have already been attempts at a cease-fire, what is required now is a more vigorous and stringent order that will keep the peace.

This was the last meeting with the emissary before his second journey to Cairo to meet Nasser. He returned only on January 31.

51 THE EMISSARY RETURNS FROM CAIRO—Jan. 31, 1956

When the emissary returned from Egypt on January 31, he met me and Sharett to give us his impressions of his meeting with Nasser.

The Emissary: On my return to Cairo I had a session with Nasser from 10:30 p.m. until midnight. I told him that the Prime Minister of Israel had said several times that he was trying to put himself in Nasser's shoes, and that the Israeli Foreign Minister was interested to know what Nasser was doing for his own country. Nasser was pleased at your personal interest. I told him about the content of our talks: that I had told you that he said he had no hostile intentions and wanted to reduce border tension and consider the problems of a settlement; that I had explained to you his concern for public opinion; and that you said that you understood this, but you were worried about the arrival of Soviet arms. Nasser replied that he understood your position, and he was trying to see the position from your viewpoint.

I told him that I thought both sides understood the problem of the borders and the refugees, and that I understood that in his opinion the problem of the refugees was not insoluble; I said I felt that room could be given for a certain measure of choice on the basis of family reunification. This was a kind of hope—as one of you said, "a ray of light." Nasser replied that there is hope for a solution, and that a certain measure of free choice should be accepted. I explained your absorption difficulties. I told him I had visited an Arab village and seen something of the way Arabs, like Jews, were being absorbed. I said both sides understood that the refugee problem should be discussed on a basis of give and take.

I tried to get more details about the refugees, and I saw that he was prepared to discuss the matter, but had not considered the subject in detail. He mentioned the Blandford Plan,★ and Syria and Iraq as possible countries of absorption, but said that he did not have the details of the matter in his head and would have to obtain additional information. His officials do not take notes of the talks and do not bring notes to the sittings.

Sharett: And what about territory?

The Emissary: I only told Nasser that this was a big question between the two

---

★ Translator's note: John B. Blandford was appointed Director of the UN Relief and Works Agency for Arab refugees in 1951 and announced a plan to spend $100 million in 12 months to resettle 150,000–250,000 refugees in Arab countries. Later he proposed a three-year plan to spend $200 million on resettlement. These plans were blocked by the Arab states and Blandford resigned in February 1953.

countries. I repeated what I had said about flexibility (though I know that flexibility worries Ben-Gurion) and told him that I had not reached a final conclusion, since sooner or later there would ultimately have to be a meeting of the two sides, and that in my opinion there were many other problems that ought to be considered first. I told him that you ascribed great importance to a personal meeting, that in your opinion it was desirable that the heads of state should meet, and that I had told you about his difficulties and you had shown understanding, although you regarded a meeting of this kind as very important. I proposed a reconsideration of the question of establishing direct contact. Nasser said he was prepared to consider it, but he did not know yet whom he could choose. He said he had taken one more person into his confidence, namely Ali Sabri, the head of his bureau. (In speaking about the refugees he said that Sabri and Zacharia Muḥi el-Din would collect the material on absorption for him.)

Nasser asked who would be let into the secret. I told him that you, out of goodwill, had expressed your readiness for a meeting any time, anywhere, even in Egypt. He said that helped. His difficulty was that his Intelligence and Police did not know about the matter (I myself came to Egypt as an ordinary tourist). I pressed him to tell me if he was worried about any other aspect of the matter. He said: Yes, he had another worry. At the first meeting he had not seemed inclined to talk about it, and I could not press him. But this time I pressed him, and said that if I was to do any good I must know everything (he was so concerned for secrecy that he urged Zacharia Muḥi el-Din and Sabri to go on with their daily work during our talks so that they should not arouse attention). When I pressed him he said: Yes, I will tell you.

At the first meeting I had told him that there had already been previous channels of communication, so that he could renew contact without anxiety. At the second meeting, after I pressed him to tell me what he thought, he said that at the time when the channel of communication existed, he had been misled as a result. That was at the time of the trial.* The accused had had to be tried. He had not thought it wise to impose the death penalty, but if the Court passed that sentence, he could not quash it. He had thought it was clear to you that the utmost he could do was to use his influence on the Court before the trial, but he could not quash the sentence. When the Gaza affair took place he was caught with his pants down. I asked if I could tell the Israelis this. He answered in the affirmative.

I said that the most important thing was to create mutual trust. I pointed out

* See note on p. 294.

that I had the promise of Ben-Gurion and others that if direct contact was established, it would be kept secret, no matter what the results, and I asked him to act accordingly. He agreed. I asked if it was desirable that there should be a responsible person through whom progress in this direction could be reported (Kermit Roosevelt, who participated at some meetings, was present at this one), and he agreed. I said that this was a step forward and that in the past perhaps there had been misunderstandings in the process of transmission. He replied that he had understood that the reaction to the death penalty would only take the form of a protest and that his attitude had been understood. He said he did not want what had happened to Abdullah to happen to him; and the only charge against Abdullah had been that he had held negotiations.

Sharett: Does he believe that we revealed the negotiations with Abdullah?

The Emissary: No, but he is afraid of a breach of secrecy at a time when he is not prepared for it. I cannot emphasize sufficiently his political anxiety; namely, that there are people in his country and other countries who will exploit any opportunity they get. But I told him that although I understood his problem I wanted him to assure me that the question of establishing contact would remain open.

Nasser agreed. I understood that he was about to expand the circle of men in his confidence. I also know (he did not say this to me and I am telling you this in confidence) that he told a certain Arab that he was now doing something which was no less important than anything he had done in his life, and he hoped for positive results. He did not give his friend the details, but he told him that what he was doing now was of the utmost importance and he was hopeful.

I told him that I could not advise him whom to take into his confidence, but the problem before us was such that it could not be finally solved with the participation of only a few men. And up till now nothing has been published.

He is preparing a letter that he intends to send to the President of the United States, in which he will say that he has no hostile intentions and that he wants to do everything to prevent difficulties on the borders. His position is difficult because of the attitude of the other Arab countries. He asked whether Israel was prepared to publish some statement. I replied in the affirmative.

As for border incidents, I made it clear that I was not thinking of a formal cease-fire, but of orders to prevent shooting and the use of technical means—flying a flag or some other sign, and that you had promised to consult the Army officers about it. He appreciated this and said that any technical means would help. But he again repeated that each side should move a few kilometers from the border. I told him that this was a technical matter, which Burns should deal with, and that all I wanted was to prevent border incidents. He said he had done this and already dispatched orders to his men to take steps to prevent border incidents.

Sharett: Does he understand that shooting is also a border incident?

The Emissary: Yes. He added that he must be honest and say that it would be difficult so long as there are refugees. There had been cases of refugees crossing from the Gaza Strip to Jordan without his men advising them to do so. It had been proposed that he should send military forces to the Strip, but his forces were limited. The refugees were extreme and would raise a lot of noise against any settlement. Even if it came to the signature of final peace, there was a danger of incidents by the refugees—until they were dispersed and settled. (He told Kermit Roosevelt that there had been acts of violence by refugees against Egyptian soldiers because they thought the Egyptians were not doing enough for them.)

I said to Nasser: You are looked on with suspicion because you received arms from Czechoslovakia. I want to ask you a straight question, and I want you to understand the moral responsibility that will rest on me in accordance with your reply. Have you hostile intentions for the use of these arms? He replied: No! I continued: Are you sincere in your desire to work for a peace settlement? He said: Yes. I said that on both sides there was the problem of moral responsibility, and that I had asked each side about its intentions toward the other. I must be confident of the intentions of both sides, for a great responsibility lay and would continue to lie on the United States, and I must be sure that his intentions were good.

I went on to ask him whether, in his opinion, it was possible to make progress with the Johnston Plan,* which was to the advantage of both sides. He replied: Yes, so far as his influence extended. All the Arabs except Syria had agreed to the plan. The difficulty was that there was no internal stability in Syria and there was no knowing from whom a reply could be received. I asked about Jordan. He said that Jordan was not opposed, and the obstacle was Syria. I asked if he was prepared to continue the talks with the Arabs for the implementation

---

* Translator's note: Eric Johnston was sent to the Middle East in 1953 by President Eisenhower as a special envoy to seek agreement on the utilization of the water resources of the Jordan and its tributaries for the development of Israel, Jordan, Lebanon and Syria, particularly with a view to refugee settlement. In 1955 he presented a Unified Water Plan agreed to by the experts of the four countries. Israel accepted the proposals, but the Arab League refused to approve them. Israel and Jordan proceeded with their water development works in accordance with the plan.

of the Johnston Plan. He said he would do that, but the question of the instability of the Syrian Government still stood.

At this juncture I mentioned that B. G. had told me that he wanted to assist the economic progress of the region, that he wanted to help Egypt and Egypt should help Israel, and that joint action of this kind was the best way for both countries. Nasser said that was good, but practical implementation depended on the readiness of both peoples to reach agreement. And both peoples were very nationalistic. The people were unwilling to take advice from the outside. I said to Nasser that talks should be held on a number of other problems which I would define as being of lesser importance, like the reunion of the villages with the agricultural areas that had been cut off from them. I said he had expressed to me the idea that the territorial partition of Jerusalem was preferable to an international zone. The protection of the Holy Places could be discussed. It was very important that there should be a continuation, and that there should be an acceleration in our efforts to reach the goal. I asked if he would keep in touch with Kermit to maintain continuity and acceleration. He said he would.

Finally I said: We have talked a great deal; I have been here and there. Many things have remained without a solution. Are we nearer a solution now than we were before? He sat in silence and scratched his head for a couple of minutes, and said: Yes, we are nearer; but he felt obliged to add that in a week or two he would be able to give a much more agreeable answer. He added that after he observed Israel's behavior in the next few weeks he could give a reply. I said the other side was also waiting to see what he would do. He said it was better to give a sincere reply and in one, two or three weeks he would see to what extent he was optimistic.

I said that we were leaving unanswered the question of direct negotiations and other problems. We wanted to continue so that we should get closer to what we wanted to do. He said: Yes, he wanted to leave Cairo for a while.

On the Suez question I asked: Could I assume that in case of a settlement the Canal would be opened to Israel shipping? He said: Correct; that was a secondary boycott connected with the state of belligerency. In his opinion, the question of the trade between other Arab countries and Israel was their own affair. I told him that B. G. looked forward to the time when trains would travel from Cairo to Beirut, and the question of contact would not exist any more than it did between the United States and Canada. Nasser said: This is a desirable aim. I told him that the question of flights across these countries was one we would have to normalize in days of peace. He said that he had no objection, and it would be like in all other countries.

The two problems are refugees and boundaries. The question of negotiations depends on the time it will take him to get others to agree, and my success in convincing him that secrecy is assured. I must also convince him that there will be no misunderstanding; that is, that he will not be misled again, as he believed he was before. That is the situation. My plans are flexible, but it is clear that things will have to move.

Sharett: When Nasser spoke about the Gaza incident, did you understand that he believes that it was done in revenge for the death penalty?

The Emissary: I cannot say exactly that he believes that the Gaza affair was due only to the trial, but basically, that is how he sees it.

Sharett: If the Gaza operation came as a surprise, on what does he base his attitude? In my written approach there was a threat that if the death penalty was carried out, it would arouse shock and indignation. I explained to you the reasons for the Gaza operation. What grounds did he have for assuming that we would not react?

The Emissary: He believed that the reaction would be in the form of a sharp protest and an appeal to international law, but not that it would lead to incidents. I said I had been told that the Gaza affair took place shortly after B. G.'s return to the Ministry of Defense, but I had been assured that B. G. did not return to the Government to create incidents. You wanted Nasser to understand this. He said that that was actually how he understood it. I told him that I simply wanted him to understand this.

I told Nasser that the number of casualties in the Gaza incident had shocked you. I would not be honest if I did not tell you that the Gaza affair was painful. Nasser said that the really serious deterioration started with that event. Until then people in Egypt did not take an interest in Palestine.

Nasser said he had thought a great deal about the question of punishing violators of the cease-fire.

Kollek: Did you mention to Nasser the possibility that we may get arms for defense? And what about Bnot Yaakov?★

The Emissary: I did not raise this question directly. As for the second question, I spoke of it in connection with Arab cooperation in the development plan. I must add that if you do anything that annoys Syria, Jordan and others, the possibility of the plan being approved will be adversely affected.

Ben-Gurion: Now I want to think aloud. We carry a terrible responsibility. Nasser is a dictator. Our colleagues do not know and will not know about these

---

★ See note on p. 316.

discussions of ours, but the questions are fateful. You have undertaken a mission of hope and tremendous danger. I will not speak about secondary matters. Is there hope, and is it near, and what must we do to realize it? Everything can be explained in two ways. It is possible that Nasser is really afraid of his people and the Arab countries—Iraq and its Syrian ally and the Saudi Arabians. If there is hope for peace—that would be the greatest thing in our lives. Several years before the establishment of the State I tried to formulate our principal aims: 1) the security of our people; 2) the founding of a Jewish State; 3) a Jewish-Arab alliance. There is a connection between the three. I always see a Jewish-Arab alliance as the ultimate goal. And therefore, if there is the slightest possibility of achieving peace with Egypt, we must do everything toward that end. But there are things that make it difficult to see hope. I have tried to dissipate all doubts—but if you cannot stop the shooting . . .

The Emissary: Has there been shooting during the last few days?

Ben-Gurion: Yes, every day.

The Emissary: Have people been killed?

Ben-Gurion: No, but rifles and machine guns are fired every day. I have suspicions, but I am prepared to understand. We have to understand. We have to understand Nasser's difficulties and do all in our power to make it easier for him to meet us and try to reach a settlement. As a democratic leader I find it very difficult not to tell these things to my colleagues. In the United States it is easier, for there is a president there. But if this is only a matter of secrecy, we can wait a month, a year, five years.

The ideal is so great that we must do nothing to jeopardize peace. But your mission also involves the danger of war. It is possible that there will be no peace—and yet no war either. I want to believe him, and one should, in order to bring peace nearer. It is possible that he is sincere, but there are forces that are brought to bear on him. If I told our people about your mission, they would be glad. Nasser cannot do that, just as he is unable to bring to trial men who commit acts of violence.

In another six months he will be very strong. Three days ago Egypt, Saudi Arabia and Syria declared that they would fight if we continued work at Bnot Yaakov. We can understand that there is no contradiction between this and Nasser's attitude. But in another six months, when he and his army feel that they are strong enough to defeat Israel, the pressure on him is liable to be too great.

I am sure that when he sent a letter and said that in the trial [of the Jews in Cairo] there would be no severe penalties, he said it in all sincerity. As President of the State he could have commuted the sentence, but because of public opinion he apparently cannot do what he would like to do.

In 1940 Roosevelt wanted to join in the war, but he could not do so until Pearl Harbor. The same applies to Nasser. He is not a free agent. If he is sincere, and the time comes when he believes he can destroy Israel, he will be unable not to do it. Saudi Arabia, his own army, Syria, and perhaps by that time Jordan too—they will all be pressing him. We will be responsible before our people and our history if we do not do everything to prevent that from happening. We shall be to blame for wanting to believe Nasser in order to help you and the President. I know that what you are doing is not easy, but if a war breaks out we shall be asked why we did not do everything to protect our country against disaster. I believe that if it were possible to arrange a meeting, then perhaps in a few days we would reach agreement. But we have not yet arrived at this stage. The danger is steadily approaching—unless we do all in our power to avert it.

I have read the President's statement at Denver, and as I read it I felt that the man who made that statement is the man I met at Frankfurt [immediately after World War II]. The danger can be averted if we get enough defensive arms. Then we shall be able to do everything to help you to carry out your mission. Possibly we shall have to start work on the Jordan. I have not the slightest doubt that Eisenhower's sole aim is to bring about peace. Arms—that is one of your functions and it is very complicated—that is the main thing. Without that we cannot do what we ought to do for peace. The danger of war must be eliminated. If we have the arms, we can keep the secret, even from our colleagues, and not do many things that we should otherwise have to do.

Let us suppose that the danger of war has been eliminated. As the first step on the road to peace, the shooting must be stopped. There is shooting every day, and it is a miracle that people are not being killed. If anything is required of us, it will be done. I give you a categorical undertaking. In our country only the army bears arms. There will be no shooting from our territory, and none of us will cross the border. If Nasser issues an order to cease fire, you can give a categorical undertaking in our name. If that is done, the atmosphere will be changed for the better. Next, communications should be established to deal with minor matters—if anything happens, he could transfer information to me and I to him. Although this is difficult for him, we must arrange direct communications for the transfer of messages from both sides. Then the third stage should come: a meeting between representatives. No mediation, not even the most ideal, could bring about what the two parties can achieve in a direct meeting.

I do not present the Jordan Plan as a prior condition, for that will create difficulties for Nasser with Syria. It would be a good thing if he could influence Syria, but I do not present this as a condition for relations between us. If we get to the third stage, to a meeting between representatives, the time will come when questions will be asked and it will be necessary to make decisions. Nasser is interested in the refugee question and in territory. I have explained our attitude, but I may possibly have some ideas for him—for the attainment of the things he wants without harming us. Then I shall have to tell my colleagues. There will be a need for contact between people on both sides who are capable of bearing responsibility. It will take perhaps a year to achieve: 1) elimination of the danger of war; 2) a cease-fire; 3) the establishment of communications; 4) a meeting of representatives; 5) a meeting of persons with the authority to decide.

If you succeed in ensuring peace, you will have done one of the greatest things in the history of our time. We are grateful to the President, and we must do all in our power to help you. Our greatest difficulty is the danger of war. Time is the main factor, and if within four or six weeks we do not get a minimum of planes and tanks we shall not be able to do what is needed for a settlement.

The Emissary: I understand your difficulties and the pressure that weighs upon you. The decisions are indeed fateful. I am sure you know that the President's attitude and that of the United States Government is to preserve the existence of Israel and to bring about peace. I am sure you understand that our Government's thinking is as thorough as possible in regard to the problems you presented and the best way to protect the security of your country and establish a stable and enduring peace. I would say that it is very important to evaluate the responsibility with the most profound and farsighted vision, for anything that is less than that might avert disaster only for the shortest term. We must let no other consideration influence our judgment to the same extent as the decisions that can lead us on the way to a settlement. All of us should recognize Egypt's desire to play a senior role in Arab unity.

We must decide how to establish ties the level of which will constantly rise, bearing in mind our knowledge of Nasser's apprehensions. It seems to me that he believes that if he puts the information in untrustworthy hands, he will give that person the best possible means for blackmail.

I have passed over one point. If, during the period before direct communications are established, you have anything you want to convey to Nasser, word for word, he has agreed that you should pass it on through us, for direct communication to him. We shall quote exactly what you want to tell him. I know that this is not a satisfactory solution.

It is very important to turn his attention to problems other than those of refugees or territory—to areas in which agreement can be found, and that will help to clear the air. That confirms what you said, for I do not believe that there are substantial differences between Egypt and Israel. To facilitate my talks on the questions on which there is a chance of agreement, I want to ask a few questions. If we assume that there will be a division in the sovereignty over Jerusalem, do you see any difficulty in arriving at an agreement over the Holy Places and have you thought about any formula?

Sharett: Is that Nasser's concern?

The Emissary: Not his direct concern, but it will help him with Jordan.

Sharett: Whatever Jordan agrees to, we will agree to as well. Let us try to find a blueprint for a settlement between Israel and Egypt. Then we shall be able to examine questions between Israel and other Arab countries.

The Emissary: Good. I believe you have answered my question about Jerusalem. I understand your attitude on the question of transit.

Sharett: On a basis of reciprocity.

The Emissary: I should like to get your reaction to Dulles' speech on 26 August. In connection with guarantees for the borders I assure you that the moment a settlement is reached, it will be possible to rely on them to a very large extent.

Sharett: Do you mean as a substitute for arms?

The Emissary: Not as a substitute, but as a primary reliance.

Ben-Gurion: As a substitute, I say: No. If there is a danger of war, we could be attacked within five minutes. Before the guarantee can become effective twenty-four hours could pass. Inside that time it could all be over.

The Emissary: What you say is that you will continue to be anxious in the area of legitimate self-defense.

Ben-Gurion: On some questions there will be differences of opinion among our people. I believe that Sharett's view and mine will be accepted. But there is a feeling among the whole people that unless we have sufficient arms in good time to deter an Egyptian attack, no guarantees will be sufficient. Three-quarters of our people live in Tel Aviv, Haifa and Jerusalem.

The Emissary: What we are trying to do is to reduce the danger.

Ben-Gurion: A guarantee is important only after the arms are there.

Sharett: Besides, according to Dulles' speech the guarantee is possible only with border rectifications, and that is doubtful. Agreement may or may not be reached. This is a supposition—and a distant one.

Ben-Gurion: Try to put yourself in our place and you will realize what we are bound to feel in the existing situation.

The Emissary: I grasp what you say, but the really important deterrence is to arrange a meeting.

Sharett: I am seriously concerned that if the meeting falls through, the whole affair might end in nothing. If the iron is hot, we must strike immediately. If not—who knows? In the papers two annoying reports have appeared. The one was a UP report which gives the impression of a leakage. On reading this report, Nasser is liable to get alarmed at once. If he is not sincere, he will snatch at any excuse to call off all the talks. Another piece of news that appeared tells about a meeting between Nasser and Trevelyan, the British Ambassador, which is described as a most important talk that lasted two and a half hours. What worries us all the time is the Guildhall speech [Prime Minister Anthony Eden's speech, which proposed the truncation of Israel's territory] and Nasser's approach. Nasser may think that he can get more from the British than from you. God knows what ideas Trevelyan may put into his head.

The Emissary: That danger always exists. I did not go to any hotel, because I am known. Nasser asked what would happen if it became known that I was in Egypt. I replied that I would say that I had come to see him about mining licences.

Mr. Sharett, suppose we arrive at the point where we are trying to do something practical. Do you think it would be better to amend the Armistice Agreement by a UN decision or in some other way?

Sharett: For a long time we have thought that the armistice agreement method is worth while. But if Nasser thinks there is a better way, we will not object. There are two ways to use the Armistice Agreement: one way, through Article 12 [which specifies a procedure for amending the agreement], the second is to begin with secret negotiations and, if we succeed, to consider what is the best way to extend the Agreement in the light of the additions both sides agree to. That is a matter for discussion.

I want to come back to the question of previous contacts, and to emphasize: 1) There was no leakage about these contacts; 2) My letter to Nasser was meant to point out the great shock that would be aroused if the death penalties were executed; 3) In regard to Gaza, he underestimated the impression that would be made by the penetrations into our territory.

The Emissary: Can I say that if there was a misunderstanding it is regretted?

Ben-Gurion: I believe you can get an understanding from Nuri Sa'id that he will not use the fact of negotiations against Nasser.

The Emissary: I have reason to believe that you are right.

Ben-Gurion: There is no reason to fear Jordan, Lebanon and Saudi Arabia. It is possible that only a few people in Syria will object.

The Emissary: I hope you will not start the works on the Jordan so long as the talks continue. That might affect the possibility of the acceptance of the Johnston Plan.

Ben-Gurion: You have mentioned the works on the Jordan. It is possible that we will not carry them out, for the sake of the United States and for the sake of peace. If we are freed from the anxiety of war, we shall be able to do things for peace that we could not do on their own merits, and we can explain this to our people. Without arms we cannot do that, for our people know that there is danger. If those who can help us do not do so, you cannot expect us to refrain from things that have to be done on their own merits. For the sake of peace I am prepared to call on my people to do anything, but only if we are freed from this anxiety. I am not discussing now the works at Bnot Yaakov; however, if we get arms, you can come to me about that matter too. And it is possible that we will reach agreement. If we meet [with Nasser] I will propose things that Nasser does not even think about. Most important things.

The Emissary: Do you believe that the basic issues can be placed on the table only when the responsible men meet?

Ben-Gurion: Yes.

The Emissary: And what about trade?

Ben-Gurion: I will go so far as to say that there will be no customs barriers. I am not an expert in economics, but what I am thinking of is far-reaching. We shall behave like separate countries insofar as it affects our national independence, but as one large unit for economic and political cooperation.

The Emissary: Haifa for the use of Jordan?

Ben-Gurion: Eilat too—and Alexandria as well, for our use.

The Emissary: I shall consider whether to return from Athens to Cairo. If not, I shall contact you. Let us examine the areas in regard to which there is agreement, so that we can approach a solution.

Ben-Gurion: If you return, something is liable to happen. You must know that Nasser is under the supervision of the Soviets, and it is possible that he is playing with the United States to win time. The cease-fire is important, but not decisive. The question is what will come afterward.

The Emissary: Whether I return or not, I will convey your feelings about the cease-fire. As for the letter to the President, I read a draft in pencil of Nasser's letter. It says "No hostile intentions against Israel and an undertaking to refrain from border incidents." That was when Nasser told me that he did not want to introduce a paragraph about punishment. This is a general letter, can I say that you will also submit a letter of this kind?

Kollek: Will he agree that copies should be conveyed to both sides?

The Emissary: I shall be able to discuss the general content. When Nasser says that he must relieve the pressure, he is thinking of two things: the Baghdad Pact and the Gaza affair. He has set the propaganda machine in motion, and he argues that he cannot get up one morning and describe Egypt in one way, and next morning say the opposite.

Ben-Gurion: If he is not involved with the Russians why is he afraid of the Baghdad Pact?

The Emissary: Because Iraq joined it first.

Ben-Gurion: Why does he not understand the Soviet danger to the frontiers of Iraq?

The Emissary: He sees the danger that all the Arab countries may join the Baghdad Pact and Egypt will be isolated. He wants to be the big noise in the League.

After I had left the meeting—Sharett had departed earlier—the emissary told Kollek and Herzog that Nasser wanted to know from Kermit Roosevelt what he (the emissary) thought about him (Nasser). Kermit replied that the emissary had not disclosed this. Nasser said that he was more optimistic now than he had been in past years.

On February 1 the talk with the emissary was held in Yaakov Herzog's house. Present were: the emissary, Moshe Sharett, Teddy Kollek and Herzog.

Sharett: Time is a factor of supreme importance. First, there are many unforeseeable factors, which could destroy all our labors. Secondly, you have shaken him and undermined the morbid idea that Israel is a merciless enemy. If we piece together scraps of information, we shall see that he is now in the grip of a new idea. Just as he previously saw greatness in the conquest of Israel, so he must now be shown the greatness of peace. Yesterday the Prime Minister showed endless tolerance in his anxiety to examine every possibility for peace, so that the responsibility for the failure of the negotiations should not fall on us. But that is not all. War grows in the womb of peace. The President took a revolutionary step by sending a man like you to be his emissary. And that is appropriate to the occasion—if it succeeds or starts a process that promises results. This initiative was born out of a sense of grave urgency, and the President made a move for a settlement as one of the most important aims of United States policy.

The Emissary: My task is to continue to press, but to avoid actions that might be counterproductive. I very much appreciate the factor of time.

Sharett: Nasser ought to begin to understand that your mission is a great opportunity. He should be made to understand that it should not be missed.

The Emissary: Nasser understands the advantage of communications and contact. His concern is the maintenance of secrecy. He is afraid that if he gives information to the wrong person, he may be blackmailed, and he is very much afraid of that. I said to him: Is the question open and will you continue to look for ways to renew the contact? He said: Yes, and in the meantime letters can be conveyed through Kermit Roosevelt.

Sharett: I ascribe great importance to a further effort to eradicate his suspicions of deceit. Some kind of practical undertaking should be extracted from him, something that will change the situation for the better.

The Emissary: The important thing is that we are changing the trend that existed before, and trying to bring about an improvement. The moment a change begins, steps should be taken to reach the goal.

Sharett: There is another point. He must understand that if we get arms of the same class as he has, it is only for the sake of self-defense. We cannot possibly get the quantity of arms in his possession.

The Emissary: We have to persevere in the effort. But I am not sure that I can convince him.

52 LETTER TO EISENHOWER—FEB. 14, 1956

The emissary returned to Washington during the first week in February. After his departure I sent President Eisenhower on February 14 the following reply to his letter of January 9:

"Dear Mr. President,

"Thank you for your letter of 9 January, which you sent through your emissary, X. L. Because of his stay for a few days in Cairo, the letter reached me only a few days ago.

"By sending us a faithful friend of excellent personal qualities and with great experience in affairs of state, a man by whose integrity, wisdom and nobility I have been deeply impressed, you have shown your interest in Israel's needs and in the improvement of Arab-Israel relations, as well as your sincere desire to help both sides arrive at agreement.

"From the city which in ancient days was the cradle of the prophetic vision of peace among all the nations, and which today still aspires to be a source of spiritual inspiration once more, I welcome your initiative with profound gratitude and esteem.

"Your emissary has no doubt told you already about the long talks he has held in both capitals and the progress that has been achieved.

"We on our part have expressed our unconditional readiness to start negotiations at once with the Prime Minister of Egypt or with responsible representatives appointed by the Prime Minister of Egypt with a view to reaching a settlement or at least revealing its possibilities. We have made it clear that we are prepared to engage in such negotiations without presenting prior conditions in regard to the scope and conditions of a settlement to be agreed upon. And since we long to arrive at a fixed, permanent and final peace if the other side wants the same, we are prepared to accept, if the other side also wants it, a partial approach to the problem, which will pave the way to peace by partial agreements.

"In our aspiration to advance the coming of peace, we are motivated not only by its great importance for Israel and the region, but also by an understanding of the value of peace and progress in the Middle East to the position of the Western democracies, with which fate and necessity bind Israel in unbreakable unity.

"But two parties are required for peace. And no praises of the importance of peace will avail if the goodwill of one side is lacking.

"I hope, therefore, that you will agree with me that if the Prime Minister of Egypt is sincere in saying that he does not want to push our region into war and that the destruction of Israel is not his aim, but, on the contrary, his policy is aimed at peace, there is no doubt that his reply to your emissary, who demanded in your name, Mr. President, direct contact between Jerusalem and Cairo, should be the arrangement of such a meeting at the earliest possible opportunity.

"Frankness compels me to tell you that if the Prime Minister of Egypt rejects this proposal, grave doubts will be aroused about his goodwill, and the question will arise whether he only wants to win time until he receives all the Czech arms. It is a painful and definite fact that, while your personal emissary has been staying in our midst, the Egyptian forces have been continuing to fire into Israel territory, and they have been doing so day by day until this very day. And the world does not know that the Egyptian armies along the border have been ordered to cease fire in accordance with the decision of the United Nations.

"On our part I wish to state that we have decided to observe the Armistice Agreement so long as it has not been replaced by a permanent peace settlement, and until then we shall refrain from any violation of the agreement.

"Even if Nasser's personal sincerity can be trusted, there is no certainty that his moral strength will enable him to oppose the pressure of the ruling junta and the army around it, after the desire to destroy us has grown in the knowledge that the new arms they are receiving give them decisive superiority over Israel, for we do not have the arms with which to defend ourselves.

"No Government responsible for the fate and survival of its people can watch with equanimity an enormous accumulation of arms in the hands of the neighboring power, which vigorously insists on war, without every effort being made to acquire arms, if not in the same quantity, at least of the same quality.

"The outstanding fact is that the Czech-Egyptian deal, which has so seriously damaged the position of the West in the Middle East and beyond—the planes and other arms that are flowing from the Soviet Union to Egypt—will soon place the towns and villages of Israel at Nasser's mercy—a danger that no people aware of the problem of its security can accept with equanimity.

"The strengthening of Israel will not weaken the prospects of peace but, on the contrary, will enhance them. A weak and helpless Israel, which Egypt could easily destroy, or at least cripple, will not be regarded as a partner for a settlement based on give and take. On the other hand, an Israel capable of defending herself—which cannot be destroyed—can bring peace nearer.

"I therefore appeal to you, Mr. President, in the name of my Government and my people, not to leave Israel without adequate capacity for self-defense, which only arms from a great power can provide, and to issue instructions to supply Israel with arms from the United States, which are essential to enable Israel to prevent or repel an attack.

"I remember the statement you made at Denver on 9 November, that the Government of the United States must examine the requirements of the peoples of the Near East in the sphere of self-defense. Three months have passed since then. Our request to acquire arms from the United States Government has remained without a reply, while the danger to Israel from continual Egyptian rearmament grows from month to month. I told your emissary that while we are prepared to do anything possible to promote his mission, we feel that the leading position of the United States in the society of democratic nations and the responsibility it bears for the defense of peace and the protection of small countries like Israel, impose on it the definite duty not to leave our call unanswered, but to reply adequately and in good time.

"Only defensive arms, especially planes like those that Egypt is receiving from Russia, will give us a sense of security and serve as a deterrent against attack. In our case, as everywhere else where national independence and democracy are in danger, peace depends on a definite and known capacity for self-defense.

"I must apologize for appealing to you at such length, but I thought it was justified because of the gravity of the danger that threatens us.

"With cordial greetings, I send you, on behalf of myself, all my colleagues in the Government and all the members of my people, heartfelt wishes for your health and strength."

53 THE EMISSARY'S LAST VISIT—MAR. 9, 1956

At the beginning of March, the emissary returned to the Middle East and, after visiting Cairo, arrived in Israel on the 9th. On the same day he met Sharett and me in Jerusalem. Kollek and Herzog were also present.

The Emissary: I have had two meetings with Nasser—Zacharia Muḥi el-Din and Ali Sabri were present at both. I arrived in Cairo on Saturday night and met Nasser at 11 o'clock. The second meeting was on Sunday night. I stayed until Monday and left for Greece, where I remained until Wednesday. At the first meeting I asked Nasser what was the meaning of the Glubb affair [the sudden dismissal of this British officer from the command of the Arab Legion in Jordan]. Nasser expressed great surprise at the nature of this incident. He would not have wondered, he said, if this had happened some time later, because Glubb had become unpopular, but he was surprised it had happened so soon. Nasser said that there was a group of officers in Jordan who were opposed to the King, and the King had dismissed Glubb in order to win their sympathy. He had acted without the knowledge of his Prime Minister.

I asked Nasser whether he had talked to Selwyn Lloyd [the British Foreign Secretary] and to what extent the talks had been satisfactory. Nasser replied that he did not know much more now about British policy than he had known before. Lloyd had not been clear and had spoken in generalities. He explained that he had not come to discuss a specific policy.

Our talk was concerned with the rapid implementation of the Johnston Plan. I said the United States hoped that Nasser would act vigorously on the plan and that would be evidence of his sincerity and reliability, and many people would congratulate him on it. I spoke about the importance of water. He agreed, but said that the problem was the instability in Syria and now, to a certain extent, in Jordan as well. He had spoken with the Syrians, but there was no leader there who would take responsibility. I advised him to approach the Council of the Arab League. Nasser said the matter would be brought up for discussion at the Council, but he was not certain that it would reach any decision.

He thought the Jordanians would hesitate more than before, because they were waiting for the results of the Glubb affair.

I repeated that we were very anxious that he should advance toward a settlement with Israel (my people had been in contact with him in my absence). Israel saw a need for direct contact. In previous talks he had argued that he could not meet you, and then I had agreed. Now I proposed that I should come to Israel and propose the appointment of an important non-governmental personality, whose absence from the country would not be felt (as would the absence of Sharett), and we would undertake to bring him to Egypt. Nasser did not react and only said that he would consider this further next day. He was tired, because he was engaged in talks with a Syrian delegation and next day he had to receive a delegation from Saudi Arabia.

We met again on Sunday evening. He was more concerned than before for his personal position. He said he had thought about the proposal to bring someone official. He felt that he could not agree, because his personal security and the security of his Government were at stake. Four times during the conversation he mentioned the murder of Abdullah and said: "I cannot stake myself and my Government on this game." I must understand, he said, that in all the Arab countries there were people who would argue that this was against the good of the Arabs. He was very willing to talk to me and the United States, and the United States could talk to Israel, but he could not take the risk of bringing an Israeli to Egypt.

I said that the people of Israel and the responsible leaders of its Government wanted peace and a settlement, and believed that it could only be reached by the two Governments. I could only prepare the ground. That was the limited part of the goal that I could reach.

On this occasion I raised the problem of border incidents. The Syrians had attacked and captured an Israeli police boat. I said that my Government regarded the incident with great concern and hoped that he would discuss it that evening with the Syrian delegation in Cairo and influence them to return the boat and its crew. He replied that he did not know the details, but he would talk to the Syrians.

He came back to his idea that the armies should be withdrawn one kilometer from the border and then the incidents would stop. I told him my opinion on this matter: the country is small and the villages are situated on the borders. He said the United Nations should propose withdrawal and the reinforcement of the UN forces for the protection of the borders. I said that the UN might want to examine other articles in the Armistice Agreement. He said that could help, but the withdrawal of the armies would solve the question.

I asked what would be the attitude of other Arab states if talks took place between Egypt and the US and Israel and the US. He replied that he had no control over the Arab states and that he would have to consult them on all questions. He remarked that Jordan and other Arab states were liable to show greater sensitivity on certain issues.

I went on to the refugee question, territorial continuity, overflights and the Suez Canal, to see if there had been any change in his views. He said that Israel would be treated like any other country if a settlement was reached. There were two serious questions: refugees and territorial continuity. I said I understood that on these questions there was no change in Israel's approach.

Mr. Prime Minister, I did what I could to find a way to establish high-level contact between Israel and Egypt, and offered the assistance of my Government. I have never seen him so resolute as on this question of a personal meeting. I cannot give you any undertaking about a meeting at any near date. Nasser says all the time that he will speak frankly with the representatives of the United States. If your Government is prepared to follow this way of mediation, tell me so. I told Nasser of your attitude, that a settlement can be reached only by personal contact. From Nasser's reference to the refugees, I had the feeling that he is more concerned about this problem than before. I also heard from Labouisse [the head of UNRWA] that there had been more unrest among the refugees.

I think we have got to the point. I will renew my efforts to ensure a meeting between Egypt and Israel at a fairly high level. I am not particularly encouraged, because he has rejected every effort on my part. Only you and your Government can advise me if you want mediation. Nasser says he is ready to talk to you through the United States. I am prepared to undertake the arrangements, if you believe it would be productive. During my visit to Egypt, Nasser said to me on several occasions that Egypt would not take part in an aggressive war against Israel and that, if war broke out, her reaction would be defensive. I again expressed my apprehension at the possibility of renewed shooting without intention. A shoots, B shoots back, the commanders defend the actions of their men, and so it starts. He admitted the existence of such a possibility, but said that he would not engage in an aggressive war.

Now, Mr. Prime Minister, what is the nature of the procedure we shall adopt if you believe that a continuation through a mediator may be productive?

The emissary handed me a letter from President Eisenhower, dated February 27, in reply to my letter of February 14. The text read as follows:

"Dear Mr. Prime Minister:
"I wish to acknowledge with appreciation your letter of February 14, 1956. My Secretary of State and I have had the benefit of a careful and detailed report by Mr. X. L. of his conversations, and we have discussed with him the steps which might next be taken in pursuit of the peaceful settlement of which you have written so earnestly.

"Mr. X. L.'s exploratory conversations in the Near East have not advanced as far toward a resolution of the issues confronting us as I had hoped, but a foundation has been laid on which we may hope to build. Meanwhile, the need for a solution has become even more pressing. It is my deepest wish that the United States make whatever contribution it can in this profoundly disturbing situation. With this desire in mind, Mr. X. L. plans to return to the Near East for further discussions within the next few days.

"I have taken full and sympathetic note of your statement of Israel's need for arms. Your request is being given the most careful consideration in light of the need both to ensure Israel's security and to create a situation which will be most conducive to peace in the area.

"Permit me to renew my warmest good wishes and heartfelt thanks for your friendly cooperation."

The Emissary: I had a long talk with the President. I spent a complete afternoon and evening with him. I want to assure you that the President is profoundly concerned, and that he is considering the most effective ways of safeguarding Israel's security and liberty. Dulles is also thinking seriously and sincerely along these lines. I know that the President and Dulles understand your concern for arms, and the question of arms is an open question.

Ben-Gurion: Have you seen the President's statement?

Sharett: A negative reaction.

The Emissary: In my opinion you must accept Dulles' words as very sincere and candid. The question of arms is not closed, but open.

Ben-Gurion: When did you see the President?

The Emissary: Before he left for Georgia.

Ben-Gurion: Before he announced that he would run again?

The Emissary: Yes. Dulles believes that, in the long view, the inequality is such that in any arms race the numerical factor of population would be decisive against Israel. Israel's hope is in peace, as you have said, and I quoted to the President your statement that if only the two sides sit together, the Egyptians will be surprised by the things Israel will have to say. I hope you will accept Dulles' words as sincere, deeply thoughtful, and adequately expressing his view of the problem.

Ben-Gurion: I agree that you have done your best. I doubt whether anyone else would have done better. And not only you. You were sent by the President of the United States. I do not know if there is a higher position in our days than that of the President. In this question the President is backed by the will to peace of the entire people in the United States. If peace is not achieved, it will certainly not be your fault or the President's. Secondly, I agree with you that we need peace not only because we are a small nation, but because peace is one of our most precious ideals. It has been our most profound belief in the two thousand five hundred years since our Prophets. The trouble is that for peace two sides are needed. It is not enough that one side wants it. On the other hand, for war the ill will of one side is sufficient.

Peace does not depend on the attitude and will of the people. I am convinced that the great majority of the American people wants peace, but it must be strong in order to ensure it—and not only the Americans, but their allies also want peace and have an ideal in life.

We are in a different position from the United States; I know that there are many people in many countries who are friendly to Israel and have goodwill toward us for many reasons, but unlike the United States no one depends on us. To a certain extent we are alone. It has always been like that. For example, the peoples of Latin America, although they quarrel among themselves, are one family. The same applies to the Scandinavian peoples, the Slav peoples, the English-speaking peoples, the Moslems—there is unity of race, there is geographical proximity, there is community of language and religion. We are alone. Possibly this was deliberately done by the Architect of our people's destiny. We were different from the Egyptians, the Arabs, the Babylonians. We have no regrets about this, although we have suffered.

Nasser spoke of dangers. We are not in any danger of assassination. If we made peace with Nasser, certain circles in our people would not like it and would say we were traitors. But there would be no danger, and even if there was we would not be afraid. We have tried to help you since you came to us. Sharett and I have made statements that were not understood by our people. Perhaps, too, they did not agree with what we said. But we did it to help you. Apart from Ḥerut, even the moderate General Zionists said that the longer we wait the greater the danger grows: Egypt is getting stronger, and the only solution, they said, is to forestall them. We said: No! There were several debates in the Knesset this week on the question of Bnot Yaakov. We are all vitally interested in this question of constructive development. I talked to Biggart* and told the Foreign Affairs and Security Committee that I would prefer less water by agreement to more water by war, though water matters more to us than gold. We thought there was a possibility of agreement.

* Translator's note: In September 1953 Israel started work on a canal near the Bnot Yaakov Bridge over the Jordan about 15 miles north of Lake Kinneret in connection with the national water project. The Syrians objected and General Vagn Bennike, then Chief of Staff of the UN

If there was no danger, I would not care. But Migs, Ilyushins and Stalins are streaming into Egypt from the Soviet bloc; so are Centurions from Britain, and the American tanks reaching Saudi Arabia can be transferred to Egypt, for 'Amer is the supreme commander of the two armies. You have Nasser's promise not to attack. Perhaps he is sincere and perhaps he is not. Let us assume that he is sincere. Hasn't he said that he fears for his life, and if he is afraid, will he not make war? He has told his people that Israel must be destroyed; he will not risk his life to keep the promise he gave you. Our very existence is in danger. He is playing for the time he needs. In four months he will be stronger than now. Three hundred Egyptians are training in the Soviet bloc in the use of Migs and missiles, and there are also Soviet experts in Egypt. A report has appeared in the London *Times* about the number of planes the Egyptians can already use.

We cannot help seeing war approaching, inevitably, as in a Greek drama. I do not believe in the Greek idea of fate, or *moira*, so I have helped you, although your mission was not logical. At worst, we shall be destroyed; at best—if we win, which is possible—the work we have done in eight years will be wiped out. Yesterday I spoke to settlers from Kurdistan. They are remote from us in the spiritual sense, but they feel that they are brothers and regard us as brothers who are trying to help them. The settlements will be destroyed, the cities laid waste, and the best of our youth will be killed.

We cannot rely solely on Nasser saying that he will not attack. He has admitted to you that he is not his own master. He has defended Syria, now he defends Jordan. We must see the conclusions. With the flow of arms, he may not be able to resist the pressure to start war, as he is now unable to make peace. If he has the arms in his possession he will be asked by his colleagues why he does not destroy Israel. There are powerful factors that will compel him. He has imperial ambitions. He was responsible for the Glubb incident, even if not directly; there were demonstrations in Jordan in his honor when Glubb was dismissed. Syria looks to Nasser, and perhaps Iraq also expects from him the bullet that will put an end to Nuri Sa'id.* Nasser is afraid of the suppressed political parties in Egypt and the jealousy of other officers. All these constitute such a pressure that

---

Truce Supervision Organization, called for the suspension of the works until agreement was reached with the Syrians. In October 1955 it was reported that Israel was about to restart the works, but on February 16, 1956, Prime Minister David Ben-Gurion told Homer Biggart, the *New York Times* correspondent, that Israel would hold up the works in the hope of agreement on the Johnston water plan (see note on p. 299). This statement was criticized in the Israeli press and the Knesset.

*Translator's note: Nuri Sa'id was indeed murdered during the Iraqi revolution of July 14, 1958.

if he thinks he is capable of attacking he will do so. In any case, no one in our position and no honest person who can understand our position will deny the magnitude of the danger. Nasser will go on talking through diplomatic channels. Hammarskjöld could not get him to give an undertaking for a cease-fire. You could not get it. The shooting goes on every day. Burns went to Cairo and could not get a cease-fire.

I can see only one way to prevent war. To bring about peace is almost impossible, but there is a way to prevent war. The prevention of war defers the danger, and if there is peace in the world, that may influence the position in our region. The only way to prevent war is for Israel to have defensive arms. For that there is no need for a stable government in Syria, and Nasser does not need to be afraid that they will kill him. It depends only on you. I do not see how you, seeing the danger, can morally refuse to give us arms. Perhaps I should not say this, because it is a question of conscience for you.

If you hope for peace, God bless you, and carry on, but only if we are safe against war this summer. I do not think that anything will happen, because the instability in Syria will continue and the pattern of Jordan will not change. Eden's attitude of appeasement will also continue. Appeasement can be good if something is achieved, but not Runciman's* appeasement. Will diplomatic means succeed if the President's emissary fails? There is no harm in the continuation of the effort, if you do everything to block the road to war.

As for the numerical inequality of the populations, I want to point out that 60 percent of army conscripts in Egypt are disqualified for health reasons and 90 percent of army recruits cannot read or write, so that they need more time for military training than educated people. For this reason we can absorb no less tanks, bombers and planes than the Egyptians.

The Emissary: Do you believe that even with more arms Nasser will not be able to build a large army?

Ben-Gurion: If he got a thousand planes he would not be able to train the pilots for them. We have not reached the limit of our capacity and he has come to the end of his.

The Emissary: Do you think he has reached the limit of his absorptive capacity?

Ben-Gurion: Almost. If we get the same number of planes as he has, we are capable of absorbing them. Besides, even if we get half the planes that he has, it is not so terrible. The difference in the size of the populations is not the basis for estimating military strength. In the light of the situation in Syria and Jordan, the

---

*Translator's note: Viscount Runciman, sent to Prague in 1938 by Prime Minister Neville Chamberlain to mediate between the Czechoslovak Government and the Sudeten Germans.

Egyptian hatred of Iraq, and Nasser's aspiration to build an empire, war is almost inevitable. Recently there have been incidents on Lake Kinneret and shooting on the Gaza border. If they shoot to kill, we will be compelled to reply, because we are human beings, and we have the right to live and not to be killed. War can be prevented, and if it is prevented you can go on if you believe it is worth while. I can hardly believe that there is any chance of success. My faith in miracles is melting away. I hoped that a miracle was possible because of the President's intervention. There is no harm in your continuing, if you act so that there should be no war.

As for the illusions of the Tripartite Declaration,* can we be confident that Britain will go to war against Egypt or Jordan if Israel is attacked? I have little respect for Glubb, but he would not start a war between Jordan and ourselves, even if Eden was Prime Minister of Britain at the time. I cannot imagine Britain attacking Egypt and Jordan. When Britain wanted to protect Jordan, she signed an alliance with her. Five years ago we proposed to Britain that we should have the same status as New Zealand. Britain refused. We are isolated, while the Arabs have alliances between themselves and with others.

The United States Government would need time to consult Congress, while Nasser's planes can bomb us within ten minutes. Besides, I do not believe that you would go to war against Egypt if they attacked us. I know that the United States can understand other countries; why does she not understand our position? If we can defend ourselves, why should we not get the arms we need? It is a matter of human dignity. Why should American boys come from the United States to fight for us? I assume that there is goodwill toward us from the Governments of France, the United States, and the Scandinavian countries as well. I cannot say the same about Britain.

How can you ask us to rely on a tripartite agreement that was not made with us? You have treaties with many countries in the world, even with Laos and Cambodia. I suppose you have your own reasons for not wanting a treaty with us. We cannot be told that our existence is safe because there is a tripartite agreement, for so far as our security is concerned, the agreement is empty and meaningless. It is a moral affront to us to suppose that we feel secure because such an agreement exists. We can defend ourselves if we have the necessary arms. You can say: Israel will attack. Let us discuss that. Let your Government say: We

---

* Translator's note: On May 25, 1950, the United States, Britain and France undertook, inter alia, to take immediate action to prevent violation of frontiers or armistice lines in the Middle East by any state in the area.

will give them arms, but we want to receive a guarantee that they will not attack their neighbors. If you do not want to rely on our word and the fact that peace is of vital necessity to us, let us discuss the means of guaranteeing it.

If I were to sum up your mission, I would say: You have done your best. The President sent one of the best men he could have chosen—and the situation is the same as it was: it has not changed for the better; even the President's intervention has not changed it. Nasser says that to discuss peace means putting his life in danger. That is a fact of political significance. He has contributed to it by a campaign of hatred on the radio, in the press and in speeches. For the time being the only way is to give us arms, perhaps not in the same quantity as Nasser has. I see no reason why we should not receive the same quantity of arms when we are no less capable of absorbing it than the Egyptians. But we shall be content with less, if it is sufficient for our defense. You can continue with your mediation, if you first avert the danger of war. If not, you will only be making fools of us. If in a few weeks you give us arms, you can continue with your efforts to improve the situation, and that can come about this year or next.

Sharett: I am in complete agreement with the Prime Minister about the dangers in store for us. I want to expand the scope of the possibilities. What Ben-Gurion said about Nasser, that he is not capable of resisting pressures, is a profound truth. Nasser could start an attack even taking into account the possibility of intervention within a few days. For in a few hours he could do such damage to our cities and installations that the clock would be set back several years.

But the problem of Western intervention is not so simple nowadays. Nasser has brought in the Soviets, and they are now an established fact in the region. Western intervention might involve Soviet intervention. The possibility of such counter-intervention is bound to lead Nasser to doubt the likelihood of Western intervention. It is hard to see how the West would intervene. There is first of all the question of time. In addition, there is the possibility of a Soviet veto on action by the Security Council. If the West nevertheless decides to intervene, the Soviets will argue that they have the right to do the same. If Western intervention was based on a treaty, that would be another matter. But there is no such treaty.

If we assume that Nasser would not risk an open attack, he could strike at us even without that. That would be the solution so long as he knows that we have no arms. The penetration into our territory will be intensified if he thinks that, for fear of war, we shall not react as we did at Gaza or Khan Yunis. He could make life intolerable in the border settlements, and when we were compelled to act, he would say that we had started. He is not demobilizing the fedayeen. They are going on with their training. If he sent them deep into our country, to terrorize our settlements and shatter their morale, an intolerable situation would be created. We would be compelled to react, and he would argue that he was not responsible. I am not sure that this is not the motive for his proposal about the withdrawal of the armies one kilometer, for that would open an area of penetration to the fedayeen. If we reacted by military force, where would that lead to? If not, that would be surrender and our lives would become unbearable. The only way to deter him from taking the first step is that he should know that war is possible and that we have arms and the means to stop him.

Four months and ten days ago I discussed our situation in Geneva with Dulles. It seems to me our prospects of obtaining arms have worsened since then. True, even if the Americans do not give us arms, we shall get some. The French have promised to supply us with 12 Mystères. On November 9 the President said at Denver that he was prepared to examine a request for arms for legitimate self-defense. Now, the day before yesterday, he said that Israel's security should not depend only on arms. Is security conceivable without arms? This is a retreat in comparison with November. We are told that we cannot absorb the same as the Arabs can. Is the impossibility of receiving the maximum sufficient reason to deny us the minimum?

This is the situation: 1) We do not need the same quantity of arms as Egypt has in order to deter an attack. Possibly, 60 or 75 aircraft in our hands would be sufficient against Nasser's 200 Migs. 2) The inequality in populations has no effect whatever on the absorptive capacity of each side. 3) We are certainly capable of absorbing the quantity required to deter an attack. And thus there is no basis for the demographic and military argument.

Almost two months have passed since I first had the pleasure of meeting you. Your mission has had a most unequal effect. Nasser has not lost a moment and has gone on with the training of his men—300 of them are training in the Soviet bloc and 200 Soviet instructors are busy in Egypt with the absorption of the arms—as well as the consolidation of the alliance with Syria and Saudi Arabia and penetration into the Jordan Kingdom.

Even if Nasser was not behind the removal of Glubb, such an incident would have been inconceivable if Nasser had not existed in the Middle East. The Legion officers acted on the Egyptian pattern. Jordan may join the Egyptian-Syrian-Saudi alliance, and Jordan and Syria may cooperate in Nasser's adventures. Up till now they have paralyzed the work at Bnot Yaakov.

We have shown great trust in you. We have undertaken a crushing responsibility in concealing your mission even from the members of the Government. The Prime Minister and I have refrained from considering our own positions so long as you are on your mission. We can now be accused of having lost precious time of national importance because of the illusion that we believed in. If you want to continue, and you come to us one day and say that there is hope, no one will be happier than we. But your activity can no longer be included in our evaluation of the realities. We cannot help doubting Nasser's sincerity. In October he promised me to persuade the Syrians—and they were no more stable then than they are now. Can our economic development wait indefinitely? Nasser has a relentless policy meant to gain time, with his goal clear in front of him.

We must now give serious consideration to our position. The United States can no longer use your mission as an excuse. We feel that Eban's talk with Dulles and our talk with Ambassador Lawson about arms are becoming humiliating. We have reached a point at which we are entitled to a clear answer. The lack of a reply can no longer be justified by reference to your mission. We are entitled to a reply. We hope to God that the reply will be affirmative, but it would be better to get a negative reply than to remain without any at all. If the reply is in the affirmative, it should be implemented immediately, for time is short.

(I showed the emissary a report of what the Egyptian Consul in Cyprus had said in a talk about Egypt's intentions vis-à-vis Israel.)

The Emissary: I understand your position. You have made it clear that any negotiations through any channel can take place from now on only if you have more arms in your possession or in other circumstances on which you can confidently rely for the prevention of war between the two countries. I want to say again: the United States has devoted and will continue to devote the best thought of which it is capable to the way which, in the opinion of the President and the Secretary of State, is the most effective for the preservation of the liberty to which you, like others, are entitled.

On the other hand, do not regard the question as a very simple one, for you understand, as I do, the danger of Soviet penetration into the Middle East and Africa. We have responsibilities toward broad areas of the world. The resources of the Middle East are absolutely essential if Nato is to continue to be a barrier against Soviet aggression. We are always considering how to ensure your safety and this is not only concern for the interests of the United States; it is a matter of profound, fervent and vital thought. While I understand that you need to know our decision, I hope that you will also take into account broader considerations which have not yet been finally decided.

We hoped that from this mission we would be able to start a development that would give you security, reduce tension and lead to a settlement, for nothing can spring from war but disaster. Whether the hopes are great or small, the main thing is to avoid war and to sit down and talk, not only about your claim for arms, but also about the interests of the free peoples against the malignant danger of Soviet penetration. Freedom is indivisible. While the fronts may be various, the allocation of resources for the preservation of world freedom must be seen in the context of all these problems that surround our people.

Mr. Prime Minister, I want to ask you a delicate question. According to your best estimate of Egypt, do you regard the possibility Mr. Sharett mentioned—an aggressive war, action designed to serve as a provocation—as the most likely? The extracts you read me from the report of the talk with the Egyptian Consul in Cyprus and your own words have given me the impression that you believe that these possibilities are immediate. Do you expect Egyptian action in the near future, direct or by deliberate provocation, to lead to war in the area?

Sharett: You have not mentioned the possibility of sending fedayeen. If we do not have arms, Nasser will try to terrorize our country and win in that way.

The Emissary: What about the other two possibilities?

Ben-Gurion: Before giving my answer I must make two remarks: 1) Let us assume that after you submit your report we receive a negative answer or none at all, then we will have only one task: to look to our security. Nothing else will interest us. We shall strengthen our morale, fortify our settlements, build shelters in the cities and see what we can do. Nothing else will interest me until I know that we can defend ourselves. If we get help—good. But we must be prepared to defend ourselves without help from the outside. 2) There is not such a great danger that Egypt will become Communist, but the present regime in Egypt is a great danger to the world, because it has no ideals; it has no concern either for freedom or for Communism. It is simply nationalist; and nothing else concerns it. For that reason it has no restraints. The Soviets have always wanted to penetrate into Africa. They are already in Egypt. Whether Nasser likes it or not, whether he knows it or not, he will bring the Russians to Sudan and Syria and perhaps to Jordan too. But the main thing is Africa, where there are conditions for a Communist regime. The British are blind. There are some people in your country who sense the danger, but I doubt if they all do.

If the Soviets gain control of the region, our existence will be impossible. Poland under Soviet rule is suppressed, but it will survive. The Czechs will also survive. But if Russia occupies the countries around us, that will be the end of us. Our people in Russia is the only people which is not allowed to have schools and newspapers. If they come to dominate this part of the world, they will not allow us to continue to maintain a free regime, or immigration, for apart from our being Israelis we belong to the free world.

And now for your questions. I have not the slightest doubt what Egypt will do if she has the strength. There is no need to declare war. The danger is as real as anything in this world. Knowing, on the one hand, the position of one great power, Russia, and, on the other hand, the hesitations of the Western countries, Nasser will feel free to do whatever he pleases. He will have every reason to make war. From now on we shall devote all our time to safeguard our survival. If we have to fight, we shall fight desperately, as no other people have fought. I am not desperate. But we will have to devote the last drop of our energy to prepare our people to meet Nasser with all his Migs.

Sharett: The last possibility—of the fedayeen—means war, because we shall not submit.

The Emissary: There is only one thing I want to say. I shall be in Washington on Tuesday. I do not know whether the Secretary of State will be there or whether he will only arrive a few days later. While he has a full appreciation of your anxiety for Israel's security, I must say that the question of arms is not and will not be excluded. Mr. Sharett wants us to say: Yes, you will get all you need, or: No, you will get nothing. This is not a problem of yes or no; it will continue to be considered with attention to the vital matter of safeguarding Israel's existence in the family of nations, and with full weight to our responsibility for all the associated problems, which are vital to your freedom as they are for ours. I know the President's view and the Secretary of State's. It is not a question of deferring the day of decision. We do not lack moral courage, but our leaders have responsibilities toward many nations.

I believe I told Nasser that I would not return unless he wanted to talk to me.

Ben-Gurion: Did Nasser make it a condition for his readiness to talk to you that you should not give us arms?

The Emissary: No, the only condition he made was secrecy. The question of arms was hardly discussed with Nasser. I only told him that it was pretty clear that if he was receiving arms from the Soviets and you were getting none, he must realize that you would feel that time was working against you.

According to your analysis, Israel says: We are prepared to meet tomorrow. Nasser says: Yes, but neither the time, the conditions nor the men are ripe. In other words, he is not ready for meetings. On the other hand he says: Here are documents for Israel—while Israel says that direct contact is essential. So we get into a procedural blind alley. I hoped that if meetings were arranged there would be more confidence. I cannot evaluate people's statements when they say that they will not start an offensive war. I told Nasser that you want to sit down and discuss with him. I understand your attitude. If there are specific conditions for a settlement, which Nasser wishes to submit through me or through my Government, I shall send them on to you, and I understand your attitude that you do not want to bind yourselves until you are free from concern for security. If you have any ideas I shall be grateful if you will convey them to me.

Ben-Gurion: You must understand the difference between two kinds of nationalism. There were two ways for Nasser to build Egypt: from the economic and social point of view, or to gain power by building the army. We hoped he would follow the first course. To our regret he chose the second.

Sharett: Try to examine the prospects of peace after we have arms—it is an American doctrine that only force deters an attack.

Ben-Gurion: The shooting must be stopped, and the Armistice Agreement must be observed.

The Emissary: The President and the Secretary of State will receive a full and detailed report from me.

That was the end of the meeting on March 9, 1956.

54 THE SINAI CAMPAIGN AND AFTER—1956-62

On a careful reading of the emissary's account of his proposals to Nasser and the latter's replies, it is clear that, although Nasser never definitely rejected the proposals, he did not accept them either: it was plain, in fact, that he was opposed to them. This was the case with President Eisenhower's proposal for a meeting between leaders on both sides to promote a peace settlement, with which the talks began, and the proposals for the prohibition of shooting across the border and the observance of the Armistice Agreement, with which they ended. There was no doubt left in our minds that Nasser was intent on war against Israel and that this was the purpose for which he was getting, with Russian backing, a wealth of arms from Czechoslovakia.

The tension and the danger grew in the months that followed. The operations of the fedayeen were intensified; Egyptian army detachments carried out incursions across the border and their batteries bombarded our villages along the edge of the Gaza Strip. Public opinion in France, Britain and America awoke to the danger of war and the UN Secretary-General made several attempts to secure a cease-fire, but all efforts to stop the escalation of violence were fruitless. Arab rulers repeatedly declared that they were about to destroy Israel. Despite the rulings of the UN Security Council, we were still denied navigation rights in the Suez Canal and freedom of transit for our ships and cargoes to and from Eilat.

Toward the end of October 1956, the danger became even more immediate when a military pact was signed between Egypt, Jordan and Syria and their armies were placed under Egyptian command—with one clear end in view: war to the death against Israel. The noose that had been prepared for us was being tightened; it was obvious that Nasser would stop at nothing to destroy us. We could no longer delay urgent and effective measures for our self-defense.

The operations we undertook in the Sinai desert and the Gaza Strip, which started on October 29 and were brought to a successful conclusion on November 5, are a part of history. In one week we cleared out the fedayeen nests, crushed the forces that had been poised to attack us, and spiked the Egyptian guns stationed at Sharm el-Sheikh to shell our shipping in the Gulf of Akaba. The immediate danger was over, though I felt it my duty to warn our people that there were still many perils and difficulties in store.

In my address to the Knesset on the morrow of the Sinai Campaign I declared that there was no dispute whatever between the people of Israel and the people of Egypt. While the Armistice Agreement that Nasser had repeatedly and flagrantly violated was dead and buried, Israel was ready to enter into negotiations with Egypt for a stable peace, cooperation and good-neighborly relations. We were asking no more than compliance with the accepted norms of international behavior: respect by each nation for the sovereignty of the other and its right to live in peace, and the resolution of differences by negotiation instead of by war and the threat of war.

The international community, led by the United States and the Soviet Union, thought otherwise, however. The United Nations, created to promote the peaceful solution of all international problems, did not call on Egypt to apply these principles to its relations with Israel. Instead, we were faced with concerted pressure to withdraw, without peace or even the assurance of peace negotiations, from our new defensive positions.

In the end Israel withdrew her forces from the Gaza Strip and the Sinai Peninsula, including Sharm el-Sheikh. But a deadly threat to her survival had been crushed, and the denial of her elementary rights to security, peaceful development and unhampered trade had been brought to the attention of the world. A United Nations Emergency Force was stationed on the borders of the Gaza Strip and at Sharm el-Sheikh. Equally important was the recognition, publicly expressed by the principal maritime powers, with the exception of the Soviet Union, that the Gulf of Akaba and the Straits of Tiran constituted an international waterway, in which all nations had the right to free passage, and that if this right was violated by force Israel would be entitled to exercise the right to self-defense under Article 51 of the UN Charter. Thus, peace reigned on Israel's southwestern border for ten years, and ships sailed unmolested through the Straits on their way to and from Eilat, which expanded into an international port and oil pipeline terminal.

However, despite our withdrawal to the boundaries that existed before the Sinai Campaign, Nasser and the other Arab rulers still refused to accept Israel's right to exist. In defiance of the Security Council's rulings, Israeli ships and cargoes were barred from the Suez Canal. Day in, day out, the Arab press and radio denounced the "Zionist danger" and, in Nazi parlance, "the machinations of international Jewish capital." At mass demonstrations in Cairo, Nasser announced his growing preparations to destroy Israel. These open threats were backed by an incessant flow of arms, especially from the Soviet Union. Hundreds of "instructors" came from Soviet-bloc countries to Egypt, Syria and Iraq, while hundreds of officers from these countries were sent out to the USSR, Czechoslovakia and other Soviet satellites to learn the trade of war.

55 APPROACH TO PRESIDENT TITO—1962-63

In 1962 I made another attempt to get negotiations started with Egypt, which was not revealed at the time in order to facilitate secret and confidential discussions if the other side would agree. Knowing of the close friendship between Nasser and Marshal Tito, President of Yugoslavia, with which Israel had good relations, I asked one of Tito's associates to explore the prospects of breaking the deadlock with his help. On December 28 I wrote to him as follows:

"Dear Mr. President,
"Knowing your attitude to the advancement of peace and social progress, I sent my friend Dan to Yugoslavia in November to enquire into the possibility of a meeting—open or secret—between us to discuss ways of advancing peace between ourselves and our neighbours in the Middle East. Dan met his friend, Mr. X, on November 28, 1962, and asked him to find out whether such a meeting was possible in the near future. Mr. X told Dan at the time that the suggestion was very interesting, that you wished to receive in writing a clearer explanation of what was involved. I am accordingly taking the liberty of approaching you in this letter.
"Four Arab nations—Lebanon, Syria, Jordan and Egypt—are situated on Israel's borders, and after the War of Independence in 1948 we signed Armistice Agreements

with them. According to the first article in each agreement, this was to be the first step towards permanent peace. Iraq was also one of the Arab States that invaded our country in 1948, on the morrow of the Proclamation of Independence on May 15, 1948, but she refused even to conclude an Armistice Agreement. Non-recognition of Israel's existence, and the desire to destroy her is the declared policy of each of these countries.

"I do not know to what extent these declarations are serious or are only a matter of internal or inter-Arab policy. I believe that there are some elements—by no means negligible—in these countries that wish for peace between the Arab States and Israel. But one fact is clear beyond any doubt: no Arab country, even Iraq, will dare to come to terms with Israel before Egypt, which is the strongest of all the Arab States in our area. When the Egyptian revolution took place in 1952, and King Farouk was deposed from his throne, I expressed in our legislature the hope that perhaps conditions had now been created for relations of peace and cooperation between ourselves and Egypt. My expectations were disappointed, but President Abdul Nasser's speeches after the dissolution of the union between Syria and his country again aroused my hopes for a settlement that would establish peace and cooperation between ourselves and Egypt. President Abdul Nasser stated repeatedly that from now on he wished to concentrate first and foremost on the solution of Egypt's internal problems and the establishment of a Socialist regime in his country. I know something of Egypt's problems in agriculture, health, development and education. I have no desire to cast doubts on the sincerity of President Abdul Nasser's Socialist aspirations. Egypt's needs are essentially the same as those of the other Arab countries in our neighbourhood, but I have no doubt that if Egypt overcame her difficulties, that would contribute towards the progress of the other Arab States.

"In area and population the State of Israel is one of the smallest countries in our area. I will not discuss here the special difficulties and grave problems that we have confronted since the renewal of our independence, but despite them all we have succeeded in establishing in Israel a progressive and democratic country, which has many achievements to its credit in agriculture, industry, education, scientific research and social progress. I cannot yet call Israel a Socialist country, for we also encourage private capital, but in agriculture, industry and transport we can claim Socialist achievements, and even the beginnings of a truly communist society in the labour settlements known as 'kibbutzim,' to which—so far as I know—there is no parallel anywhere else in the world.

"One of the factors that hinder economic development in our area (including, to no small extent, our own country) is the burden of defence and the arms race between our neighbours and ourselves—especially between ourselves and Egypt. And I am convinced that nothing would more effectively further the development and progress of the Arab countries in our area—of Egypt, especially—than peace and cooperation between them and Israel. Our country is both small and poor, but through the pioneering and Socialist initiative of our labour movement, which has held the leading place in the State since its establishment, we have succeeded in overcoming our internal difficulties and created a progressive society, unique in the whole of the Asian continent, as well as making a modest contribution to the advancement of the new States in Africa and Asia—and I have not the slightest doubt that under conditions of peace and cooperation with our neighbours, we could offer no little assistance to their progress.

"Since I believe in the sincerity of President Abdul Nasser's desire to advance Egypt and the neighbouring countries along the path of social progress, I assume that he understands the importance of peace with his neighbours as a force making for progress.

"The whole world knows you as one of the foremost fighters for world peace—nor need I expatiate on your Socialist achievements in Yugoslavia and the aid you have given to other countries in the advancement of Socialism. You are also well known, Mr. President, as one of President Nasser's closest friends, and I believe that you could play an outstanding role in bringing together Israel and Egypt to negotiate a peaceful settlement.

"For this purpose, I should like to come to your country, openly or incognito, to discuss the matter, at any time you think fit.

"I assume as a matter of course that complete secrecy must be observed in the preliminary steps, as well as in any contact—direct or indirect—between President Nasser and myself. In case the attempt is not successful, that should not lead to a deterioration in the relations between ourselves and Egypt, or between Egypt and the other countries in the area.

"In spite of all the obvious difficulties, I believe that by direct negotiations it is possible to arrive at mutual understanding and an agreed settlement between ourselves and Egypt.

"For this purpose, Mr. President, I have asked, through my friend Dan, for a meeting with you in the near future, whenever you can find the time.

"In profound respect and esteem."

The hope of such a step toward a dialogue with Egypt was not realized, however. Four months later, I received from President Tito the following disappointing reply, dated April 14, 1963:

"Mr. Prime Minister:
"I would like to acknowledge receipt of your letter and to apologize for my having been unable, for several reasons, particularly lack of time, to reply to you earlier.
"Mr. Prime Minister:
"I appreciate your desire to arrive at a settlement of your relations with neighboring countries, for our Government has always shown a keen interest in the settlement of conditions in the Near East and in a constructive solution of existing problems,

as this is in keeping with a policy of peaceful settlement of problems in conflict. We have, within our means, and at appropriate opportunities, made our concrete contribution thereto, within the framework of the United Nations and outside it. But I wish to point out that I am afraid that you are overrating my personal capacity to promote a speedy and concrete settlement of the problems in conflict as they exist between you and your neighboring countries, notwithstanding my goodwill in this respect.

"In view of present conditions in this part of the world and the significant developments and tensions now prevailing, outside intervention, in my view, could not produce the desired results. We nevertheless hope that the unsettled problems will not take the course of aggravation and deterioration, and that realism and readiness for a peaceful settlement will prevail.

"As far as concerns our relations, I may note with satisfaction that there are normal relations between our countries and that our economic collaboration is developing in the interest of both sides.

"Please accept, Mr. Prime Minister, the expression of my high esteem."

On June 16, 1963, I resigned, for personal reasons, from the premiership. Since then I have been a private citizen and the responsibility for the conduct of Israel's affairs has been in other hands.

BIOGRAPHICAL AND OTHER NOTES

Abdul Hadi, Auni (b. 1888), Palestinian Arab lawyer, member of Arab Higher Committee.

Abdullah (1882–1951), Emir of Transjordan, later King of Jordan; murdered by a supporter of the Mufti of Jerusalem.

"Actions Committee," Zionist General Council, q.v.

Agudat Israel, non-Zionist organization of Orthodox Jews.

Akaba, on the Red Sea, Jordan's only port.

Alami, Musa (b. 1895), Palestinian civil servant and Arab leader; dismissed from Palestine civil service in 1937 and left the country; member of Palestinian Arab delegation to the London Conference in 1939.

Allen of Hurtwood, Lord (1889–1939), British Labour leader, chairman Independent Labour Party 1922–26.

Allenby, General Sir Edmund, H.H., Fieldmarshal and later Viscount (1861–1939), commander of the British forces which conquered Palestine in 1918.

American Jewish Committee, a non-Zionist body founded in 1906 to protect Jewish civil and religious rights and "secure for Jews equality of economic, social and educational opportunity."

Andrews, Lewis Y. (1896–1937), District Commissioner for Galilee; his murder was one of the turning points of the Arab revolt.

Antonius, George (1899–1942), Christian Arab writer from Lebanon, living in Jerusalem at the time referred to; author of *The Arab Awakening*.

Arlosoroff, Chaim (1899–1933), Labor Zionist leader, head of the Jewish Agency's Political Department from 1931.

Armstrong, Captain Harold C. (1892–1943), British officer and writer; later official in British War Office.

Arslan, Shekib (1869–1947), Syrian Druze pan-Arabist leader; had close ties with Fascist Italy and Nazi Germany.

Asch, Sholem (1880–1957), noted Yiddish novelist and dramatist; member of the Council of the enlarged Jewish Agency.

Aswan High Dam, modern Egypt's largest development project. After the Egyptian-Soviet arms deal in 1955, the United States and the World Bank cancelled plans to help finance it and President Nasser, in retaliation, nationalized the Suez Canal, precipitating the Suez Crisis of 1956. The Dam was completed in 1970 with Soviet assistance.

Bakstansky, Lavy (1904–1971), General Secretary, British Zionist Federation.

Baldwin, Stanley, Earl of (1867–1947), British Prime Minister 1923–24, 1924–29 and 1935–37.

Balfour Declaration, issued by the British Government on November 2, 1917. It stated: "His Majesty's Government view with favour the establishment in Palestine of a national home for the Jewish people, and will use their best endeavours to facilitate the achievement of this object, it being clearly understood that nothing shall be done which may prejudice the civil and religious rights of existing non-Jewish communities in Palestine, or the rights and political status enjoyed by Jews in any other country."

Basle Program, adopted at the First Zionist Congress, 1897. Its main clause was: "The aim of Zionism is to create for the Jewish people a home in Palestine secured by public law."

Bearsted, Walter Horace Samuel, 2nd Viscount (1882–1948), English Jewish philanthropist.

Ben-Zvi, Izhak (1884–1963), Socialist Zionist pioneer; a leader of Palestine Jewry and second President of Israel.

Berlin (Bar-Ilan), Meyer (1880–1949), a leader of the Mizrachi religious Zionist movement.

Bevin, Ernest (1881–1951), British Labour leader; Foreign Secretary 1945–51.

Bilu, Hebrew initials of *Beit Ya'akov, Lekhu ve-Nelkhah* ("House of Jacob, come ye and let us go," Isa. 2:5), the watchword of one of the earliest groups of pioneers, who settled in Palestine in 1882.

Bludan Conference, 1937, conference of pan-Arab organizations which decided on support for Palestinian Arabs.

Blum, Léon (1872–1950), French Jewish Socialist leader; Prime Minister 1936–37, 1938, and 1946–47.

Blumenfeld, Jonathan (b. 1895), official in Administration of Palestine.

Brandeis, Louis Dembitz (1856–1941), American Zionist leader; member of U.S. Supreme Court.

Brit Shalom ("Peace Alliance"), society founded in Jerusalem in 1925 to foster good relations between Jews and Arabs and seek an agreed solution to the Palestine problem. Its opponents accused it of readiness to surrender essential Jewish rights.

Brodetsky, Prof. Selig (1888–1954), member of Zionist and Jewish Agency Executive 1928–49; President of Board of Deputies of British Jews 1939–49.

Byroade, Henry (b. 1913), U.S. Ambassador to Egypt 1952–55.

Chamberlain, Joseph (1863–1914), British statesman; in 1903, as Colonial Secretary, he offered a territory in East Africa ("Uganda") for autonomous Jewish settlement.

Chamberlain, Neville (1869–1940), British Prime Minister 1937–40.

Chancellor, Sir John (1870–1952), High Commissioner of Palestine and Transjordan 1928–31.

Clayton, Sir Gilbert (b. 1875), British civil servant; during the McMahon (q.v.)-Ḥussein talks a political adviser on the staff of the British forces in Egypt.

Cranborne, Viscount, later Marquess of Salisbury (b. 1893), British Undersecretary for Foreign Affairs 1935–38; held various other offices.

Darwazah, Izzat, member of Istiqlal movement; supporter of the Mufti.

Degania, the first *kvutza* (collective village), established in 1909.

Dubnow, Simon (1860–1941), Russian Jewish historian.

Dulles, John Foster (1888–1959), U. S. Secretary of State 1952–59.

Dunam, 1,000 square meters, or one-quarter acre.

Eden, Sir Anthony, later Lord Avon (b. 1897), British Foreign Secretary 1935–38, 1940–45, and 1951–55; Prime Minister 1955–57.

Eilat, Israel's Red Sea port, near sites of biblical Elath and Ezion-Geber, gateway to East Africa and Asia.

Eisenhower, Dwight David (1890–1969), Supreme Commander Allied Forces in Europe during World War II and President of the United States 1953–61.

Elath (Epstein), Eliahu (b. 1903), head of Jewish Agency's Near East Bureau; later Jewish Agency representative in U. S., Israel Ambassador in Washington and in London, and President of the Hebrew University.

Erez Israel, "Land of Israel," the Hebrew name for the homeland of the Jewish people.

Eshkol (Shkolnik), Levi (1895–1969), Director, Settlement Department Jewish Agency 1949–63; Israel Minister of Agriculture 1951–52; Minister of Finance 1952–63; Prime Minister 1963–69.

Fawzi, Mahmud (b. 1900), Egyptian diplomat and statesman; Foreign Minister 1952–64; Prime Minister under President Sadat 1970–72.

Faisal I (1883–1933), son of Sherif Hussein of Mecca; leader of the Arab revolt against the Turks in World War I; King of Iraq 1921–33.

Fedayeen (also spelled *fedaiyun*—sing. *fedaye*—"suicide fighters"), medieval Islamic term, used particularly in recent years by Palestinian Arab terrorists fighting against Israel.

Fishman, Rabbi Yehuda-Leib, later Maimon (1876–1962), leading member of Mizrachi (religious Zionist) Party; elected to Jewish Agency Executive in 1953; Israel's first Minister of Religious Affairs.

French, Lewis (1873–1945), appointed in 1931 as Director of Development in Palestine; his recommendations were regarded by the Zionists as sterile and unconstructive.

Frumkin, Gad (1887–1960), only Jewish member of the Palestine Supreme Court.

Fuad (1868–1936), King of Egypt from 1917.

General Zionists, center party in the Zionist movement, at first consisting of Zionists without a clearly defined social ideology; later divided into A (moderate) and B (right-wing) groups; in Israel merged in 1961 into the Liberal Party.

Ghazi I (1912–1939), King of Iraq, son of Faisal.

Ghussein, Jacob (b. 1900), member of Arab Higher Committee; chairman of Arab Youth Congress 1933–44; son of Tewfik Ghussein.

Glubb, Sir John Bagot (b. 1897), British soldier, commander of the Transjordanian (later Jordanian) Arab Legion 1932–56.

Goldmann, Nahum (b. 1894), Zionist leader; in 1934 representative of the Jewish Agency in Geneva; later President of World Jewish Congress and World Zionist Organization.

Gort, Viscount (1886–1946), British High Commissioner for Palestine 1944–45.

Greenbaum, Yizhak (1879–1970), Polish Jewish and Zionist leader, member of Jewish Agency Executive 1933–48, Minister of the Interior in Provisional Government of Israel 1948–49.

Haganah ("Defense"), semi-underground Jewish defense force in Palestine under the control of the official Jewish authorities before the establishment of the State of Israel.

Halifax, Marquess of (1881–1940), British Foreign Secretary 1938–40.

Halutz, plural Halutzim, pioneer of Jewish resettlement in the Land of Israel.

Hammarskjöld, Dag (1905–1961), Secretary-General of the United Nations 1953–60.

Hamza, Fuad Bey (b. 1899), born in Lebanon, diplomat in the Saudi Arabian service.

Hankin, Yehoshua (1865–1945), pioneer in the purchase of land for Jewish settlement in the Land of Israel.

Hapo'el Haza'ir ("The Young Worker"), Zionist labor party in Erez Israel, founded in 1905. It opposed the class struggle theory and affiliation to international socialism. Among its leaders were A. D. Gordon and Yosef Sprinzak, q.v. In 1930 it merged with Ahdut Ha'avodah to form Mapai.

Hauran, plateau east of the Sea of Galilee and the Jordan River.

Henderson, Arthur (1863–1935), British Labour leader and statesman; Foreign Secretary 1929–31; largely responsible for the neutralization of the Passfield (q.v.) White Paper by the MacDonald (q.v.) Letter.

Herzl, Theodor (1860–1904), founder of the World Zionist Organization and of modern political Zionism; author of *Der Judenstaat* (1896).

Herzog, Isaac Halevi (1888–1959), Chief Rabbi of Palestine (later, Israel) from 1936.

Herzog, Yaakov (b. 1921), Director, U.S. Division, Israel Foreign Ministry 1954–57; Minister in Washington 1957–60; Director-General Prime Minister's Office since 1964.

Hess, Moses (1812–1875), German-Jewish Socialist leader; a forerunner of modern Zionism; author of *Rome and Jerusalem* (1862).

Hexter, Morris (b. 1891), non-Zionist member of Jewish Agency Executive 1929–38.

Hilmi, Ahmed, member of Arab Higher Committee; manager of Arab Bank in Jerusalem.

Histadrut ("Organization"), full name: *Ha-Histadrut ha-Kelalit Shel ha-Ovedim ha-Ivriyyim be-Erez Israel;* the General Federation of Jewish Workers in the Land of Israel; founded in 1920 to deal with all the interests of the workers, including not only trade-union activity but also mutual aid, social services, and the establishment of agricultural settlements and industrial, transport and other concerns, with a view to the development of a socialist society.

Hoz, Dov (1894–1941), Labor Zionist leader; established close contact with leaders of the British Labour Party.

el-Husseini, Haj Amin (b. c.1895), Palestinian Arab leader; Mufti (Moslem religious head) of Jerusalem 1921–37; fled to escape arrest in 1937; was one of the fiercest opponents of Jewish settlement in Palestine; collaborated with the Nazis during World War II.

Husseini, Jamal (b. 1893), cousin of the above; member of Arab Higher Committee; in 1939 leader of Palestine Arab delegation to the St. James' Palace Conference.

Husseini, Musa (b. 1903), official in Education Department of Palestine Administration.

Hyamson, Albert (1874–1954), English Jewish official in Palestine Administration; author of history of British Jewry.

Ibn Saud, Abdel-Aziz (1880–1953), Sultan of Nejd 1921–32, King of Saudi Arabia from 1932.

I.C.A., Jewish Colonization Organization, founded in 1902 by Baron Hirsch to promote Jewish resettlement in Argentina and elsewhere; in 1899 it took over the administration of Baron Edmond de Rothschild's aid to Jewish villages in Palestine.

Istiqlal ("Independence"), pan-Arabist movement; Palestinian branch established in 1932 by Auni Abdul Hadi.

Jabotinsky, Vladimir Ze'ev (1880–1940), Zionist leader, founder of the Revisionist movement in Zionism, of which the Irgun Zeva'i Leumi ("National Military Organization") and the Herut ("Freedom") movement in Israel were offshoots.

Jacobs, Mrs. Rose (b. 1888), a founder of Hadassah, American Women Zionists' Organization; member of Jewish Agency Executive 1935–37.

Jarblum, Marc (b. 1887), French Labor Zionist leader.

Jewish Agency for Palestine (later: for Israel), body recognized by the Mandate for Palestine (Article 4) "as a public body for the purpose of advising and cooperating with the Administration of Palestine in such economic, social and other matters as may affect the establishment of the Jewish National Home and the interests of the Jewish population in Palestine, and, subject always to the control of the Administration, to assist and take part in the development of the country." At first the Zionist Organization was recognized in this capacity, but in 1929 the enlarged Jewish Agency was constituted by adding non-Zionists willing to assist in the establishment of the Jewish National Home. The two bodies had the same president and, in time, the same executive. In 1971, a reconstituted Jewish Agency was established.

Joseph, Bernard (Dov) (b. 1899), Zionist leader and Israeli statesman; at time referred to was adviser to Political Department of Jewish Agency; later held important positions in Jewish Agency Executive and Israel Cabinet.

Kalvarisky, Hayim Margalit (1868–1947), Jewish agronomist in Palestine, leader of Brit Shalom.

Kan'an, Dr. Habib (b. 1883), Christian Arab supporter of the Mufti.

Kaplan, Eliezer (1891–1952), member of Jewish Agency Executive 1933–52, Finance Minister of Israel 1948–52.

Kaplansky, Shelomoh (1884–1950), Socialist Zionist leader; head of the Technion, Institute of Technology, Haifa.

Katznelson, Berl (1887–1944), ideological leader of the Jewish Labor movement in Palestine; among founders of Histadrut and Mapai; first editor of *Davar*, the Hebrew Labor daily.

Kefar Tavor, Jewish village in Galilee, founded in 1902.

Khalidi, Dr. Hussein (1895–1962), Mayor of Jerusalem 1934–37; member of Arab Higher Committee; opponent of the Mufti.

Kinneret, Lake (also known as Lake Tiberias, the Sea of Galilee and the Lake of Gennesaret), in the north of Israel; the River Jordan flows through it. Under the 1949 Israel-Syrian Armistice Agreement, the Armistice Demarcation Line was drawn a few meters east of the shore, leaving the entire lake in Israeli territory, but there were numerous incidents due to Syrian encroachment on the lake and firing on Israeli fishermen.

Kirkbride, Sir Alec (b. 1897), from 1937 District Commissioner in Galilee; from 1939 British representative in Transjordan and later in Jordan.

Kisch, Colonel (later Brigadier) Frederick H. (1888–1943), member of British military delegation at the Versailles Peace Conference; Chairman of the Palestine Executive of the Zionist Organization and the Jewish Agency 1923–31.

Kollek, Theodor (Teddy) (b. 1911), Director-General Prime Minister's Office 1952–64; Mayor of Jerusalem since 1965.

el-Kuwatly, Shukri (1892–1967), President of Syria 1943–49 and 1955–58.

Labor Palestine movement, general name for the Labor movement in Palestine and its supporting parties abroad, which appeared as a bloc at the Zionist Congresses.

Laski, Neville (1890–1969), President of the Board of Deputies of British Jewry 1933–39.

Lavon (Lubianiker), Pinhas (b. 1904), Secretary-General of the Histadrut 1949–51 and 1956–61; Minister without Portfolio 1951–52; Minister of Agriculture 1952–54; Minister of Defense 1954–55.

Lawrence, Thomas Edward (1888–1935), organizer of the Arab revolt against the Turks in World War I.

Lipsky, Louis (1876–1963), American Zionist leader; member Zionist Organization and Jewish Agency Executive 1923–31 and 1933–35.

Litani, river which flows southwestward from the Lebanese mountains and then, close to the headwaters of the Jordan, turns westward to the Mediterranean; the latter section forms the natural boundary between the Lebanese mountains and Galilee.

Lloyd, (John) Selwyn (Brooke) (b. 1904), British Foreign Secretary 1955–60.

Locker, Berl (b. 1887), Labor Zionist leader, member of Jewish Agency Executive in

London 1931–48; Joint Chairman Jewish Agency Executive 1948–56.

Longuet, Jean (1876–1938), French Socialist leader; grandson of Karl Marx.

Lourie, Arthur (b. 1903), Political Secretary of Jewish Agency in London 1933–40; later Israeli diplomat.

MacDonald, James Ramsay (1866–1937), British Prime Minister 1924 and 1929–35; author in 1931 of the MacDonald Letter, which largely met Zionist objections to the Passfield White Paper of 1930.

MacDonald, Malcolm (b. 1901), son of the above, British Colonial Secretary 1935 and 1938–40; author of the 1939 White Paper.

Machover, Dr. John M. (1880–1971), Jewish lawyer, Jewish State Party representative at St. James' Palace Conference.

McMahon, Sir Henry (1862–1949), British High Commissioner in Egypt 1914–16; negotiated with Sherif Hussein of Mecca in 1915 on Arab aid to the Allies in return for Allied support for Arab independence. McMahon subsequently testified that Palestine was excluded from the area in which Arab independence was promised and that this was understood by Hussein.

Magnes, Dr. Judah Leib (1877–1948), first President of the Hebrew University in Jerusalem; leader of Brit Shalom, q.v.; active in attempts to reach agreement with the Arabs.

Mandate for Palestine, approved by the League of Nations in 1922, confirming Britain as the Mandatory responsible for putting the Balfour Declaration (q.v.) into effect and giving recognition "to the historical connexion of the Jewish people with Palestine and to the grounds for reconstituting their national home in that country."

Mardam, Jamil (1890–1960), first Syrian Foreign Minister after independence; later Ambassador in Cairo and Chairman of the Council of the Arab League.

Meir (Myerson), Golda (b. 1898), Israel Minister in Moscow 1948–49; Minister of Labor 1949–56; Foreign Minister 1956–66; Prime Minister since 1969.

Melchett, Alfred, 1st Baron, formerly Sir Alfred Mond (1868–1930), British Jewish industrialist and politician; supporter of Zionist work in Palestine.

Menahemiah, Jewish village in Galilee, founded in 1902.

Mikveh Israel ("Hope of Israel"), agricultural school, founded in 1870 near Jaffa by the Alliance Israélite Universelle.

Mohammed Ali, Prince (b. 1875), member of Egyptian royal family.

Mossinsohn, Dr. Ben-Zion (1878–1942), headmaster Herzliyah Gymnasiah (high school), Tel Aviv; General Zionist representative at St. James' Palace Conference.

Mufti, Moslem religious dignitary; *the* Mufti, in this book, denotes the Mufti of Jerusalem, Haj Amin el-Husseini, q.v.

Muhi el-Din, Zacharia (b. 1918), associate of Nasser in the 1952 revolution, held various posts, including premiership and vice-presidency, from 1953 to 1967.

Nahas Pasha, Mustafa (1876–1965), leader of the Egyptian Wafd Party; Prime Minister in 1928, 1930, 1936–37, 1942–44 and 1950–52.

Namier, Professor Lewis B. (1888–1960), distinguished British historian; member of the Zionist Organization and Jewish Agency Political Department in London 1919–31.

Nashashibi, noted Jerusalem Arab family, traditional rivals of the Husseinis; Ragheb Nashashibi (1875 or 1881–1951) was Mayor of Jerusalem 1920–34; in 1934 was defeated in the municipal elections and formed the National Defense Party, which he represented on the Arab Higher Committee.

Nasser, Gamal Abdel (1918–1970), President of Egypt (later United Arab Republic) 1956–70, a leading member of the group of officers that revolted and deposed King Farouk in 1952; he became Prime Minister and deposed Mohammed Nagib, the titular leader of the revolt, in 1954.

Nes Ziona, village, later town, south of Tel Aviv, founded in 1882.

Newcombe, Col. S. F. (1878–1956), British officer serving in the Middle East; in the 1930s represented Palestinian Arab interests in London.

Niẓanah (Auja el-Ḥafir), outpost at the point where the Beersheba—el-'Arish road crosses the Israel-Sinai border. Under the Israel-Egyptian Armistice Agreement the surrounding area was to be a demilitarized zone, but the Egyptians made frequent encroachments; they were expelled by the Israel Defense Forces on September 21, 1955 and again, after they had returned, on November 3, 1955.

Novomeysky, Moshe (1873–1961), founder of the Dead Sea Potash Works.

Nuri Pasha, see el-Sa'id Nuri.

Ormsby-Gore, William G. A., later Lord Harlech (1885–1964), member of British delegation to the Versailles Peace Conference; British representative on the League of Nations Mandates Commission; Colonial Secretary 1936–38; generally favorable to Zionist aims.

Passfield, 1st Baron, formerly Sidney Webb (1859–1947), Colonial Secretary 1929–31; author of the Passfield White Paper, 1930. Its anti-Zionist tone and policies led to the resignation from the presidency of the Zionist Organization and the Jewish Agency of Dr. Weizmann, who declared that it went far toward "denying the rights and sterilizing the hopes of the Jewish people in regard to the National Home in Palestine."

Perlzweig, Maurice (b. 1895), deputy member Jewish Agency Executive 1935–46.

Petaḥ Tikva ("Gateway of Hope"), first modern Jewish village in Palestine (now town), founded in 1878.

Philby, H. St. John B. (1885–1960), British Arabist; British representative in Transjordan 1921–24; became a Moslem in 1930 and lived chiefly in Arabia as friend of Ibn Saud.

Piaster, popular name for 10 mils, one-hundredth of a Palestine pound.

Pinsker, Judah-Loeb Leon (1821–1891), Russian-Jewish pioneer of Zionism; leader of the Ḥibbat Zion ("Love of Zion") movement; author of *Autoemanzipation* (1882).

Plumer, 1st Viscount (1857–1932), British High Commissioner of Palestine 1925–28.

Po'alei Zion, Socialist Zionist movement, founded in 1907; in Palestine it amalgamated in 1919 with a non-party group to form Ahdut Ha-avodah; in other countries it continued to exist as a party within the Zionist movement, allied with Labor.

Radical Zionists, Zionist party of the 1920s and 1930s, headed by Yizhak Greenbaum.

Reading, Gerald Rufus, Marquess of (1889–1960), British Jewish statesman, non-Zionist member of Jewish delegation at St. James' Palace Conference.

Rehovot, town (at first village) south of Tel Aviv, founded 1890; later seat of the Weizmann Institute of Science.

Rishon le-Zion ("First in Zion"), one of the first modern Jewish villages (later a town) in Palestine, founded in 1882.

Roosevelt, Kermit (b. 1916), consultant to U.S. Secretary of State on Middle East and Communist affairs, 1947–57.

Rosh Pina, one of the first modern Jewish villages (later a town) in Palestine, founded in 1882.

Rotenstreich, Dr. Ephraim Fischel (1882–1938), General Zionist member of Jewish Agency Executive from 1935.

Ruppin, Dr. Arthur (1876–1943), Zionist leader and Jewish sociologist; head of Zionist Organization's Palestine Office 1908–15; member of Zionist and Jewish Agency Executive 1929–35.

Rutenberg, Pinhas (1879–1942), Jewish leader in Palestine, founder of Palestine Electric Corporation.

Sabri, Ali (b. 1920), associate of Nasser in the 1952 revolution; held various important positions, including premier and vice-president, until deposed by Anwar el-Sadat in 1970.

Sacher, Harry (1881–1971), English Zionist leader, member of Zionist Executive 1927–29.

el-Sa'id, Nuri Pasha (1888–1958), Iraqi politician, frequently Foreign Minister and Prime Minister, murdered in Iraqi revolution.

Salah, Abdul Latif (b. 1880), Jericho lawyer, member of Istiqlal movement.

Samuel, Edwin, 2nd Viscount (b. 1898), official in Palestine Administration, 1920–48.

Samuel, Herbert Louis, 1st Viscount (1870–1963), British statesman and Jewish leader; member of British Cabinets, 1909–16 and 1931–32; first High Commissioner for Palestine and Transjordan 1920–25; created viscount in 1937.

Sarafend, British military camp near Tel Aviv, used for, inter alia, interning political prisoners.

Sejera (Hebrew name: Ilaniyah), founded in 1899; first modern Jewish village in Lower Galilee.

Senator, David Werner (1896–1953), German Jewish social worker; member Jewish Agency Executive 1930–45; member of Brit Shalom.

Shahbander, Dr. Abdel-Rahman (?–1940), leader of pan-Arab movement in Syria; in the 1930s in opposition to the Syrian Government.

Sharett (Shertok), Moshe (1894–1965), head of Jewish Agency Political Department 1933–48; Foreign Minister of Israel 1948–56; Prime Minister 1953–55.

Shaw Commission, appointed after the Arab riots of 1929; its report, issued in 1930, ascribed the riots to Arab opposition to Jewish settlement and was the basis for the anti-Zionist Passfield White Paper.

Simpson, Sir John Hope (b. 1868), British expert sent to Palestine in 1930 to investigate questions of immigration, land settlement and development; he reported that there was "with the present methods of Arab cultivation no margin of land available for cultivation by new immigrants."

Smilansky, Moshe (1874–1953), Jewish farmers' leader in Palestine and Hebrew writer, member of Brit Shalom.

Snell, Harry, later Lord (1865–1944), British Labour M.P., member of Shaw Commission; wrote a minority report favorable to Zionist work.

Sokolow, Nahum (1860–1937), Zionist leader and Hebrew publicist; President of World Zionist Organization and Jewish Agency 1931–35.

Sprinzak, Yosef (1885–1959), Labor Zionist leader; prominent in Hapo'el Haza'ir, q.v.; first speaker of the Knesset, Israel's parliament.

Stein, Leonard (b. 1887), Political Secretary World Zionist Organization 1920–29; Legal Adviser Jewish Agency 1929–39.

al-Sulh, Riad (1894–1951), a leader of pan-Arabist Istiqlal movement: Prime Minister of Lebanon 1943–45 and 1946–51.

Suprasky, Joshua (1879–1948), leading member of right-wing General Zionist Party in Palestine.

Suweidi, Nagi Pasha (b. 1882), Iraqi statesman, for a time Prime Minister.

Sykes-Picot Agreement, on the post-war division of the Middle East, concluded in May 1916 between Sir Mark Sykes, representing Great Britain, and Georges Picot, for France. Several Arab states were to be established, under French or British control or influence, but the greater part of Western Palestine—from the Sea of Galilee to south of Hebron—was to be placed under an Anglo-Russian-French condominium.

Tabenkin, Yizhak (1889–1971), Socialist Zionist pioneer.

Tamimi, Amin (1882–1944), member of Arab Higher Committee; supporter of the Mufti.

Thomas, James Henry (1874–1949), British trade union leader; Colonial Secretary, 1924, 1931 and 1935–36.

Thon, Dr. Jacob J. (1880–1950), Palestine Jewish community leader.

"Uganda" Project, offer by Joseph Chamberlain, on behalf of British Government, to Theodor Herzl in 1903 to provide land in East Africa (not actually in Uganda) for the establishment of a Jewish colony. The project aroused fierce controversy among Zionists and the 7th Zionist Congress, in 1905, rejected the offer, ruling that all Zionist effort must be concentrated in Palestine.

United Nations Relief and Works Agency for Palestine Refugees in the Near East (UNRWA), established in 1949. Its plans for the resettlement of refugees in Arab countries were dropped owing to Arab opposition and the Agency confined itself to relief, social services and education.

Ussishkin, Menahem Mendel (1863–1941), Zionist leader, General Zionist (B group), President of Jewish National Fund, 1923–41.

Va'ad Le'umi, National Council of Palestine Jews, the executive organ of Knesset Israel, the officially organized Jewish community in Palestine.

Vansittart, Sir Robert, later Lord (1881–1957), Permanent Undersecretary for Foreign Affairs 1935–38; Chief Diplomatic Adviser to Foreign Secretary 1938–41.

Vilensky, Nahum (d. 1961), Jewish Agency official, later journalist.

Wahba, Sheikh Hafiz (b. 1899), Education Minister in Saudi Arabian Cabinet; Saudi Ambassador in London 1930–56.

Wahhabi, puritanical Moslem sect dominant in Saudi Arabia.

Warburg, Felix M. (1871–1937), American Jewish banker and philanthropist; Chairman, Administrative Committee of Jewish Agency 1929–30.

Wauchope, General Sir Arthur S. (1874–1947), British High Commissioner for Palestine and Transjordan 1931–38, a period of rapid growth for the Jewish National Home.

Weizmann, Chaim (1874–1952), President of the World Zionist Organization and (from 1929) of the Jewish Agency, 1920–31 and 1935–46; first President of Israel, 1948–52.

White Paper, statement of official British Government policy; Palestine White Papers included those of: 1922, issued by Winston Churchill; 1930, issued by Lord Passfield, q.v.; 1938, stating that the Government was not bound to accept the Peel Commission's proposals for partition and announcing the appointment of the Woodhead Commission; and 1939, issued by Malcolm MacDonald, which the Zionist movement regarded as a betrayal of Britain's obligations under the Mandate.

Wise, Rabbi Stephen S. (1874–1949), American Zionist leader; a founder of the American Jewish Congress and the World Jewish Congress.

Yavne'el, Jewish village in Galilee, founded in 1902.

Yevsektzia, abbreviation for Yevreiskaya Sektzia, the Jewish section of the Soviet Communist Party up to 1930; it was particularly assiduous in anti-Zionist activity.

Zikhron Ya'akov, one of the first modern Jewish villages in Palestine, founded in 1882.

Zionist Congress, supreme governing body of the World Zionist Organization and later of the Jewish Agency; held annually, 1897–1913, bi-annually, 1921–39, and since 1951 quadrennially. It elects the Executive of the W.Z.O. and (until 1968) of the Jewish Agency.

Zionist General Council ("Actions Committee"), body representing all Zionist parties, wielding authority in periods between congresses.

APPENDIX

The following is a list of the passages appearing in this work, which are quoted from available English documents:

	Beginning on page
Weizmann-Faisal agreement	1
Faisal statement to Reuter correspondent	5
Arlosoroff letter	12
High Commissioner's reply to Arab delegation	40
Sharett and Joseph's meeting with Musa Alami	93
Memorandum of "the five"	98
Ben-Gurion–Philby correspondence	136
Weizmann-Sharett exchange of cables	141
Hyamson-Newcombe proposals and correspondence with Lourie and Laski	142
Hyamson letter	149
Sharett-Magnes correspondence	152
Bakstansky memorandum	156
Magnes letter	167
Proceedings of London Conference	199
Eisenhower letter	314
Ben-Gurion letter to Tito	327

CANCELLED

73-143   301.29569
                              B43

Ben-Gurion, David
   My talks with Arab leaders

**GOLDY AND MAX SMITH LIBRARY
BRITH EMETH
27575 SHAKER BLVD.
PEPPER PIKE, OHIO 44124**